Essential German Grammar

Essential *German* Grammar

MARTIN DURRELL
Professor of German, University of Manchester

KATRIN KOHL
Fellow in German, Jesus College, University of Oxford

GUDRUN LOFTUS
German Language Instructor, University of Oxford

McGraw·Hill

New York   Chicago   San Francisco   Lisbon   London   Madrid   Mexico City
Milan   New Delhi   San Juan   Seoul   Singapore   Sydney   Toronto

Library of Congress Cataloging-in-Publication Data
is available from the United States Library of Congress.

First published in Great Britain in 2002 by Arnold, a member of the Hodder Headline
Group, 338 Euston Road, London NW1 3BH.

3 4 5 6 7 8 9 0   2 1 0 9 8 7 6 5 4 3

ISBN 0-07-141338-3

The advice and information in this book are believed to be true and accurate at the date of
going to press, but neither the author nor the publisher can accept any legal responsibility
or liability for any errors or omissions.

McGraw-Hill books are available at special quantity discounts to use as premiums and
sales promotions, or for use in corporate training programs. For more information, please
write to the Director of Special Sales, Professional Publishing, McGraw-Hill, Two Penn
Plaza, New York, NY 10121-2298. Or contact your local bookstore.

This book is printed on acid-free paper.

Contents

Preface

This book is designed to introduce the basic grammatical structures of German and give a wide range of examples to illustrate how they are used in practice. As the title *Essential German Grammar* indicates, this is not a comprehensive reference work. The focus is on presenting the most useful rules clearly. Much of the material is given in tables, which use two colours in order to make it easier to focus on key points and memorize rules. Explanations are intended both to clarify individual points, and to develop an appreciation of how German grammar operates as a system. Each chapter finishes with an authentic text that illustrates how the grammar points work in context. A separate section with exercises and answers enables learners to test themselves on what they have learnt.

The book is intended to be suitable for use as a stand-alone grammar in post-GCSE courses and at undergraduate level, and it is simultaneously designed as a foundation grammar for *Hammer's German Grammar and Usage*, by Martin Durrell. *Hammer* gives the advanced learner a deeper understanding of German grammar, and explains complex areas of the language not covered in the more elementary book. But the learner will still find it useful to keep referring back to the tables and summaries in *Essential German Grammar*.

The authors would like to thank the students at Manchester University and the University of Oxford, whose questions have helped to shape this book. We should also like to thank Dr Sonia Brough and Erica Parsons for their constructive criticisms and helpful suggestions. Our thanks go finally to Lesley Riddle, Elena Seymenliyska, Eva Martinez and Anke Ueberberg at Arnold for bringing this project to fruition.

Acknowledgements

The authors and publisher would like to thank the following for permission to use copyright material in this book.

Texts

Texts are abbreviated and/or adapted.

Chapter 1: Martin Luther, *Biblia. Das ist die gantze Heilige Schrift. Deudsch auffs new zugericht*, Wittenberg 1545, reprint ed. H. Volz (Munich: DTV, 1974), p. 25. Franz Kafka, *Die Verwandlung*, in: *Sämtliche Erzählungen*, ed. Paul Raabe (Frankfurt/M., Hamburg: Fischer 1970), p. 56. *Der Spiegel*, No. 21, 24.5.1999, p. 234. **Chapter 2:** Circus Krone, Programme December 2000/January 2001, p. 39. **Chapter 3:** 'Besser als vor 25 Jahren?', *Bravo Sport*, No. 8, 9.4.1999, pp. 8f. **Chapter 4:** 'Suchtfalle Internet', *Cosmopolitan*, No. 5, May 1999, p. 160 . **Chapter 5:** Column 'Bizznezz : Geld–Job–Zukunft', *Popcorn* No. 5, May 1999, p. 82. **Chapter 6:** Katja Franke, 'Meine Eltern lieben mich kaputt', *Brigitte Young Miss*, No. 5, May 1999, pp. 60–64. **Chapter 7:** Jacob and Wilhelm Grimm, 'Hänsel und Gretel', in: Brüder Grimm, *Kinder- und Hausmärchen. Ausgabe letzter Hand mit den Originalanmerkungen der Brüder Grimm*, ed. H. Rölleke, 3 vols (Stuttgart: Reclam 1984), vol. I, pp. 106f. **Chapter 8:** Claus Jacobi, 'Des Teufels Alternative', *Der Spiegel special*, No. 10, 1998, pp. 26–32. **Chapter 9:** Christian Spaeth, *Säugetiere der Vorzeit*, Was ist Was 38 (Nürnberg: Tessloff 1995), p. 5. **Chapter 10:** Franz Kafka, *Der Heizer*, in: *Sämtliche Erzählungen*, ed. Paul Raabe (Frankfurt/M., Hamburg: Fischer 1970), p. 32. **Chapter 11:** *Duden. Das große Wörterbuch der deutschen Sprache in 10 Bänden*, 3rd edition (Mannheim, Leipzig, Wien, Zürich: Dudenverlag, 1999), vol. I (dustcover), vol. II (dustcover). **Chapter 12:** *Popcorn* No. 5, May 1999, p. 86. **Exercises:** *Fernsehwoche*: No. 34, 26.8–1.9.2000, p. 5 (Chapter 1); No. 27, 8.–14.7.2000, p. 5 (Chapter 4); No. 21, 27.5.–2.6.2000, p. 12 (Chapter 5); No. 23, 10.–16.6.2000, p. 6 (Chapter 6); No. 36, 9.–15.9.2000, pp. 10f. (Chapter 7); No. 23, 10.–16.6.2000, p. 7 (Chapter 7).

Illustrations

Chapter 1: Martin Luther, *Biblia. Das ist die gantze Heilige Schrift. Deudsch auffs new zugericht*, Wittenberg 1545, reprint ed. H. Volz (Munich: DTV, 1974), p. 24. Franz Kafka, sketch, in: *Sämtliche Erzählungen*, ed. Paul Raabe (Frankfurt/M., Hamburg: Fischer 1970), p. 411. Ashley Walker, 'Promised Land'. **Chapter 2:** Circus Krone, Programme December 1999/January 2000, title page and pp. 20f. **Chapter 3:** FC Bayern, team photograph 1999. **Chapter 4:** Photograph: Terry Griffiths. **Chapter 5:** Photograph: Terry Griffiths. **Chapter 6:** *Brigitte Young Miss*, No. 5, May 1999, p. 62. **Chapter 7:** *Acht der schönsten Grimms Märchen*, illustrated by anon (no publisher, no date), p. 13. **Chapter 8:** *Der Spiegel special*, No. 10, 1998, pp. 29, 30. **Chapter 9:** NASA/GSFC/MITI/ERSDAC/JAROS, and US/Japan ASTER

Science Team, © California Institute of Technologie. **Chapter 10:** Cartoon, *Bravo Sport*, Nr. 8, 9. April 1999, p. 32. 'Statue of Liberty', photograph © Martin Kerans. **Chapter 11:** Jacob and Wilhelm Grimm, *Deutsches Wörterbuch*, vol. I (Leipzig: Hirzel 1854), facsimile reprint (Munich: dtv 1984), frontispiece and column 18. *Duden. Das große Wörterbuch der deutschen Sprache in 10 Bänden*, 3rd edition (Mannheim, Leipzig, Wien, Zürich: Dudenverlag 1999), vol. I, p. 67. **Chapter 12:** *Popcorn* No. 5, May 1999, p. 86. **Chapters 1–9 and 11–12:** Cartoons by Erik Liebermann, in: *Unverhofft kommt oft*, ed. Gesamtverband der Deutschen Versicherungswirtschaft e.V. (GDV), Cologne 1986.

Why grammar?
Some frequently asked questions

Can language learning be made easy?

The simple answer is no – whatever certain methods promise you. You can quickly learn a few useful phrases, but you can't learn to communicate properly without a lot of effort. As with a musical instrument, you also need to practise regularly what you learn in order not to forget it. But you can enhance your efficiency:

◆ Develop an awareness of what types of learning work best for you.

◆ Vary the ways you learn.

◆ Use your teacher and any (other) native speakers to help you.

Are there any shortcuts to learning a language?

Yes – learning its grammar! For each rule you learn to apply correctly, you can get a vast number of individual utterances right.

Does German have 'more grammar' than English, French or Spanish?

No. The grammar of a language is its basic framework which allows you to combine a finite number of words in an infinite number of ways – and still be understood immediately. But in different languages, different parts of the framework are developed in more or less complex ways. This means that difficulties can lie in different aspects of the language and confront the learner at different stages. German seems to have 'more grammar' at the beginning because it's an 'inflecting' language: the structure of certain words changes (typically, different endings are used) depending on their function in the sentence. But other areas of German grammar are comparatively simple, and developing your vocabulary in German is helped by the big 'word families' you can build up with the rules of word formation.

Isn't it best to concentrate on communicating and forget about those silly little endings?

Even without the details, it's possible to reach the stage where you succeed in ordering the right drink in a restaurant, manage to tell people where you went on holiday, and get the gist of simple conversations or films. But you'll never get your command of German to a point where you can take part in more complex conversations (or business negotiations) or understand sophisticated texts or documentaries. You're also not taken as seriously if you make mistakes – just look at people's reaction to foreigners who speak ungrammatical or inaccurate English. If you're aiming for a good command of German in the long term, you need to get into the habit of caring about the detail from the start. But it's a good idea to vary your aims: set aside times for switching into 'basic communication' mode.

Is it best to learn grammar in context, by listening to German and reading it?

It's very important to see how grammar works in context. But it's essential to learn the rules systematically, by rote, if you want to make fast progress. After all, you wouldn't expect to learn to play football or tennis just by watching matches on television.

Is it best to avoid translating when learning grammar?

You can't assume that an English phrase or construction can be transposed directly into German, though in fact the two languages are in many ways similar. But it's very useful to learn grammar by comparison. After all, you've spent thousands of hours mastering the grammar of your native language (even if much of it is subconscious), so make use of that knowledge when learning German. Some people think translation is an 'unnatural' way to learn – but even small children will use it if they're learning a second language. Practising translating from German into English and vice versa is a good way of comparing German and English grammar 'in action'.

Do I need to go abroad to learn the language?

For most people, spending some time using the language in a country where it is spoken is the most interesting and motivating way to learn it – and that means potentially the fastest. But your progress will be best if you underpin any time abroad with systematic learning. It's not unknown for students to spend a whole year in Germany without significantly improving their command of German!

Can't we do without all that jargon used in grammar books?

Without the 'metalanguage' (the terms we use to talk about language) explanations become very longwinded. It's worth spending some time familiarizing yourself with the concepts explained in the Glossary and in the introductory chapter (Words and sentences). You'll probably forget them again, so keep coming back to them when you meet them in the later chapters. You should also get a good, comprehensive bilingual dictionary and familiarize yourself with the terms and abbreviations it uses.

How can I make learning German grammar less boring?

Vary the way in which you learn and use the media you find most interesting. Make the rules stick in as many ways as possible:

◆ See if you can identify examples of a rule by analysing e.g. German advertisements, a German website, a magazine article on a topic that interests you, a short Grimm's fairy-tale, or even a poem.

◆ Have regular learning competitions with a friend, with prizes.

◆ Find a pen-pal or email-pal and work on getting your written German right.

◆ See if you can get hold of a 'parallel text' or a translation of a German story (e.g. by Franz Kafka), and compare the beginning with the original. You could even try translating a passage from the original and compare your translation with the published translation.

◆ Read examples out loud so that they sink in via your ear as well as via your eye.

◆ Write important rules out on cards, using colour to highlight irregularities.

◆ Use cards to test yourself by writing examples of a rule on one side of the card and the rule on the other.

◆ Use cards to learn vocabulary, with one word per card and the translation on the back. Write the words out with colour-coding, e.g. with noun genders blue for masculine, red for feminine, green for neuter, or with types of verb blue for weak, green for strong and red for irregular. Put aside the cards once you have learnt the words, and then check through them at regular intervals.

◆ It helps to learn words in context, in little phrases or sentences – especially verbs.

◆ Set aside regular slots for learning grammar and stick to them. It helps to have a routine, and to be systematic. That way you'll be able to see progress.

Keep going back and forth between the rules and actual usage in spoken and written language. Spot the differences without allowing them to frustrate you!

Did you know…?

▶ By the time a child is 5 years old, it will on average have spent 9,100 hours learning its native language.

▶ An adult can learn a foreign language far more efficiently than a child learns its native language.

▶ German is spoken as a first language by nearly 100 million people in 15 European countries.

▶ Because many British companies assume that 'everyone speaks English' and lack staff with a knowledge of German, Britain has an enormous export deficit with Germany. Germans will sell their goods in English – but when they're the customers, they prefer to operate in the language they know best.

▶ In 1999, graduates in German had the best employment record for any university subject in the UK, with the exception of medical subjects.

▶ Aside from Dutch, German is the language that is most closely related to English.

Abbreviations and spelling

Abbreviations

acc.	accusative case	**jdn.**	*jemanden* (accusative)
adj.	adjective	**masc.**	masculine
aux.	auxiliary verb	**nom.**	nominative case
dat.	dative case	**neut.**	neuter
esp.	especially	**pl.**	plural
etw.	*etwas* (something)	**prep.**	preposition
fem.	feminine	**sb.**	somebody
gen.	genitive case	**sg., sing.**	singular
jd.	*jemand* (nominative)	**sth.**	something
jdm.	*jemandem* (dative)		

Spelling

The reformed German spelling is used throughout, e.g. *dass, musste,* not *daß, mußte* (see **12.2** and **12.5**).

Glossary

In order to learn a foreign language, you need to gain an understanding of the way in which languages are structured. It helps to analyse your own native language since you have a native-speaker command of it – even if you aren't aware of the 'metalanguage' linguists use to talk about what you are doing in practice. In *The Cambridge Encyclopedia of Language*, David Crystal gives the following example of a word you probably know how to use correctly in five different grammatical contexts:

◆ It's your **round**. I'll have a whiskey.   **Noun**

◆ Mary bought a **round** table.   **Adjective**

◆ We walked **round** to the shop.   **Adverb**

◆ The car went **round** the corner.   **Preposition**

◆ The yacht will **round** the buoy soon.   **Verb**

This glossary explains these 'word classes' as well as other grammatical concepts you'll come across in the following chapters, with examples. It's a good idea to familiarize yourself with these concepts thoroughly – they're your tools! But you will need to do so gradually, as you move through the chapters.

The explanations include references to sections of chapters where you will find more detailed explanations. Further references are given in the index.

accusative *Akkusativ*	typically, the **CASE** which shows the **DIRECT OBJECT** of **TRANSITIVE VERBS**: *Ich sehe den Hund*; *Ich sehe ihn* (see **1.3**, **8.1**). It is also used after some **PREPOSITIONS**: *Ich gehe durch den Wald*, *in die Stadt* (see **5.1**, **5.3**), and in some **ADVERBIAL** constructions: *Sie kommt jeden Tag* (see **4.9**).
adjective *Adjektiv*	a word which qualifies, or describes a **NOUN**: *die schöne Stadt*; *die Stadt ist schön* (see **4.1–4.2**).
adverb *Adverb*	a word which qualifies a **VERB**, an **ADJECTIVE** or a whole **CLAUSE**, often giving extra information on how, when, where or why: *Sie singt gut*; *Sie war sehr freundlich*; *Sie ging trotzdem nicht* (see **4.8–4.14**).
adverbial *Adverbialbestimmung*	any part of a **SENTENCE** which has the function of an **ADVERB**. It can be a single word (an **ADVERB**), or a **PHRASE**, or a whole **CLAUSE**: *Sie sang gut*; *Sie sang mit einer hellen Stimme*; *Sie sang, als sie ins Zimmer kam* (see **4.8–4.14**).

agreement *Kongruenz*	copying a grammatical feature from one word to another, so that some words have ENDINGS according to the words they are used with or refer to. In German, DETERMINERS, ADJECTIVES and many PRONOUNS 'agree' with their NOUN for GENDER, NUMBER and CASE: *dieses Buch; mit meinem neuen Auto; Welchen Rock kaufst du? Den da* (see chapter **3** and **4.1–4.2**). VERBS also 'agree' with their SUBJECT for PERSON and NUMBER: *ich singe, du singst, er/sie/es singt* (see **1.2**).
article *Artikel*	the most important of the DETERMINERS. In German, like English, there is a definite article *der, die, das,* etc. (= English 'the'), and an indefinite article *ein, eine,* etc. (= English 'a') (see **3.1–3.3**).
attributive adjective *attributives Adjektiv*	used before a NOUN: *die klassische CD, mein großer Zeh* (see **4.1–4.2**).
auxiliary verb *Hilfsverb*	a verb used in combination with the INFINITIVE or PAST PARTICIPLE of another verb, especially to form COMPOUND TENSES and the PASSIVE, e.g. *Karin hat einen Hund gekauft.* The main auxiliary verbs in German are *haben, sein, werden* and the MODAL AUXILIARIES, like *können* and *müssen* (see chapter **6**, esp. **6.2, 6.5–6.7**).
bracket *Verbalklammer*	the 'bracket' construction is typical of German CLAUSES, with most words and phrases in a clause bracketed between two parts of the VERB: *Wir [kommen um 17 Uhr in Innsbruck an]; Sie [hat ihn in der Stadt gesehen]* (see **1.8, 9.1**).
cardinal number *Kardinalzahl*	numerals used in counting: *eins, zwei, …, hundert* (see **4.17**).
case *Kasus/Fall*	indicates the function of a NOUN PHRASE in the CLAUSE (e.g. whether it is the SUBJECT or DIRECT OBJECT, or dependent on a particular PREPOSITION) by using ENDINGS. German has four cases: NOMINATIVE *der Igel;* ACCUSATIVE *den Igel;* GENITIVE *des Igels* and DATIVE *dem Igel* (see **2.11**).
central section *Mittelfeld*	the main part of a MAIN CLAUSE, between the BRACKETS formed by the FINITE VERB in second position and any other parts of the verb at the end of the clause, e.g. *Bald wird Disneys Kult-Klassiker in den Kinos ein tolles Comeback feiern* (see **1.8, 9.4–9.9**).
clause *Satz*	a part of a SENTENCE with a VERB and its COMPLEMENTS. A MAIN CLAUSE can stand on its own. A SUBORDINATE CLAUSE is dependent on another clause in the sentence (see **1.7**).
commands *Befehle*	use the IMPERATIVE mood of the VERB. The FINITE VERB is in first position: *Komm hierher! Seid vorsichtig! Steigen Sie bitte ein!* (see **1.9, 6.3**).
comparative *Komparativ*	the form of an ADJECTIVE or ADVERB used to express a comparison: *schneller, höher, weiter* (see **4.6, 4.16**).

complement
Ergänzung

an element in a **CLAUSE** which is closely linked to the **VERB** and completes its meaning. The most important complements of the verb are its **SUBJECT** and **OBJECTS**, but German also has **DIRECTION COMPLEMENTS**, **PLACE COMPLEMENTS** and **PREDICATE COMPLEMENTS** (see **1.1**).

compound tense
zusammengesetzte Verbform

a **TENSE** formed by using an **AUXILIARY VERB** with the **INFINITIVE** or **PAST PARTICIPLE** of another verb. The main compound tenses in German are the **PERFECT**: *Sie hat geschlafen; Sie ist gekommen*, the **PLUPERFECT**: *Sie hatte geschlafen; Sie war gekommen* and the **FUTURE**: Sie wird schlafen; *Sie wird kommen* (see **6.2**).

compound word
Kompositum

a word formed by joining two or more words: *Kindergarten, Computerfachmann, dunkelrot* (see **11.1**, **11.3**).

conditional
würde-Form

a compound form of **SUBJUNCTIVE II** formed from the subjunctive II form of the **AUXILIARY VERB** *werden*, i.e. *würde*, and the **INFINITIVE** of another verb: *Ich **würde geben**; Die Kinder **würden schlafen*** (see **6.9**, **7.11**).

conjugation
Konjugation

the forms of a **VERB**, in particular the pattern of endings and/or vowel changes which indicate **AGREEMENT** with the **SUBJECT**, and show the various **TENSES**, the **MOOD**, etc., e.g. *ich **kaufe**, du **kaufst**; ich **sehe**, du **siehst*** (first and second person singular, present, indicative); *ich **kaufte**; ich **sah*** (first person singular, past, indicative) (see chapter **6**).

conjunction
Konjunktion

a word used to link **CLAUSES** within a **SENTENCE**. Coordinating conjunctions link **MAIN CLAUSES** (e.g. *und, aber, denn, sondern*), and subordinating conjunctions introduce **SUBORDINATE CLAUSES** (e.g. *dass, obwohl, weil, wenn*) (see **10.1–10.4**).

copula
Kopulaverb

a linking **VERB**, which typically links the **SUBJECT** with a **PREDICATE COMPLEMENT**: an **ADJECTIVE** or a **NOUN** in the **NOMINATIVE** case. The most frequent copulas in German are *sein, werden* and *scheinen*: *Er ist ein guter Lehrer; Die alte Frau wurde blass; Das scheint mir plausibel* (see **8.10**).

dative
Dativ

a **CASE** used to mark some **OBJECTS** of the verb, especially the **INDIRECT OBJECT** of a verb which also has a **DIRECT OBJECT**: *Sie hat **meiner Schwester** die CD gegeben*. Some German verbs just have an object in the dative case (you have to learn these): *Ich helfe **meinem Bruder*** (see **1.4**, **8.3**). The dative case can also indicate possession: *Sie zog **dem Kind** die Jacke aus* (see **8.4**). It is used after some **ADJECTIVES**: *Er sieht **meinem Vater** ähnlich* (see **4.4**); and after many **PREPOSITIONS**: *Er will mit **diesen Kindern** spielen* (see **5.2–5.3**).

declension
Deklination

the pattern of **ENDINGS** on a **NOUN**, an **ADJECTIVE** or a **DETERMINER** which show **GENDER**, **NUMBER** and **CASE**, e.g. *der gute Hund* (masculine singular nominative) *den guten Hunden* (masculine plural dative) (see chapters **2**, **3**, and **4.1–4.2**).

demonstrative *Demonstrativpronomen*	a **DETERMINER** or **PRONOUN**, like English 'this' and 'that', which points to something specific, e.g. *dieser, jener* (see **3.4**, **3.9**).
determiner *Determinativ*	a function word used with **NOUNS**, including the **ARTICLES** *der* and *ein*, the **DEMONSTRATIVES**, like *dieser*, the **POSSESSIVES**, like *mein*, and **INDEFINITES** like *einige* and *viele*. They typically come before **ADJECTIVES** in the **NOUN PHRASE** (see **3.1–3.6**).
direct object *direktes Objekt*	a verb **COMPLEMENT**, typically a person or thing directly affected by the action. It is in the **ACCUSATIVE** case. *Der Löwe fraß **den Esel**; Die böse Frau schlug **den Hund*** (see **1.3**, **8.1**).
direction complement *Direktivergänzung*	a typical **COMPLEMENT** with verbs of motion, indicating where the **SUBJECT** is going or where the **DIRECT OBJECT** is being put: *Sie **fährt nach Prag**; Er **stellte** den Besen **in die Ecke*** (see **8.9**).
ending *Endung*	a **SUFFIX** on a **NOUN**, **VERB** or **ADJECTIVE** which helps to indicate the grammatical role of the word in the phrase or sentence: *mit **kaltem** Wasser; **Kommst** du morgen? seit **Jahren**.*
feminine *Femininum*	one of the three **GENDERS** into which **NOUNS** are divided, shown by the **ENDING** of the **DETERMINER** and/or **ADJECTIVE** in the **NOUN PHRASE**: *die Frau, eine kleine Lampe*. A feminine thing is referred to by a feminine **PRONOUN**, not the neuter pronoun *es*, e.g. ***Die Diskette ... Sie** ist kaputt* (see **2.3**, **3.7**).
finite verb *finites Verb*	a form of the verb which has an **ENDING** in **AGREEMENT** with the **SUBJECT**: ***Ich komme**; **Wir haben** geschlafen; **Sie wurden** betrogen; **Ihr könnt** gehen* (see **1.2**, **6.2**).
future tense *Futur*	a **TENSE** which refers to the future or expresses a supposition. It is formed with the **AUXILIARY VERB** *werden* and an **INFINITIVE**: *Ich **werde** das Buch nicht **lesen**; Franz **wird** wieder krank **sein*** (see **6.2**, **7.2**).
future perfect *Futur II*	a **TENSE** formed with the **AUXILIARY VERB** *werden* and a compound **INFINITIVE**, indicating what will have happened by a point in the future, or a supposition in the past: *Sie **wird** das Buch **gelesen haben*** (see **6.2**, **7.2**).
gender *Geschlecht/Genus*	a division of **NOUNS** into three classes, called **MASCULINE**, **FEMININE** and **NEUTER**. The gender of a noun is shown by the **ENDING** of the **DETERMINER** and/or **ADJECTIVE** in the **NOUN PHRASE**: *der Mann, diese Frau, klares Wasser* (see **2.1**).
genitive *Genitiv*	a **CASE** which is mainly used to show possession or to link **NOUNS** together: *das Buch **meines Vaters**; die Geschichte **dieser Stadt*** (see **2.11**). A few verbs have a genitive **OBJECT** (see **8.5**); and it is used after a few **PREPOSITIONS**: *trotz **des Wetters*** (see **5.4**).

imperative
Imperativ

a **MOOD** of the **VERB** used to give commands or instructions, or make a request: *Komm hierher! Seid vorsichtig! Steigen Sie bitte ein!* (see **6.3**, **7.10**).

indefinite
Indefinitpronomen

an indefinite **PRONOUN** or **DETERMINER** is one which does not refer to a specific person or thing: *etwas, jemand, irgendwelcher* (see **3.6**, **3.9**).

indicative mood
Indikativ

the most usual **MOOD** of the **VERB**, used to make statements and ask questions: *Sie kam gestern. Siehst du das Licht?* This 'default' mood (see chapters **6** and **7**) is contrasted with the **IMPERATIVE** mood and the **SUBJUNCTIVE** mood (see **7.10**).

indirect object
indirektes Objekt

a verb **COMPLEMENT**, typically a person indirectly affected by the action expressed by the **VERB**, especially someone being given something (the **DIRECT OBJECT**) or benefiting from the action. It is in the **DATIVE** case: *Sie gab **ihrem Vater** das Geld* (see **1.1**, **1.4**, **8.3**).

infinitive
Infinitiv

the basic form of a **VERB**, ending in *-en* or *-n*: *kommen, machen, untergehen, betteln, sein.* This is the form of the verb given in dictionaries (see **6.1**).

infinitive clause
Infinitivsatz

a **SUBORDINATE CLAUSE** containing an **INFINITIVE**, typically preceded by the particle *zu*: *Sie hat mir geraten, **nach Hause zu gehen*** (see **1.10**, **10.6–10.8**).

inflection
Flexion

changing the form of words, most often by **ENDINGS**, to indicate their grammatical role in a phrase or sentence. In German, for example, **DETERMINERS** and **ADJECTIVES** inflect to show **GENDER**, **NUMBER** and **CASE**, and **VERBS** inflect to show **PERSON**, **NUMBER**, **TENSE** and **MOOD**. The inflection of **NOUNS**, **ADJECTIVES** and **DETERMINERS** is called **DECLENSION**, while the inflection of verbs is called **CONJUGATION**.

inseparable verb
untrennbares Verb

a prefixed verb whose **PREFIX** is not stressed and always remains attached to the verb: *besuchen, erwarten, verstehen* (see **6.4**, **11.5**).

interrogative
Interrogativ-

interrogative **ADJECTIVES**, **ADVERBS** or **PRONOUNS** are used to ask a **QUESTION**: *Welches Hemd kaufst du? Warum geht er nicht? Wem sagst du das?* (see **1.9**).

intransitive verb
intransitives Verb

a verb is intransitive if it does not have a **DIRECT OBJECT** in the **ACCUSATIVE** case: *Wir **schwimmen**; Dort **stand** er und **wartete** auf Luise; Meine Schwester **hilft** mir* (see **8.1**).

irregular verb
unregelmäßiges Verb

a verb with forms that do not consistently follow the pattern of **WEAK VERBS** or **STRONG VERBS**, e.g. *kennen – kannte – gekannt* has a vowel change like a strong verb, but a past participle ending in *-t* like a weak verb. Other verbs are quite irregular, e.g. *sein, wissen, gehen, tun* (see **6.1**, **6.11**).

main clause *Hauptsatz*	can form a **SENTENCE** on its own, or join up with other main clauses or **SUBORDINATE CLAUSES**. The **FINITE VERB** is the second element in a German main clause: ***Heute kommt sie nicht zur Arbeit**, weil sie krank ist* (see **1.8**).
main verb *Hauptverb*	the verb with the main meaning, which constitutes the main verb of a **CLAUSE**, as opposed to **AUXILIARY VERBS** or **MODAL AUXILIARIES**. In simple (i.e. one-word) **TENSES**, the main verb is the **FINITE VERB** of the clause, e.g. ***Er schreibt** mir eine E-Mail*. In **COMPOUND TENSES** the main verb is generally at or near the end of the clause in the **PARTICIPLE** or **INFINITIVE** form, e.g. ***Er hat** mir eine E-Mail **geschrieben**; **Er will** mir eine E-Mail **schreiben*** (see **1.8**, **6.2**).
masculine *Maskulinum*	one of the three **GENDERS** into which **NOUNS** are divided, shown by the **ENDING** of the **DETERMINER** and/or **ADJECTIVE** in the **NOUN PHRASE**: *der Mann, ein alter Baum*. A masculine thing is referred to by a masculine **PRONOUN**, not the neuter pronoun *es*, e.g. ***Der Computer ... Er** ist teuer* (see **2.2**, **3.7**).
modal auxiliaries *Modalverben*	*dürfen, können, mögen, müssen, sollen* and *wollen* are the modal auxiliary verbs. As **AUXILIARY VERBS** they are normally only used with the **INFINITIVE** of another verb: *Sie **darf spielen**; Ich **musste gehen**; Du **sollst** das Fenster **aufmachen***. They typically express ideas like possibility, obligation, desire or permission (see **7.13**).
modal particle *Modalpartikel*	a small word which indicates the speaker's attitude to what is being said: *Es gibt ja hier nur zwei gute Restaurants* (assumes agreement on something uncontroversial); *Das Bier ist aber kalt!* (surprise) (see **4.21**).
mood *Modus*	forms of the **VERB** which indicate the speaker's attitude. German has three moods: **INDICATIVE** (neutral, factual): *Er geht nach Hause*; **IMPERATIVE** (commands, requests): *Geh nach Hause!*; and **SUBJUNCTIVE** (possibly not factual): *Wenn er nach Hause ginge, ...* (see **7.10**).
neuter *Neutrum*	one of the three **GENDERS** into which **NOUNS** are divided, shown by the **ENDING** of the **DETERMINER** and/or **ADJECTIVE** in the **NOUN PHRASE**: *das Buch, ein gutes Drama*. A neuter noun is referred to by a neuter **PRONOUN**, even if its natural gender is masculine or feminine, e.g. ***Das Mädchen ... Es** ist sehr klein* (see **2.4**, **3.7**).
nominative *Nominativ*	the nominative **CASE** most often indicates the **SUBJECT** of a **VERB**: ***Du** lügst; **Der Hund** bellt; **Der Regen** fällt* (see **1.2**, **8.1**). It is also used in the **PREDICATE COMPLEMENT** of **COPULAS**: *Ich bin **der neue Lehrer*** (see **8.10**).
non-finite *infinite Verbform*	a form of the **VERB** which does not have an **ENDING** in **AGREEMENT** with the **SUBJECT**, i.e. the **INFINITIVE** and the **PARTICIPLES** (see **6.1–6.2**).

noun *Substantiv*	a type of word which typically refers to a person, a living being, a thing, a place or an idea and can normally be used with a definite ARTICLE: *der Tisch, die Idee, das Pferd* (see chapter **2**).
noun phrase *Nominalgruppe*	a group of connected words containing a NOUN (or a PRONOUN) and any other words accompanying it (i.e. a DETERMINER and/or an ADJECTIVE): *Brot, weißes Brot, das weiße Brot* (see chapter **3**).
number *Numerus*	the grammatical distinction between SINGULAR and PLURAL: *der runde Tisch – die runden Tische* (see **2.6–2.10**).
object *Objekt*	objects are among the most important COMPLEMENTS of the VERB, especially the DIRECT OBJECT, INDIRECT OBJECT and PREPOSITIONAL OBJECT (see **8.1**).
ordinal number *Ordinalzahl*	a form of a numeral used as an ADJECTIVE: *das zweite Mal, sein zwanzigster Geburtstag* (see **4.18**).
participle *Partizip*	NON-FINITE forms of the VERB. German has two participles: the PRESENT PARTICIPLE, e.g. *spielend*, and the PAST PARTICIPLE, e.g. *gespielt* (see **6.1–6.3**).
passive (voice) *Passiv*	a form of a VERB where the doer of the action is not necessarily mentioned and the SUBJECT is typically a person or thing to which something happens. The most common German passive construction uses the AUXILIARY VERB *werden* and the PAST PARTICIPLE: *Die Schlange **wurde** **getötet*** (see **6.8**, **7.4–7.8**).
past tense *Präteritum*	the simple (i.e. one-word) TENSE used to relate an action, state or event in the past, e.g. *Ich kam an; Sie sah mich; Wir warteten lang* (see **6.2–6.3**, **7.3**).
past participle *Partizip II*	a NON-FINITE form of the VERB, typically with the PREFIX *ge-* and the ending *-t* (WEAK VERBS) or *-en* (STRONG VERBS). It is most often used with an AUXILIARY VERB to form COMPOUND TENSES or the PASSIVE: *Sie hat es **gekauft**; Wir sind **gekommen**; Er wurde **angezeigt*** (see **6.1–6.2**). It can also be used as an ATTRIBUTIVE ADJECTIVE, with the appropriate ending: *der **gekühlte** Saft* (see **4.1**) or as a NOUN (see **11.2**).
perfect tense *Perfekt*	a COMPOUND TENSE formed with the PRESENT TENSE of the AUXILIARY VERB *haben* or *sein* and the PAST PARTICIPLE, e.g. *Ich habe sie gesehen; Sie sind gekommen*. It can be used to link a past action, state or event to the present, or (especially in spoken German) relate an action, state or event in the past (see **6.2**, **6.7**, **7.3**).
person *Person*	a category of the VERB indicating the person speaking (first person, i.e. *ich* or *wir*), the person addressed (second person, i.e. *du, ihr, Sie*) or other persons or things spoken about (third person, i.e. *er, sie, es*). (see chapter **6**).

personal pronoun *Personalpronomen*	simple words standing for the various **PERSONS** or referring to a **NOUN PHRASE**, e.g. *ich*, *mich*, *mir*, *du*, *sie* (see **3.7**).
place complement *Lokativergänzung*	a typical **COMPLEMENT** with verbs that indicate position, indicating where something is situated: *Die Flasche **steht auf dem Tisch**; Ich **wohne in Berlin*** (see **8.8**).
pluperfect tense *Plusquamperfekt*	a **COMPOUND TENSE** formed with the **PAST TENSE** forms of the **AUXILIARY VERB** *haben* or *sein* and the **PAST PARTICIPLE**, e.g. *Ich hatte sie gesehen; Sie waren gekommen*. It is generally used in the context of a past-tense statement to report an action, state or event in the more distant past, e.g. *Ich rief ihn an, nachdem wir gegessen hatten* (see **6.2**, **7.3**).
plural *Plural*	a grammatical term referring to more than one person or thing, whereas **SINGULAR** refers to just one. The **PRONOUNS** *wir*, *uns*, *ihr* are plural, as are the **NOUN PHRASES** *die kleinen Hunde* and *die Kinder* (see **2.6–2.10** and chapter **3**).
possessive *Possessivpronomen*	a word used to indicate possession, either as a **DETERMINER**, e.g. *sein Fahrrad*, or as a **PRONOUN**, e.g. *das ist meines* (see **3.5**, **3.9**).
predicate complement *Prädikatsergänzung*	the typical verb **COMPLEMENT** with a **COPULA** (usually *sein*, *werden*, *scheinen*), normally consisting of an **ADJECTIVE**, or a **NOUN PHRASE** in the **NOMINATIVE CASE**, which is descriptive of the **SUBJECT**: *Mein neuer BMW **ist schön**; Er **wird** bestimmt **ein guter Tennisspieler*** (see **8.10**).
prefix *Präfix*	an element added to the beginning of a word to form another word: *Urwald, unglücklich, verbessern, weggehen* (see **11.1**).
preposition *Präposition*	a (usually small) word used to introduce a **NOUN PHRASE** and typically indicating position, direction, time, etc.: *an, auf, aus, neben, ohne*, etc. In German each preposition is followed by a noun phrase in a particular **CASE**: *Er kam **ohne seinen Hund*** (acc.); *Er kam **mit seinem Hund*** (dat.); *Er kam **trotz seines Hundes*** (gen.) (see chapter **5**).
prepositional adverb *Pronominaladverb*	a compound of *da(r)-* with a **PREPOSITION**, typically used in the function of a **PRONOUN** referring to things: e.g. *damit* 'with it', 'with them' (see **5.5**).
prepositional object *Präpositionalobjekt*	a **COMPLEMENT** of the **VERB** introduced by a **PREPOSITION**. Prepositional objects occur with many German verbs. Typically, the preposition does not have its usual meaning, and the choice of preposition depends on the individual verb: *Wir warten **auf meine Mutter**; Sie warnte mich **vor dem großen Hund*** (see **1.5**, **8.7**).
prepositional phrase *Präpositionalgruppe*	a **NOUN PHRASE** introduced by a **PREPOSITION**: *an diesem Tag, aus dem Haus, zwischen den Häusern* (see **chapter 5**).
present participle *Partizip I*	a **NON-FINITE** form of the **VERB**, with the suffix *-d* added to the **INFINITIVE**, corresponding to English forms in '-ing': *leidend, schlafend*. It is used most often as an **ATTRIBUTIVE ADJECTIVE**, with the appropriate ending: *das fahrende Auto* (see **4.1**, **6.3**, **11.2**).

present tense *Präsens*	the **TENSE** used to relate something going on at the moment of speaking, or which takes place regularly or repeatedly, e.g. *Jetzt kommt sie*; *In Irland regnet es viel* (see **6.3**, **7.2**).
principal parts *Stammformen*	the three main forms in the **CONJUGATION** of a **VERB**, i.e. **INFINITIVE** – **PAST TENSE** – **PAST PARTICIPLE**: *machen – machte – gemacht* (**WEAK VERB**); *kommen – kam – gekommen* (**STRONG VERB**). The other verb forms can usually be constructed on the basis of these three forms (see **6.1**).
pronoun *Pronomen*	typically a little word which stands for a whole **NOUN PHRASE** already known from the context, e.g. **PERSONAL PRONOUNS**: *ich*, *mich*, *sie*; **DEMONSTRATIVE** pronouns: *dieser*; **POSSESSIVE** pronouns: *meiner*, *seines*; **INDEFINITE** pronouns: *man*, *niemand* (see **3.7**–**3.9**).
questions *Fragen*	have the **FINITE VERB** in first position, e.g. *Kommt er heute mit in die Disko?* However, if the question starts with an **INTERROGATIVE** word or phrase, the finite verb comes second, e.g. ***Wieviel kostet das Aquarium?*** (see **1.9**).
reflexive pronoun *Reflexivpronomen*	a **PRONOUN** in the **ACCUSATIVE** or **DATIVE** case referring back to the **SUBJECT** of the verb: *Sie **wäscht sich**; Ich habe es **mir** so **vorgestellt***. In the third person there is a special form for the reflexive pronoun, *sich*. For the other persons the **PERSONAL PRONOUNS** are used as reflexive pronouns (see **3.8**, **8.2**).
reflexive verb *reflexives Verb*	a verb used in combination with a **REFLEXIVE PRONOUN**: *sich erinnern* (remember), *sich weigern* (refuse) (see **8.2**).
register *Register/Textsorte*	a concept that distinguishes 'levels' of language, e.g. differences of usage appropriate to different situations and addressees. An important distinction is that between spoken and written language (see **12.8**).
relative clause *Relativsatz*	a **SUBORDINATE CLAUSE** used rather like an **ADJECTIVE** to describe a **NOUN**: *der Mann, der dort spielt*. Relative clauses are introduced by a **RELATIVE PRONOUN** (= English 'who', 'which', 'that'). The usual relative pronoun in German is *der*, which agrees in **GENDER** and **NUMBER** with the noun it refers to: *die Männer, **die dort spielen***. Its **CASE** is determined by its function within the clause: *der Mann, **den ich sah**; die Männer, **denen wir helfen*** (see **1.10**, **10.5**).
relative pronoun *Relativpronomen*	type of **PRONOUN** that introduces a **RELATIVE CLAUSE** and is equivalent to English 'who', 'which', 'that'. The most common relative pronoun has the same forms as the **DEMONSTRATIVE** pronoun *der*, *die*, *das*; *was* is also used as a relative pronoun (see **10.5**).
reported speech *indirekte Rede*	reporting what someone else said within a sentence rather than giving the speaker's original words ('direct speech'). Compare direct speech: *Er sagte: „Ich bin heute krank."* with the corresponding reported

speech (sometimes called 'indirect speech'): *Er sagte, dass er krank sei* (see **7.12**).

root *Stamm*	the base form of a word, without **PREFIXES** and **SUFFIXES**, e.g. *wiederkommen, arbeiten, uninteressant* (see **11.1**).
sentence *Satz*	the longest unit of grammar, ending with a full stop in writing. It may consist of one **MAIN CLAUSE**, which can stand on its own, or of a number of clauses. A **SUBORDINATE CLAUSE** is dependent on another clause in the sentence (see **1.7**).
separable verb *trennbares Verb*	a verb with a stressed **PREFIX** which detaches from the **FINITE VERB** in **MAIN CLAUSES** and is placed at the end of the **CLAUSE**, e.g. ***ankommen***: *Wir **kommen** morgen um zwei Uhr in Dresden **an*** (see **6.4**, **11.6**).
singular *Singular*	a grammatical term referring to one person or thing, whereas **PLURAL** refers to more than one. The pronouns *ich, du, er, sie, es* and the noun phrases *der kleine Hund* and *das Kind* are singular (see chapters **2** and **3**).
strong adjective declension *starke Adjektivdeklination*	a set of **ENDINGS** used with **ATTRIBUTIVE ADJECTIVES** which are like the endings of the definite **ARTICLE** and used when there is no **DETERMINER** in the **NOUN PHRASE**, or when the determiner has no ending of its own: ***starkes** Bier, **guter** Wein, mein **alter** Freund* (see **4.1**).
strong verb *starkes Verb*	a verb which has vowel changes in the **PAST TENSE** and often the **PAST PARTICIPLE**, and the ending *-en* on the past participle: *bitten – bat – gebeten* (see **6.1**, **6.10–6.11**).
subject *Subjekt*	the **NOUN PHRASE** or **PRONOUN** in the **NOMINATIVE CASE** with which the **FINITE VERB** agrees for **PERSON** and **NUMBER**: ***Du kommst** morgen*; ***Die Leute beschwerten** sich über diese Preise*. Typically it is the person or thing carrying out the action expressed by the verb (see **1.2**, **8.1**).
subjunctive mood *Konjunktiv*	a **MOOD** of the verb typically used to indicate that an action, event or state may not be factual. There are two forms of the subjunctive in German: **SUBJUNCTIVE I** is used most often to mark **REPORTED SPEECH**: *Sie sagte, er sei nicht gekommen*; **SUBJUNCTIVE II**, which indicates unreal conditions: *Ich würde lachen, wenn sie käme* (see **6.9**, **7.10–7.12**).
subordinate clause *Nebensatz*	unlike a **MAIN CLAUSE**, a subordinate clause cannot form a **SENTENCE** in its own right. It is dependent on another clause in the sentence, and usually introduced by a **CONJUNCTION**. In German, the verb is typically at the end: *Wir kommen nicht, **weil wir keine Zeit haben**. Ich weiß, **dass sie heute nicht kommt***. Other types of subordinate clause are the **RELATIVE CLAUSE** and the **INFINITIVE CLAUSE** (see **1.10**, **10.3–10.8**).
suffix *Suffix*	an element added to the end of a word or **ROOT** to form a new word or word-form: *freundlich, Freundlichkeit, schneller* (see **11.1**).

superlative *Superlativ*	the form of an **ADJECTIVE** or **ADVERB** which expresses the highest degree. In German it is formed by adding the ending *-st* to the adjective or adverb: *der **höchste** Baum, das Auto fährt am **schnellsten*** (see **4.6**, **4.16**).
tense *Tempus*	a form of the **VERB** which indicates the time of an action, event or state in relation to the moment of speaking. German has six tenses: **PRESENT** *ich warte*; **PAST** *ich wartete*; **FUTURE** *ich werde warten*; **PERFECT** *ich habe gewartet*; **PLUPERFECT** *ich hatte gewartet*; **FUTURE PERFECT** *ich werde gewartet haben* (see **6.2–6.7**, **7.1–7.3**).
topic *Thema*	the first element in a **MAIN CLAUSE**, before the **FINITE VERB** – something we are emphasizing because we want to say something about it. This position can be occupied by many types of word or phrase, e.g. *Max fuhr gestern nach Rom; Gestern fuhr Max nach Rom; Nach Rom fuhr Max gestern* (see **9.3**).
transitive verb *transitives Verb*	a verb is transitive if it has a **DIRECT OBJECT** in the **ACCUSATIVE** case: *Sie **sah mich**; Ich grüsste **meinen Freund**; Meine Schwester **kauft mir die Bücher*** (see **8.1**).
valency *Valenz*	the construction used with a particular **VERB**, i.e. the number and type of **COMPLEMENTS** which it requires to form a fully grammatical **CLAUSE** or **SENTENCE** (see chapter **8**).
verb *Verb*	a type of word which refers to an action, event, process or state: *schlagen, passieren, recyceln, schlafen* (see chapters **6** and **7**).
verbal bracket *Verbalklammer*	refers to the 'bracket' construction that encloses most words and phrases in a clause between two parts of the **VERB**: *Sie [haben Tom die Diskette nicht gegeben]* (see **1.8**, **9.1**).
weak adjective declension *schwache Adjektivdeklination*	a set of **ENDINGS** used with the **ATTRIBUTIVE ADJECTIVE** when there is a **DETERMINER** with its own ending preceding it in the **NOUN PHRASE**. There are only two endings for the weak adjective: *-e*, used principally in the **NOMINATIVE SINGULAR**, *das **starke** Bier*; and *-en*, used elsewhere: *mit meinem **alten** Freund; die **jungen** Frauen* (see **4.1**).
weak masculine noun *schwaches Maskulinum*	one of a small set of **MASCULINE** nouns which have the **ENDING** *-(e)n* in the **ACCUSATIVE**, **GENITIVE** and **DATIVE** cases in the **SINGULAR** as well as in the **PLURAL**: *der **Affe**, den **Affen**, des **Affen**, dem **Affen**, die **Affen***, etc. (see **2.12**).
weak verb *schwaches Verb*	the mainly regular verbs of German, which form their **PAST TENSE** with the **ENDING** *-te* and their **PAST PARTICIPLE** with the **ENDING** *-t*: *machen – machte – gemacht* (see **6.1**).

Words and sentences 1

In all languages a limited number of basic elements, **words**, are combined in a limited number of patterns. This framework of combinations is the **grammar** of the language. The grammatical patterns show how each element in the sentence relates to the others, ensuring that what we say can be understood. In the English sentence 'The boy has given his friend the videos' we know **who** is doing **what** to **whom** because of the order of the phrases and the endings on the words. The same is true of the German sentence *Der Junge hat seinem Freund die Videos gegeben*. But in German more work is done by special **endings** on words and less by their order in the sentence than in English – so you can change *Der Hund hat den Mann gebissen* to *Den Mann hat der Hund gebissen* without making the man bite the dog.

To use a foreign language properly we need to master its grammar so that we can construct comprehensible sentences and understand the speakers of the other language. This chapter shows the basic patterns of German, demonstrates how sentences are built up from a simple combination of elements, and explains the terminology used for talking about grammar.

◆ The first part of the chapter explains how German shows the links between the elements of a sentence so that we can tell who is doing what to whom – see sections **1.1–1.6**.

◆ The second part of the chapter explains how different types of German sentence are constructed – see sections **1.7–1.10**.

▶ **This chapter is intended to give you an overview** so you can see how all the areas of grammar fit together. Don't worry if you find all these concepts confusing to start with – they will be explained more fully in later chapters.

1.1 Words and their relationships: complements, case, valency

Like other languages, German has different types of word:

determiner	adjective	noun	verb
Der	**böse**	**Wolf**	**schläft**.
The	*bad*	*wolf*	*is sleeping.*

determiner	adjective	noun	verb	determiner	noun
Der	**böse**	**Wolf**	**frisst**	**die**	**Großmutter**.
The	*bad*	*wolf*	*eats*	*the*	*grandmother.*

pronoun	verb	pronoun
Er	**frisst**	**sie.**
He	*eats*	*her.*

Verb

The VERB is the main word in a sentence telling you what is happening or being done, e.g. *spielen* (play) or *kaufen* (buy) or *fressen* (eat – by animals). It may have more than one part, as in this sentence: *Ich **habe gespielt*** (I have played).

Complements

The COMPLEMENTS of the VERB tell you **who** is doing **what** to **whom**. They usually consist of a NOUN PHRASE, which might be a single noun or a longer phrase ending in a noun: *Computer* (NOUN), *der Computer* (DETERMINER + NOUN), *der neue Computer* (DETERMINER + ADJECTIVE + NOUN). It may also consist simply of a PRONOUN, which is a word that 'stands for' the noun, like *er* or *ich*. The most important complements are as follows:

▶ The SUBJECT does the action.

▶ The DIRECT OBJECT is typically the person or thing to which the action is done.

subject	verb	direct object
Der Wolf	frisst	**die Großmutter.**
Rotkäppchen	hat	**eine Großmutter.**
Ich	kaufe	**einen Computer.**

▶ The INDIRECT OBJECT is typically the person who 'benefits' from the action in a sentence such as 'Little Red Riding Hood takes a cake **to the grandmother**'.

subject	verb	indirect object	direct object
Rotkäppchen	bringt	**der Großmutter**	**einen Kuchen.**

There are also a few other types of complement, notably:

▶ The PREPOSITIONAL OBJECT, which consists of a preposition such as *in, an, auf* and a noun phrase, e.g. *Der Wolf wartet **auf Rotkäppchen***, 'The wolf waits **for Little Red Riding Hood**'.

▶ The PREDICATE COMPLEMENT, which is used after certain verbs like *sein* (be), *Rotkäppchen ist **ein Mädchen*** or *Der Wolf ist **böse***.

Case

In English, the position of a noun phrase shows its function in the sentence. For example, in 'Craig kisses Sheila' or 'The guy kisses the girl' the subject has to come first, then the verb, then the direct object, so we know who is kissing whom. If the noun phrase consists of a pronoun, its form or CASE also helps to indicate its function: '**He** kisses **her**' rather than '**She** kisses **him**'.

In German, **case is indicated by the form of the whole noun phrase**, so it may change the form of DETERMINERS, ADJECTIVES, NOUNS and PRONOUNS. Because case does the work in showing the function of the noun phrase in the sentence, word order is much more flexible. You can't rely on finding the subject before the verb in German.

German has four cases:

▶ NOMINATIVE (the SUBJECT is in the nominative case)

▶ ACCUSATIVE (the DIRECT OBJECT is in the accusative case)

▶ GENITIVE (a rare type of object is in the genitive case, see **8.5**)

▶ DATIVE (the INDIRECT OBJECT is in the dative case).

You'll find the most important different types of COMPLEMENT and their cases explained in sections **1.2–1.6**. For more detail, see chapter **8**.

Valency

Like English, German has different types of verb – ranging from self-sufficient verbs that only need a subject to verbs which need one or more extra complements to make their meaning complete. Compare:

schlafen (sleep)	**Mutter** schläft.
	Mother is sleeping.
bauen (build) + direct object	**Der Ingenieur** baute **den Tunnel**.
	The engineer built the tunnel.
geben (give) + direct object + indirect object	**Der Student** gab **seinem Freund** die **CD**.
	The student gave the CD to his friend.
danken (thank) + indirect object + prepositional object	**Sie** dankte **dem Mann** für das **Video**.
	She thanked the man for the video.

Every verb needs specific complements to make a grammatical sentence, i.e. it has a particular sentence structure associated with it. This sentence structure is known as the VALENCY (in the US: valence) of the verb – a term borrowed from chemistry. German, with its cases, has a wider range of verb valency than English.

Some verbs have more than one possible valency, often with variations in meaning, e.g. *stürzen*:

stürzen (fall)	**Das Pferd** stürzte. *The horse fell.*
stürzen (bring down, overthrow) **+ direct object**	**Der Reichstag** stürzte **den Kanzler**. *Parliament brought down the Chancellor.*
stürzen (rush) **+ prepositional object**	**Lena** stürzte **aus dem Haus**. *Lena rushed out of the house.*

NB The different uses and meanings will be listed in your dictionary.

When you learn a German verb, you should always note which complements it needs to make its meaning complete. For every verb you learn, also learn sentences that will remind you which complement or complements it is used with.

The verb and its complements make up the core of the sentence. In addition to them, a sentence can have one or more ADVERBIALS. These tell us, for example, when, where or how something is done (see chapter **4**), e.g. *Sie drehten den Film **letzten Sommer in Afrika mit einem großen Kamerateam*** (They made the film **last summer in Africa with a large camera team**). Adverbials add information, but the sentence remains grammatical without them.

▶ COMPLEMENTS are elements closely linked to the action of a verb.

▶ CASE indicates the function of a noun phrase in the sentence.

▶ The VALENCY of a verb is the type and number of complements it needs to make a grammatical sentence.

You will find these concepts explained more fully in chapter **8**.

1.2 The subject and the finite verb

Some verbs only need one noun phrase to complete the sentence. This means that the simplest type of German sentence has two elements: a verb and a noun phrase in the NOMINATIVE case:

Schnee fällt.	*Snow falls/is falling.*
Ich kam.	*I came.*
Der Film beginnt.	*The film begins/is beginning.*
Sein großer Hund bellte.	*His large dog barked/was barking.*

The noun phrase in red in these sentences is the SUBJECT of the verb, the person or thing that is the 'doer' of the action. It is the element in the sentence which is most closely linked to the verb, and the verb has an ENDING that shows this link – the verb **agrees** with the subject. A verb with an ending that agrees with the subject is called a FINITE VERB (see **6.2**). Simple sentences like these have the following pattern:

The SUBJECT of the verb

▶ is typically the **doer of the action** and has the forms of the NOMINATIVE case (see **2.11** and chapter **3**);

▶ has ENDINGS on the verb which **agree** with it (see chapter **6**).

In more complex sentences, you may find several noun phrases, and several verb forms (see **1.8**). In order to get your bearings when reading or translating a sentence, it's always a good idea to start off by trying to identify the FINITE VERB and its SUBJECT

1.3 Accusative objects

Many verbs need two noun phrases to complete the sentence:

Astrid kaufte **einen Roman**.	*Astrid bought a novel.*
Der Mann schlug **mich**.	*The man hit me.*
Ich tötete **die giftige Schlange**.	*I killed the poisonous snake.*

The noun phrases in red have a different relationship to the verb from the subject. They are persons or things which undergo the·action expressed by the verb. They are the DIRECT OBJECT of the verb, and they are in the ACCUSATIVE case. The sentences have the following pattern:

The DIRECT OBJECT of the verb

▶ is typically the **person or thing to which something is done**;

▶ has the forms of the ACCUSATIVE case.

Verbs which can be used with a direct object are known as TRANSITIVE VERBS, and those which cannot be used with a direct object are called INTRANSITIVE VERBS (see **8.1**).

Because the subject and the direct object are distinguished from each other by their case, their order in the sentence is flexible. This means that the direct object can come before the subject, e.g. 'the shark ate the diver' might appear like this: ***Den Taucher*** (acc.) *fraß **der Hai*** (nom.). That's why it's essential to pay attention to case endings!

1.4 Dative objects

Some verbs (typically those of giving and taking – in the widest sense) require a subject, a direct object (in the accusative case) and a further object in the DATIVE case. This is the INDIRECT OBJECT:

Er verkaufte **Anke den BMW**.	*He sold the BMW to Anke.*
Sie gab **Herrn Schmidt das Geld**.	*She gave Herr Schmidt the money.*
Leihst **du mir deine Klamotten?**	*Will you lend me your clothes?*
Er zeigte **dem jungen Arzt die Hand**.	*He showed the young doctor his hand.*

The objects in red are typically persons who are benefiting from the action expressed by the verb. Sentences like this have the following pattern:

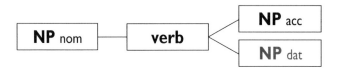

In English, the difference between the direct and the indirect object can be shown by the word order, with the indirect object first, e.g. 'She gave **Mr Smith** the money'. Alternatively, we can use a phrase with 'to', e.g. 'She gave the money **to Mr Smith**'. German has nothing to correspond to this second construction in English, and the indirect object is normally indicated simply by using the dative case, **not by using a preposition**.

A number of German verbs have no accusative object, but a single object in the dative case:

Der Papagei antwortete **mir**.	*The parrot answered me.*
Der Student half **dem Mann**.	*The student helped the man.*
Das Auto gehört **meiner Kusine**.	*The car belongs to my cousin.*

These sentences have the following structure:

There is no equivalent to this construction in English since English does not distinguish accusative and dative cases by endings. It is therefore necessary to learn German verbs used in this way (see **8.3**).

▶ Dative objects typically indicate a person **who benefits from the action of the verb**.

▶ INDIRECT OBJECTS have the forms of the DATIVE case. They are not marked by using a preposition.

▶ Some verbs **only have a dative object** and no direct object.

Dative objects are explained in section **8.3**.

1.5 Prepositional objects

A large number of verbs have a complement with a noun phrase which is linked to the verb with a specific preposition like the following:

Ich erinnerte sie **an den Termin**.	*I reminded her of the appointment.*
Sie dankte ihm **für die Blumen**.	*She thanked him for the flowers.*
Er verliebte sich **in sie**.	*He fell in love with her.*
Der Pudding schmeckt **nach Fisch**.	*The dessert tastes of fish.*
Er warnte mich **vor dem Hund**.	*He told me to beware of the dog.*

NB Each preposition takes a specific **CASE**, e.g. *für* + acc., *nach* + dat. (see chapter **5**).

The prepositions used in these **PREPOSITIONAL OBJECTS** do not have their full meaning. They just link the noun phrase to the verb. The nearest equivalent English verbs often have a different preposition (or another construction with no preposition).

Some verbs only have a prepositional object, e.g. ***nach etwas*** *schmecken* (taste **of something**). The sentence then has the following structure:

Other verbs additionally have an **ACCUSATIVE OBJECT** or a **DATIVE OBJECT**, e.g. ***jemanden*** *an jemanden/etwas erinnern* (remind someone of someone/something) or ***jemandem*** *für etwas danken* (thank someone for something). Sentences with these verbs have the following structures:

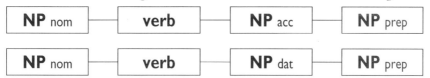

Verbs with prepositional objects

▶ are used with a **specific preposition**;

▶ may additionally have an accusative or a dative object;

▶ **need to be learnt with the preposition (and its case)**

Prepositional objects are explained in section **8.7**.

1.6 *sein* (and similar verbs) and their complements

Sentences with the verb *sein* (be) are unlike other sentences. The verb *sein* links the subject (which is in the nominative case) with another **NOUN PHRASE** which is also in the **NOMINATIVE** case, or with an **ADJECTIVE** that describes the subject:

Der Mann war **mein Rivale**.	*The man was my rival.*
Er ist **der beste Skifahrer**.	*He is the best skier.*
Das Essen ist **schlecht**.	*The food is bad.*

A few other common verbs link the subject with a noun phrase or an adjective in the same way, notably:

bleiben	*remain*	heißen	*be called*
scheinen	*seem*	werden	*become*

These are **COPULAR VERBS** (or simply **COPULAS** – which just means 'links'). The complement which follows them is called the **PREDICATE COMPLEMENT**. The structure of sentences with these verbs is as follows:

▶ *sein*, *bleiben*, *heißen*, *scheinen* and *werden* are **COPULAR VERBS**.

▶ They are used with a noun phrase or adjective – the **PREDICATE COMPLEMENT**.

▶ The noun phrase following these verbs is in the **NOMINATIVE** case.

Copulas and predicate complements are explained in section **8.10**.

1.7 Sentences and clauses

It is usual to distinguish between sentences and clauses. A **SENTENCE** is the longest unit of grammar and, in writing, it ends with a full stop. A sentence may consist of one clause or several clauses.

A **CLAUSE** is a segment of a sentence with a single **FINITE VERB** (the verb with an ending that agrees with the subject of the clause or sentence, see **1.2**). A **MAIN CLAUSE** can stand on its own and form a sentence. A **SUBORDINATE CLAUSE** is dependent on a main clause and cannot stand on its own.

Some sentences only have one clause, which is always a main clause:

Die Prinzessin **schlief**.	*The princess slept.*
An ihrem fünfzehnten Geburtstag	*On her fifteenth birthday*
traf sie die alte Frau im Turm.	*she met the old woman in the tower.*

But many sentences have two, three, or even more clauses, each with its own verb. These are called **complex sentences**. In German, the clauses are usually separated by commas:

Er **weiß**, dass sie **schläft**.	*He knows that she is sleeping.*
Als der Prinz **kam**,	*When the prince came,*
teilte sich die Dornenhecke,	*the thorny hedge parted*
und er **ging** in das Schloss,	*and he went into the castle*
wo Dornröschen **lag**.	*where Sleeping Beauty was lying.*

Conjunctions

Clauses can be linked up with CONJUNCTIONS ('linking' words). Two (or more) parallel main clauses can be linked by a **coordinating conjunction** like *und* (and) or *aber* (but):

Er **sah** sie **und** er **küsste** sie.	*He saw her and he kissed her.*
Die Prinzessin **starb** nicht,	*The princess did not die,*
aber sie **fiel** in einen tiefen Schlaf.	*but she fell into a deep sleep.*

A subordinate clause may be linked to a main clause by a **subordinating conjunction** like *dass* (that), *weil* (because) or *als* (when):

Er **sah** sofort, **dass** die Prinzessin schön **war**.	*He immediately saw that the princess was beautiful.*
Sie **wachte** auf, **als** der Prinz sie **küsste**.	*She woke up when the prince kissed her.*

Sentences are made up of one or more clauses:

▶ Each CLAUSE has its own VERB.

▶ MAIN CLAUSES can stand on their own. They can be linked by a **coordinating conjunction**.

▶ SUBORDINATE CLAUSES function as part of another clause and are dependent on it. They may be linked to the clause they depend on by a **subordinating conjunction**.

Complex sentences and conjunctions are explained in chapter **10**.

1.8 Main clauses

In order to get your mind round German sentence structure, you need to pay attention to **word order**. This differs for MAIN CLAUSES and SUBORDINATE CLAUSES.

    German **main clause statements** are not constructed in the same way as in English. The following diagram shows their structure:

In a German main clause, the FINITE VERB is always the **second element** in the clause. What comes before the verb can be a single word, a phrase or a subordinate clause. This **first element** is the TOPIC of the sentence – what we want to say something about. It can be the subject, but it does not need to be – unlike in English:

Mein Bruder fährt mit dem ICE nach Leipzig.	*My brother is going to Leipzig by Intercity Express.*
2 Millionen Buchtitel gibt es auf unserer Website.	*You can get two million book titles from our website.*
An dem Abend fiel der Meteor auf die Erde.	*That evening the meteor hit the earth.*
Wohin sie ihn brachten, **weiß** mein Vater nicht.	*My father doesn't know where they took him.*

Verb forms consisting of two parts

As in English, some verb forms consist of a FINITE VERB and a PAST PARTICIPLE or INFINITIVE (these are 'non-finite' verb forms):

Ich **habe** ihn **gesehen**.	*I have seen him/I saw him.*
Du **bist gekommen**.	*You have come.*
Die Rakete **wurde** in den Weltraum **geschossen**.	*The rocket was launched into space.*
Bettina **kann** heute nicht **surfen**.	*Bettina can't surf today.*

In these examples, the finite verb in second position is an AUXILIARY VERB (see chapter **6**). The verb with the main meaning, the MAIN VERB, is in the infinitive or past participle form, and comes **at the end of the clause**.

Unlike English, German has a type of compound verb with a first section that can be detached, e.g. **an**kommen (arrive), **auf**stehen (get up) or **weg**laufen (run away). These are called SEPARABLE VERBS (see **6.4**). In a main clause with a separable verb, the finite verb in second position consists only of the main part of the verb, while the PREFIX detaches and stands **at the end of the clause**:

Der Zug **kommt** in fünf Minuten **an**.	*The train is arriving in five minutes.*
Der Dieb **lief** ganz schnell **weg**.	*The thief ran away very quickly.*

The verbal bracket – key to German word order

In *The Awful German Language*, Mark Twain complained that the average sentence in a German newspaper consisted of a mass of words occupying a quarter of a column, '*after which comes the* VERB, *and you find out for the first time what the man has been talking about*'. He recommended getting rid of the 'all-inclosing king-parenthesis'. Modern German sentences generally make do with a couple of lines – but the 'bracket' has stayed.

An English main clause unfolds from the subject and complete verb at the front. The German main clause needs to be understood as a whole, once it is complete. This principle is clearest where the verb consists of two parts. **The two parts of the verb enclose** all the other elements in the clause – forming a kind of BRACKET around the CENTRAL SECTION of the clause:

topic	verb[1]	central section	verb[2]
Ich	**habe**	heute hart an meinem Projekt	**gearbeitet.**
Am Montag	**wollte**	er mit seiner Freundin ins Kino	**gehen.**
Nach 100 Jahren	**wachte**	die Prinzessin aus ihrem Schlaf im Turm	**auf.**

Note the word order in English:

*I **have worked** hard on my project today.*
*On Monday he **wanted to go** to the cinema with his girlfriend.*
*After 100 years the princess **woke up** from her sleep in the tower.*

German main clauses have a different structure to that of English:

▶ The FINITE VERB is **always the second element**.

▶ Only one element – the TOPIC – comes **before the finite verb**.

▶ other parts of the verb – INFINITIVE, PAST PARTICIPLE, SEPARABLE PREFIX – are placed **at the end of the clause**.

Word order is explained in chapter **9**, and you should familiarize yourself in particular with the **word order table** at the end of that chapter.

1.9 Questions and commands

The only difference between the structure of questions and commands on the one hand and of main clause statements on the other is that in the former **the finite verb is in first position**. Any other parts of the verb are at the end of the clause, and the two parts of the verb enclose all the other elements in the clause:

The following sentences illustrate this:

verb¹	central section	verb²
Arbeitet	er an seinem Projekt?	
Willst	du ins Kino	**gehen?**
Surfen	Sie im Internet!	

In some types of question (those which can't be answered by *ja/nein*), the verb is not in first position, but is preceded by an INTERROGATIVE word or phrase (typically beginning with *w*-):

Wer hat das City-Cup-Finale **gewonnen?**	*Who won the City Cup Final?*
Mit wem bist du zum Skifahren **gefahren?**	*Who did you go skiing with?/With whom …*
Welches Rad willst du?	*Which bike do you want?*
In welcher Kneipe hast du sie **getroffen?**	*Which bar did you meet her in?*
Warum studierst du Japanisch?	*Why are you studying Japanese?*
Wie lange wollt ihr Karten **spielen?**	*How long do you want to play cards?*

NB Question words belong to different word classes: pronouns (e.g. *wer*, see **3.9**), adjectives (e.g. *welcher*, see **3.4**), adverbs (e.g. *warum*, see **4.15**). The pronouns and adjectives change their form, while adverbs remain unchanged.

1.10 Subordinate clauses

The structure of subordinate clauses differs from that of main clauses. Subordinate clauses introduced by a **subordinating** CONJUNCTION have the following structure:

conjunction	central section	verb²	verb¹

All the parts of the verb are at the end of the clause. The FINITE VERB follows the infinitive or past participle, and is in **final position**. Separable prefixes join up with the main verb. All the other words and phrases are enclosed by the conjunction and the verb(s):

conjunction	central section	verb²	verb¹
..., **dass**	meine Freundin jetzt in Konstanz		arbeitet
..., **weil**	die meisten Frauen nicht mit Robotern	schlafen	wollen
..., **ob**	der Minister diesen Brief an den Kanzler	abgeschickt	hat
..., **wenn**	Dornröschen nach 100 Jahren		aufwacht

> ... *that* my girlfriend now **works** in Konstanz
> ... *because* most women **do** not **want to sleep** with robots
> ... *whether* the minister **has sent off** this letter to the Chancellor
> ... *when* Sleeping Beauty **wakes up** after 100 years

„Er hat es immer noch nicht kapiert, dass er
nur die Post reinholen soll!"

Relative clauses

The structure is similar in so-called RELATIVE CLAUSES. This is a type of subordinate clause that typically gives additional information about a noun in the preceding clause. It is introduced not by a conjunction, but by a RELATIVE PRONOUN, equivalent to the English 'who', 'that' or 'which' (see **10.5**):

relative pronoun	central section	verb²	verb¹
Alfred Nobel ..., **der**	im Jahre 1867 das Dynamit		**erfand**
eine Frau ..., **die**	in ihrer Kindheit Zirkusakrobatin	**werden**	**wollte**
ein Film ..., **in dem**	Humphrey Bogart die Hauptrolle	**gespielt**	**hatte**

*Alfred Nobel, **who invented dynamite in the year 1867***
*a woman **who wanted to become** a circus acrobat in her childhood*
*a film **in which Humphrey Bogart had played the main part***

Infinitive clauses

Some subordinate clauses do not contain a finite verb but an INFINITIVE preceded by *zu*. There is no initial conjunction or pronoun, but the infinitive with its particle *zu* is placed at the end of the clause. With separable verbs, *zu* is inserted in the infinitive form of the verb, after the prefix. If there is an auxiliary, this is in the infinitive form and it comes second:

Ich hoffe **Elefanten in freier Wildbahn zu** filmen.
Der Prinz beabsichtigt, **Dornröschen aus dem Schlaf** aufzuwecken.
Der Metzger behauptet, **in der Kirche einen verdächtigen Typ** gesehen **zu** haben.

*I hope **to film elephants in the wild**.*
*The prince intends **to wake up Sleeping Beauty from her sleep**.*
*The butcher claims **to have seen a suspicious man in the church**.*

German subordinate clauses have a distinctive structure:

▶ The FINITE VERB is in **final position**.

▶ The CONJUNCTION or RELATIVE PRONOUN and the VERB **enclose all the other elements**.

▶ In infinitive clauses, the INFINITIVE with *zu* **follows all other words**.

The structure of the various types of subordinate clause is explained in sections **9.1–9.2** and in chapter **10**.

WORDS AND SENTENCES IN CONTEXT

Die Schöpfung

Am Anfang schuf Gott Himmel und Erde.
Und die Erde war wüst und leer
und es war finster auf der Tiefe.
Und der Geist Gottes schwebte auf dem
   Wasser.
Und Gott sprach: Es werde Licht! und es
   ward Licht.
Und Gott sah, dass das Licht gut war.
(Aus: Martin Luther, *Die ganze Heilige Schrift*,
1545, modernized spelling)

Die Verwandlung

Als Gregor Samsa eines Morgens aus unruhigen
Träumen erwachte, fand er sich in seinem Bett
zu einem ungeheueren Ungeziefer verwandelt.
(Aus: Franz Kafka, *Die Verwandlung*, 1912)

Andere Welten

Der ultramoderne Luxusliner ist gestrandet, das Personal läuft verwirrt umher, tief unten

im Bauch des Gefährts tickt eine Bombe. Das interstellare Computerspiel "Raumschiff Titanic", das der britische Kultbuchautor Douglas Adams erfunden hat, kommt jetzt in einer deutschen Ausgabe auf den Markt. Deutsche Sprecher gaben den Robotern die Stimmen.
(Aus: *Der Spiegel*)

TYPES OF WORD

article	adjective	noun	verb	adverb	preposition	article	noun
Das	interstellare	Spiel	kommt	jetzt	auf	den	Markt.
The	*interstellar*	*game*	*comes*	*now*	*onto*	*the*	*market.*

MAIN CLAUSES (**finite verb is 2nd element**, other parts of verb at the end)

topic	verb¹	central section	verb²
Gott	**schuf**	Himmel und Erde.	
Am Anfang	**schuf**	Gott Himmel und Erde.	
der Geist Gottes	**schwebte**	auf dem Wasser.	
Als…,	**fand**	er sich zu einem Ungeziefer	**verwandelt.**
das Personal	**läuft**	verwirrt	**umher.**

NB *umherlaufen* is a SEPARABLE VERB.

SUBORDINATE CLAUSES (all parts of verb at the end, **finite verb last**)

conjunction/relative pronoun	central section	verb²	verb¹
…, **dass**	das Licht gut		**war.**
Als	Gregor Samsa eines Morgens		**erwachte,**
[das Spiel], **das**	der Kultbuchautor	**erfunden**	**hat,**

COMPLEMENTS OF THE VERB AND THEIR CASES: who does **what** to **whom**?

subject	Am Anfang schuf **Gott** Himmel und Erde. **Der Geist Gottes** schwebte auf dem Wasser. Als **er** erwachte, … tief unten im Bauch tickt **eine Bombe**. …, das **der Autor** erfunden hat,	nominative case
direct object	Gott schuf **(den) Himmel** und **(die) Erde**. Sprecher gaben den Robotern die **Stimmen**.	accusative case
indirect object	Sprecher gaben **den Robotern** die Stimmen.	dative case

NB The GENITIVE case generally shows **possession**: *im Bauch des Gefährts*.

Nouns 2

NOUNS are words which name living creatures, things, places, ideas or processes. In written German they can be distinguished easily because they are written with a capital letter. A noun is usually preceded by an **ARTICLE** or other **DETERMINER** and often also by one or more **ADJECTIVES** or a longer adjectival phrase. Together, these form the **NOUN PHRASE**:

determiner	adjective/adjectival phrase	noun
		Gott
die		**Erde**
das	ultramoderne	**Raumschiff**
ein	vom Kultbuchautor Adams erfundenes	**Computerspiel**

This chapter gives you details about the main features of nouns:

◆ the **GENDER** of nouns (**2.1–2.5**)

◆ how nouns form their **PLURAL** (**2.6–2.10**)

◆ **CASE** and how nouns and noun phrases show it (**2.11–2.12**).

▶ Study carefully how your **dictionary** gives information about the gender of each noun, its change of form indicating case, and its formation of the plural.

2.1 Gender

All German nouns are divided up into three categories, called genders: **MASCULINE**, **FEMININE** and **NEUTER**.

masculine	feminine	neuter
der **Mann**	die **Frau**	das **Kind**
der **Mund**	die **Nase**	das **Auge**
der **Löffel**	die **Gabel**	das **Messer**

The names for the genders are misleading. Nouns denoting male animals or humans are usually masculine, and nouns denoting female animals or humans are usually feminine – but not always:

die **Wache** ...	sentry	... is *feminine*
das **Mädchen** ...	girl	... is *neuter*
die **Person** ...	person	... is *feminine*
der **Mensch** ...	human being	... is *masculine*

To confuse matters further, words denoting things can be masculine, feminine or neuter and there is often no logical explanation at all:

der **Apfel**	apple	der **Computer**	computer
die **Birne**	pear	die **Diskette**	diskette
das **Obst**	fruit	das **Faxgerät**	fax machine

Only around 20% of German nouns are neuter, so:

▶ You should not assume that things are neuter.

The gender of each noun affects the endings of any articles or adjectives used with that noun, and you should therefore

▶ always check the gender of a noun in your dictionary. It will normally be indicated by *m* (masculine), *f* (feminine) or *n* (neuter);

▶ **always learn a noun with its definite article** – learning it aloud helps you remember it!

However, the **ending** on a noun, or its **meaning**, may give a clue to its gender (though there are often exceptions). The most useful of these clues are explained in sections **2.2–2.5**.

2.2 Masculine nouns

The following nouns are usually MASCULINE.

▶ Nouns with the following **meanings**:

Male humans and animals	der Vater	der Arzt	der Lehrer	der Hahn
Seasons, months, days of the week	der Sommer	der Mai	der Mittwoch	
Wind and weather	der Wind	der Regen	der Hagel	der Sturm
Makes of car	der Ford	der BMW	der Mercedes	der Toyota

▶ Nouns with the following **endings**:

-ant	der Konson**ant**	*-ismus*	der Sozial**ismus**
-ast	der Kontr**ast**	*-ling*	der Lieb**ling**
-ich	der Tepp**ich**	*-or*	der Mot**or**
-ig	der Hon**ig**	*-us*	der Rhythm**us**

2.3 Feminine nouns

The following nouns are usually FEMININE.

▶ Nouns with the following **meanings**:

Female humans and animals	die Mutter	die Ärztin	die Lehrerin	die Henne
Aeroplanes, motorbikes, ships	die Boeing	die BMW	die Suzuki	die „Bismarck"
Rivers in Germany	die Donau	die Elbe	die Mosel	die Ruhr
Names of numerals	die Null	die Eins	die Hundert	die Million

NB Exceptions: *der Airbus, der Rhein, der Main*

▶ Nouns with the following **endings**:

-a	die Pizza	-schaft	die Herrschaft
-anz/-enz	die Eleganz	-sion/-tion	die Explosion
-ei	die Bücherei	-tät	die Universität
-heit/-keit	die Krankheit	-ung	die Bedeutung
-ie	die Biologie	-ur	die Natur
-in	die Freundin		

2.4 Neuter nouns

The following nouns are usually NEUTER.

▶ Nouns with the following **meanings**:

Young persons and animals	das Baby	das Kind	das Lamm
Continents, countries, towns	das alte Europa	das neue Polen	das geteilte Berlin
Metals, chemical elements, scientific units	das Gold	das Kobalt	das Ampère
Letters of the alphabet, musical notes	das A	das Ypsilon	das hohe C
Other parts of speech used as nouns	das Du	das Gehen	das neue Deutsch

▶ Nouns with the following **endings**:

-chen	das Mädchen	-tel	das Viertel
-lein	das Büchlein	-tum	das Eigentum
-ma	das Drama	-um	das Album
-ment	das Appartement		

NB Exceptions: *der Irrtum, der Reichtum*

2.5 Other clues to gender

Some other clues to gender are useful, though there are more exceptions.

▶ Nouns **ending in -e** are over 90% **feminine**

die Lamp**e**	die Sahn**e**	die Reis**e**	die Bühn**e**	die Tann**e**	die Diskett**e**

NB Most exceptions are masculine nouns for people, e.g. *der Junge* (see **2.12**).

▶ Nouns with the **prefix *Ge-*** are over 90% **neuter**

das **Ge**bäude	das **Ge**setz	das **Ge**spräch	das **Ge**wicht	das **Ge**bot

NB A few common exceptions, especially *die Geschichte, der Geruch*.

▶ 75% of nouns **ending in -*nis*** are **neuter**

das Bedürf**nis**	das Ereig**nis**	das Erleb**nis**

NB The rest are feminine – common are *die (Er)kenntnis, die Erlaubnis*.

2.6 Noun plurals

In English, most nouns simply add -*s* to form the plural. There is no similar rule in German, and there are **seven ways of forming the plural**:

HOW NOUNS FORM THEIR PLURAL IN GERMAN

no ending (–)	der **Lehrer** das **Segel**	die **Lehrer** die **Segel**
no ending, with *Umlaut* (¨)	der **Vogel** der **Bruder**	die **Vögel** die **Brüder**
add -e (–e)	der **Arm** das **Jahr**	die **Arme** die **Jahre**
add -e, with *Umlaut* (¨e)	der **Stuhl** die **Hand**	die **Stühle** die **Hände**
add -er, with *Umlaut* if poss. (–er)/(¨er)	das **Tal** das **Kind**	die **Täler** die **Kinder**
add -n or -en (-n)/(-en)	die **Frau** die **Wiese**	die **Frauen** die **Wiesen**
add -s (–s)	der **Streik** das **Auto**	die **Streiks** die **Autos**

There is no reliable way of telling which noun will have which ending for the plural, and you should therefore:

▶ always check the plural formation of a noun in your dictionary. The plural ending, with *Umlaut* indicated where applicable, is normally listed after the gender and the genitive case ending;

▶ **always learn a noun with its plural form** – saying it aloud helps to make it stick!

In practice, the gender and form of a noun can give helpful clues to its plural. These are shown in the table below, and sections **2.7–2.10** give you more details.

plural	masculine	feminine	neuter
no ending (–)	Those ending in **-el, -en, -er**	**NONE**	Those ending in **-el, -en, -er, -chen, -lein**
no ending, with *Umlaut* (⸚)	About **20**	**TWO:** *Mutter, Tochter*	**ONE:** *Kloster*
Add -e (-e)	**MOST**	very rare *Kenntnis -nisse*	**MOST**
Add -e, with *Umlaut* (⸚e)	Many **monosyllables** that can have *Umlaut*	about **30**	**ONE:** *Floß*
Add -er, with *Umlaut* **if poss.** (-er)/(⸚er)	About **12**	**NONE**	Many **monosyllables**
Add -n or -en (-n)/(-en)	All in **-e**, and a few others, mainly animate beings	**MOST**	About **12**

2.7 The plural of masculine nouns

▶ Most masculine nouns ending in *-el*, *-en* and *-er* form their plural **without adding an ending or** *Umlaut*:

der **Onkel** – die **Onkel**	der **Bäcker** – die **Bäcker**
der **Haken** – die **Haken**	der **Computer** – die **Computer**

▶ About twenty nouns ending in *-el*, *-en* and *-er* add *Umlaut* in the plural, but no ending:

der **Apfel** – die **Äpfel**	der **Laden** – die **Läden**
der **Mantel** – die **Mäntel**	der **Bruder** – die **Brüder**
der **Vogel** – die **Vögel**	der **Hammer** – die **Hämmer**
der **Garten** – die **Gärten**	der **Vater** – die **Väter**

▶ Most other masculine nouns **add -*e*** in the plural:

der Arm	–	die Arme	der Schuh	–	die Schuhe
der Hund	–	die Hunde	der Tisch	–	die Tische
der König	–	die Könige	der Termin	–	die Termine

If the noun has one syllable and a vowel which can have *Umlaut*, it frequently **adds *Umlaut*** as well as the **ending -*e*** – but not always. In practice, about 75% of the nouns which could have *Umlaut* do so:

der Arzt	–	die Ärzte	der Stuhl	–	die Stühle
der Bart	–	die Bärte	der Tanz	–	die Tänze
der Sohn	–	die Söhne	der Wolf	–	die Wölfe

But quite a lot of common nouns which could have *Umlaut* don't:

der Arm	–	die Arme	der Punkt	–	die Punkte
der Besuch	–	die Besuche	der Tag	–	die Tage
der Monat	–	die Monate	der Verlust	–	die Verluste

▶ About a dozen masculine nouns **add -*er*/-̈*er*.** The most common ones are:

der Geist	–	die Geister	der Rand	–	die Ränder
der Gott	–	die Götter	der Wald	–	die Wälder
der Mann	–	die Männer	der Wurm	–	die Würmer

▶ A number of masculine nouns **add -*n*/-*en*.**

Most of these are 'WEAK' MASCULINE NOUNS (see **2.12**) which denote humans or animals:

der Affe	–	die Affen	der Junge	–	die Jungen
der Bär	–	die Bären	der Mensch	–	die Menschen
der Franzose	–	die Franzosen	der Student	–	die Studenten

A few others ending in -*e* which have an irregular singular (see **2.12**):

der Buchstabe	–	die Buchstaben	der Gedanke	–	die Gedanken
der Funke	–	die Funken	der Name	–	die Namen

Some other nouns with a regular singular. The most common are:

der **Nerv**	– die **Nerven**	der **Strahl**	– die **Strahlen**
der **Pantoffel**	– die **Pantoffeln**	der **Typ**	– die **Typen**
der **Schmerz**	– die **Schmerzen**	der **Zeh**	– die **Zehen**

2.8 The plural of feminine nouns

▶ Most feminine nouns **add** *-n/-en* in the plural:

die **Arbeit**	– die **Arbeiten**	die **Frau**	– die **Frauen**
die **Bühne**	– die **Bühnen**	die **Last**	– die **Lasten**
die **Eule**	– die **Eulen**	die **Regel**	– die **Regeln**

NB The spelling of words with the ending *-in: die Lehrerin – die Lehrerinnen.*

▶ About 30 feminine nouns have a plural in *-e* **with** *Umlaut*. Some of these are very common:

die **Bank**	– die **Bänke**	die **Maus**	– die **Mäuse**
die **Hand**	– die **Hände**	die **Nacht**	– die **Nächte**
die **Kuh**	– die **Kühe**	die **Stadt**	– die **Städte**
die **Luft**	– die **Lüfte**	die **Wand**	– die **Wände**
die **Macht**	– die **Mächte**	die **Wurst**	– die **Würste**

NB *Bank* here means 'bench'. The plural of *Bank* meaning 'bank' is *die Banken*.

▶ Two common feminine nouns **add** *Umlaut* in the plural, with no ending:

die **Mutter**	– die **Mütter**	die **Tochter** – die **Töchter**

2.9 The plural of neuter nouns

▶ Most neuter nouns ending in *-el*, *-en* and *-er* and *-chen* or *-lein* form their plural **without adding an ending or** *Umlaut*:

das **Segel**	– die **Segel**	das **Mädchen**	– die **Mädchen**
das **Kissen**	– die **Kissen**	das **Büchlein**	– die **Büchlein**
das **Messer**	– die **Messer**		

▶ Most other neuter nouns **add** *-e* **in the plural**:

das **Bein**	– die **Beine**	das **Klavier**	– die **Klaviere**
das **Boot**	– die **Boote**	das **Schaf**	– die **Schafe**
das **Jahr**	– die **Jahre**	das **Verbot**	– die **Verbote**

▶ About a dozen neuter nouns **add -n/-en** in the plural. The most common are:

das Auge – die Augen	das Herz – die Herzen
das Bett – die Betten	das Interesse – die Interessen
das Hemd – die Hemden	das Ohr – die Ohren

▶ Around 50 neuter nouns consisting of only one syllable form their plural in *-er/-̈er*:

das Blatt – die Blätter	das Kind – die Kinder
das Dach – die Dächer	das Rad – die Räder
das Dorf – die Dörfer	das Schloss – die Schlösser
das Ei – die Eier	das Tal · – die Täler
das Haus – die Häuser	das Wort – die Wörter

NB A few neuter nouns of more than one syllable also have this ending, notably *das Gehalt, das Geschlecht, das Gesicht, das Gespenst.*

2.10 Plurals in -s (and other foreign plurals)

▶ Many words from French and English **add -s** in the plural:

das Baby – die Babys	der Park – die Parks
der Balkon – die Balkons	das Skateboard – die Skateboards
das Hotel – die Hotels	das Team – die Teams

▶ Words ending in a full vowel and abbreviations also **add -s** in the plural:

das Auto – die Autos	der LKW – die LKWs
der Azubi – die Azubis	der Uhu – die Uhus
das Kino – die Kinos	die Uni – die Unis

▶ Many foreign words ending in *-us*, *-a* or *-um* **replace this by** *-en* in the plural:

der Rhythmus – die Rhythmen	das Thema – die Themen
der Virus – die Viren	die Villa – die Villen
das Drama – die Dramen	das Museum – die Museen
die Firma – die Firmen	das Zentrum – die Zentren

2.11 Case

You saw in chapter **1** that German has four cases: nominative, accusative, genitive and dative. They indicate the **function of a noun phrase in the sentence**, and their main uses are summarized in the following tables:

NOMINATIVE

marks the subject of the verb (see **1.2, 8.1**)	**Der Fußballspieler** schoss ein Tor. *The footballer scored a goal.*
used in the complement of copular verbs like *sein* (see **8.10**)	Brecht ist **ein großer Dichter.** *Brecht is a great writer.*
with the noun in isolation	**Dein Freund,** wann siehst du ihn wieder? *Your friend, when will you see him again?*

ACCUSATIVE

marks the direct object of the verb (see **8.1**)	Ich kaufe **einen kleinen Fernseher.** *I'm buying a small television.*
after some prepositions (see **5.1, 5.3**)	Sie tat es für **ihren Bruder.** *She did it for her brother.*
in many adverbial phrases (see **4.9**)	Anita blieb **den ganzen Tag** zu Hause. *Anita stayed at home the whole day.*
in conventional greetings and wishes	**Guten Tag! Herzlichen Glückwunsch!** *Good morning/afternoon! Congratulations!*

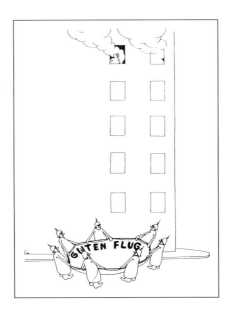

GENITIVE

links nouns, **especially to show possession** (see **8.6**)	Der Ton **des Radios** ist furchtbar. *The sound of the radio is awful.*
after a few prepositions (see **5.4**)	Sie lief **trotz ihres hohen Alters** schnell. *She ran fast despite her advanced age.*

DATIVE

marks the indirect object **of the verb** (see **8.3**)	Ich gebe **dem Hamster** sein Futter. *I'm giving the hamster its food.*
marks the sole (dative) object **of some verbs** (see **8.3**)	Sie will **ihrem Freund** helfen. *She wants to help her friend.*
can show possession, **esp. with clothing and parts of the body** (see **8.4**)	Sie zogen **dem Verletzten** die Hose aus. *They took the injured man's trousers off.*
after some prepositions (see **5.2–5.3**)	Wir suchten überall **nach dem Geld**. *We looked everywhere for the money.*
with many adjectives (see **4.4**)	Dieses Gespräch war **mir** sehr unangenehm. *This conversation was very unpleasant for me.*

2.12 Case marking on the noun

The four cases are marked through **endings in the noun phrase**. In practice, it is the endings of the ARTICLES, DETERMINERS and ADJECTIVES (chapters **3** and **4**) which indicate case most clearly, but sometimes there are **endings on the noun** to show case, too.

Regular nouns have the following forms in the four cases:

	masculine		feminine		neuter	
	singular	plural	singular	plural	singular	plural
nom.	der Vater	die Väter	die Frau	die Frauen	das Kind	die Kinder
acc.	den Vater	die Väter	die Frau	die Frauen	das Kind	die Kinder
gen.	**des Vaters**	der Väter	der Frau	der Frauen	**des Kindes**	der Kinder
dat.	dem Vater	**den Vätern**	der Frau	den Frauen	dem Kind	**den Kindern**

As the table shows, there are two special case endings with regular nouns:

▶ Masculine and neuter nouns **add -(e)s in the genitive singular**

▶ All nouns **add -n in the dative plural** (unless the plural ends in -n or -s).

Weak masculine nouns

This is a small group of masculine nouns that differ from the above pattern. They form their **plural with** -(e)n and also have this ending -(e)n **in all the singular cases except the nominative**. Their declension looks like this:

	singular	plural	singular	plural	singular	plural
nom.	der Junge	die Jungen	der Student	die Studenten	der Herr	die Herren
acc.	den Jungen	die Jungen	den Studenten	die Studenten	den Herrn	die Herren
gen.	des Jungen	der Jungen	des Studenten	der Studenten	des Herrn	der Herren
dat.	dem Jungen	den Jungen	dem Studenten	den Studenten	dem Herrn	den Herren

NB *Herr* is irregular: it has the ending -*n* in the singular, but -*en* in the plural.

These nouns typically denote **humans or animals**. There are three main groups:

▶ **All masculine nouns ending in** -e, e.g. *der Affe, der Bote, der Erbe, der Experte, der Franzose, der Genosse, der Hase, der Hirte, der Insasse, der Jude, der Junge, der Kunde, der Laie, der Riese, der Zeuge.*

▶ Foreign masculine nouns with the following **stressed SUFFIXES**:

-ant	der Diamant, der Demonstrant	-et	der Komet, der Planet
-aph	der Photograph/Fotograf	-ist	der Journalist, der Tourist
-arch	der Monarch, der Patriarch	-krat	der Demokrat, der Bürokrat
-at	der Automat, der Soldat	-nom	der Astronom, der Ökonom
-ent	der Dirigent, der Präsident	-ot	der Idiot, der Exot

▶ Some German masculine nouns ending in a consonant. The following are the most common:

der Bauer (gen. -n, pl. -n)	*farmer, peasant*	der Herr (gen. -n, pl. -en)	*gentleman*
der Fürst (gen. -en, pl. -en)	*prince*	der Mensch (gen. -en, pl. -en)	*human being*
der Held (gen. -en, pl. -en)	*hero*	der Nachbar (gen. -n, pl. -n)	*neighbour*

Don't confuse these WEAK MASCULINE NOUNS with **adjectives used as nouns** like *der Deutsche* 'the German'. These are explained in section **4.3**.

Irregular masculine nouns

There are a few irregular masculine nouns **ending in** -e that have a declension like the weak nouns, but their **genitive singular ends in** -ns:

	singular	plural
nom.	der Name	die Namen
acc.	den Namen	die Namen
gen.	des Namens	der Namen
dat.	dem Namen	den Namen

These nouns are:

der Buchstabe	*letter* (of alphabet)	der Glaube	*belief*
der Funke	*spark*	der Name	*name*
der Gedanke	*thought*	der Wille	*will*

NB The neuter noun *das Herz* (plural *die Herzen*) is similarly irregular: *des Herzens* (genitive singular), *dem Herzen* (dative singular).

▶ **Your dictionary will normally list the genitive ending** after the gender and before the plural ending for a noun. This tells you how it changes its form depending on case, e.g.

Vater *m* **-s, ̈** ⟶ des **Vaters**	**Franzose** *m* **-n, -n** ⟶ des **Franzosen**

NOUNS IN CONTEXT

EURE GUNST UNSER STREBEN

Eine moderne Arche Noah

Zirkus – auch als Theater des Volkes bezeichnet – ist eine der ältesten Formen der Unterhaltungskunst und Träger internationaler Kultur. Zirkus – das heißt Akrobaten, Clowns und vor allem Tiere, denn der Ursprung des Zirkus liegt in der Präsentation von Tieren.

CIRCUS CARL KRONE
der Circus den die ganze Welt kennt

CARL KRONE
der Schöpfer u. alleinige Eigentümer
des Unternehmens mit seinem
Lieblings-Elefanten ASSAM

Unser Zirkus ist so etwas wie eine moderne Arche Noah. Die Tiere sind unsere Partner, unsere Freunde und gehören mit zu unserer großen Familie.

Alle unsere Tiere haben die beste Pflege, gutes Futter, geräumige Stallungen und Außengehege, optimale Betreuung durch qualifizierte Tierärzte und Hufschmiede und vor allem ständige Ansprache von Tierlehrern und Tierpflegern. Alle unsere Dressuren basieren auf natürlichen Verhaltensweisen der Tiere. Partnerschaft zwischen Mensch und Tier ist die Grundlage der Dressurarbeit.

In einer Zeit, in der Exoten immer mehr aus ihrer natürlichen Umgebung verdrängt werden, ist es von größter Wichtigkeit, dass wir ihnen Lebensraum bei uns geben. So tragen wir dazu bei, die einzige Unterhaltungsform für die ganze Familie auch in Zukunft zu erhalten – den Zirkus.

(Aus: Circus Krone München, *Programmheft*)

GENDER

masculine	feminine	neuter
der Partner	die Partner**in**	das Leben
der Arzt	die Umgeb**ung**	das Volk
der Lehrer	die Wichtig**keit**	das Tier
der Freund	die Partner**schaft**	das Futter
der Akrobat	die Präsenta**tion**	das Gehege
der Clown	die Kultur	das Theater
der Mensch	die Sprach**e**	
der Zirkus	die Kunst	
der Raum	die Arbeit	
der Ursprung (!)	die Zeit	

NB *der Ursprung* is masculine: '-*ung*' is part of the 'root' *Sprung*, not an ending.

▶ Male humans/animals are MASCULINE

▶ Female humans/animals are FEMININE and often end in -*in*

▶ Nouns with the ending -*ung* are FEMININE and relate to verbs (e.g. *umgeben* – *die Umgebung*)

▶ Nouns ending in -*keit*, -*schaft*, -*sion*/-*tion*, -*ur* are FEMININE

▶ Most nouns with the ending -*e* are FEMININE

▶ **Only 20%** of German nouns are NEUTER

PLURALS

no ending, **sometimes with *Umlaut***	**Partner**
add -e, **sometimes with *Umlaut***	**Freunde, Räume**
add -er, **with *Umlaut* if possible**	**Völker**
add -n/-en **(esp. feminine)**	**Sprachen, Zeiten**
add -s **(esp. foreign)**	**Clowns**

CASE

masculine and neuter nouns add -(e)s in the **genitive singular** -n in the **dative plural** (except after **-n-** or **-s**)	des **Partners**, des **Volk(e)s** den **Partnern**, den **Völkern**
'weak' masculine nouns add -(e)n **in all cases** other than nom. sing.	der **Mensch** – **Menschen** der **Akrobat** – **Akrobaten** der **Exot** – **Exoten**

The noun phrase: determiners and pronouns 3

A **NOUN PHRASE** may simply consist of one noun on its own, e.g. *Rache ist süß*, or of a **PRONOUN**, which 'stands for' a noun, e.g. *Sie ist süß*. As in English, it is usual for a noun to be preceded by a **DETERMINER** such as the following:

◆ an **ARTICLE** – *der* (the) or *ein* (a)

◆ a **DEMONSTRATIVE** such as *dieser* (this)

◆ a **POSSESSIVE** such as *mein* (my) or *dein* (your)

◆ an **INTERROGATIVE** such as *welcher* (which) or *wie viele* (how many).

Between the determiner and the noun you may find one or more **ADJECTIVES** (see chapter 4) or even – unlike English – long **adjectival phrases** that give additional information about the noun:

dieser tolle neue Film	*this brilliant new film*
Der 1867 von dem schwedischen Chemiker Alfred Nobel erfundene und kurz darauf für die Erbauung des Gotthard-Tunnels benutzte Sprengstoff heißt Dynamit.	*The explosive invented in 1867 by the Swedish chemist Alfred Nobel and used shortly afterwards for the construction of the Gotthard Tunnel is called dynamite.*

Determiners play an important part in indicating the **role of the noun phrase** in the sentence. To do this they have **endings** that indicate GENDER, NUMBER and CASE. Similarly, the form of pronouns changes depending on their grammatical role. In order to understand German well and produce comprehensible sentences, you need to learn these forms and pay attention to the endings in their context.

This chapter gives you details about the following:

◆ definite and indefinite **ARTICLES** (**3.1–3.3**)

◆ other **DETERMINERS** (**3.4–3.6**)

◆ **PRONOUNS**, notably **PERSONAL PRONOUNS** and **REFLEXIVE PRONOUNS** (**3.7–3.9**).

3.1 The definite article

The definite article (= English 'the') has different forms to show the GENDER, NUMBER and CASE of the noun it is used with.

	masculine	feminine	neuter	plural
nominative	der	die	das	die
accusative	den	die	das	die
genitive	des	der	des	der
dative	dem	der	dem	den

With certain prepositions, the definite article is often contracted and written as a single word. The following are the most usual:

ans = an + das	**ins** = in + das	**zum** = zu + dem	**beim** = bei + dem
am = an + dem	**im** = in + dem	**zur** = zu + der	**vom** = von + dem

3.2 The indefinite article

The indefinite article (= English 'a'/'an') has forms corresponding to the GENDER and CASE of the noun. There is no plural, because (as in English) indefinite plural nouns are used without an article, e.g. *Ich habe **ein Ei** gekauft*, but *Ich habe **Eier** gekauft*.

	masculine	feminine	neuter
nominative	ein	eine	ein
accusative	einen	eine	ein
genitive	eines	einer	eines
dative	einem	einer	einem

Kein(e) (*not a/not any*)

There is a **negative form of the indefinite article**, *kein*, which corresponds to English 'not … a', 'not … any' or 'no' with a noun. It has the same endings as *ein* in the **singular**, but unlike *ein* it can also be used in the **plural**, where it has case endings like those of *mein* (see **3.5**). The following examples illustrate the use of *kein*:

Ich habe **keinen Garten**.	*I haven**'t** got **a** garden.*
Wir haben **keine frischen Brötchen**.	*We haven**'t** got **any** fresh rolls.*
Keine Franzosen sind gekommen.	***No** French people came.*

Remember:

▶ The German equivalent for '**not a**' and '**not any**' is *kein* (i.e. not *nicht ein*).

3.3 Uses of the articles

Generally speaking, articles are used in German much as they are in English. But there are certain differences, with usage being affected by context and style. These are the main differences to watch out for in German:

▶ The definite article is often used before **abstract nouns**:

Die Demokratie ist in einer Krise.	*Democracy is in a state of crisis.*
Sie glaubt an **das Leben** nach **dem Tod**.	*She believes in life after death.*

▶ The definite article is often used before **infinitives used as nouns**:

Das Fotografieren ist verboten.	*It is not permitted to take photographs.*
Ich liebe **das Drachenfliegen**.	*I love hang-gliding.*

▶ The definite article is used with names of **languages** if these are in an 'inflected' form, i.e. with a case ending:

eine Übersetzung aus **dem Russischen**	*a translation from Russian*
Im Deutschen sagt man das nicht.	*You don't say that in German.*
BUT: Ich kann **Deutsch**.	*I can speak German/I know German.*

▶ The definite article is used with names of **months and seasons**:

Der April war verregnet.	*April was rainy.*
Im Winter friert der Bach zu.	*In winter the stream freezes over.*

▶ The definite article is used with **street names** and with **feminine and plural names of countries**:

Ich wohne in **der Marktstraße**.	*I live in Market Street.*
Wir wohnen jetzt in **der Schweiz**.	*We live in Switzerland now.*
Sie lebt in **den Niederlanden**.	*She lives in the Netherlands.*

▶ The definite article is used with all **proper names qualified by an adjective or adjectival phrase**:

das heutige **Deutschland**	*Germany today/modern Germany*
der junge **Heinrich Mann**	*the young Heinrich Mann*
das zerstörte **Dresden**	*the destroyed city of Dresden*
das zur Hauptstadt ernannte **Berlin**	*Berlin, which has been made the capital*

▶ The definite article is used in **colloquial** speech before the **names of people**:

„Ich finde **den Udo** total unmöglich.“	*"I find Udo totally impossible."*
„Ist **die Frau Berlinger** da?“	*"Is Frau Berlinger there?"*

▶ The definite article is often used with **parts of the body and articles of clothing**, where English uses a possessive:

Sie machte **die Augen** zu.	*She closed her eyes.*
Hast du dir **die Zähne** geputzt?	*Have you cleaned your teeth?*
Er steckte **die Hand** in **die Tasche**.	*He put his hand in his pocket.*

▶ A definite article is used in some **set prepositional phrases** where the English equivalent has no article:

Wir gingen **in die Schule**.	*We went to school.*
Er trank den Kaffee **im Stehen**.	*He drank his coffee standing up.*
Wir fahren **mit dem Bus**.	*We're going by bus.*

▶ **No article** is used in the PREDICATE COMPLEMENT of *sein*, **werden** or **bleiben** with nouns denoting **professions**, **nationality or classes of people**:

Er ist **Arzt/Bäcker/Installateur**.	*He is a doctor/baker/plumber.*
Mein Schwager ist **Deutscher**.	*My brother-in-law is (a) German.*
Anne ist doch **Engländerin**, oder?	*Anne is an Englishwoman, isn't she?*
Helmut blieb **Junggeselle**.	*Helmut remained a bachelor.*
Er wurde **Sozialdemokrat**.	*He became a Social Democrat.*

NB If the noun is preceded by an adjective, the indefinite article is used, e.g. *Er ist ein guter Arzt*.

▶ **No article** or determiner need be used in the **plural** where English uses 'some' or 'any':

Ich habe **Äpfel** gekauft.	*I bought **some** apples.*
Brauchen Sie **Marken**?	*Do you need **any** stamps?*

3.4 Demonstratives

Demonstratives are words used to **point to something or someone**, like English 'this' and 'that'. This section deals with demonstrative DETERMINERS. See **3.9** for demonstrative PRONOUNS.

Der/die/das

This is the most frequent demonstrative in spoken German. It has the same written forms as the definite article (see **3.1**), but it is typically pronounced with heavy stress and a full vowel while pointing at the object. It corresponds to English 'this' or 'that'. Compare:

Ich möchte ein Stück von der **Wurst**.	*I'd like a piece of the **sausage**.*
Ich möchte ein Stück von **der** Wurst.	*I'd like a piece of **this/that** sausage.*

Dieser

Dieser generally corresponds to English 'this'. It is especially common in written German (where *der* would be ambiguous), but it is used in speech, too. It has different forms to show the GENDER, NUMBER and CASE of the noun it is used with.

	masculine	feminine	neuter	plural
nominative	dieser	diese	dieses	diese
accusative	diesen	diese	dieses	diese
genitive	dieses	dieser	dieses	dieser
dative	diesem	dieser	diesem	diesen

These endings are also used for a large number of other determiners:

alle	*all*	**jener**	*that*	**viele**	*much, many*
beide	*both*	**mancher**	*some, many*	**welcher**	*which*
einige	*some*	**mehrere**	*several*	**wenige**	*few*
jeder	*each, every*	**sämtliche**	*all*		

In practice, *dieser* is often used where we would say 'that' in English if it is not necessary to make a clear distinction between something close by and something further away:

Ich habe **diese Erklärung** nicht verstanden.	*I didn't understand this/that explanation.*
Diese Schokolade schmeckt aber gut!	*This/that chocolate really does taste good!*

Other demonstratives

Jener (**that**) is used mainly in formal written German. It has the same endings as *dieser*.

Seit **jenen Tagen** hatte Herr Arndt ihn nicht mehr gesehen.	*Mr Arndt had not seen him since those days.*

Solcher (**such**) is used mainly in the plural, with the same endings as *dieser*. In the singular it is usually used with *ein* and has the same endings as an adjective (see **4.1**, 'weak' declension).

Solchen Leuten kann man alles erzählen.	*You can tell people like that anything.*
Eine solche Kamera würde ich nie kaufen.	*I'd never buy a camera like that.*

So ein is the most common equivalent for '**such a**' in spoken German, with the endings of the indefinite article *ein* (see **3.2**). It is often accompanied by a gesture indicating the size.

Sie hat mir **so ein großes Eis** gekauft.	*She bought me an ice-cream **this** big!*

Derjenige (**that**) is most often followed by a relative clause. The first part declines like *der* (see **3.1**), the second has the endings of an adjective (see **4.1**, 'weak' declension).

Gerade **diejenige Frau**, die mir helfen wollte, ist verschwunden.	*The very woman that was going to help me has disappeared.*

Derselbe (**the same**). Both parts decline, like *derjenige*.

Er besucht **dieselbe Schule** wie dein Bruder.	*He's at the same school as your brother.*

3.5 Possessives

Possessives indicate 'possession' of the following noun, e.g. *mein Buch* 'my book', *Ihre Tochter* 'your daughter'. As in English, there is a possessive form corresponding to each PERSONAL PRONOUN, e.g. *ich* (I) or *du* (you) (see **3.7**). This section deals with possessive DETERMINERS. See **3.9** for possessive PRONOUNS.

singular			plural		
ich	mein	*my*	**wir**	unser	*our*
du	dein	*your*	**ihr**	euer	*your*
er	sein	*his*	**Sie**	Ihr	*your* (polite)
sie	ihr	*her*	**sie**	ihr	*their*
es	sein	*its*			

NB For the personal pronouns *ich*, *du* etc. see **3.7**.
NB The polite form *Sie* (you) and its possessive *Ihr* (your) can be used to address one person, or two or more people (see **3.7**).
NB The *-er* at the end of *unser* and *euer* is part of the stem, not an ending. The endings are added to the stem, e.g. *in unserem Haus*, *eu(e)re Reise*.

Like other determiners, possessives change their endings in accordance with the GENDER, NUMBER and CASE of the following noun:

Mein Vater	traf	meine **Schwestern**.
(masc., sg., nom.)		*(fem., pl., acc.)*
My father	*met*	*my sisters.*
Der Bruder **meines Vaters**	traf	den Lehrer **meiner Schwestern**.
(masc., sg., gen.)		*(fem., pl., gen.)*
*The brother **of my father***	*met*	*the teacher **of my sisters**.*
OR: **My father's** *brother*	*met*	**my sisters'** *teacher.*

The **case endings** of possessive determiners are like those of *ein* and *kein*:

	masculine	feminine	neuter	plural
nominative	mein	meine	mein	meine
accusative	meinen	meine	mein	meine
genitive	meines	meiner	meines	meiner
dative	meinem	meiner	meinem	meinen

Possessives can also be used as PRONOUNS (i.e. as the equivalent to English 'mine' rather than 'my'), but they then have different endings (see **3.9**).

3.6 Other determiners

Most of the other common determiners in German have the **same endings as *dieser*** (see **3.4**). Many of them are used only or chiefly in the plural.

Alle (**all/all the**) is used in the plural with endings like *dieser*:

Sie hat **alle guten Bonbons** aufgegessen.	*She's eaten up all the good sweets.*

It can also be used without an ending in the singular and in the nominative/accusative plural, followed by a definite article, e.g. *mit **all dem** Geld, **all die** braven Kinder.*

Beide (**both**) is used in the plural with endings like *dieser*:

Ich möchte **beide T-Shirts** kaufen.	*I'd like to buy both T-shirts.*

Ein paar (**a few**) does not decline. The determiner *ein paar* should not be confused with *ein Paar* (a pair), e.g. *ein Paar Schuhe*:

Wir fahren in **ein paar Tagen** nach Griechenland.	*We're going to Greece in a few days' time.*

Einige (**some**) has endings like *dieser* and is more common in the plural:

Nach **einigem Überlegen** (sg.) hat sie **einige Bücher** (pl.) gekauft.	*After some deliberation she bought some books.*

Irgendein/irgendwelche (**some/some ... or other/any ... at all**) emphasizes indefiniteness. *Irgendein* is only used in the singular and has the endings of *ein* (see **3.2**). *Irgendwelche* is used in the plural and has endings like *dieser*:

Er hat **irgendeinen Job** bei einer Zeitung.	*He's got some job with a newspaper.*
Sie hat mir Fotos von **irgendwelchen Filmstars** gezeigt, von denen ich noch nie gehört habe.	*She showed me photographs of some filmstars I've never heard of.*

Jeder (**each/every/any**) has endings like *dieser* and is only used in the singular:

Wir spielen **jeden Tag** Monopoly.	*We play Monopoly every day.*

Mancher (**some/many, in the sense of 'a fair number'**) has endings like *dieser* and is more common in the plural:

An **manchen Tagen** bleibt Alfred einfach im Bett.	*Some days Alfred simply stays in bed.*

Mehrere (**several**) has endings like *dieser* and is used in the plural:

Er brauchte zur Reparatur des Computers **mehrere Monate**.	*He needed several months to mend the computer.*

Sämtliche (**all, referring to the members of a particular set**) has endings like *dieser*:

In der Kreidezeit sind **sämtliche Dinosaurier** ausgestorben.	*All the dinosaurs died out in the Cretaceous period.*

Viel/viele (**much/many/a lot of**) usually has no ending in the singular, but endings like *dieser* in the plural:

Viel Glück! Ich hoffe, du fängst **viele Fische**.	*Good luck! I hope you catch lots of fish.*

Was für (ein) (**what sort of**). The word *ein* declines like the indefinite article (see **3.2**). It is absent in the plural:

Was für Tiere magst du am liebsten?	*What kind of animals do you like best?*
Was für ein Mann ist er denn?	*What sort of a man is he?*

Welcher (**which**) is an interrogative determiner and has the same endings as *dieser*. It can be used in the singular and plural:

Welche Partei wählst du dieses Mal?	*Which party will you vote for this time?*

Wenig/wenige (**little/few/not much/not many**) usually has no ending in the singular, but the endings of *dieser* in the plural:

Das Flugzeug landet in **wenigen Minuten**.	*The plane will be landing in a few minutes.*
Er hat **wenig Zeit**.	*He doesn't have much time.*

3.7 Personal pronouns

PRONOUNS are typically little words which stand for nouns or noun phrases. The PERSONAL PRONOUNS in English and German fall into three groups:

▶ **First person**: the speaker (or a group including the speaker)

▶ **Second person**: the person(s) being addressed

▶ **Third person**: the other person(s) or thing(s) being spoken about.

Like nouns, they have special forms to indicate gender (in the third person), plural and case:

	person	nominative		accusative	dative
	1st	ich	*I*	mich	mir
	2nd	du	*you*	dich	dir
singular	3rd masculine	er	*he*	ihn	ihm
	feminine	sie	*she*	sie	ihr
	neuter	es	*it*	es	ihm
	1st	wir	*we*	uns	uns
	2nd familiar	ihr	*you*	euch	euch
plural	polite (sg./pl.)	Sie	*you*	Sie	*Ihnen*
	3rd	sie	*they*	sie	ihnen

NB There are genitive forms of the personal pronouns (*meiner, deiner, seiner*, etc.), but they are rarely used nowadays even in very formal registers.

Er, sie, es

Because words for things can have any of the three genders in German, we find all three used where we would use 'it' in English.

▶ In the singular, the **third person pronouns take their gender from the noun** which they refer to.

This means that *er, sie* and *es* do not correspond exactly to English 'he', 'she' and 'it'. Look carefully at these sentences:

Dein Geldbeutel? Ach, **er** lag vorhin auf dem Tisch, aber irgendjemand muss **ihn** weggenommen haben. (der Geldbeutel)   *Your purse? Oh, it was lying on the table earlier, but someone must have taken it.*
Die Katze sah **die Maus**, fing **sie** und biss **ihr** den Kopf ab. (die Maus)   *The cat saw the mouse, caught it and bit its head off* [literally: *bit off the head from it*].
Darf ich **Ihr Buch** noch eine Woche behalten? Ich habe **es** noch nicht gelesen. (das Buch)   *May I keep your book for another week? I haven't read it yet.*
Der Prinz sah **Dornröschen** und küsste **es**. (das Dornröschen)   *The prince saw Sleeping Beauty and kissed her.*

NB Whether the pronoun is masculine, feminine or neuter in principle depends on grammatical gender, e.g. ***das** Dornröschen* is ***es*** despite being female (nouns with the diminutive ending *-chen* are always neuter). Especially in spoken German, however, people often use the pronoun appropriate to the person's natural gender.

Prepositional adverbs

Personal pronouns are not normally used to refer to **things after a preposition**. The prepositional adverb (a compound of ***da(r)*** + PREPOSITION) is used instead:

Ich sitze darauf.	*I am sitting **on it**.*
Ich sitze **auf ihm**.	*I am sitting **on him**.*
Ich spiele damit.	*I am playing **with it**.*
Ich spiele **mit ihm**.	*I am playing **with him**.*
Ich spreche darüber.	*I am talking **about it**.*
Ich spreche **über ihn**.	*I am talking **about him**.*

NB *dar-* is sometimes contracted to ***dr-***, e.g. *drunter und drüber.*

Du/Sie

German distinguishes between **familiar** and **polite** forms of the second person pronouns:

du (and its plural *ihr*) are used

▶ when speaking to children (up to age 14), animals and God

▶ between relatives and close friends

▶ between fellow students at college and university

▶ between blue-collar workmates

Sie is used in all other instances, in particular

▶ to address adult strangers

▶ to address colleagues in middle-class professions, though close colleagues will often use first names and *du*

The forms of **Sie** are the same whether you are speaking to one or more people. In general, the use of **du/ihr** (and the corresponding use of first names) is much less widespread in German-speaking countries than the use of first names in English-speaking countries.

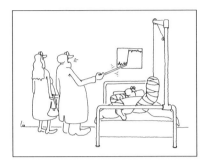

„Zu diesem Zeitpunkt erfuhr Ihr Mann, dass Sie ihn besuchen wollten."

Man

When referring to people in general, it is normal to use the indefinite pronoun *man* 'one' (not *du* or *Leute*):

Bei Rot soll **man** nicht über die Straße gehen.	*One/You shouldn't cross the road when the lights are red.*
Heutzutage ist **man** toleranter.	*Nowadays people are more tolerant.*

Man only exists in the nominative form. For the other cases **einen** (accusative) and **einem** (dative) are used:

Die Politik macht **einen** geradezu depressiv.	*Politics make one positively depressed.*
Der Staat sollte **einem** viel mehr Geld geben.	*The state ought to give people far more money.*

3.8 Reflexive pronouns

Sometimes a pronoun refers back to the subject of the sentence, e.g. *Ich wasche mich* (I wash myself/I'm washing myself) or *Er schadet sich* (He's harming himself). These are called REFLEXIVE PRONOUNS, and verbs used with reflexive pronouns are called REFLEXIVE VERBS. In terms of valency this means that their direct or indirect object refers to the same person(s) as their subject (see **8.2**).

Reflexive pronouns are used more widely in German than English, and they have a special form – *sich* – in the third person:

accusative			dative		
ich	freue	**mich**	**ich**	schade	**mir**
du	freust	**dich**	**du**	schadest	**dir**
er/sie/es	freut	**sich**	**er/sie/es**	schadet	**sich**
wir	freuen	**uns**	**wir**	schaden	**uns**
ihr	freut	**euch**	**ihr**	schadet	**euch**
sie/Sie	freuen	**sich**	**sie/Sie**	schaden	**sich**

The function of the reflexive pronouns becomes clear when we compare, for instance, *fragen* (to ask) with *sich fragen* (to wonder):

Vater fragt ihn	*father is asking him (i.e. someone else)*
Vater fragt sich	*father is wondering (i.e. asking himself)*

3.9 Demonstrative, possessive and indefinite pronouns

Most of the **demonstratives and indefinite determiners** listed in sections **3.4** and **3.6** can be used as PRONOUNS, with the **same endings** to indicate GENDER, NUMBER and CASE. This means that instead of being used with a following noun, they can substitute for a noun, often referring back to a noun or noun phrase already mentioned:

Ich will **eine andere Tasche. Diese** hier mag ich nicht.	*I want a different bag. I don't like **this one**.*
Die Ameisen sind ja riesig. **Solche** habe ich noch nie gesehen.	*The ants are enormous. I've never seen **ones like that**.*
Sie hat **einige** gekauft.	*She bought **some of them**.*
Jeder hier kennt ihn.	***Everyone** here knows him.*
Ich habe **viel** gelesen.	*I've read **a lot**.*
Hast du **alles**, was wir brauchen?	*Have you got **everything** we need?*
Derjenige, der das getan hat, soll sich melden.	***The one** who (i.e. whoever) did this should put up their hand/give themselves up.*

Unfortunately for the learner, some of the demonstratives, possessives etc. have special forms when used as pronouns.

Der/die/das

When used as a PRONOUN, the DEMONSTRATIVE *der* has special forms in the genitive case and the dative plural:

	masculine	feminine	neuter	plural
nominative	der	die	das	die
accusative	den	die	das	die
genitive	dessen	deren	dessen	deren
dative	dem	der	dem	denen

NB These are also the forms of the RELATIVE PRONOUN, see **10.5**.

Die sind viel zu teuer.	***Those ones** are far too expensive.*
Hast du gestern **den Film** gesehen?	*Did you see the film yesterday?*
Der war toll, was?	***It** was great, wasn't it?*
Das Buch liegt auf **dem Tisch** –	*The book is lying on the table –*
ja, auf **dem** da drüben.	*yes, on **that one** over there.*

NB The genitive is generally used to replace an ambiguous possessive, e.g. *Er kam mit **seinem Freund** und **dessen Sohn**.* He came with his friend and **the friend's** son.

Possessives

When used as PRONOUNS, the POSSESSIVES have distinct forms in the masculine nominative singular and the neuter nominative/accusative singular:

	masculine	feminine	neuter	plural
nominative	meiner	meine	mein(e)s	meine
accusative	meinen	meine	mein(e)s	meine
genitive	meines	meiner	meines	meiner
dative	meinem	meiner	meinem	meinen

Wenn du ein Auto brauchst, kann ich dir mein(e)s (*neut., sg., acc.*) **leihen.**	
*If you need a car, I can lend you **mine**.*	
Das ist nicht mein Koffer, sondern deiner (*masc., sg., nom.*).	
*That isn't my suitcase, but **yours**.*	
Ich fahre in deinem Wagen. In seinem **habe ich immer Angst** (*masc., sg., dat.*).	
*I'll go in your car. I'm always frightened in **his**.*	

Einer/keiner

The PRONOUNS *einer* 'one' and *keiner* 'none' have the **same endings as the possessive pronouns**. This means that unlike the indefinite article, they have endings in the masculine nominative singular and the neuter nominative/accusative singular:

Das sind **gute Birnen**. Willst du **eine**?	*These are good pears. Do you want **one**?*
Habt ihr **einen Hund**? – Nein, wir haben **keinen**.	*Have you got a dog? – No, we don't have **one**.*
einer dieser Männer .../**eine dieser Frauen** .../	*One of these men/women/children*
eines dieser Kinder	
Sie sprach mit **keiner dieser Damen**/... mit	*She talked to **none of** these ladies/men.*
keinem dieser Männer.	

Other common pronouns

Etwas (**something, anything**) has no case forms. It is often shortened to *was* in speech:

Ich habe **etwas** für Sie./Ich hab **was** für dich.	*I've got something for you.*
Er sagte ihr **etwas**.	*He told her something.*
Hast du **was** gesagt?	*Did you say something?*

Jemand (**somebody, someone**) can have endings in the accusative (*jemanden*) and dative cases (*jemandem*), but it is used just as frequently without in both spoken and written German:

Ich habe **jemand(en)** gesehen.	*I saw someone.*
Wir haben mit **jemand(em)** gesprochen.	*We spoke to someone.*

Nichts (**nothing**) has no case forms:

Nichts gefiel ihr dort!	*Nothing there was to her liking.*
Aber ich habe **nichts** gesagt.	*But I did**n't** say **anything**.*

NB Distinguish this from the negation with *nicht*, e.g. *Es gefiel ihr **nicht*** (She did**n't** like it); *Das habe ich **nicht** gesagt* (I did **not** say that).

Niemand (**nobody, no one**) is used like *jemand*:

Sie hat **niemand**(en) getroffen.	*She met **no one**.*
Er hat sich bei **niemand**(em) bedankt.	*He did **not** thank **anybody**.*

Was (**what**) refers to things. It has no case forms. After prepositions it is replaced by a compound formed with **wo(r)**- in standard German, e.g. **wofür** and **wobei** rather than *für was* and *bei was*:

Was hast du gesehen?	*What did you see?*
Womit schreibst du? Mit einem Bleistift?	*What are you writing **with**? With a pencil?*
Worüber sprechen Sie? – Über die Römer.	*What will you be talking **about**? – About the Romans.*

Welcher (**some, any**) declines like *dieser* (see **3.4**). It is frequent in speech:

Ich brauche Marken. Hast du **welche**?	*I need some stamps. Have you got some?*

Wer (**who**) refers to persons. It has the case forms *wen* (accusative), *wessen* (genitive) and *wem* (dative):

Wen hast du dort gesehen?	*Who(**m**) did you see there?*
Wessen Bücher sind das?	*Whose books are those?*
Mit **wem** hast du gespielt?	*Who did you play with?*

THE NOUN PHRASE IN CONTEXT

Besser als das „Dream Team"?

Die Zeichen stehen gut: Die Münchner führen mit großem Vorsprung die Bundesligatabelle an. Die Wahrscheinlichkeit, dass die Bayern ihre 15. Deutsche Meisterschaft erringen, liegt bei 99,9 Prozent! Und wenn alles ideal läuft, können die Bayern das schaffen, was in Deutschland noch niemand geschafft hat: das „Triple" – Deutscher Meister, DFB-Pokalsieger und Champions-League-Sieger in einem Jahr! Sich endlich einmal wieder am Gipfel des europäischen Fußballs zu sonnen, darauf sind sie in München alle super heiß – vom Platzwart bis zum Präsidenten!

Keine Frage, mit diesem außergewöhnlichen Erfolg würde die Mannschaft in die Annalen des Fußballs eingehen. Rekordnationalspieler Lothar Matthäus, der seinen Platz im Geschichtsbuch längst sicher hat: „Wir haben die Chance, eine große Ära des FC Bayern

einzuläuten – das muss Motivation genug für jeden Spieler sein." Zur Erinnerung: Das Weltrenommée, das die Münchner heute haben, erspielten sie sich zwischen 1974 und 1976, als das damalige Team um die Topstars Franz Beckenbauer, Gerd Müller und Sepp Maier dreimal in Folge den Europapokal der Landesmeister holte …

Die aktuelle Mannschaft soll noch besser sein als das „Dream Team" – davon ist zumindest der inzwischen zum Bayern-Präsidenten avancierte Franz Beckenbauer überzeugt: „Wir hatten damals sieben oder acht gute Leute. Heute sind es 15 bis 17 Topspieler!" Die Bayern – stark wie nie?

(Aus: *Bravo Sport*)

THE NOUN PHRASE

determiner	adjective/adjectival phrase	noun/pronoun
		Motivation
die		**Chance**
		sie
eine	große	**Ära**
der	inzwischen zum Bayern-Präsidenten avancierte	**Franz Beckenbauer**

DETERMINERS

type of determiner	gender, number, case in the text:
definite article (3.1)	**die** Chance (*f. sg. acc.*), **das** Team (*n. sg. nom.*) **des** Fußballs (*m. sg. gen.*), **den** Pokal (*m. sg. acc.*) **die** Topstars (*pl. acc.*) **am**, **im**, **vom**, **zum**=an/in/von/zu **dem** (*m./n. sg. dat.*) **zur**=zu **der** (*f. sg. dat.*)
indefinite article (3.2)	**eine** Ära (*f. sg. acc.*), **einem** Jahr (*n. sg. dat.*) **keine** Frage (*f. sg. nom.*)
demonstrative (3.4)	**diesem** Erfolg (*m. sg. dat.*)
possessive (3.5)	**ihre** Meisterschaft (*f. sg. acc.*) **seinen** Platz (*m. sg. acc.*)
other determiners (3.6)	**jeden** Spieler (*m. sg. acc.*)

PRONOUNS

type of pronoun	person/gender, number, case in the text:
personal pronoun (3.7)	**sie** (*3rd pl. nom.*), **wir** (*1st pl. nom.*), **es** (*3rd sg. nom.*)
reflexive pronoun (3.8)	**sich** (*3rd pl. acc.*) sonnen **sich** (*3rd pl. acc.*) etwas erspielen
demonstrative pronoun (3.9)	Wir haben die Chance … – **das** (*n. sg. nom.*) muss … können die Bayern **das** (*n. sg. acc.*) schaffen, was …
relative pronoun (3.9, also 10.5)	Lothar Matthäus, **der** … (*m. sg. nom.*) das Weltrenommée, **das** … (*n. sg. acc.*) das …, **was** (*n. sg. acc.*)
other pronouns (3.9)	**alle** (*pl. nom.*) sind heiß; **alles** (*n. sg. nom.*) läuft ideal das hat **niemand** (*m. sg. nom.*) geschafft

Adjectives, adverbs and adverbials 4

This chapter gives you details about the formation and use of adjectives, adverbs and other adverbials in German. **ADJECTIVES** generally qualify or describe nouns as part of noun phrases, while **ADVERBS** and **ADVERBIALS** may qualify verbs, adjectives or other adverbs – or fulfil other functions such as introducing questions or indicating the attitude of the speaker. Topics covered in this chapter are:

◆ **ADJECTIVES** – their use and declension (**4.1–4.5**)

◆ the **comparison** of adjectives and adverbs (**4.6–4.7** and **4.16**)

◆ **ADVERBS** and **ADVERBIALS** – their formation and use (**4.8–4.14**)

◆ **INTERROGATIVE** adverbials (**4.15**)

◆ numerals (**4.17–4.20**)

◆ **MODAL PARTICLES** (**4.21**).

4.1 Adjective declension

ADJECTIVES typically **qualify or describe a noun**. They can be used in two main ways in German:

▶ They can be placed **before** the noun as **ATTRIBUTIVE ADJECTIVES**. In this position they have an **ending** which indicates the **GENDER**, **NUMBER** and **CASE** of the noun, e.g. *der **helle** Tag, eine **alte** Frau, **reines** Gold, mit **kaltem** Wasser*. Even an extended adjectival phrase has such an ending:

> Er erfand den **für die Erbauung des Gotthard-Tunnels benutzt**en Sprengstoff.
> *He invented the explosive that was used for the construction of the Gotthard Tunnel.*

> Der **inzwischen zum Bayern-Präsidenten avancierte** Beckenbauer ist davon überzeugt.
> *Beckenbauer, who has meanwhile risen to the position of president of Bayern München, is convinced of that.*

NB In such phrases, a present participle or a past participle (e.g. *benutzt, avanciert*) is used as an adjective.

▶ They can be used as a complement of the verb (i.e. as a **PREDICATE COMPLEMENT**, see **1.6**). They then come **after** the verb and have **no ending**: *Das Wasser ist kalt. Das Auto ist schnell*

When used with a noun, adjectives have **two basic types of declension**:

▶ The 'weak' **declension** is used if the adjective is preceded by a **DETERMINER which has its own ending**.

▶ The 'strong' **declension** is used if the adjective is not preceded by a determiner, or if the determiner has no ending.

Weak declension

The weak declension is typically used **after the definite article** and all **determiners which decline like *dieser***. There are only two endings, *-e* (used in the nominative singular and the accusative singular feminine and neuter) and *-en* (used everywhere else):

	masculine	feminine	neuter	plural
nom.	der gute Wein	die gute Suppe	das gute Brot	die guten Weine
acc.	den guten Wein	die gute Suppe	das gute Brot	die guten Weine
gen.	des guten Weines	der guten Suppe	des guten Brotes	der guten Weine
dat.	dem guten Wein	der guten Suppe	dem guten Brot	den guten Weinen

Strong declension

The strong declension is almost identical to the **endings of *dieser*** (see **3.4**). It is typically used if there is **no determiner**, or if the **determiner has no ending**, like singular *viel* or *wenig* (e.g. *mit viel kaltem Wasser*):

	masculine	feminine	neuter	plural
nom.	guter Wein	gute Suppe	gutes Brot	gute Weine
acc.	guten Wein	gute Suppe	gutes Brot	gute Weine
gen.	guten Weines	guter Suppe	guten Brotes	guter Weine
dat.	gutem Wein	guter Suppe	gutem Brot	guten Weinen

Mixed declension

There is also a so-called 'mixed' declension, which is used **after the indefinite article *ein***, the **negative *kein*** and the POSSESSIVES. After these determiners, adjectives have weak endings **except** in the nominative singular masculine and the nominative/accusative singular neuter. Here they have the strong endings because the determiner has no ending:

	masculine	feminine	neuter	plural
nom.	sein guter Wein	seine gute Suppe	sein gutes Brot	seine guten Weine
acc.	seinen guten Wein	seine gute Suppe	sein gutes Brot	seine guten Weine
gen.	seines guten Weines	seiner guten Suppe	seines guten Brotes	seiner guten Weine
dat.	seinem guten Wein	seiner guten Suppe	seinem guten Brot	seinen guten Weinen

4.2 Adjective declension: some special cases

There are a few instances where adjective declensions do not follow the patterns outlined in section **4.1**.

▶ Adjectives have **strong endings** after *einige*, *manche*, *mehrere*, *viele* and *wenige* used in the plural.

This runs counter to the usual rule that adjectives always have weak endings after a determiner which has an ending itself:

nom.	einige gute	Weine
acc.	einige gute	Weine
gen.	einiger guter	Weine
dat.	einigen guten	Weinen

▶ Adjectives ending in *-el*, *-er* (and sometimes those in *-en*) can drop the *-e-* when an ending is added:

dunkel	ein **dunkler** Wald	*a dark forest*
trocken	die **trockne/trockene** Wäsche	*the dry washing*
teuer	ein **teurer** Computer	*an expensive computer*

▶ The adjective ***hoch*** 'high' has the special form *hoh-* when endings are added:

Der Berg ist **hoch** **BUT** ein **hoher** Berg	*The mountain is high/a high mountain*

4.3 Adjectives used as nouns

▶ In German, almost any adjective can be used as a noun:

der Alte *the old man*	**die Alte** *the old woman*	**die Alten** *the old people*

▶ Adjectives used as nouns like this have a capital letter, but they keep their **adjectival ending**.

This ending is 'weak' or 'strong' depending on the determiner, as the table below shows for *der Jugendliche* 'the young man':

declension with ...		definite article		indefinite article	
singular	nominative	der	**Jugendliche**	ein	**Jugendlicher**
	accusative	den	Jugendlichen	einen	Jugendlichen
	genitive	des	Jugendlichen	eines	Jugendlichen
	dative	dem	Jugendlichen	einem	Jugendlichen
plural	nominative	die	Jugendlichen		**Jugendliche**
	accusative	die	Jugendlichen		**Jugendliche**
	genitive	der	Jugendlichen		**Jugendlicher**
	dative	den	Jugendlichen		**Jugendlichen**

NB The feminine equivalent has the feminine adjective endings, e.g. in the nominative case singular *die Jugendliche, eine Jugendliche*. Correspondingly, neuter adjectival nouns have the appropriate neuter adjective endings, e.g. *das Schöne* (the beautiful thing/quality).

Der Jugendliche (*sg. nom.*) war nach Paris gefahren.	*The young man had gone to Paris.*
Bei **den Jugendlichen** (*pl. dat.*) handelte es sich um Deutsche.	*The young people in question were Germans.*
Ein Jugendlicher (*sg. nom.*) wurde verletzt.	*One young man was injured.*
Jugendlichen (*pl. dat.*) ist der Zutritt nicht gestattet.	*No admission under 18.*

▶ **Masculine and feminine** adjectives used as nouns usually refer to **people**.

In the English equivalent, we often have to supply a noun like *man, woman* or *people*. However, a large number of these adjectival nouns in common use correspond to simple nouns in English, for example:

der/die Abgeordnete	*representative*	**der/die Reisende**	*traveller*
der Beamte/die Beamtin	*civil servant*	**der/die Staatsangehörige**	*citizen*
der/die Bekannte	*acquaintance*	**der/die Überlebende**	*survivor*
der/die Deutsche	*German*	**der/die Verlobte**	*fiancé/fiancée*
der/die Erwachsene	*adult*	**der/die Verwandte**	*relative*
der/die Fremde	*stranger*	**der/die Vorgesetzte**	*superior*
der/die Geistliche	*clergyman*	**der/die Vorsitzende**	*chair(man)*

NB The female form of *der Beamte* is the regular noun *die Beamtin*

▶ **Neuter** adjectival nouns usually denote **abstract ideas**.

The English equivalents often require a word like *things*:

Es ist schon **Schlimmes** passiert.	*Bad things have already happened.*
Er hat **Hervorragendes** geleistet.	*He has achieved outstanding things.*

They are often used after indefinites, with the appropriate **weak** or **strong** ending depending on the ending of the determiner:

alles **Gute**	*everything (that is) good/all the best*
etwas **Schönes**	*something beautiful/something nice*
nichts **Neues**/von nichts **Neuem**	*nothing new/of nothing new*
wenig **Interessantes**	*nothing much of interest*

4.4 Adjectives with the dative

▶ Many adjectives can be used **with a noun dependent on them** in the DATIVE case:

Er ist **seinem Bruder** sehr **ähnlich**.	*He is very much like his brother.*
Dieser Mann war **ihr** nicht **bekannt**.	*This man was not known to her.*
Dieses Gespräch war **mir** sehr **nützlich**.	*This conversation was very useful to me.*

A large number of adjectives appear with a noun in the dative. Some common ones are:

ähnlich	*similar*	**fremd**	*strange*	**peinlich**	*embarrassing*
angenehm	*agreeable*	**gefährlich**	*dangerous*	**treu**	*loyal*
bekannt	*familiar*	**klar**	*clear*	**überlegen**	*superior*
bewusst	*known*	**möglich**	*possible*	**verständlich**	*comprehensible*
dankbar	*grateful*	**nützlich**	*useful*	**willkommen**	*welcome*

▶ Some adjectives expressing **sensations** are used with the DATIVE in constructions with the verb **sein**.

This is how you say things in German like *I am warm, I am cold,* etc.:

Mir ist **kalt.**/Es ist **mir kalt.**	*I'm cold.*
Mir ist zu **warm.**/Es ist **mir** zu **warm.**	*I'm too warm.*
Mir ist **schlecht.**	*I feel sick.*
Mir ist **schwindlig.**	*I'm dizzy.*

4.5 Adjectives with prepositions

Many adjectives can be **linked to a noun** by using a PREPOSITION:

Das ist **von** dem Wetter **abhängig.**	*That is dependent on the weather.*
Sie war **mit** meinem Entschluss **einverstanden.**	*She was in agreement with my decision.*
Das Land ist **reich an** Bodenschätzen.	*The country is rich in natural resources.*

The preposition used with a particular adjective often differs from that in the equivalent English construction. A few of the commonest examples are given below – your dictionary will give you many more!

angewiesen auf	*dependent on*	**gewöhnt an**	*accustomed to*
arm an	*lacking in*	**interessiert an**	*interested in*
bereit zu	*ready for*	**neidisch auf**	*envious of*
besorgt um	*anxious about*	**scharf auf**	*keen on*
böse auf	*angry at*	**stolz auf**	*proud of*
dankbar für	*grateful for*	**typisch für**	*typical of*
eifersüchtig auf	*jealous of*	**überzeugt von**	*convinced of*
fähig zu	*capable of*	**verliebt in**	*in love with*
gespannt auf	*eager for*	**vorbereitet auf**	*prepared for*

4.6 Comparison of adjectives

As in English, qualities can be compared using special forms of adjectives. These are formed with the **endings** *-er* **and** *-st-*, followed by a **case ending** if the adjective precedes a noun:

Mein Auto ist **schnell**,	dein Auto ist **schneller**,	aber sie hat das **schnellste** Auto.
My car is fast,	*your car is faster,*	*but she's got the fastest car.*

The form in *-er* is called the COMPARATIVE, and the form in *-st-* is called the SUPERLATIVE. These endings are used in German with **all adjectives**, irrespective of length, unlike English, where we use 'more'/'most' with long adjectives: 'fast**er**'/'fast**est**' but '**more** beautiful'/'**most** beautiful':

positive	comparative	superlative
tief (*deep*)	**tiefer**	(das) **tiefste**
schön (*beautiful*)	**schöner**	(das) **schönste**
langsam (*slow*)	**langsamer**	(das) **langsamste**
freundlich (*friendly, kind*)	**freundlicher**	(das) **freundlichste**
unwiderstehlich (*irresistible*)	**unwiderstehlicher**	(das) **unwiderstehlichste**

NB It's easy to confuse case ending and comparative ending. The case ending is added on to the comparative ending, e.g. *ein* **schneller** *Drucker* (masc. sg. nom., 'a fast printer') but *ein* **schnellerer** *Drucker* (a faster printer).

A few adjectives differ slightly from this pattern in forming their comparative and superlative:

▶ Some common adjectives **add** *Umlaut* in the comparative and superlative, e.g. *arm – ärmer – (***das***) ärmste*:

alt	*old*	**jung**	*young*	**rot**	*red*
arg	*bad*	**kalt**	*cold*	**scharf**	*sharp*
arm	*poor*	**klug**	*clever*	**schwach**	*weak*
dumm	*stupid*	**krank**	*sick, ill*	**schwarz**	*black*
grob	*coarse*	**kurz**	*short*	**stark**	*strong*
hart	*hard*	**lang**	*long*	**warm**	*warm*

▶ Adjectives in *-el*, *-en*, *-er* usually **drop -e- in the comparative**:

dunkel (*dark*) – **dunkler**	**trocken** (*dry*) – **trockner**
edel (*fine*) – **edler**	**teuer** (*expensive*) – **teurer**

▶ Adjectives ending in *-d*, *-t*, *-s*, or *-z* add *-est* **in the superlative**:

mild (*mild*) – **das mildeste**	**süß** (*sweet*) – **das süßeste**
sanft (*gentle*) – **das sanfteste**	**stolz** (*proud*) – **das stolzeste**

▶ A few comparative and superlative forms are **irregular**:

groß (*big*)	**größer**	(das) **größte**
gut (*good*)	**besser**	(das) **beste**
hoch (*high*)	**höher**	(das) **höchste**
nah (*near*)	**näher**	(das) **nächste**

4.7 Some uses of the comparative and superlative

▶ The **comparative particle** (= English 'than') is *als*:

Mein Auto ist **schneller als** deins.	*My car is faster than yours.*
London ist **schmutziger als** Zürich.	*London is dirtier than Zurich.*

▶ **Equality** is expressed by *so ... wie* (= 'as ... as'):

Peter ist **so alt wie** Thomas.	*Peter is as old as Thomas/the same age as Thomas.*
Ich bin **so groß wie** du.	*I'm as tall as you.*

NB Equality can be reinforced by using *ebenso* or *genauso* (= 'just as ...'), e.g. *Ich bin **genauso/ebenso groß wie** du.*

▶ **Progression** (= more and more) is expressed by using *immer* **with the comparative**:

Das Wetter wird **immer schlechter**.	*The weather is getting worse and worse.*
Meine Arbeit wird **immer schwieriger**.	*My work is getting more and more difficult.*

▶ **Superlatives** used as PREDICATE COMPLEMENTS of the **verb** *sein* (see **1.6**) are most often in the form *am ... sten*:

Dieser Weg ist **am steilsten**.	*This path is the steepest.*
Ein Mercedes wäre **am teuersten**.	*A Mercedes would be the most expensive.*

▶ **Proportion** (= 'the more ... the more') can be expressed by *je ... desto/umso* with a comparative adjective:

Je länger man Deutsch lernt,	*The longer you learn German,*
desto/umso leichter wird es.	*the easier it becomes.*

▶ **Comparative adjectives** often have the meaning '**fairly**', '**quite**':

eine **ältere** Frau	*an elderly woman, a fairly old woman*
eine **größere** Stadt	*a fair-sized town, quite a large town*
Ich habe **längere** Zeit dort gewohnt.	*I lived there for a while/for a number of years.*

4.8 Adverbs and adverbials

Many sentences contain elements which give added detail about the action or event, telling us when, where, why or how something happened or was done. **Unlike complements, they are not required grammatically.** They simply provide extra information and, as long as they make sense in their context, the same words or phrases could in principle be added to any sentence with any verb:

Der Schauspieler spricht deutlich.	*The actor speaks clearly.*
Das war finanziell eine Katastrophe.	*Financially that was a catastrophe.*
Er kaufte trotzdem eine Karte.	*He bought a ticket all the same.*
Ich traf sie um zwei Uhr.	*I met her at two o'clock.*
Ich wartete vor dem Kino auf ihn.	*I waited for him in front of the cinema.*

These words and phrases are known as ADVERBIALS, which is a useful term covering both ADVERBS (single words) and longer ADVERBIAL PHRASES (e.g. both *heute* and *am heutigen Tage* are adverbials). Adverbials can be distinguished according to their function:

adverbs	use	examples
time	*answering the question **when***	**damals, lange, oft, gestern, heute, vor einer Woche, am Freitag**
place	*answering the question **where***	**hier, dort, oben, draußen, überall, im Garten, neben der Kirche**
direction	*answering the question **where to/from***	**dorthin, dorther, hinein, herauf, woandershin, irgendwohin**
attitude	***commenting** on what is said, or answering a **yes/no** question*	**hoffentlich, leider, wahrscheinlich, natürlich, ohne Zweifel**
reason	*answering the question **why***	**dadurch, daher, deshalb, folglich, trotzdem, aus diesem Grund**
manner	*answering the question **how***	**irgendwie, anders, telefonisch, durch einen Freund, mit einer Axt**
degree	*answering the question **how much/small**... (often with adjectives)*	**sehr, außerordentlich, relativ, etwas, ziemlich, in höchstem Maße**
interrogative	*wh-words introducing questions*	**wann?, wie lange?, bis wann?, weshalb?, wieso?, von wo?**

4.9 Time adverbials

Time adverbials answer the question '**when**?' They can indicate:

▶ a **point in time**

augenblicklich	*at the moment, at once*	heute	*today*
bald	*soon*	jetzt	*now*
demnächst	*soon, very shortly*	morgen	*tomorrow*
früher	*formerly*	neulich	*recently*
gerade	*just (now)*	sofort	*immediately*
gestern	*yesterday*	vorher	*before(hand)*

Note the German equivalents for English 'then':

damals *refers to past time only ('at that time')*	**Sie war damals sehr arm.** *She was very poor then.*
dann *is used for all other meanings of 'then'*	**Wenn sie kommt, was machst du dann?** *If she comes, what will you do then?*

▶ **duration**

bisher	*up to now*	lange	*for a long time*
inzwischen	*meanwhile*	seitdem	*since then*
kurz	*for a short time*	vorläufig	*for the time being*

▶ **frequency**

gelegentlich	*occasionally*	nie	*never*
häufig	*frequently*	nochmals	*again*
immer	*always*	oft, öfters	*often*
irgendwann	*sometime or other*	selten	*seldom, rarely*
manchmal	*sometimes*	unaufhörlich	*incessantly*
meistens	*mostly*	wieder	*again*

Many time adverbials take the form of **prepositional phrases**, especially with *an*, *in* and *zu*, e.g. *am* Montag, *in* vierzehn Tagen, *zu* dieser Zeit. These are explained in chapter **5**.

The ACCUSATIVE case is used to form **adverbials without a preposition**:

▶ to denote **length of time** (often = English 'for'), and *lang* is often added:

Ich war einen Monat lang im Gefängnis.	*I was in prison for a month.*
Ich bin jede Woche einen Tag in Ulm.	*Each week I spend one day in Ulm.*
Ich blieb vier Tage in der Schweiz.	*I stayed in Switzerland for four days.*
Er lag den ganzen Tag (lang) im Bett.	*He lay in bed all day long.*

▶ to indicate a specific **point in time**:

Ich habe sie letzte Woche gesehen.	*I saw her last week.*
Ich habe Jakob letzten Freitag gesehen.	*I saw Jakob last Friday.*
Er hatte sie einen Augenblick zuvor gesehen.	*He had seen her a moment earlier.*
Wir verreisen dieses Jahr nicht.	*We aren't going away this year.*

4.10 Adverbs of place

Adverbs of place indicate **position** and answer the question '**where?**'. In some important contexts German and English usage differs.

▶ *hier*, *dort*, *da* for English '**here**' and '**there**':

hier = English 'here'	**Wir wohnen schon lange hier in Potsdam.** *We've lived here in Potsdam for a long time.*
dort = English 'there'	**Ich sah deine Schwester dort stehen.** *I saw your sister standing there.*
da less emphatic alternative to **dort**	**Ich sah ihn da an der Ecke stehen.** *I saw him standing there on the corner.*

However, *da* is often used to point in a general way when the difference between 'here' and 'there' is not crucial. In such contexts it can correspond to English 'here':

Herr Meyer ist momentan nicht da.	*Mr Meyer is not here at the moment.*

▶ *oben*, *unten* for English '**top**' and '**bottom**'

German lacks nouns corresponding to 'top' and 'bottom', and often uses phrases with *oben* or *unten* instead:

Sie stand oben auf der Treppe.	*She was standing at the top of the stairs.*
Sein Name steht unten auf der Liste.	*His name is at the bottom of the list.*

▶ *mitten* for English '**middle**'

The adverb *mitten* is often the most usual equivalent for the English noun 'middle'. It is usually followed by an appropriate preposition:

Mitten im Garten ist ein Teich.	*There's a pond in the middle of the garden.*
Die Polizei kam mitten in der Nacht.	*The police came in the middle of the night.*
Sie stellte die Vase mitten auf den Tisch.	*She put the vase in the middle of the table.*

▶ Other common **adverbs of place**:

außen	*on the outside*	**irgendwo**	*somewhere*
innen	*on the inside*	**nirgendwo/nirgends**	*nowhere*
draußen	*outside*	**anderswo/woanders**	*somewhere else*
drinnen	*inside*	**überall**	*everywhere*

4.11 Adverbs of direction

German usually makes a clear distinction between **position**, **movement away from the speaker** and **movement towards the speaker** by combining *hin* (away from) and *her* (towards) with other adverbs or prepositions to form adverbs of direction.

▶ *-hin* and *-her* are **suffixed** to other adverbs of place to indicate **direction**:

Wo wohnst du?	*Where do you live?*
Wohin gehst du?	*Where are you going (to)?*
Woher kommst du?	*Where do you come from?*
Komm doch hierher!	*Just come here!*
Ich bin gerade auf dem Weg dahin.	*I'm just on my way there.*
Wie können wir dorthin kommen?	*How can we get there?*
Er geht irgendwohin.	*He's going somewhere or other.*
Den Typ kenne ich irgendwoher.	*I know that guy from somewhere or other.*
Morgen fahren wir woandershin.	*Tomorrow we're going somewhere else.*

NB In spoken German you'll often hear: *Wo gehst du hin?* and *Wo kommst du her?*

▶ *hin-* and *her-* can be **prefixed** to PREPOSITIONS to form **directional adverbs**, e.g. *heraus*.

These directional adverbs can in turn be used as PREFIXES with **verbs of motion**. They link the direction indicated by the preposition with the idea of movement away from or towards the speaker:

Er kam ins Zimmer herein.	*He came into the room.*
Sie ging aus dem Zimmer hinaus.	*She went out of the room.*
Er fuhr unter der Brücke hindurch.	*He drove underneath the bridge.*
Er zog eine Pistole unter dem Bett hervor.	*He pulled a pistol out from under the bed.*
Wir sind die Treppe hinaufgestiegen.	*We climbed up the stairs.*
Sie kamen die Treppe heruntergerannt.	*They came running down the stairs.*

NB In spoken German, speakers will tend to shorten *hinunter/herunter* and *hinauf/herauf* to *runter* and *rauf.*

As the examples show, the directional adverbs with *hin* and *her* sometimes repeat the direction given by a preceding preposition.

You can use a noun phrase in the ACCUSATIVE case (without a preposition) to form adverbials which express **distance**. This is common in combination with directional adverbs in *hin-* and *her-:*

Er ging den ganzen Weg zu Fuß.	*He walked the whole way.*
Er wohnt einen Kilometer davon entfernt.	*He lives one kilometre away from it.*
Er kam die Stufen herunter.	*He came down the steps.*
Sie ging den Berg hinauf.	*She went up the mountain.*

4.12 Adverbs of attitude

Adverbs of attitude are used to comment on a statement, e.g. whether it is probable (*wahrscheinlich*), to be hoped for (*hoffentlich*) or obvious (*natürlich, selbstverständlich*).

▶ The suffix **-erweise** can be added to adjectives to form adverbs expressing the **attitude** or **opinion** of the speaker:

bedauerlicherweise	*regrettably*	**interessant**erweise	*interestingly*
dummerweise	*unfortunately*	**komischer**weise	*funnily (enough)*
erstaunlicherweise	*astonishingly*	**möglich**erweise	*possibly*
glücklicherweise	*fortunately*	**normal**erweise	*normally*

4.13 Adverbs of manner

Most German **adjectives** can be used **as adverbs** without any ending corresponding to English *-ly*. In practice, most of these are adverbs of manner, indicating '**how**' something was done:

Der Krankenwagen ist schnell gekommen.	*The ambulance came quickly.*
Die Band hat toll gespielt.	*The band played brilliantly.*
Sie haben einen schön geschnitzten Schrank.	*They have a beautifully carved cupboard.*

▶ Many adverbs of manner are formed with **-weise** from nouns:

ausnahmsweise	*by way of exception*	**stunden**weise	*by the hour*
beispielsweise	*for example*	**teil**weise	*partly*
probeweise	*on approval*	**zwangs**weise	*compulsorily*

NB The corresponding nouns are *die Ausnahme, das Beispiel, die Probe, die Stunde, der/das Teil, der Zwang*. Some require a linking element (*-s-, -n-*) or drop a letter but this follows no fixed rule.

4.14 Adverbs of degree

Adverbs of degree are used to emphasize, amplify or tone down. Their main use is to qualify adjectives or other adverbs:

Das Wetter war ganz schön.	*The weather was quite good.*
Susi war von den Affen total begeistert.	*Susi was dead keen on the monkeys.*
Ich bin ziemlich k.o.	*I'm pretty shattered.*
Barbara fährt sehr gut Ski.	*Barbara can ski very well.*

Oddly, *ganz* can either tone down an adjective or intensify it: *ein ganz guter Film* means 'quite a **good** film' or, if the adverb is stressed, 'a **very good** film'.

4.15 Interrogative adverbials

These **introduce questions**, corresponding to the English '**wh-**' **words**. They fall into the same groups as other adverbs:

time	wann? seit wann?	*when?* *since when?*	bis wann? wie lange?	*until when?* *how long?*
place/direction	wo? woher?	*where?* *where from?*	wohin? von wo?	*where (to)?* *where from?*
reason	warum? weshalb?	*why?* *why?*	wieso? *(colloquial)* wozu?	*why?* *what...for?*
manner	wie?	*how?*		

4.16 Adverb comparison

When **adjectives** are used **as adverbs**, they form the COMPARATIVE like the equivalent adjectives (see section **4.6**):

Er will **schneller** fahren als Schumacher.	*He wants to drive faster than Schumacher.*
Gestern hat es noch **stärker** geregnet als heute.	*Yesterday it rained even harder than today.*
Mit Lifting sehen Sie **jünger** aus!	*A face lift will make you look younger!*
Pavarotti hat **besser** gesungen.	*Pavarotti sang better.*

In the **superlative**, the form *am ... sten* is used:

Gabi ist **am schnellsten** gelaufen.	*Gabi ran fastest.*
Am Südpol ist es **am kältesten**.	*It's coldest at the South Pole.*

Some adverbs have an **irregular comparative** (in addition to those also used as adjectives, see **4.6**):

bald	eher	am ehesten
gern	lieber	am liebsten
oft	öfter(s)	am öftesten
viel	mehr	am meisten

4.17 Cardinal numbers

Cardinal numbers have the following forms in German:

0	null	10	zehn	20	zwanzig	30	dreißig
1	eins	11	elf	21	einundzwanzig	40	vierzig
2	zwei	12	zwölf	22	zweiundzwanzig	50	fünfzig
3	drei	13	dreizehn	23	dreiundzwanzig	60	sechzig
4	vier	14	vierzehn	24	vierundzwanzig	70	siebzig
5	fünf	15	fünfzehn	25	fünfundzwanzig	80	achtzig
6	sechs	16	sechzehn	26	sechsundzwanzig	90	neunzig
7	sieben	17	siebzehn	27	siebenundzwanzig	100	hundert
8	acht	18	achtzehn	28	achtundzwanzig	101	hundert(und)eins
9	neun	19	neunzehn	29	neunundzwanzig	102	(ein)hundertzwei

151	(ein)hunderteinundfünfzig
200	zweihundert
535	fünfhundertfünfunddreißig
999	neunhundertneunundneunzig

1000	(ein)tausend
1099	tausend(und)neunundneunzig
1100	(ein)tausendeinhundert/elfhundert
2305	zweitausenddreihundertfünf

564 297 fünfhundertvierundsechzigtausendzweihundertsiebenundneunzig

1 000 000	eine Million	1 000 000 000	eine Milliarde
2 000 000	zwei Millionen	1 000 000 000 000	eine Billion

Usage with the numerals

▶ **Long numbers** are hardly ever written out in full (except on cheques). If they are, they are written as a **single word**.

▶ **Numbers from ten thousand** are written with **spaces** or, sometimes, a **point** every three digits: **564 297 or 564 297**. Note that this differs from English, where a comma is used instead of a point.

▶ *Eine Million*, *eine Milliarde*, *eine Billion* are treated as separate **nouns**. They are written (and spoken) separately, and have plural endings where appropriate.

▶ *Zwo* is often used for *zwei* in speech (especially on the telephone) in order to distinguish it from *drei*).

▶ *Eins* is the **only numeral to decline** regularly for gender, number and case. It has the same forms as the indefinite article (see **3.2**) when used with a following noun.

▶ **Decimals** are written with a **comma**: **2,7** (*zwei Komma sieben*), **0,8** (*null Komma acht*), **34,75** (*vierunddreißig Komma sieben fünf*). Note that this differs from English, where a point is used instead of a comma.

4.18 Ordinal numbers

Ordinal numbers are **adjectival** forms of numerals. They are formed by adding the **suffixes -te** or **-ste** to the cardinal numbers.

▶ For the numbers **up to 20**, the suffix **-te** is used:

der zweite (*2nd*)	**der zwölfte** (*12th*)	**der fünfzehnte** (*15th*)

There are three irregular forms:

der erste (*1st*)	**der dritte** (*3rd*)	**der siebte** (*7th*)

▶ For the **numbers over 20**, the suffix **-ste** is used:

der zwanzigste (*20th*)	**der vierunddreißigste** (*34th*)	**der hundertste** (*100th*)

▶ In writing, **ordinal numbers** are indicated by a **point**:

der 2. (zweite)	**der 23.** (dreiundzwanzigste)

▶ The **point** is used when giving **dates**:

am 4. September (*spoken*: vierten)	**am 4.9.** (*spoken*: vierten neunten)

Note also the following uses of ordinal numbers:

erstens, zweitens, drittens …	*firstly, secondly, thirdly …*
zu zweit/zu dritt/zu viert **Zu zweit** ist es billiger. Wir wohnen **zu viert** hier.	*in twos/threes/fours/as a twosome …* *It's cheaper for two.* *There are four of us living here together.*
zweit-/dritt-/viert- + *superlative* Die Donau ist der **zweitlängste** Fluss Europas.	*second/third/fourth* + *superlative* *The Danube is the second longest river* *in Europe.*

4.19 Fractions

▶ Fractions are formed by **adding -el** to the stem of the **ordinal number**. They are neuter nouns:

ein Drittel **ein Viertel**	*a third* *a quarter*	**ein Achtel** **ein Zehntel**	*an eighth* *a tenth*

▶ Fractions can be written together with common measurement words – or separately, with a small initial letter:

in fünf Hundertstelsekunden **in fünf** hundertstel **Sekunden**	**mit einem Achtel**liter **mit einem** achtel **Liter**

NB *Eine Dreiviertelstunde* is often treated as an independent noun, e.g. *nach einer Dreiviertelstunde* ('after/in three-quarters of an hour').

4.20 Clock times, days of the week and months

▶ In **everyday speech** the **twelve-hour clock** is used:

1.00	**Es ist ein Uhr/Es ist eins**	*It's one (o'clock)*
3.00	**Es ist drei (Uhr)**	*It's three (o'clock)*
3.05	**fünf (Minuten) nach drei**	*five (minutes) past three*
3.07	**sieben Minuten nach drei**	*seven minutes past three*
3.10	**zehn (Minuten) nach drei**	*ten (minutes) past three*
3.15	**Viertel nach drei** **viertel vier** (S. and E. Germany)	*quarter past three*
3.20	**zwanzig nach drei** **zehn vor halb vier**	*twenty past three*
3.25	**fünf vor halb vier**	*twenty-five past three*
3.30	**halb vier**	*half past three/half three*
3.35	**fünf nach halb vier**	*twenty-five to four*
3.40	**zwanzig vor vier** **zehn nach halb vier**	*twenty to four*
3.45	**Viertel vor vier** **dreiviertel vier** (S. and E. Germany)	*quarter to four*
3.47	**dreizehn Minuten vor vier**	*thirteen minutes to four*
3.50	**zehn (Minuten) vor vier**	*ten (minutes) to four*
3.55	**fünf (Minuten) vor vier**	*five (minutes) to four*

NB *viertel vier – halb vier – dreiviertel vier* look forward to the next full hour. Don't confuse **halb vier** with 'half four'!

▶ In **official contexts** (timetables, TV and radio programmes, theatres, cinemas, business hours, etc.) the **twenty-four-hour clock** is used:

0.27	**null Uhr siebenundzwanzig**	*12.27 a.m.*
5.15	**fünf Uhr fünfzehn**	*5.15 a.m.*
10.30	**zehn Uhr dreißig**	*10.30 a.m.*
13.07	**dreizehn Uhr sieben**	*1.07 p.m.*
21.37	**einundzwanzig Uhr siebenunddreißig**	*9.37 p.m.*
24.00	**vierundzwanzig Uhr**	*12.00 midnight*

▶ **Days** of the week:

Sonntag	*Sunday*	**Donnerstag**	*Thursday*
Montag	*Monday*	**Freitag**	*Friday*
Dienstag	*Tuesday*	**Samstag** (esp. S. Germany)	
Mittwoch	*Wednesday*	**Sonnabend** (esp. N. Germany)	*Saturday*

▶ **Months** of the year:

Januar	*January*	Juli	*July*
Februar	*February*	August	*August*
März	*March*	September	*September*
April	*April*	Oktober	*October*
Mai	*May*	November	*November*
Juni	*June*	Dezember	*December*

NB When discussing dates on the phone, confusion between *Juni* and *Juli* is sometimes avoided by using *Juno* and *Julei*. In Austria, January is *Jänner*.

4.21 Modal particles

Modal particles indicate the **speaker's attitude** to what is being said. They are a typical feature of **spoken German**, being used to persuade the other person, establish common ground, or soften a statement or question. They can be a minefield for the learner because their meaning depends on **context** and **emphasis**. These little words can also occur as other parts of speech (e.g. *aber* 'but' as a conjunction, and *vielleicht* 'perhaps' as an adverb). When used as modal particles, they are difficult to give equivalents for because **English tends to use tone of voice, rather than words, to achieve similar effects**. Get into the habit of listening out for them. These examples give an idea of how they may be used:

aber *expressing* **surprise***, makes statement into exclamation*	Sabines **Freund** ist aber **nett**! *Sabine's boyfriend's really nice, isn't he!*
auch *in yes/no questions,* **seeks confirmation**	Ist Michael auch **wirklich** Sieglindes **Freund**? *Is Michael really Sieglinde's boyfriend?*
denn *in questions, expresses* **personal interest***,* **incredulity**	Ist denn **Mike** Sonjas **Freund**? *Is Mike Sonja's boyfriend?*
doch *in statements,* **appeals for agreement** *if uncertain*	Moritz ist doch Stellas **Freund**, oder? *Moritz is Stella's boyfriend, isn't he?*
eben/halt *emphasises a* **known or inescapable fact**	Max ist eben/halt Saras **Freund**. *Well, Max is Sara's boyfriend, after all.*
eigentlich *makes questions sound* **casual**	Ist Mark eigentlich Susis **Freund**? *Is Mark Susi's boyfriend, do you happen to know?*
etwa *in questions, implies undesirability and* **invites 'no'**	Ist Magnus etwa Sophias **Freund**? *Surely Magnus isn't Sophia's boyfriend?*
ja *in statements,* **assumes agreement** *on sth. uncontroversial*	Manfred ist ja Steffis Freund. *Manfred is Steffi's boyfriend, of course.*
mal **tones down** *commands, requests, questions*	Sag mal, ist Mario Sigrids **Freund**? *Tell me, is Mario Sigrid's boyfriend?*

schon *gives commands an **insistent** tone*	Sag schon, ist Martin Sylvias **Freund**? *Go on then, tell me, is Martin Sylvia's boyfriend?*
überhaupt *in questions, **casts doubt** on an assumption*	**Ist** Matthias überhaupt Silkes Freund? *Is Matthias **actually** Silke's boyfriend, anyway?*
vielleicht *adds **emotional force** to exclamations*	**Das** ist vielleicht ein **Mist**kerl! *He's a real bastard, isn't he!*
wohl *expresses **probability** or **supposition***	Besser wär's wohl, sie macht mit ihm Schluss. *It would probably be better if she dumped him.*

ADJECTIVES, ADVERBS AND ADVERBIALS IN CONTEXT

Suchtfalle Internet – die Zahl der Internet-Surfer wächst

Ab wann ist man denn internetsüchtig und wie kommt es überhaupt dazu? Nacht für Nacht sitzen Sie bis zwei Uhr früh am Bildschirm. Sie wollen raus aus dem Netz, schaffen es aber einfach nicht. Wenn Sie längere Zeit off-line sind, werden Sie unruhig, depressiv und loggen wieder ein. Besonders gefährdet sind Menschen, die depressiv oder einsam sind. Manche haben Eheprobleme, andere ersetzen eine frühere Sucht, z.B. abstinente Alkoholiker.

Gibt es Unterschiede zwischen Männern und Frauen? Während Männer eher zu Sexseiten pilgern und stundenlang Bilder herunterladen, ziehen Frauen Chatrooms vor. Viele beginnen auf diesem Weg virtuelle Affären, denn man kommt sich viel schneller näher als im richtigen Leben. Deshalb kann Internetsucht in nur wenigen Monaten eine Ehe zerstören.

Was tun, wenn der Partner nicht mehr vom Computer loskommt? Dann muss man den abhängigen Surfer mit seiner Sucht konfrontieren. Doch leider leugnen die Süchtigen in der Regel das Problem. Sport, Kinobesuche oder ein Urlaub zu zweit können Unterstützung bieten. Wenn gar nichts hilft, gibt es allerdings nur eins: professionelle Hilfe von einem Psychologen.
(Aus: *Cosmopolitan*)

ADJECTIVES QUALIFYING NOUNS

before the noun	**weak ending** if determiner shows gender, number, case	im **richtigen** Leben (*n. sg. dat.*) eine **frühere** Sucht (*f. sg. acc.*) den **abhängigen** Surfer (*m. sg. acc.*)
	strong ending if there is no determiner	**professionelle** Hilfe (*f. sg. acc.*) **abstinente** Alkoholiker (*pl. nom.*) **virtuelle** Affären (*pl. acc.*)
as a complement of the verb (usually *sein* or *werden*)	**without ending**	Sie sind **off-line** Sie werden **unruhig, depressiv** Menschen, die **depressiv** oder **einsam** sind

ADJECTIVES USED AS NOUNS

der Süchtige (*m.*)/die Süchtige (*f.*)	*person who is addicted*
die Süchtigen (*pl.*)	*people who are addicted*

COMPARISON

adjective	lange Zeit eine frühe Sucht	**längere** Zeit eine **frühere** Sucht	die längste Zeit die frühste Sucht
adverb	schnell nah(e)	**schneller** **näher**	am schnellsten am nächsten

NB Forms used in the text are in **bold**.

ADVERBS/ADVERBIAL PHRASES give added detail about the action/event:

time	stundenlang, **Nacht für Nacht**, längere Zeit, bis zwei Uhr früh, in nur wenigen Monaten, nicht mehr, in der Regel
place/direction	**heraus/raus, im Büro**
attitude	**leider**
reason	**deshalb**
manner	schnell, auf diesem **Weg**, zu zweit
degree	**eher, viel**

INTERROGATIVE ADVERBIALS

wann?	*when?*	**wie?**	*how?*

NUMERALS

eins, **zwei**, drei, vier …

MODAL PARTICLES indicate the speaker's attitude (usually unstressed)
Meaning depends on context! Here:

denn, **überhaupt**	*similar to 'in fact'/'actually'*
einfach	*similar to 'simply'*

Prepositions 5

PREPOSITIONS are a small set of little words which typically occur **before a noun phrase** and help to link it to the rest of the sentence. The resulting PREPOSITIONAL PHRASES frequently express notions of time, place and direction, and they often **depend on a preceding noun, adjective or verb**:

Seit zwei Jahren lernt William Deutsch.	*William has been learning German for two years.*
Ute wohnt **in einem alten Haus am Waldrand**.	*Ute lives in an old house on the edge of the forest.*
Um halb acht gehen wir ins **Fitness-Studio**.	*We're going to the gym at half past seven.*
Wir freuten uns sehr **über seinen Besuch**.	*We were delighted at his visit.*

In German, the NOUN PHRASE following each preposition is in a particular CASE – the preposition **governs** a case. Prepositions are **never followed by the nominative case**. Most are followed by the dative or accusative; prepositions governing the genitive are confined to formal language. One important group of common prepositions is followed by the accusative or dative case, with variations in meaning.

Prepositions are troublesome for the learner because they have so many meanings and often lose their 'normal' meaning when they are part of a stock expression – as in English. In fact, German has rather less variety than English (check 'get' and all the associated prepositions and meanings in your dictionary!). This chapter explains the most important meanings and uses of the common German prepositions, arranged according to the case they govern:

◆ prepositions with the ACCUSATIVE (**5.1**)

◆ prepositions with the DATIVE (**5.2**)

◆ prepositions with the DATIVE or the ACCUSATIVE (**5.3**)

◆ prepositions with the GENITIVE (**5.4**).

Prepositions may also join up with the prefix *da(r)-* to form PREPOSITIONAL ADVERBS such as *dafür* (for it) or *darüber* (over it, about it). These are explained in section **5.5**. Many prepositions may themselves act as PREFIXES for verbs, e.g. *durchfahren* (to drive through), *aufstellen* (to set up) (see **11.6–11.7**).

The following table lists the most common prepositions with their cases:

prepositions governing the ...			
accusative	bis durch	für gegen	ohne um
dative	aus außer bei	gegenüber mit nach	seit von zu
accusative or dative	an auf hinter	in neben über	unter vor zwischen
genitive	statt trotz	wegen während	

NB The preposition *entlang* is used with the accusative or dative case depending on its function, and it often comes after the noun. For details see the end of section **5.3**.

NB With certain prepositions, the definite article is often contracted, e.g. *ins = in das; zum = zu dem* (see **3.1**).

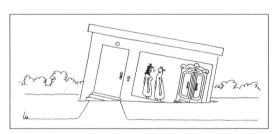

„Das Geld für das schwere Möbelstück hätten wir besser in das Hausfundament gesteckt!"

5.1 Prepositions with the accusative

Bis

Bis is never followed by a determiner. Except with names, adverbs and a few time words, it has another preposition with it (most often *zu*).

▶ referring to place = 'as far as', '(up) to':

Ich fahre nur **bis Marbach**.	*I'm only going as far as Marbach.*
Wir gingen **bis zum Fluss**.	*We went as far as the river.*
Der Weg führt **bis ins Tal**.	*The path leads right down to the valley.*

NB The **last** preposition governs the case of the following noun phrase, e.g. *bis + zu + dative.*

▶ referring to time = 'by', 'until':

Bis 1945/bis zu seinem Tod lebte er in Wien.	*Until 1945/until his death he lived in Vienna.*
Ich habe es **bis heute Abend** fertig.	*I'll have finished it by tonight.*

Durch

▶ referring to place = 'through', 'across' (often with *hindurch* after the noun):

Sie gingen **durch den Wald** (**hindurch**).	*They went through the forest.*
Wir wateten **durch den Fluss**.	*We waded across the river.*

▶ referring to cause or means = 'by (means of)', 'through':

Er wurde **durch das Fernsehen** bekannt.	*Television made him famous.*
Das Haus wurde **durch Bomben** zerstört.	*The house was destroyed by bombs.*

Für

▶ corresponds to English 'for' in many senses, especially 'on behalf of', 'having regard to':

Sie hat viel **für mich** getan.	*She did a lot for me.*
Für sein Alter ist er ganz fit.	*For his age he's quite fit.*

▶ referring to time, indicates a period of time from 'now':

Ich miete die Wohnung **für zwei Jahre**.	*I'm renting the flat for two years.*

Gegen

▶ referring to place = 'against', 'into':

Ivan presste sie **gegen die Wand**.	*Ivan pressed her against the wall.*
Sie stieß **gegen den Tisch**.	*She bumped into the table.*

▶ referring to time, expresses approximation = 'about', 'towards':

Sie kamen **gegen halb vier** an.	*They arrived at about half-past three.*
Gegen Abend erreichten sie die Hütte.	*They reached the hut towards evening.*

▶ expresses opposition = 'against':

Sie handelte **gegen meinen Willen**.	*She acted against my wishes.*
Das ist ein gutes Mittel **gegen Husten**.	*This medicine is good for coughs.*

Ohne

▶ corresponds to English 'without':

Das tat sie **ohne mein Wissen**.	*She did that without my knowledge.*
Er ging **ohne Mantel** aus dem Haus.	*He left the house without his coat.*

Um

▶ referring to place = '(a)round', 'about':

Sie gingen **um die Ecke**.	*They went round the corner.*
Er hat gern viele Mädchen **um sich**.	*He likes having a lot of girls around him.*

▶ referring to time: expresses a point in time with clock times (= 'at'), otherwise expresses an approximation (= 'about'):

Sie riefen **um halb vier** an.	*They phoned at half-past three.*
Sie kamen **um die Mittagszeit (herum)**.	*They came around lunchtime.*

▶ corresponds to English 'about', 'concerning', 'in respect of' after certain verbs and nouns:

Hier **ging** es nur **um Geld**.	*This was simply a question of money.*
Es war ein **Streit um die Erbschaft**.	*It was a quarrel about the inheritance.*

5.2 Prepositions with the dative

Aus

▶ referring to direction = 'out of', 'from':

Sie kamen **aus dem Café**.	*They were coming out of the café.*
Ich bin **aus der Übung** gekommen.	*I've got out of practice.*

▶ referring to material = '(made) of':

Die Kaffeekanne war **aus Silber**.	*The coffee-pot was made of silver.*

▶ expresses a cause, a reason or a motive = 'for', 'from', 'out of':

Sie tat es **aus Überzeugung**.	*She did it from conviction.*
Ich frage nur **aus Interesse**.	*I'm only asking out of interest.*

Ausser

▶ expresses a restriction = 'except (for)', 'apart from':

Niemand sah ihn **außer mir**.	*Nobody saw him except for/apart from me.*

Bei

▶ referring to place, indicates approximate location = 'by', 'at', including reference to where somebody lives or works:

Potsdam liegt **bei Berlin**.	*Potsdam is near Berlin.*
Ich wohne **bei meinen Eltern**.	*I live at my parents'.*

▶ indicates attendant circumstances, i.e. = 'in view of', 'on the occasion of' or simply 'while doing something':

Bei diesem Wetter muss er hier bleiben.	*In view of the weather he'll have to stay here.*
Das besprechen wir **bei einem Glas Wein**.	*We'll discuss that over a glass of wine.*

▶ used with a verbal noun, corresponds to 'when':

Bei seiner Ankunft küsste sie ihn.	*She kissed him when he arrived.*
Beim Fahren benutze ich nie das Handy.	*I never use my mobile when I'm driving.*

Gegenüber

The position of *gegenüber* is unusual: it **follows** a PRONOUN, and can **precede or follow** a NOUN Especially with nouns denoting people, it tends to follow the noun.

▶ referring to place = 'opposite':

Ich wohne **gegenüber dem Sportplatz**.	*I live opposite the sportsground.*
Ich saß **ihr/dem Herrn gegenüber**.	*I sat opposite her/the man.*

▶ expresses a comparison or a relation = 'in respect of', 'toward':

Gisela gegenüber ist Anne im Vorteil.	*Anne has the advantage over Gisela.*
Das ist eine neue Politik **gegenüber den USA**.	*This is a new policy towards the USA.*

Mit

▶ corresponds to English 'with' in most senses:

Sie öffnete die Tür **mit ihrem Schlüssel**.	*She opened the door with her key.*
Mit ihr spiele ich oft Tennis.	*I often play tennis with her.*

▶ indicates means of transport = 'by':

Wir sind **mit der Bahn** dahin gefahren.	*We went there by train.*

Nach

▶ referring to direction = 'to' (with neuter names of cities and countries only, or with points of the compass or place adverbs):

Wir fahren **nach Duisburg/nach England**.	*We're going to Duisburg/to England.*
Die Straße führt **von Osten nach Westen**.	*The road goes from east to west.*

▶ referring to time = 'after':

Emine kam **nach dem Abendessen**.	*Emine came after dinner.*

▶ corresponds to English 'according to'. In this sense it can follow the noun, especially in some set phrases:

Nach meiner Uhr ist es schon zehn.	*According to my watch it is already ten.*
Meiner Meinung nach ist das nutzlos.	*In my opinion that's futile.*

Seit

▶ referring to time = 'for' (a period of time up to 'now' or 'then'), 'since'. It is normally used with the PRESENT or PAST TENSES, unlike English, which uses the perfect or pluperfect (often progressive):

Seit einer Stunde stand sie im Flur.	*She had been standing in the hall for an hour.*
Seit 1990 wohnt sie wieder in Rostock.	*She has been living in Rostock again since 1990.*

Von

▶ referring to direction or time = 'from'. In time phrases it is often used with a following *an*:

Sie fuhren **von Augsburg** nach München.	*They drove from Augsburg to Munich.*
Das wusste ich **von Anfang an**.	*I knew that from the start.*

▶ corresponds to English 'of'. In this sense a phrase with *von* may be an **alternative** to the GENITIVE case, especially in colloquial speech or if a genitive is not possible (see section **8.6**):

Ich fahr' mit dem Wagen **von meinem Vater**.	*I'll go with my father's car.*
(*less colloquial*: mit dem Wagen meines Vaters)	
Kann einer **von euch** mir helfen?	*Can one of you help me?*
Millionen **von Lesern** waren begeistert.	*Millions of readers were enthralled.*
Das ist die Königin **von England**.	*That's the Queen of England.*

▶ referring to the **agent** in PASSIVE constructions:

Er wurde **von dem Angeklagten** erwürgt.	*He was strangled by the accused.*
Das Auto wurde **von der Polizei** abgeschleppt.	*The car was towed away by the police.*

Zu

▶ referring to direction = 'to' (in that direction, or to someone's house):

Dieser Bus fährt **zum Rathaus**.	*This bus goes to the town hall.*
Heute Abend gehen wir **zu Fatima**.	*Tonight we're going to Fatima's.*

▶ referring to time, indicates a point in time = 'at':

Der Osterhase kommt nur **zu Ostern**.	*The Easter bunny only comes at Easter.*
Das war **zur Zeit** der letzten Wahlen.	*That was at the time of the last election.*

▶ referring to **purpose** = 'for':

Zu diesem Zweck heirate ich den Millionär.	*For that reason I'm marrying the millionaire.*
Ich lade ihn **zu meinem Geburtstag** ein.	*I'm inviting him to my birthday.*

Other prepositions governing the dative

A few less common prepositions also govern the dative:

ab (*from*)	ab nächster **Woche**	*from next week*
dank (*thanks to*) (*also used with genitive*)	dank seinem **Einfluss** dank seines **Einflusses**	*thanks to his influence*
entgegen (*contrary to*)	entgegen allen **Erwartungen**	*contrary to all expectations*
gemäß (*according to*) (*precedes or follows the noun*)	den Anweisungen gemäß gemäß den Anweisungen	*in accordance with the instructions*
laut (*according to*) (*also used with genitive*)	laut unserem **Bericht** laut unseres **Berichtes**	*according to our report*
zufolge (*according to*) (*follows the noun*)	dem Wetterbericht zufolge	*according to the weather forecast*

5.3 Prepositions with the accusative or the dative

With one group of prepositions, using a different case changes the meaning. These prepositions govern

▶ the DATIVE if they express **position**;

▶ the ACCUSATIVE if they express **direction**.

accusative **expressing** direction	dative **expressing** position
Ich hänge das Bild **an die Wand**.	Das Bild hängt **an der Wand**.
Wir gehen **in dieses Zimmer** (hinein).	Wir essen **in diesem Zimmer**.

In **other meanings**, e.g. to express time or relationships, most of these prepositions are used with the DATIVE (except *auf* and *über*, which are normally used with the accusative). A few important verbs use *an* + accusative (see section **8.7**).

An (+ dative)

▶ referring to position = 'on (the side of)', 'at', 'by':

Ich wartete **am Fenster**.	*I was waiting at the window.*
Das Fahrrad steht **an der Mauer**.	*The bicycle is standing by the wall.*

▶ expressing time = 'on', 'in' (esp. with days or parts of the day):

Sie kam am **Montag**/am **Abend**.	*She came on Monday/in the evening.*

An (+ accusative)

▶ referring to direction = 'to', 'on' (i.e. to a position on the side of something, or next to it):

Ich ging an **das**/ans **Fenster**.	*I went to the window.*
Ich schrieb einen Brief an **meine Mutter**.	*I wrote a letter to my mother.*

NB *an… vorbei* is used with the dative even though it expresses movement, e.g. *Er geht* **am Bahnhof vorbei**.

Auf (+ dative)

▶ referring to position = 'on (top of)':

Die Katze saß auf **dem Schrank**.	*The cat was sitting on the cupboard.*
Wir wohnen auf **dem Land**.	*We live in the country.*

Auf (+ accusative)

▶ referring to direction = '(on)to' (i.e. onto the top of something):

Die Katze sprang auf **den Schrank**.	*The cat jumped onto the cupboard.*
Wir fuhren auf **das Land**/aufs **Land**.	*We went into the country.*

Hinter (+ dative)

▶ referring to position = 'behind':

Der Wagen steht **hinter dem Haus**.	*The car is behind the house.*

Hinter (+ accusative)

▶ referring to direction = 'behind' (i.e. to the back of something):

Sie fuhr den Wagen **hinter das Haus**.	*She drove the car round to the back of the house.*

In (+ dative)

▶ referring to position = 'in':

Die Milch ist im **Kühlschrank**.	*The milk is in the fridge.*
Heute waren wir in **der Stadt**.	*We were in town today.*

▶ expressing time = 'in' (a period of time):

In zwei Stunden sind wir in Wien.	*We'll be in Vienna in two hours.*
Im Moment hab' ich keine Lust zu arbeiten.	*At the moment I don't feel like working.*

In (+ *accusative*)

▶ referring to direction = '(in)to' (i.e. to a position inside something):

Ich stellte die Milch **in den Kühlschrank**.	*I put the milk in(to) the fridge.*
Heute gehen wir **in die Stadt**.	*We're going to town today.*

Neben (+ *dative*)

▶ referring to position = 'next to', 'beside':

Ich saß **neben ihrem Mann**.	*I was sitting next to her husband.*

Neben (+ *accusative*)

▶ referring to direction = 'next to', 'beside':

Ich setzte mich **neben ihren Mann**.	*I sat down next to her husband.*

Über (+ *dative*)

▶ referring to position = 'over', 'above':

Das Poster hängt **über meinem Schreibtisch**.	*The poster hangs above my desk.*
Über dem See schwebte ein Ballon.	*A balloon hovered over the lake.*

Über (+ *accusative*)

▶ referring to direction = 'over', 'across':

Ich hängte das Poster **über meinen Schreibtisch**.	*I hung the poster over my desk.*
Das Flugzeug flog **über den See**.	*The aeroplane flew over the lake.*

▶ corresponds to English 'about', 'concerning' (with verbs and nouns of speaking and writing):

Ich schreibe ein Buch **über Afrika**.	*I'm writing a book about Africa.*
Er beschwerte sich **über den Fernseher**.	*He complained about the television.*

▶ expressing quantity = 'over', 'more than':

Das Päckchen wiegt **über 500 Gramm**.	*The package weighs over 500 grams.*

Unter (+ *dative*)

▶ referring to position = 'under(neath)', 'below', 'among(st)':

Der Hund lag **unter dem Tisch**.	*The dog was lying under the table.*
Hier bist du **unter deinen Freunden**.	*You're among your friends here.*

▶ expressing quantity = 'under', 'below', 'less than':

Das Päckchen wiegt **unter 500 Gramm**.	*The package weighs less than 500 grams.*

Unter (+ accusative)

▶ referring to direction = 'under', 'below', 'among(st)':

Der Hund kroch **unter den Tisch**.	*The dog crept under the table.*
Sie mischte sich **unter die Gäste**.	*She mingled with the guests.*

Vor (+ dative)

▶ referring to position = 'in front of', 'ahead of':

Marco wartete **vor dem Kino**.	*Marco was waiting in front of the cinema.*
Vor ihm in einiger Entfernung stand Ute.	*Ute stood some distance ahead of him.*

▶ referring to time = 'before', 'ago':

Wir haben es **vor einer Woche** gekauft.	*We bought it a week ago.*
Ich sah ihn einen Tag **vor seiner Abreise**.	*I saw him a day before his departure.*

▶ expressing cause or reason (especially with verbs and adjectives):

Vor lauter Angst ist er weggerannt.	*He was so afraid he ran away.*
Vor Nebel war nichts zu sehen.	*Nothing could be seen for the fog.*

Vor (+ accusative)

▶ referring to direction = 'in front of':

Er fuhr **vor das Kino**.	*He drove up in front of the cinema.*
Sie stellte sich **vor mich** hin.	*She stood (positioned herself) in front of me.*

Zwischen (+ dative)

▶ referring to position = 'between', 'among(st)':

Sie saß **zwischen mir** und **meiner Frau**.	*She was sitting between me and my wife.*

Zwischen (+ accusative)

▶ referring to direction = 'between', 'among(st)':

Sie setzte sich **zwischen mich** und **meine Frau**.	*She sat down between me and my wife.*

Uses of entlang

The preposition *entlang* is normally used to indicate movement alongside or down the middle, and it then **follows** a noun in the ACCUSATIVE case:

Sie gingen **den Bach** entlang.	*They walked along the stream.*
Wir fuhren **den Weg/die Straße** entlang.	*We drove along the path/the road.*

A common alternative is **an** [+ **dative**] ... **entlang**, which indicates movement alongside (but not down the middle):

Sie gingen **am Fluss** entlang.	*They walked along the river.*
Wir fuhren **an der Mauer** entlang.	*We drove along the wall.*

5.4 Prepositions with the genitive

Prepositions followed by a noun phrase in the genitive are largely restricted to **formal written** language.

Four frequent prepositions governing the genitive

(An)statt corresponds to English 'instead of':

Statt eines Briefes schickte er ihr eine E-Mail.	*Instead of a letter he sent her an e-mail.*

Trotz corresponds to English 'despite', 'in spite of':

Trotz des Regens fand das Festival statt.	*The festival took place despite the rain.*

Während refers to time = English 'during':

Während des Sommers blieben sie in Bozen.	*They stayed in Bolzano during the summer.*

Wegen corresponds to English 'because of':

Sie konnten wegen des Schnees nicht kommen.	*They couldn't come because of the snow.*

In colloquial speech these prepositions are often used with the DATIVE.

Other prepositions governing the genitive

Eight further prepositions expressing **position** govern the genitive:

außerhalb des Rings	*outside*	**innerhalb** Berlins	*inside, within*
oberhalb des Hauses	*above*	**unterhalb** des Knies	*underneath, below*
diesseits der Grenze	*on this side of*	**jenseits** des Meeres	*on the other side of*
beiderseits der Tür	*on either side of*	**unweit** der Stadt	*not far from*

These are often used with a following *von* instead of a genitive, especially in spoken German:

Sie wohnt **außerhalb des Ortes/außerhalb von dem Ort**.	*She lives outside the village/town.*

There are also a large number of other prepositions which govern the genitive, but these are restricted in the main to very formal, especially official and commercial language. The following are not infrequent:

angesichts der Kälte	*in view of*	**kraft** seiner Autorität	*by virtue of*
anlässlich ihres Todes	*on the occasion of*	**längs** der Straße	*along(side)*
bezüglich des Briefes	*with reference to*	**seitens** des Angeklagten	*on the part of*
hinsichtlich der Preise	*with regard to*	**ungeachtet** der Tatsache	*notwithstanding*

5.5 Prepositional adverbs

Prepositional adverbs (sometimes called 'pronominal adverbs') are formed by prefixing *da(r)*- to a PREPOSITION, e.g. *damit* (with it), *daran* (on/at it). They typically substitute for **preposition + third person pronoun**, except when the pronoun refers to a person (see **3.7**). Compare:

Wir warten **auf den Mann.**	→ Wir warten **auf ihn.**	*We're waiting **for him**.*
Wir warten **auf den Computer.**	→ Wir warten **darauf.**	*We're waiting **for it**.*

▶ The pronoun *es* is not normally used after prepositions:

Er freut sich **über das Geschenk.**	→ Er freut sich **darüber.**	*He's pleased **about it**.*

▶ The prepositional adverb is always used to refer to **whole sentences**:

Er ist in Paris. Anna weiß nichts **davon.**	*He's in Paris. Anna knows nothing **about it**.*

▶ If motion is involved, separable prefixes (see **11.6**) with *hin-* or *her-* are used rather than the prepositional adverb:

Sie erreichten den Tunnel und fuhren **hindurch.**	*They reached the tunnel and drove **through** it.*

▶ The prepositional adverb is often used to anticipate a following *dass*-**clause** or **infinitive clause** (see **8.7**, **10.3** and **10.6**):

Ich warte **darauf, dass er mich anruft.**	*I'm waiting for him to ring me up.*
	(literally: *I'm waiting **for it that he rings me up**.*)
Sie sehnte sich **danach Georg wiederzusehen.**	*She yearned to see Georg again.*
	(literally: *She yearned **for it to see Georg again**.*)

An equivalent compound is formed with *wo(r)*- **+ preposition**, e.g. *womit, wovon, worüber*. This is used instead of **preposition +** *was* (see **10.5**):

interrogative pronoun	**Wofür** benutzt man dieses Werkzeug? ***What** do you use this tool **for**?*
relative pronoun	Er hat gefragt, **worüber** wir gesprochen haben. *He asked **what** we talked **about**.*

PREPOSITIONS IN CONTEXT

Zeitungsvolontär/-in — ein Job mit Zukunft

Der Wunsch, als Journalist sein Geld zu verdienen, das Tagesgeschehen aus nächster Nähe mitzuerleben und immer am Ball zu sein, wenn es um aktuelle Informationen aus aller Welt geht, ist für viele das Berufsziel Nummer 1! Ohne Abitur hat man nur geringe Chancen. Dem Ziel näher kommt man durch ein Hochschulstudium (z.B. Publizistik), eine Ausbildung an einer Journalistenschule oder ein Volontariat bei einer Zeitung, nach dessen Ende man als Redakteur übernommen werden kann. Die Zukunftsaussichten sind gut, da es trotz des Internets immer Zeitungen geben wird. Mirjam (22) hat Glück gehabt. Sie berichtet von ihren Erfahrungen.

Welche Stationen durchläufst du als Volontärin? Ich fing in der Lokalredaktion an. Zuerst während eines mehrwöchigen Praktikums, dann als freie Mitarbeiterin und später für

fünf Monate während meines Volontariats. Jetzt bin ich seit kurzem in der Wirtschaftsredaktion. Am meisten freu' ich mich auf die Kultur, denn ich interessiere mich vor allem für Kunst und Theater!

Mit welchen Themen beschäftigst du dich zurzeit? Zuletzt habe ich kleinere Meldungen über aktuelle Aktien-kurse geschrieben.

Was empfiehlst du Interessenten an einem Volontariat? Man sollte sich möglichst durch ein Praktikum vorbereitet haben. Lasst Euch nicht entmutigen, wenn's nicht auf Anhieb mit der Bewerbung um ein Volontariat klappt. Etwas hartnäckig muss man schon sein!
(Aus: *Popcorn*)

PREPOSITIONS GOVERNING THE...

...accusative	durch für ohne um
...dative	aus bei mit nach seit von zu
...accusative **or** dative	an auf in über vor
...genitive	trotz während

NB These are contracted forms: ***am = an dem***, ***zur = zu dem*** (see **3.1**).

PREPOSITIONAL PHRASES AS STOCK EXPRESSIONS

aus nächster **Nähe**	*on the spot* (lit. *from very close by*)
am **Ball** sein/bleiben	*be where the action is* (football: *be in possession of the ball*)
seit kurzem	*here: for a few weeks* (lit. *since recently*)
vor allem	*above all*
auf **Anhieb**	*straight away, instantly*

PREPOSITIONS AS VERBAL PREFIXES (see also **11.5–11.7**)

inseparable prefixes	**durch**laufen	*pass through*
	übernehmen	*take over*
separable prefixes	**an**fangen	*begin*
	miterleben	*experience (together with others)*

NB *durch-* and *über-* are in fact variable prefixes.

PREPOSITIONAL OBJECTS

sich beschäftigen mit	*be concerned with, occupy oneself with*
sich freuen auf	*look forward to*
gehen um (es geht um ...)	*concern (it concerns...), be a matter of*
sich interessieren für	*be interested in*
das Interesse an	*interest in*
der Interessent an	*someone interested in*
die Bewerbung um	*application for*

Verbs: forms 6

You saw in chapter **1** how central VERBS are to the sentence – they are where the 'action' is! The verb adjusts its endings to the 'doer' of the action (the SUBJECT of the sentence or clause) and directs the action at the accusative or dative OBJECTS and the other COMPLEMENTS (see VALENCY, chapter **8**). The verb (together with adverbials) also indicates:

▶ the **time** when the action takes place, through TENSE

▶ the **perspective** on the action, through the active or PASSIVE VOICE

▶ the **speaker's attitude** to what they are saying, through the INDICATIVE, IMPERATIVE or SUBJUNCTIVE MOOD (with most sentences being in the indicative).

This chapter gives you details about verb **forms**, i.e. the endings and other changes which indicate tense, voice and mood:

◆ STRONG, WEAK and IRREGULAR VERBS, with their PRINCIPAL PARTS (**6.1**)

◆ how the TENSES of the verb are formed (**6.2–6.7**)

◆ how the PASSIVE is formed (**6.8**)

◆ how the SUBJUNCTIVE is formed (**6.9**)

◆ the forms of STRONG and IRREGULAR VERBS (**6.10–6.11**).

Chapter **7** explains the meaning and use of these forms.

6.1 Principal parts: weak, strong and irregular verbs

Each German verb has three major forms – the PRINCIPAL PARTS. If you know these, you can construct the forms for all the other tenses, the passive and the subjunctive. The principal parts are:

▶ the INFINITIVE. This is the form of the verb given in the dictionary, and the forms of the PRESENT TENSE and SUBJUNCTIVE I are based on it. It is used to form the FUTURE TENSE and the CONDITIONAL.

▶ the PAST TENSE in the **first person singular**. The forms of SUBJUNCTIVE II are based on this.

▶ the PAST PARTICIPLE. This is used to make the compound PERFECT TENSES and the PASSIVE.

infinitive	past tense	past participle
machen	machte	gemacht
warten	wartete	gewartet
singen	sang	gesungen
fahren	fuhr	gefahren

NB These forms are equivalent to the English forms **make – made – made**; **wait – waited – waited**; **sing – sang – sung**; **drive – drove – driven**.

The table shows that there are two main types of verb:

	past tense	past participle
weak verbs **regular** **MOST** verbs	ending -*te*	ending -*t*
strong verbs **not regular** **many COMMON** verbs	vowel change	(vowel change) + ending -*en*

Because many of the most common verbs are strong and hence not fully regular, it is necessary to **learn the principal parts for each strong verb** (see sections **6.10** and **6.11**). Luckily, the new verbs coming into German from English such as *surfen*, *skaten* or *mailen* are weak.

There are also a few IRREGULAR VERBS which follow different patterns:

▶ The common verbs *sein* 'be', *haben* 'have' and *werden* 'become', which are also used as AUXILIARY VERBS to form compound tenses and the passive (see section **6.3**).

▶ The MODAL AUXILIARY verbs *dürfen*, *können*, *mögen*, *müssen*, *sollen*, *wollen* have an irregular present tense (see section **6.5**).

▶ A few WEAK VERBS have **vowel changes**, e.g. *kennen – kannte – gekannt* (know) (see section **6.11**).

▶ A few other verbs such as *gehen* and *tun* are quite irregular (see section **6.11**), including the verb *wissen* 'know', which is given with all its forms in section **6.5**.

There is no way around learning these forms – learn them like times tables. The sooner and the more thoroughly you learn them, the more quickly you will be able to understand German and produce correct sentences of your own. Learning the verb forms also allows you to learn associated vocabulary more easily. For example, *sprechen – sprach – gesprochen*, with the present tense *er spricht*, gives you the forms of associated verbs such as *absprechen*, *besprechen*, *entsprechen*, *versprechen*, nouns such as *die Sprache* and *das Sprichwort*, and adjectives such as *das versprochene Geld*. To enable you to vary your learning processes, strong and irregular verbs are listed both in **patterns** (**6.10**) and **alphabetically** (**6.11**).

6.2 Tenses: general

The tense of the verb helps to indicate the **time** when the action or event took place. German has six tenses of the verb:

▶ Two **simple** tenses, PRESENT and PAST, which consist of single word forms – the MAIN VERB.

▶ Four **compound** tenses:

◆ the PERFECT and PLUPERFECT, constructed respectively from the simple present and past tenses of the auxiliary *haben* or *sein* with the past participle of the main verb;

◆ the FUTURE TENSE, constructed from the present tense of the auxiliary *werden* with the infinitive of the main verb;

◆ the FUTURE PERFECT, constructed from the present tense of *werden* with the infinitive of *haben* or *sein* and the past participle of the main verb.

	weak verb and auxiliary *haben*	strong verb and auxiliary *sein*	
present	ich **mache**	ich **bleibe**	*I make/stay*
past	ich **machte**	ich **blieb**	*I made/stayed*
perfect	ich **habe gemacht**	ich **bin geblieben**	*I (have) made/stayed*
pluperfect	ich **hatte gemacht**	ich **war geblieben**	*I had made/stayed*
future	ich **werde machen**	ich **werde bleiben**	*I will make/stay*
future perfect	ich **werde gemacht haben**	ich **werde geblieben sein**	*I will have made/stayed*

NB German has **no progressive or continuous tenses** such as the English 'I am doing' or 'I have been staying' (see **7.1**).
NB Note the different order of the parts in the **future perfect** in English:

ich **werde gemacht** *haben*	I will *have* made

The MAIN VERB in the SIMPLE TENSES and the AUXILIARY VERB in the COMPOUND TENSES have **endings** which link them to the SUBJECT (note the endings in the table 'Conjugation in the simple tenses' in **6.3**). We say that the verb **agrees** with the subject (see section **1.2**). This form of the verb is known as the FINITE VERB (in the table, the verb in red). The verb forms which do not have these endings, the infinitive and the past participle, are called the NON-FINITE forms of the verb.

6.3 Conjugation of weak and strong verbs in simple tenses

The various forms of a verb are known collectively as its CONJUGATION. This section shows the conjugation of the simple verb forms, i.e. those which consist of a **single word**. These are:

▶ the two simple tenses (PRESENT and PAST)

▶ the non-finite forms (the **INFINITIVE** and the **PARTICIPLES**)

▶ the **IMPERATIVE** (used to give commands).

Regular weak and strong verbs have the forms in the table below.

▶ The **third person singular ending** (given with the pronoun *es*) is the same for all three genders.

▶ The ending for the **second person polite** (*Sie*) is the same as for the third person plural (*sie*).

CONJUGATION IN THE SIMPLE TENSES

	weak			strong
infinitive present participle past participle	machen machend gemacht	warten wartend gewartet	wandern wandernd gewandert	bleiben bleibend geblieben
present tense	ich mache du machst es macht wir machen ihr macht sie machen	ich warte du wartest es wartet wir warten ihr wartet sie warten	ich wand(e)re du wanderst es wandert wir wandern ihr wandert sie wandern	ich bleibe du bleibst es bleibt wir bleiben ihr bleibt sie bleiben
past tense	ich machte du machtest es machte wir machten ihr machtet sie machten	ich wartete du wartetest es wartete wir warteten ihr wartetet sie warteten	ich wanderte du wandertest es wanderte wir wanderten ihr wandertet sie wanderten	ich blieb du bliebst es blieb wir blieben ihr bliebt sie blieben
imperative singular plural (familiar) plural (polite)	mach(e)! macht! machen Sie!	warte! wartet! warten Sie!	wand(e)re! wandert! wandern Sie!	bleib! bleibt! bleiben Sie!

„Und ich sage dir, der Motor klingelt!"

Some otherwise regular verbs diverge slightly from this pattern, often in order to avoid series of consonants that are difficult to pronounce – try saying [*es regnt*] or [*du faxst*]! The main **variations in verb conjugation** are:

infinitive/stem	finite forms/past participle	example	
stem ends in: **-d or -t** **-n or -m** after consonant (other than 'l' or 'r')	before endings -st, -t, and past-tense ending -te: adds -e-	finden warten regnen atmen	→ du findest, sie findet → du wartest, es wartete → es regnet → er atmet (but: er filmt)
infinitive ends in: **-eln or -ern**	in some forms: drops -e- of stem/ending	klingeln wandern	→ ich klingle → ich wand(e)re
stem ends in: **-s, -ß, -x or -z**	in the *du* form of the present: ending -t (not -st)	lesen grüßen faxen sitzen	→ du liest → du grüßt → du faxt → du sitzt
strong verbs with: **-e- in stem**	*du* and *es* form of the present and imperative singular: vowel change to -i- or -ie-	lesen geben helfen	→ du liest, es liest, lies! → du gibst, es gibt, gib! → du hilfst, es hilft, hilf!
strong verbs with: **-a- or -au- in stem**	*du* and *es* form of the present: *Umlaut*	fahren laufen	→ du fährst, es fährt → du läufst, es läuft
infinitive ends in: **-ieren**	past participle: omits ge-	studieren trainieren	→ er hat studiert → es wurde trainiert

6.4 Separable and inseparable verbs

Whereas English has a wide variety of phrasal verbs like 'get up' or 'go out', German forms new verbs by adding prefixes. These can be 'inseparable' or 'separable', with a few prefixes being variable (see chapter **11**).

Inseparable verbs

Verbs with the following prefixes are known as inseparable verbs because their prefixes always remain attached to the verb:

▶ *be-, ent-/emp-, er-, ge-, miss-, ver-, zer-*.

▶ They do not add *ge-* in the **past participle**:

infinitive		past tense	past participle
bestellen	(*order*)	bestellte	bestellt
gefallen	(*please, like*)	gefiel	gefallen
verlieren	(*lose*)	verlor	verloren

Separable verbs

There are a wide variety of other prefixes that can attach to verbs, which typically look like prepositions or adverbs, e.g. *ansehen* (look at), *aufmachen* (open), *hinausgehen* (go out), *weglaufen* (run away). Verbs with prefixes like this are known as SEPARABLE because the prefixes **separate from the verb** in some forms.

▶ In the simple tenses (PRESENT, PAST) the prefix **separates** from the verb and is placed at the **end of the clause**.

▶ In non-finite forms (INFINITIVE, PRESENT PARTICIPLE, PAST PARTICIPLE) the **prefix stays with the verb**, e.g. infinitive *weglaufen*, present participle *weglaufend*, past participle *weggelaufen*.

▶ In the PAST PARTICIPLE the syllable *ge-* is inserted **between the prefix and the verb**, e.g. *weggelaufen, angesehen*.

▶ In SUBORDINATE CLAUSES, the prefix **rejoins** the verb at the **end of the clause**.

simple tense	**Ich mache einfach den Safe auf.**
infinitive	**Sie wollte den Safe heimlich aufmachen.**
present participle	**Den Safe aufmachend**, sah sie schon die Diamanten.
past participle	**Endlich hatte sie den Safe aufgemacht.**
subordinate clause	**Während sie den Safe aufmachte**, hörte sie Otto.

6.5 Conjugation of irregular verbs

The MODAL AUXILIARY verbs and *wissen* (know) have a number of irregular basic forms:

infinitive	*dürfen*		*können*	*mögen*	*müssen*	*sollen*	*wollen*	*wissen*
present tense	ich	**darf**	kann	mag	muss	soll	will	weiß
	du	**darfst**	kannst	magst	musst	sollst	willst	weißt
	es	**darf**	kann	mag	muss	soll	will	weiß
	wir	**dürfen**	können	mögen	müssen	sollen	wollen	wissen
	ihr	**dürft**	könnt	mögt	müsst	sollt	wollt	wisst
	sie	**dürfen**	können	mögen	müssen	sollen	wollen	wissen
past tense	ich	**durfte**	konnte	mochte	musste	sollte	wollte	wusste
	du	**durftest**	konntest	mochtest	musstest	solltest	wolltest	wusstest
	es	**durfte**	konnte	mochte	musste	sollte	wollte	wusste
	wir	**durften**	konnten	mochten	mussten	sollten	wollten	wussten
	ihr	**durftet**	konntet	mochtet	musstet	solltet	wolltet	wusstet
	sie	**durften**	konnten	mochten	mussten	sollten	wollten	wussten
past part.	**gedurft**		**gekonnt**	**gemocht**	**gemusst**	**gesollt**	**gewollt**	**gewusst**

The simple forms of the AUXILIARY VERBS *sein* (be), *haben* (have) and *werden* (become) are wholly irregular in their basic forms:

infinitive	sein	haben	werden
present participle	seiend	habend	werdend
past participle	gewesen	gehabt	geworden
present tense	ich **bin** du **bist** es **ist** wir **sind** ihr **seid** sie **sind**	ich **habe** du **hast** es **hat** wir **haben** ihr **habt** sie **haben**	ich **werde** du **wirst** es **wird** wir **werden** ihr **werdet** sie **werden**
past tense	ich **war** du **warst** es **war** wir **waren** ihr **wart** sie **waren**	ich **hatte** du **hattest** es **hatte** wir **hatten** ihr **hattet** sie **hatten**	ich **wurde** du **wurdest** es **wurde** wir **wurden** ihr **wurdet** sie **wurden**
imperative singular plural (familiar) plural (polite)	sei! seid! seien Sie!	hab! habt! haben Sie!	werde! werdet! werden Sie!

6.6 Compound tenses

The compound tenses are illustrated with the **weak verb *machen*** and the **strong verb *singen***, which form their perfect tenses with *haben*, and the **strong verb *bleiben***, which forms its perfect tenses with *sein*:

	with *haben*		with *sein*
perfect	ich habe gemacht du hast gemacht es hat gemacht wir haben gemacht ihr habt gemacht sie haben gemacht	habe gesungen hast gesungen hat gesungen haben gesungen habt gesungen haben gesungen	bin geblieben bist geblieben ist geblieben sind geblieben seid geblieben sind geblieben
pluperfect	ich hatte gemacht du hattest gemacht es hatte gemacht wir hatten gemacht ihr hattet gemacht sie hatten gemacht	hatte gesungen hattest gesungen hatte gesungen hatten gesungen hattet gesungen hatten gesungen	war geblieben warst geblieben war geblieben waren geblieben wart geblieben waren geblieben

	with *haben*		with *sein*
future	ich werde machen	werde singen	werde bleiben
	du wirst machen	wirst singen	wirst bleiben
	es wird machen	wird singen	wird bleiben
	wir werden machen	werden singen	werden bleiben
	ihr werdet machen	werdet singen	werdet bleiben
	sie werden machen	werden singen	werden bleiben
future perfect	ich werde gemacht haben	werde gesungen haben	werde geblieben sein
	du wirst gemacht haben	wirst gesungen haben	wirst geblieben sein
	es wird gemacht haben	wird gesungen haben	wird geblieben sein
	wir werden gemacht haben	werden gesungen haben	werden geblieben sein
	ihr werdet gemacht haben	werdet gesungen haben	werdet geblieben sein
	sie werden gemacht haben	werden gesungen haben	werden geblieben sein

NB The auxiliary verb in red is the finite verb, i.e. the part that agrees with the subject (see **6.2**). In a main clause, this comes in second position, while the other parts go to the end of the clause (see **9.1**), e.g. *Susi **bat** eine Expedition an den Nordpol **gemacht*** (Susi **has made** an expedition to the North Pole).

NB Note how in all compound tenses except for the future tense, the **main verb** is in the past participle form. In the future tense, the main verb is in the infinitive form (compare the present passive (**6.8**), which uses the past participle!).

6.7 *haben* or *sein* in the perfect?

Whether the perfect tenses are formed with *haben* or *sein* depends on the meaning of the verb. **Most verbs**, including all TRANSITIVE VERBS and REFLEXIVE VERBS, **form their perfect tenses with** *haben*, but **the following groups of verbs use** *sein*:

▶ **intransitive** verbs of **motion**:

Herr Steiger **ist** nach Köln **gefahren**.	*Herr Steiger **has gone** to Cologne.*
Sie **sind** gerade aus dem Haus **gegangen**.	*They **have** just **gone** out of the house.*
Sie **war** beim Skifahren **hingefallen**.	*She **had fallen over** while skiing.*

▶ **intransitive** verbs expressing a **change of state**:

Sie **sind** schon **eingeschlafen**.	*They **have** already **gone to sleep**.*
Das Licht **ist ausgegangen**.	*The light **has gone out**.*
Die Bombe **war** um elf Uhr **explodiert**.	*The bomb **had exploded** at eleven o'clock.*

▶ most verbs meaning '**happen**', '**succeed**', '**fail**':

Was **ist** hier **passiert**?	*What **has happened** here?*
Der Plan **war fehlgeschlagen**.	*The plan **had failed**.*

▶ the verbs *sein* and *bleiben*:

Er **ist** in der Bäckerei **gewesen**.	*He **has been** to the bakery.*
Wir **waren** in Bonn **geblieben**.	*We **had stayed** in Bonn.*

A few verbs can be used with *sein* or *haben*, with variations in meaning. The most common one is *fahren*: as an intransitive verb of motion, it forms its perfect tenses with *sein* and means 'go (by transport)', but when used as a transitive verb with *haben* it means 'drive':

Sie **ist** leider nach Stuttgart **gefahren**.	*Unfortunately she **has gone** to Stuttgart.*
Sie **hat** schon seinen neuen Porsche **gefahren**.	*She **has** already **driven** his new Porsche.*

6.8 Forms of the passive

German has two forms of the passive, with differences in usage (see section **7.8**). **The *werden*-passive is the most frequent by far**. It conveys a **process** and is normally the **equivalent of the English passive**, e.g. 'he was praised'=*er wurde gelobt*. It employs the auxiliary *werden* and the PAST PARTICIPLE of the main verb. It has the same six tenses as the active, illustrated here with the verb *loben* 'praise'. There is no imperative form:

WERDEN-PASSIVE

present			perfect			future		
ich	**werde**	gelobt	ich	**bin**	gelobt worden	ich	**werde**	gelobt werden
du	**wirst**	gelobt	du	**bist**	gelobt worden	du	**wirst**	gelobt werden
es	**wird**	gelobt	es	**ist**	gelobt worden	es	**wird**	gelobt werden
wir	**werden**	gelobt	wir	**sind**	gelobt worden	wir	**werden**	gelobt werden
ihr	**werdet**	gelobt	ihr	**seid**	gelobt worden	ihr	**werdet**	gelobt werden
sie	**werden**	gelobt	sie	**sind**	gelobt worden	sie	**werden**	gelobt werden

past			pluperfect			future perfect		
ich	**wurde**	gelobt	ich	**war**	gelobt worden	ich	**werde**	gelobt worden sein
du	**wurdest**	gelobt	du	**warst**	gelobt worden	du	**wirst**	gelobt worden sein
es	**wurde**	gelobt	es	**war**	gelobt worden	er	**wird**	gelobt worden sein
wir	**wurden**	gelobt	wir	**waren**	gelobt worden	wir	**werden**	gelobt worden sein
ihr	**wurdet**	gelobt	ihr	**wart**	gelobt worden	ihr	**werdet**	gelobt worden sein
sie	**wurden**	gelobt	sie	**waren**	gelobt worden	sie	**werden**	gelobt worden sein

NB In the passive, the form ***worden*** (without *ge-*) is used as the **past participle** of *werden*.

NB Take care not to confuse the present passive (*ich **werde** gelobt*) with the future active (*ich **werde** loben*) (see **6.6**).

Note how the above forms compare with the English passive forms:

	werden (conjugated with *sein*) +past participle of main verb	'be' (conjugated with *have*) +past participle of main verb
present	ich **werde gelobt**	I am **praised**
past	ich **wurde gelobt**	I was **praised**
perfect	ich **bin gelobt *worden***	I have ***been* praised**
pluperfect	ich **war gelobt *worden***	I had ***been* praised**
future	ich **werde gelobt *werden***	I will ***be* praised**
future perfect	ich **werde gelobt *worden* SEIN**	I will ***HAVE been* praised**

The other German passive, the ***sein*-passive**, is formed with the auxiliary *sein* and the PAST PARTICIPLE of the main verb. It describes a **state**, i.e. the result of an action, and is often equivalent to *sein* + adjective (e.g. *Die Tür **ist geöffnet** = Die Tür ist offen*, see **7.8**). In practice, only the present and past tenses are in common use. It is illustrated with the verb *verletzen* 'injure':

***SEIN*-PASSIVE**

present			past		
ich	**bin**	**verletzt**	ich	**war**	**verletzt**
du	**bist**	**verletzt**	du	**warst**	**verletzt**
es	**ist**	**verletzt**	es	**war**	**verletzt**
wir	**sind**	**verletzt**	wir	**waren**	**verletzt**
ihr	**seid**	**verletzt**	ihr	**wart**	**verletzt**
sie	**sind**	**verletzt**	sie	**waren**	**verletzt**

6.9 Forms of the subjunctive

Most forms of the SUBJUNCTIVE MOOD (see **7.10**) are uncommon except for those of the AUXILIARY VERBS, the MODAL AUXILIARY VERBS and the CONDITIONAL. Apart from the conditional, which is also used colloquially, the subjunctive tends to be confined to written German (see **7.5–7.7**). The forms of the German subjunctive fall into two groups, SUBJUNCTIVE I and SUBJUNCTIVE II, which reflect their uses:

subjunctive I	present subjunctive	**es gebe**
	perfect subjunctive	**es habe gegeben**
	future subjunctive	**es werde geben**
subjunctive II	past subjunctive	**es gäbe**
	pluperfect subjunctive	**es hätte gegeben**
	conditional	**es würde geben**

NB The traditional classifications 'present/past subjunctive' are misleading since the forms **do not indicate time** in the way the tenses of the indicative do.

The two simple forms of the subjunctive are constructed in the following way:

▶ The simple form of SUBJUNCTIVE I (traditionally the 'present subjunctive') is constructed quite regularly from the form of the INFINITIVE. Only the verb *sein* has irregular forms. All other verbs which have an irregular present indicative are regular in the subjunctive:

infinitive:		*sein*	*haben*	*können*	*werden*	*machen*
subjunctive I	ich	sei	habe	könne	werde	mache
('present'	du	sei(e)st	habest	könnest	werdest	machest
subjunctive)	es	sei	habe	könne	werde	mache
	wir	seien	haben	können	werden	machen
	ihr	seiet	habet	könnet	werdet	machet
	sie	seien	haben	können	werden	machen

▶ The simple form of SUBJUNCTIVE II (traditionally the 'past subjunctive') is formed on the basis of the normal PAST TENSE (the 'past indicative'). For weak verbs, it is identical; for strong and most irregular verbs, *Umlaut* is added to the past indicative form if possible, and there are some special endings:

infinitive:		*sein*	*haben*	*können*	*werden*	*machen*
past indicative:	**(ich)** *war*		*hatte*	*konnte*	*wurde*	*machte*
subjunctive II	ich	wäre	hätte	könnte	würde	machte
('past' subjunctive)	du	wärest	hättest	könntest	würdest	machtest
	es	wäre	hätte	könnte	würde	machte
	wir	wären	hätten	könnten	würden	machten
	ihr	wäret	hättet	könntet	würdet	machtet
	sie	wären	hätten	könnten	würden	machten

The COMPOUND TENSES and the PASSIVE of the subjunctive are constructed using the appropriate subjunctive forms of the auxiliaries *haben*, *sein* and *werden* in exactly the same way as the corresponding compound tenses of the indicative. The most important of these is the CONDITIONAL, formed from the past subjunctive of *werden* and the infinitive:

conditional		
ich	würde	machen
du	würdest	machen
es	würde	machen
wir	würden	machen
ihr	würdet	machen
sie	würden	machen

6.10 Vowel changes with strong verbs

The vowel changes with most strong verbs fall into a small number of **recurrent patterns**, and these can help you to remember the forms. These patterns are all given here, together with the verbs which follow each pattern (for each pattern there are also many other verbs, formed with prefixes, e.g. *abfallen, gefallen, wegfallen* etc.).

a – ie – a		a – u – a	
fallen – fiel – gefallen		fahren – fuhr – gefahren	
present: -ä- du fällst, es fällt		*present*: -ä- du fährst, es fährt	
blasen	lassen	graben	tragen
braten	raten	laden	wachsen
halten	schlafen	schlagen	waschen

e – a – e		e – a – o	
geben – gab – gegeben		helfen – half – geholfen	
present: -i- du gibst, es gibt		*present*: -i- du hilfst, es hilft	
-ie- du liest, es liest		-ie- du stiehlst, es stiehlt	
fressen	sehen	befehlen	stehlen
geschehen	treten	brechen	sterben
lesen	vergessen	empfehlen	treffen
messen		erschrecken	verbergen
		gelten	verderben
		helfen	werben
		sprechen	werfen
		stechen	

ei – i – i		ei – ie – ie	
beißen – biss – gebissen		bleiben – blieb – geblieben	
gleichen	schleichen	entscheiden	schreien
gleiten	schleifen	leihen	schweigen
greifen	schmeißen	meiden	steigen
kneifen	schreiten	preisen	treiben
pfeifen	streichen	reiben	verzeihen
reißen	streiten	scheinen	weisen
reiten	weichen	schreiben	
scheißen			

i – a – o	i – a – u
spinnen – spann – gesponnen	singen – sang – gesungen
beginnen schwimmen gewinnen	binden schwingen dringen sinken finden springen gelingen stinken klingen trinken ringen verschwinden schlingen zwingen

ie – io – o			
bieten – bot – geboten			
biegen	frieren	riechen	verlieren
fliegen	genießen	schieben	wiegen
fliehen	gießen	schießen	
fließen	kriechen	schließen	

6.11 List of strong and irregular verbs

Most German verbs are weak, and therefore quite regular, but many of the most **frequently used** verbs are strong or irregular in some way. There is no way of telling from the infinitive of a verb whether it is strong or irregular, and you should make a point of learning the PRINCIPAL PARTS of these verbs. By far the best way is to **learn them out loud**, so your ear helps you to memorize the vowel patterns.

The table on the following pages gives all the frequent strong and irregular verbs, including those whose vowel changes do not follow the patterns detailed in **6.10**.

▶ Remember that these forms are also used when these verbs combine with PREFIXES, e.g. *entschwinden/verschwinden*; *entscheiden/unterscheiden*; *abfahren/hinfahren/umfahren/wegfahren*.

▶ Learning these forms is time well spent as it can help you to expand your vocabulary, e.g. the forms of the verb *sitzen – saß – gesessen* (sit) provide clues to the meaning of the nouns *das Gesäß* (posterior) and *der Sessel* (armchair).

▶ The vast majority of strong verbs follow the patterns given in **6.10**, while a few strong verbs have other vowel changes. **Vowel changes are highlighted in red in the table below**.

▶ A few verbs (*brennen, kennen, nennen, rennen*) have vowel changes but weak endings: **brennen – brannte – gebrannt**.

▶ A number of very common verbs (given in red) are irregular in other ways: *bringen, denken, essen, geben, leiden, nehmen, schneiden, sitzen, stehen, tun, wissen, ziehen.*

infinitive		3rd sg. pres.	past	past participle	
befehlen	(command)	[es befiehlt]	**befahl**	**befohlen**	
beginnen	(begin)		**begann**	**begonnen**	
beißen	(bite)		**biss**	**gebissen**	
betrügen	(deceive)		**betrog**	**betrogen**	
biegen	(bend)		**bog**	**gebogen**	(hat/ist)
bieten	(offer)		**bot**	**geboten**	
binden	(bind)		**band**	**gebunden**	
bitten	(ask, request)		**bat**	**gebeten**	
blasen	(blow)	[es bläst]	**blies**	**geblasen**	
bleiben	(stay, remain)		**blieb**	**geblieben**	(ist)
braten	(fry, roast)		**briet**	**gebraten**	
brechen	(break)	[es bricht]	**brach**	**gebrochen**	(hat/ist)
brennen	(burn)		**brannte**	**gebrannt**	
bringen	(bring)		**brachte**	**gebracht**	
denken	(think)		**dachte**	**gedacht**	
dringen	(penetrate)		**drang**	**gedrungen**	(hat/ist)
empfehlen	(recommend)	[es empfiehlt]	**empfahl**	**empfohlen**	
erschrecken	(be startled)	[es erschrickt]	**erschrak**	**erschrocken**	(ist)
essen	(eat)	[es isst]	**aß**	**gegessen**	
fahren	(go, drive)	[es fährt]	**fuhr**	**gefahren**	(ist/hat)
fallen	(fall)	[es fällt]	**fiel**	**gefallen**	(ist)
fangen	(catch)	[es fängt]	**fing**	**gefangen**	
finden	(find)		**fand**	**gefunden**	
flechten	(plait)	[es flicht]	**flocht**	**geflochten**	
fliegen	(fly)		**flog**	**geflogen**	(ist/hat)
fliehen	(run away)		**floh**	**geflohen**	(ist)
fließen	(flow)		**floss**	**geflossen**	(ist)
fressen	(eat (of animals))	[es frisst]	**fraß**	**gefressen**	
frieren	(freeze)		**fror**	**gefroren**	(hat/ist)

infinitive		3rd sg. pres.	past	past participle	
gebären	(give birth)	[es gebiert]	gebar	geboren	
geben	(give)	[es gibt]	gab	gegeben	
gehen	(go)		ging	gegangen	(ist)
gelingen	(succeed)		gelang	gelungen	(ist)
gelten	(be valid)	[es gilt]	galt	gegolten	
genießen	(enjoy)		genoss	genossen	
geschehen	(happen)	[es geschieht]	geschah	geschehen	(ist)
gewinnen	(win)		gewann	gewonnen	
gießen	(pour)		goss	gegossen	
gleichen	(resemble)		glich	geglichen	
gleiten	(glide, slide)		glitt	geglitten	(ist)
graben	(dig)	[es gräbt]	grub	gegraben	
greifen	(grasp)		griff	gegriffen	
halten	(hold)	[es hält]	hielt	gehalten	
hängen	(hang)		hing	gehangen	
hauen	(hit, cut)		haute/hieb	gehauen	
heben	(raise, lift)		hob	gehoben	
heißen	(be called)		hieß	geheißen	
helfen	(help)	[es hilft]	half	geholfen	
kennen	(know)		kannte	gekannt	
klingen	(sound)		klang	geklungen	
kneifen	(pinch)		kniff	gekniffen	
kommen	(come)		kam	gekommen	(ist)
kriechen	(creep, crawl)		kroch	gekrochen	(ist)
laden	(load)	[es lädt]	lud	geladen	
lassen	(let, leave)	[es lässt]	ließ	gelassen	
laufen	(run)	[es läuft]	lief	gelaufen	(ist/hat)
leiden	(suffer)		litt	gelitten	
leihen	(lend, borrow)		lieh	geliehen	
lesen	(read)	[es liest]	las	gelesen	
liegen	(lie)		lag	gelegen	

infinitive		3rd sg. pres.	past	past participle	
lügen	(tell lies)		**log**	**gelogen**	
meiden	(avoid)		**mied**	**gemieden**	
melken	(milk)		**melkte/molk**	**gemolken**	
messen	(measure)	[es misst]	**maß**	**gemessen**	
nehmen	(take)	[es nimmt]	**nahm**	**genommen**	
nennen	(name, call)		**nannte**	**genannt**	
pfeifen	(whistle)		**pfiff**	**gepfiffen**	
preisen	(praise)		**pries**	**gepriesen**	
quellen	(well up)	[es quillt]	**quoll**	**gequollen**	(ist)
raten	(advise)	[es rät]	**riet**	**geraten**	
reiben	(rub)		**rieb**	**gerieben**	
reißen	(tear)		**riss**	**gerissen**	(hat/ist)
reiten	(ride)		**ritt**	**geritten**	(ist/hat)
rennen	(run)		**rannte**	**gerannt**	(ist/hat)
riechen	(smell)		**roch**	**gerochen**	
ringen	(wrestle)		**rang**	**gerungen**	
rufen	(call)		**rief**	**gerufen**	
saufen	(booze)	[es säuft]	**soff**	**gesoffen**	
schaffen (distinguish from **schaffen** 'manage', 'work')	(create)		**schuf** (schaffte)	**geschaffen** (geschafft)	
scheiden	(separate, depart)		**schied**	**geschieden**	(hat/ist)
scheinen	(shine, seem)		**schien**	**geschienen**	
scheißen	(shit)		**schiss**	**geschissen**	
schieben	(push)		**schob**	**geschoben**	
schießen	(shoot)		**schoss**	**geschossen**	(hat/ist)
schlafen	(sleep)	[es schläft]	**schlief**	**geschlafen**	
schlagen	(hit)	[es schlägt]	**schlug**	**geschlagen**	
schleichen	(creep)		**schlich**	**geschlichen** (ist)	
schleifen	(grind, sharpen)		**schliff**	**geschliffen**	
schließen	(shut)		**schloss**	**geschlossen**	
schlingen	(wind, wrap)		**schlang**	**geschlungen**	

infinitive		3rd sg. pres.	past	past participle	
schmeißen	(chuck, throw)		schmiss	geschmissen	
schmelzen	(melt)	[es schmilzt]	schmolz	geschmolzen	(hat/ist)
schneiden	(cut)		schnitt	geschnitten	
schreiben	(write)		schrieb	geschrieben	
schreien	(shout, scream)		schrie	geschrien	
schreiten	(stride)		schritt	geschritten	(ist)
schweigen	(be silent)		schwieg	geschwiegen	
schwellen	(swell)	[es schwillt]	schwoll	geschwollen	(ist)
schwimmen	(swim)		schwamm	geschwommen	(ist/hat)
schwinden	(disappear)		schwand	geschwunden	(ist)
schwingen	(swing)		schwang	geschwungen	
schwören	(swear)		schwor/schwur	geschworen	
sehen	(see)	[es sieht]	sah	gesehen	
senden (distinguish from **senden** 'broadcast')	(send)		sandte (sendete)	gesandt (gesendet)	
singen	(sing)		sang	gesungen	
sinken	(sink)		sank	gesunken	(ist)
sitzen	(sit)		saß	gesessen	
spinnen	(spin, be stupid, talk rubbish)		spann	gesponnen	
sprechen	(speak)	[es spricht]	sprach	gesprochen	
springen	(jump)		sprang	gesprungen	(ist)
stechen	(sting, prick)		stach	gestochen	
stehen	(stand)		stand	gestanden	
stehlen	(steal)	[es stiehlt]	stahl	gestohlen	
steigen	(climb, rise)		stieg	gestiegen	(ist)
sterben	(die)	[es stirbt]	starb	gestorben	(ist)
stinken	(stink)		stank	gestunken	
stoßen	(push)	[es stößt]	stieß	gestoßen	(hat/ist)
streichen	(stroke, paint)		strich	gestrichen	(hat/ist)
streiten	(quarrel)		stritt	gestritten	
tragen	(carry)	[es trägt]	trug	getragen	

infinitive		3rd sg. pres.	past	past participle	
treffen	(meet, hit)	**[es trifft]**	**traf**	**getroffen**	
treiben	(drive, drift)		**trieb**	**getrieben**	(ist/hat)
treten	(step)	**[es tritt]**	**trat**	**getreten**	(ist/hat)
trinken	(drink)		**trank**	**getrunken**	
tun	(do)		**tat**	**getan**	
verbergen	(hide)	**[es verbirgt]**	**verbarg**	**verborgen**	
verderben	(spoil)	**[es verdirbt]**	**verdarb**	**verdorben**	(hat/ist)
vergessen	(forget)	**[es vergisst]**	**vergaß**	**vergessen**	
verlieren	(lose)		**verlor**	**verloren**	
verzeihen	(excuse)		**verzieh**	**verziehen**	
wachsen	(grow)		**wuchs**	**gewachsen**	(ist)
waschen	(wash)		**wusch**	**gewaschen**	
weichen	(yield, give way)		**wich**	**gewichen**	(ist)
weisen	(point)		**wies**	**gewiesen**	
werben	(recruit, advertise)	**[es wirbt]**	**warb**	**geworben**	
werfen	(throw)		**warf**	**geworfen**	
wiegen	(weigh)		**wog**	**gewogen**	
wissen	(know) (see **6.5**)		**wusste**	**gewusst**	
ziehen	(pull)		**zog**	**gezogen**	(hat/ist)
zwingen	(force)		**zwang**	**gezwungen**	

VERB FORMS IN CONTEXT

Meine Eltern lieben mich kaputt

„Sie sind also der junge Mann, von dem mir meine Tochter erzählt hat?" fragt Sandras Mutter mit Haifisch-Lächeln. „Äh, weiß nicht, ja", antwortet Tino. Schweigen. „Und was machen Sie so, gehen Sie noch zur Schule?" Sandras Mutter siezt ihn und nennt ihn „junger Mann", obwohl er mit seinen 17 Jahren kaum älter ist als ihre Tochter. Sandra ist das nur noch peinlich. „Nee, ich mach' grad eine Lehre als Schreiner", sagt Tino gedehnt. Und dann, zu Sandra:

„Können wir gehen?" – „Bitte sei um elf zu Hause, du weißt, ich werde mir Sorgen machen!" ruft ihre Mutter ihnen hinterher, in einem Ton, bei dem schon wieder alles klar ist: durchgefallen.

So ist es fast immer. Wenn Sandra Klamotten anprobiert, kommt ihre Mutter mit und sagt ihr, was ihr steht und was nicht – bis sie entnervt aufgibt und genau das Teil kauft, das die Mutter gut findet. Oder damals, als sie die blöden Ballettstunden nehmen musste. Wegen ihrer schlechten Haltung, sagte ihre Mutter. Wie sie den Unterricht gehasst hatte. Am liebsten hätte sie die Schühchen in die Ecke geschmissen und wäre nie wiedergekommen.

Aber sie tat es nicht – weil sie Angst hatte, die Eltern zu enttäuschen. „Ich will doch nur dein Bestes", sagte ihre Mutter. Und: „Ich möchte eine hübsche Tochter haben."

Alle Diskussionen laufen so. Sandra weiß, dass die Eltern alles für sie tun würden. Aber sie machen ständig Druck. Durch Enttäuschung, Traurigsein oder übertriebene Fürsorge. Bei Tino dagegen hat sie das Gefühl, dass sie ohne Bedingungen akzeptiert wird.

(Aus: *Brigitte Young Miss*)

PRINCIPAL PARTS OF VERBS

	infinitive (3rd sg. pres.)	past tense	past participle
weak verbs	lie**ben** (es lie**bt**) erzählen, fragen, machen, siezen, sagen, dehnen, nerven, kaufen, hassen, enttäuschen	lie**bte**	**ge**lie**bt**
	antwor**ten** (es antwor**tet**)	antwor**tete**	**ge**antwor**tet**
	probi**eren** (es probi**ert**), akzeptieren	probi**ert**	**probiert**
strong verbs	rufen (es ruft)	rief	ge**ruf**en
	fallen (es fällt)	fiel	ge**fall**en
	kommen (es kommt)	kam	ge**komm**en
	geben (es gibt)	gab	ge**geb**en
	finden (es findet)	fand	ge**fund**en
	nehmen (es nimmt)	na**hm**	ge**nomm**en
	schmeißen (es schmeißt)	schmiss	ge**schmiss**en

strong verbs (cont.)	laufen (es läuft)	lief	gelaufen
	treiben (es treibt)	trieb	getrieben
irregular	wissen (es weiß)	wusste	gewusst
verbs	gehen (es geht)	**ging**	**gegangen**
	nennen (es nennt)	nannte	genannt
	stehen (es steht)	**stand**	**gestanden**
	tun (es tut)	**tat**	getan
auxiliary verbs	sein (es ist)	war	gewesen
(irregular)	haben (es hat)	hatte	gehabt
	werden (es wird)	wurde	worden
modal aux.	können (es kann)	konnte	gekonnt
verbs	müssen (es muss)	musste	gemusst
(irregular)	mögen (es mag)	mochte	gemocht

TENSES

present tense	Sie **lieben** mich.
	Ich **mache** gerade eine Lehre.
past tense	Die Mutter **sagte** es.
	Sie **musste** Ballettstunden **nehmen**.
perfect tense	Sie **hat** von ihm **erzählt**.
	(Er **ist**) **durchgefallen**.
pluperfect tense	Sie **hatte** den Unterricht **gehasst**.
future tense	Ich **werde** mir Sorgen **machen**.

VOICE AND MOOD

werden-passive		Sie **wird** ohne Bedingungen **akzeptiert**.
imperative		**Sei** um elf zu Hause!
subjunctive	**pluperfect subjunctive**	Am liebsten **hätte** sie die Schuhe in die Ecke **geschmissen**.
		Am liebsten **wäre** sie nie **wiedergekommen**.
	conditional	Die Eltern **würden** alles für sie **tun**.

PREFIXES

inseparable prefixes	er**zählen**	*tell, narrate*
	enttäuschen	*disappoint*
separable prefixes	**an**probieren	*try on*
	aufgeben	*give up*
	durchfallen	*fail*
	mitkommen	*come (with someone)*

Verbs: uses 7

This chapter explains the main uses of the various verb forms in German:

◆ the use of the TENSES (**7.1–7.3**)

◆ the PASSIVE and passive constructions (**7.4–7.9**)

◆ the uses of the SUBJUNCTIVE (**7.10–7.12**)

◆ the MODAL AUXILIARIES (**7.13–7.19**).

7.1 The tenses and their use

As you saw in section **6.2**, there are six TENSES of the verb in German. These correspond quite closely in form and use to the six English tenses:

present	**ich kaufe**	*I buy*
past	**ich kaufte**	*I bought*
perfect	**ich habe gekauft**	*I have bought*
pluperfect	**ich hatte gekauft**	*I had bought*
future	**ich werde kaufen**	*I shall/will buy*
future perfect	**ich werde gekauft haben**	*I shall/will have bought*

German has no forms like the extended verb forms in English, so that *ich kaufe* can correspond to English 'I buy', 'I am buying', 'I do buy'. Whereas English can distinguish an ongoing action by a **progressive tense** (e.g. 'I'm reading'), this is not possible in German. Instead you often find an adverbial such as *gerade* (e.g. *Ich lese gerade*):

Ich repariere gerade mein Fahrrad.	*I'm fixing my bike.*
Sie telefonierte gerade, als er hereinkam.	*She was telephoning when he came in.*

Otherwise, though, the use of the tenses in German is close to that of the corresponding English ones, and **in most cases the same tense is used in German as would be used in the corresponding context in English**. Sections **7.2–7.3** give you information about important instances where German and English do not agree in the use of tense.

7.2 Present and future

The PRESENT TENSE is mostly used as in English, to express an action in the present or a generalization:

Wir **beziehen** uns auf Ihr heutiges Fax.	*We refer to your fax of today.*
Ich **gehe** jeden Samstag ins Kino.	*I go to the cinema every Saturday.*

German also often uses the present tense to **refer to the future**, as long as the future meaning is clear from the context (typically through a time adverbial):

In zwei Stunden bin ich wieder da.	*I'll be back in two hours.*
Ich **schreibe** den Brief **heute Abend**.	*I'll write the letter tonight.*
Vielleicht sagt er es ihr.	*Perhaps he'll tell her.*

NB There is no equivalent in German to the '**going to** future', e.g. 'I'm going to see him tomorrow': *Ich sehe ihn morgen.*

▶ The FUTURE TENSE is used **much less** in German than in English.

The future tense is mainly used to refer to the future **if the present could be misunderstood**:

Er **wird** wieder bei der Post **arbeiten**.	*He is going to work for the post office again.*

NB *Er arbeitet wieder bei der Post* can only mean 'He is working for the post office again'.

In both English and German, the future tense may indicate not that something is going to happen in the future, but that the speaker supposes that something has happened, is happening, or will happen.

▶ In German the **most common use of the future tense** is to express a **supposition** (often with the modal particle *wohl*):

Sie **wird (wohl)** wieder krank **sein**.	*She'll be ill again./I expect she's ill again.*
Dietlinde **wird** auch **kommen wollen**.	*Dietlinde will want to come too.*

The FUTURE PERFECT can refer to an **event before another one in the future**:

Wenn wir uns wiedersehen, werden wir beide unser Abitur **gemacht haben**.	*By the time we meet again, we will both have done our Abitur.*
Bis morgen werde ich den Brief **geschrieben haben**.	*By tomorrow I'll have written the letter.*

The future perfect is also commonly used to express a **supposition about the past**:

Sie **wird (wohl)** krank **gewesen sein**.	*She'll have been ill./I expect she was ill.*
Max **wird** den Termin **vergessen haben**.	*I expect Max forgot the appointment.*

In German, the perfect tense is often used in contexts like these rather than the future perfect:

Bis morgen habe ich den Brief **geschrieben.**	*By tomorrow I will have written the letter.*
Sie **ist (wohl)** krank **gewesen.**	*I expect she was ill.*

7.3 Past and perfect

There are important **differences between English and German** in the use of the PERFECT TENSE

▶ In English the perfect tense is clearly distinct from the past tense. It links a past action to the present time in some way. Compare:

I've broken my leg (see the plaster).	*I broke my leg skiing* (it's healed up now).

The German perfect tense is **not as clearly distinct** in meaning and use from the past tense, and their uses overlap.

▶ As in English, the German perfect tense often refers to a **present state resulting from a past action**:

Ich habe ihr schon geschrieben.	*I've already written to her.*
Ich habe mir das Bein gebrochen.	*I've broken my leg.*

▶ Contrary to English, the German perfect tense is often used to refer to an **action or event wholly in the past**.

In such contexts English always uses a past tense:

Ich habe sie vorige Woche in der Stadt gesehen.	*I saw her in town last week.*
Letztes Jahr haben wir noch in Köln gewohnt.	*Last year we were still living in Cologne.*

In general, the past tense is used to **narrate** past actions or events in written German. In spoken German, the perfect tense is commonly used in such contexts:

written German	1960 gingen die Beatles nach Hamburg, wo sie in Nachtclubs spielten. Im „Top Ten" schlugen sie wie eine Bombe ein.
spoken German	1960 sind die Beatles nach Hamburg gegangen, wo sie in Nachtclubs gespielt haben. Im „Top Ten" haben sie wie eine Bombe eingeschlagen.
English	*In 1960, the Beatles **went** to Hamburg, where they **played** in nightclubs. They **went down** like a bomb/**were** a smash hit in the 'Top Ten'.*

Although the perfect tense predominates in speech in such contexts, the past tense is not unusual. The past tense is used especially in northern German and with common verbs like *sein, haben, gehen, kommen* and the modal auxiliaries *dürfen, können, mögen, müssen, sollen* and *wollen*.

Both in spoken and in written German you may find the two tenses used more or less interchangeably.

'Up-to-now' contexts

In 'up-to-now' sentences, typically with '**for**' or '**since**', English uses the perfect tense (often in the progressive). German always uses the PRESENT TENSE in such contexts (usually with **seit** or **schon**):

Ich **studiere seit 6 Wochen** dort.	*I've been studying* there *for 6 weeks*.
Er **fährt seit 1990** jedes Jahr nach Dresden.	*Since 1990 he's been going* to Dresden *every year*.
Wir **warten schon eine Stunde** auf euch!	*We've been waiting* for you *for an hour*!

7.4 The passive with *werden*

Action is typically expressed using the 'default' ACTIVE VOICE, both in English and in German. The active sentence **Die Schlange frisst den Frosch** ('The snake is eating the frog') tells us what is happening **and** who or what is doing it. But we can also use the PASSIVE VOICE and thereby present a different perspective on an action: **Der Frosch wird gefressen** ('The frog is being eaten') places the emphasis on what is going on without saying who is doing it.

   Most active sentences with a TRANSITIVE VERB can be turned into passive sentences (a transitive verb takes a direct object, in the accusative case, see **1.3**). The ACCUSATIVE OBJECT **of the active sentence** becomes the SUBJECT **of the passive sentence**:

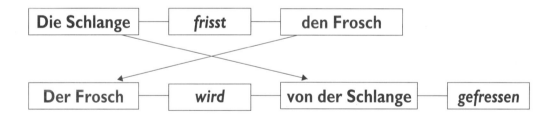

The subject of the active sentence (*die Schlange*) is either omitted altogether, or appears in a phrase using *von* or *durch* (English 'by', see **7.7**): *Der Frosch wird* ***von der Schlange*** *gefressen* ('The frog is being eaten **by the snake**'):

tense	active	passive
present	Der Arzt **heilt den Patienten**.	**Der Patient wird** (vom Arzt) **geheilt**.
	The doctor **heals the patient**.	**The patient is healed** (by the doctor).
past	Die Bauleute **rissen das Haus ab**.	**Das Haus wurde** (von den Bauleuten) **abgerissen**.
	The builders **pulled down the house**.	**The house was pulled down** (by the builders).

tense	active	passive
perfect	Die Firma **hat den Angestellten entlassen**.	**Der Angestellte ist** (von der Firma) **entlassen worden**.
	The company **has sacked the employee**.	**The employee has been sacked** (by the company).
future	Der Computer **wird das Buch verdrängen**.	**Das Buch wird** (vom Computer) **verdrängt werden**.
	The computer **will replace the book**.	**The book will be replaced** (by the computer).

NB Don't confuse the **present passive** (***werden* + past participle**, e.g. *wird ... geprüft*) with the **future active** (***werden* + infinitive**, e.g. *wird ... prüfen*).

NB Remember that you can't rely on word order to tell you which is the subject of a German sentence! The following word order changes the emphasis but not the basic meaning of the sentences 'The doctor heals the patient'/'The patient is healed by the doctor': *Den Patienten* (accusative object) *heilt der Arzt* (subject)/*Vom Arzt wird der Patient* (subject) *geheilt*.

7.5 The 'subjectless' passive

The ***werden*-passive** is often used **without a subject** to indicate that an **activity** of some kind is (or is not) taking place:

Heute **wurde** mit den Bauarbeiten **begonnen**.	*They started the building work today.*
Hier **darf** nicht **geraucht werden**.	*Smoking is not allowed here.*

This construction can be used with any verb, transitive or intransitive, which expresses an activity of some kind. If no other element is placed before the finite verb, the pronoun ***es*** is inserted as a '**dummy subject**':

Es wird wieder **gekämpft**.	*The fighting has started up again.*
Es wurde bei dem Fest kaum **getanzt**.	*People hardly danced at the party.*

7.6 The passive with dative objects

In German only the ACCUSATIVE OBJECT of a transitive verb can become the SUBJECT of the corresponding passive sentence:

Ich **lese den Roman**.	⇒	**Der Roman wird gelesen**.
I am reading the novel.		*The novel is being read.*
Meine Schwester **schrieb den Brief**.	⇒	**Der Brief wurde geschrieben**.
My sister wrote the letter.		*The letter was written.*

Verbs which **govern the dative** can be used in the passive, but the DATIVE OBJECT **remains in the dative**. The verb has no subject and is in the form of the third person singular:

Sie **dankte** *ihnen* für ihre Hilfe.	⇒	*Ihnen* **wurde** für ihre Hilfe **gedankt**.
They thanked them for their help.		*They were thanked for their help.*
Wir **helfen** *meinem Vater*.	⇒	*Meinem Vater* **wird geholfen**.
We are helping my father.		*My father is being helped.*

With verbs which have **dative and accusative objects**, only the accusative object can be the subject of the corresponding passive sentence. The dative object always stays in the dative:

Er **schenkte** *meiner Schwester* **den Hund**.	*He gave my sister the dog (as a present).*
Der Hund wurde *meiner Schwester* **geschenkt**.	*The dog was given to my sister.*
Meiner Schwester wurde **der Hund** **geschenkt**.	*My sister was given the dog.*

7.7 *von* or *durch* with the passive

The equivalent of English 'by' in passive sentences can be ***von*** or ***durch***.

▶ ***Von*** is the most usual equivalent and indicates the **agent** (i.e. the 'doer') of the action. This is usually a person, but it can be a force of nature:

Die Stadt **wurde von dem Feind zerstört**.	*The town was destroyed by the enemy.*
Sie **wurde von zwei Polizisten verhaftet**.	*She was arrested by two policemen.*
Die Stadt **wurde von einem Waldbrand bedroht**.	*The town was endangered by a forest fire.*
Er **wurde von der Lawine mitgerissen**.	*He was swept away by an avalanche.*

▶ ***Durch*** indicates the **means** by which an action is carried out (usually a thing), or an **intermediary** (if a person):

Die Stadt **wurde durch Bomben zerstört**.	*The town was destroyed by bombs.*
Die Pest **wird durch einen Virus verursacht**.	*The plague is caused by a virus.*
Ich **wurde durch einen Boten benachrichtigt**.	*I was informed by a messenger.*

7.8 The passive with *sein*

German has two passives: in addition to the usual passive formed with ***werden*** and a past participle, there is a second type, formed with the auxiliary verb ***sein*** and a past participle. The *sein*-passive is more **descriptive**, and can be equivalent in meaning to an **adjective**, e.g. *Die Tür ist geöffnet* is equivalent to *Die Tür ist offen*.

▶ The ***werden*-PASSIVE** expresses an **action** or a **process** and is normally equivalent to the English passive.

▶ The ***sein*-PASSIVE** expresses a **state resulting from an action** which has/had already taken place.

The following examples illustrate this **difference between the *werden*- and the *sein*-passive**:

Der Tisch **wird gedeckt**.	*The table is being laid.* (someone is performing the action of laying the table)
Der Tisch **ist gedeckt**.	*The table is laid.* (someone has already laid it)
Die Ostereier **wurden bemalt**.	*The Easter eggs were (being) painted.* (someone was carrying out this action, or did it regularly)
Die Ostereier **waren bemalt**.	*The Easter eggs were painted.* (someone had painted them)
Die Stadt **wurde 1944 zerstört**.	*The town was destroyed in 1944.* (the event took place in 1944)
Die Stadt **war 1944 zerstört**.	*The town was destroyed in 1944.* (someone had destroyed it by then)

The following points can help you to decide which passive to use:

▶ The ***werden*-passive** often corresponds to an **English progressive**, especially in the present tense. This is because it reports an action in progress, e.g. *Die Rose wird gepflanzt* 'The rose is being planted'.

▶ As the ***sein*-passive** expresses a state resulting from a previous action it often corresponds to an **English perfect or pluperfect**. In this way *Das Auto ist repariert* means 'The car has been repaired'.

▶ Verbs which do not express some kind of tangible or visible result cannot be used in the *sein*-passive. Thus we can say *Meine Hand ist verletzt* because the injury is clear, but we cannot say **Er ist bewundert* for 'He is admired', because it is not tangible or visible. We can only say *Er wird bewundert*.

▶ In practice, the *werden*-passive is about four times more frequent in actual use than the *sein*-passive.

▶ The equivalent of an English passive (formed with 'be') is usually not the passive formed with *sein*, but the passive formed with *werden*.

„Heißt das etwa, dass Sie nicht
angeschnallt waren?"

7.9 Alternatives to passive constructions

German has a wide range of other constructions which express a meaning like the *werden-passive*.

▶ *man* is much more frequent than English 'one':

Man sagt ...	= **Es wird gesagt ...**
People say ...	*It is said ...*
Man hatte ihn davor gewarnt.	= **Er war davor gewarnt worden.**
People had warned him of that.	*He had been warned of that.*

▶ *bekommen* (get (given)) or in spoken German *kriegen* are used to make passive sentences from verbs with dative objects:

Er bekam das Buch geschenkt.	= **Ihm wurde das Buch geschenkt.**
	He was given the book (as a present).
Sie kriegte das Geld ausgezahlt.	= **Ihr wurde das Geld ausgezahlt.**
	She was given the money/The money was paid out to her.

▶ **Reflexive verbs** are often alternatives to passives:

Mein Verdacht hat sich bestätigt.	= **Mein Verdacht wurde bestätigt.**
	My suspicion was confirmed.
Das Buch liest sich schnell.	= **Das Buch kann schnell gelesen werden.**
	The book can be read quickly.

▶ Constructions with *sich lassen* add the idea of possibility:

Das lässt sich leicht ändern.	= **Das kann leicht geändert werden.**
	That can easily be changed.
Ein Ende lässt sich nicht absehen.	= **Ein Ende kann nicht abgesehen werden.**
	An end is not in sight.

▶ Many **phrasal verbs**, especially with *kommen*, have a passive meaning:

Die Verhandlungen kommen heute zum Abschluss.	= **Die Verhandlungen werden heute abgeschlossen.**
	The negotiations will be concluded today.

▶ *sein* with an **infinitive with *zu*** adds the idea of possibility or obligation:

Die Anträge sind im Rathaus abzuholen.	= **Die Anträge können/sollen im Rathaus abgeholt werden.**
The application forms are to be collected from the Town Hall.	*The application forms can/should be collected from the Town Hall.*

▶ **Adjectives in -*bar*** express a passive possibility:

Diese Muscheln sind nicht essbar.	= **Diese Muscheln können nicht gegessen werden.**
These mussels are not edible.	*These mussels cannot be eaten.*
Das Argument ist nicht widerlegbar.	= **Das Argument kann nicht widerlegt werden.**
This argument is irrefutable.	*This argument cannot be refuted.*

7.10 **The subjunctive: general**

In addition to tense (present tense, past tense, etc.) and voice (active or passive), verb forms can vary in terms of their MOOD. This indicates whether the speaker is expressing a fact, command, wish, etc.

In German, as in English, most verbs are in the INDICATIVE MOOD, and this is used for statements that are presented as **fact** (the tenses of the indicative were explained in **7.1–7.3**).

The IMPERATIVE is used in both English and German to give **commands**, e.g. *Warte!* (familiar) or *Warten Sie!* (polite) ('Wait!') (the forms of the imperative are given in **6.3**).

The SUBJUNCTIVE MOOD can signal that the speaker regards the statement as unreal, or as merely possible, rather than as fact, e.g. 'If I *knew* he *were* at home, I *would* drop round'. The subjunctive is used more widely in German than in English. Most forms are more widespread in written than in spoken language.

▶ By using the subjunctive mood, German speakers can characterize what they are saying as **unreal**, **possible** or **not necessarily true**.

▶ The subjunctive is primarily used in CONDITIONAL sentences (**7.11**) and in REPORTED SPEECH (**7.12**).

The forms of the subjunctive in German fall into two groups, which are usually called SUBJUNCTIVE I and SUBJUNCTIVE II, and these two groups have rather different uses:

subjunctive I	present subjunctive perfect subjunctive future subjunctive	es gebe es habe gegeben es werde geben
subjunctive II	past subjunctive pluperfect subjunctive conditional	es gäbe es hätte gegeben es würde geben

As the tables in section **6.9** show, for most verbs (except *sein*) the only ending for subjunctive I which is clearly different from that for the indicative is the one for *er/sie/es*, and, in practice, this is the only form which is at all commonly used.

The past subjunctive and conditional forms are **interchangeable in meaning** in most contexts, e.g. *ich gäbe* and *ich würde geben* can both mean 'I would give'.

▶ The **one-word past subjunctive forms** are used mainly for the most common verbs, especially *wäre*, *hätte* and the **modal auxiliaries**.

▶ For other verbs, especially weak verbs, the CONDITIONAL form with *würde* **plus the infinitive** is usually preferred, especially in spoken German.

7.11 Subjunctive II: conditional sentences

▶ The main use of subjunctive II in German – in the spoken language as well as in writing – is to indicate **unreal** or **hypothetical conditions**, typically in conditional sentences with *wenn* (if):

Wenn ich Zeit **hätte**, **käme** ich gern mit.
If I had time I would gladly accompany you.
Wenn wir Zeit **hätten**, **könnten** wir einen Ausflug machen.
If we had time we could go on an excursion.
Die Europäer **wären** erleichtert, **wenn** England wieder austreten **würde**.
The Europeans would be relieved if England pulled out/were to pull out again.
Wir **würden** es begrüßen, **wenn** Sie uns besuchen **könnten**.
We would welcome it if you could visit us.
Wenn ich im Lotto gewinnen **würde**, **würde** ich eine Villa in Italien kaufen.
If I won/were to win the jackpot, I would buy a villa in Italy.

▶ In German, forms of subjunctive II are used in both the *if*-**clause** and the **main clause**.

Either the past subjunctive or the conditional form can be used in **either clause**, depending on the verb used (i.e. the 'past subjunctive' with common verbs, the 'conditional' with less common, or weak verbs, as explained above).

▶ To express a **hypothetical possibility in the past**, the pluperfect subjunctive is used:

Wenn wir schneller **gefahren wären**, **hätten** wir die Fähre **erreicht**.	*If we had driven faster we would have reached the ferry.*
Wenn sie den Zug **verpasst hätte**, **hätte** sie uns sicher **angerufen**.	*If she had missed the train she would certainly have called us.*

Generally, subjunctive II is used to show that the condition is unreal or hypothetical, though **conditional sentences may take other forms**, like those below.

▶ *Wenn* can be **omitted**:

Hätte ich Zeit, (**so**) **käme** ich gern **mit**.	*If I had time, I'd love to come with you.*
Wäre Rotkäppchen zu Hause **geblieben**, (**so**) **hätte** der Wolf es nicht **gefressen**.	*If Little Red Riding Hood had stayed at home, the wolf would not have eaten her.*

▶ The condition may be expressed through an ADVERBIAL:

Bei dem Wetter *wäre* ich zu Hause **geblieben.**	*In that weather I would have stayed at home.*
Ohne ihre Hilfe *hätte* ich den Ring nicht **gefunden.**	*Without her help I wouldn't have found the ring.*

▶ The condition may have to be **inferred** from the wider context:

Ich *wäre* lieber zu Hause **geblieben.**	*I would have preferred to stay at home.*
Ich *hätte* an deiner Stelle dasselbe **getan.**	*If I'd been you, I'd have done the same.*

7.12 Subjunctive I: reported speech

The main use of subjunctive I in German is to indicate reported speech.

▶ The standard rule is that reported speech is put into subjunctive I using **the same tense** as was used in the indicative in the **original direct speech**:

tense of direct speech		reported speech: subjunctive I
present	„**Sie weiß es.**"	**Er sagte, sie wisse es.**
	"She knows it."	*He said she knew it.*
past	„**Sie wusste es.**"	**Er sagte, sie habe es gewusst.**
	"She knew it."	*He said she had known it.*
perfect	„**Sie hat es gewusst.**"	**Er sagte, sie habe es gewusst.**
	"She knew/has known it."	*He said she had known it.*
future	„**Sie wird es wissen.**"	**Er sagte, sie werde es wissen.**
	"She will know it."	*He said she would know it.*

Note that the 'perfect subjunctive' is used if the tense of the original direct speech was the past **or** the perfect.

▶ If the form of subjunctive I is **the same as the indicative**, subjunctive II is used in place of subjunctive I:

tense of direct speech		reported speech: subjunctive II
present	„**Sie wissen es.**"	**Er sagte, sie wüssten es.**
	"They know it."	*He said they knew it.*
past	„**Sie wussten es.**"	**Er sagte, sie hätten es gewusst.**
	"They knew it."	*He said they had known it.*
perfect	„**Sie haben es gewusst.**"	**Er sagte, sie hätten es gewusst.**
	"They knew/have known it."	*He said they had known it.*
future	„**Sie werden es wissen.**"	**Er sagte, sie würden es wissen.**
	"They will know it."	*He said they would know it.*

The use of subjunctive I to indicate reported speech is limited to the **formal written language**, where it is frequent especially in newspaper reports. In other registers, and particularly in everyday speech, the indicative or subjunctive II is used:

formal writing	everyday speech
Er sagte, sie wisse es.	**Er hat gesagt, sie weiß es.** **Er hat gesagt, sie wüsste es.**
Er sagte, sie habe es gewusst.	**Er hat gesagt, sie hat es gewusst.** **Er hat gesagt, sie hätte es gewusst.**

7.13 The modal auxiliary verbs

The six modal auxiliary verbs *dürfen, können, mögen, müssen, sollen* and *wollen* indicate the attitude of the speaker to what is being said. They are used with other verbs to express ideas like **ability**, **permission**, **necessity**, **obligation** and **volition**, but in practice each has a wide range of meaning which is often idiomatic.

They have a number of special features which distinguish them from other verbs, or from their English equivalents:

▶ Their forms are quite **irregular** (see section **6.5**).

▶ They are used with a following INFINITIVE **without** *zu* (like some of the equivalent English verbs):

Ich **konnte** es nicht **tun.** Du **solltest** ihn nicht **ärgern.** Compare *(infinitive clause):* Ich **versuchte**, es nicht **zu tun.**	*I **could** not **do** it.* *You **should** not **annoy** him/You **ought** not* *to **annoy** him.* *I **tried** not **to do** it.*

▶ Their PERFECT tenses are formed with the INFINITIVE, **not** with the past participle:

Sie **hat** es schon immer **machen wollen.**	*She **has** always **wanted to do** it.*

▶ In SUBORDINATE CLAUSES, the modal auxiliary follows the infinitive of the main verb:

Wenn Sie diesen Ring **kaufen wollen,** ...	*If you **want to buy** this ring ...*

▶ In SUBORDINATE CLAUSES with a PERFECT TENSE of the modal, the auxiliary *haben* **precedes both infinitives**:

Wenn sie es **hätte kaufen** wollen, ...	*If she **had** wanted **to buy** it ...*

Modal auxiliaries have a **full range of tenses**, unlike the English modal verbs. The various possibilities are illustrated for **können**:

tense	infinitive type		
present	+ infinitive	Er kann es **machen**.	He **can do** it.
present	+ perfect infinitive	Er kann es **gemacht haben**.	He **can have done** it.
future	+ infinitive	Er wird es **machen können**.	He **will be able** to **do** it.
past	+ infinitive	Er konnte es **machen**.	He **was able** to **do** it.
perfect	+ infinitive	Er hat es **machen können**.	He **has been/was able** to **do** it.
pluperfect	+ infinitive	Er hatte es **machen können**.	He **had been able** to **do** it.
past subj.	+ infinitive	Er könnte es **machen**.	He **could do** it.
past subj.	+ perfect infinitive	Er könnte es **gemacht haben**.	He **could have done** it.
pluperf. subj.	+ infinitive	Er hätte es **machen können**.	He **would have been able** to **do** it.

Especially in everyday speech, the main verb can be omitted in certain contexts if the meaning is clear. This is common with verbs of motion (e.g. *gehen, kommen, fahren*) and with the verb *tun*:

Er **darf** nicht nach Paris. **[fahren]**	*He isn't allowed to go to Paris.*
Ich **will** heute nicht in die Disko. **[kommen]**	*I don't want to come to the disco today.*
Das **konnten** wir einfach nicht. **[tun]**	*We just couldn't do it.*

7.14 *dürfen*

▶ *dürfen* most often expresses **permission** (=ʻbe allowedʼ, ʻmayʼ):

Sie **dürfen hereinkommen**.	*They may/are allowed to come in.*
Sie **durften hereinkommen**.	*They were allowed to come in.*

▶ With *nicht*, this is the equivalent of English ʻ**must not**ʼ:

Sie **dürfen** nicht **hereinkommen**.	*They mustn't/are not allowed to come in.*

▶ The subjunctive II of *dürfen* expresses probability (=ʻwill (probably)ʼ):

Das **dürfte reichen**.	*That will probably be enough.*
Die Jacke **dürfte** ein Vermögen **gekostet haben**.	*That jacket will have cost a fortune.*

▶ With *nicht*, the subjunctive II of *dürfen* corresponds to English ʻshouldn'tʼ or ʻoughtn'tʼ:

Das **dürfte** sie gar nicht **wissen**.	*She ought not to know that.*
Das **hätte** er nicht **machen dürfen**.	*He shouldn't have done that.*

7.15 *können*

▶ *können* most often expresses **ability** (='can', 'be able to'):

Sie **kann** gut **schwimmen**.	*She can swim well.*
Ich **konnte** sie nicht **besuchen**.	*I couldn't/wasn't able to visit her.*
Ich **werde** sie morgen **besuchen können**.	*I will be able to visit her tomorrow.*
Ich **könnte** es morgen **tun**, wenn ich Zeit hätte.	*I could do it tomorrow if I had time.*
Er **hätte** es gestern **machen können**.	*He could have done it yesterday.*

NB *können* can also be used as a **main verb** with a **direct object**, e.g. *Ich **kann** Deutsch* (I know German).

▶ *können* can express possibility (='may', 'might') – this is most usual with a perfect infinitive or in the subjunctive II:

Er **kann** es **gesehen haben**.	*He may have seen it.*
Sie **könnte** krank **sein**.	*She might be ill.*
Sie **könnte** krank **gewesen sein**.	*She might have been ill.*

7.16 *mögen*

▶ *mögen* most usually expresses **liking**, most often in the subjunctive II form *möchte*:

Sie **möchte** einen neuen Wagen **kaufen**.	*She would like to buy a new car.*
Möchten Sie noch Wein?	*Would you like some more wine?*
Ich **möchte** nicht, dass sie heute kommt.	*I don't want her to come today.*

▶ *mögen* can express possibility (='may'), often with concessive force (i.e. implying a following *aber...*). This sense of *mögen* is rare in everyday speech except in set phrases:

Das **mag** vielen nicht **einleuchten** (‚aber ...)	*That may not be clear to many people (but...)*
Das **mag** (wohl) **sein** (‚aber ...)	*That may (well) be (but...)*

▶ In the present and past tenses it is most often used as a **main verb** just with a direct object:

Sie **mag** keinen Tee.	*She doesn't like tea.*
Mögt ihr den neuen Lehrer?	*Do you like the new teacher?*
Ich **mochte** ihn einfach nicht.	*I just didn't like him.*

NB It is used with a following infinitive only in the negative in this sense, e.g. *Ich **mag** diese Fragen **nicht beant-worten*** (I don't want to answer these questions).

7.17 *müssen*

▶ *müssen* expresses **necessity** or **compulsion** (='must', 'have to'):

Ich **muss** um acht **gehen**.	*I have to leave at eight.*
Ich **musste** um acht **gehen**.	*I had to leave at eight.*
Ich **habe** um acht **gehen müssen**.	*I had to leave at eight.*
Ich **werde** bald **gehen müssen**.	*I shall have to leave soon.*

▶ Negative *müssen* retains this sense of necessity (='needn't', 'don't have to'):

Wir **müssen** noch nicht **gehen**.	*We don't have to go yet.*
Ich **habe** es nicht **tun müssen**.	*I didn't need to do it.*

▶ *müssen* often expresses a logical deduction (='must', 'have to'):

Sie ist hier, also **muss** es ihr besser **gehen**.	*She's here, so she must be better.*
Das **muss** ein Fehler **sein**.	*That must/has to be a mistake.*

▶ The subjunctive II of *müssen* can express a possible compulsion or necessity or a logical deduction (='would have to', 'should', 'ought to'):

Da **müsstest** du den Chef **fragen**.	*You'd have to/need to ask the boss.*
Ich **müsste** eigentlich zum Zahnarzt **gehen**.	*I really ought to go to the dentist.*
Ich **hätte** mich anders **ausdrücken müssen**.	*I should have expressed myself differently.*

7.18 *sollen*

▶ *sollen* most commonly expresses an **obligation** (='be supposed to', 'be meant to'):

Um wieviel Uhr **soll** ich **kommen**?	*What time am I supposed to come?*
Was **soll** ich **sagen**?	*What am I (meant) to say?*
Er **soll** sofort **kommen**.	*He is (supposed) to come at once.*
Sie wusste nicht, was sie **tun sollte**.	*She didn't know what she was supposed to do.*

▶ *sollen* can also express an intention or a prediction (='be to', 'be supposed/meant to'):

Hier **soll** die Fabrik **gebaut werden**.	*They're supposed to be building the factory here.*
Es **sollte** eine Überraschung **sein**.	*It was intended to be a surprise.*

▶ In the present tense, with a present or perfect infinitive, *sollen* can express a rumour or a report (='It is said that ...'):

Er **soll** sehr arm **sein**.	*He is said to be very poor.*
Es **soll** bisher vier Tote **gegeben haben**.	*Four people are reported to have been killed.*

▶ In the subjunctive II, *sollen* expresses a possible obligation (='should', 'ought to'):

Das **hätten** Sie mir gestern **sagen sollen**.	*You ought to have told me that yesterday.*
Warum **sollte** sie nicht ins Kino **gehen?**	*Why shouldn't she go to the cinema?*
Das **sollte** ihm inzwischen klar **geworden sein**.	*He ought to have realized that by now.*

7.19 *wollen*

▶ *wollen* most often expresses a **desire** (='want/wish to'):

Sie **will** ihn um Geld **bitten**.	*She wants to ask him for money.*
Sie **wollte** ihn um Geld **bitten**.	*She wanted to ask him for money.*
Hättest du wirklich **kommen wollen?**	*Would you really have wanted to come?*

▶ In this sense it can be used without a following infinitive, as a **main verb**:

Sie **will** Geld.	*She wants money.*
Was **wollen** Sie von mir?	*What do you want from me?*

▶ *wollen* can express intention. In this sense it is close in meaning to the English future construction with 'be going to':

Wie **wollen** Sie ihm das **klarmachen?**	*How are you going to explain that to him?*
Ich **will** sie erst morgen **anrufen**.	*I don't intend to phone her till tomorrow.*
Ich **wollte** Sie danach **fragen**.	*I was going to ask you about that.*

▶ With an inanimate subject, *wollen* corresponds to English 'need' (or, when negative, 'refuse'):

Eine solche Arbeit **will** Zeit **haben**.	*A piece of work like that needs time.*
Das **will** geübt **sein**.	*That needs to be practised.*
Das Fenster **wollte** nicht **zugehen**.	*The window refused to shut.*

▶ *wollen* can be used in the sense of 'claim', typically in the present tense with a perfect infinitive:

Sie **wollen** dich in Hamburg **gesehen haben**.	*They say they saw you in Hamburg.*
Er **will** krank **gewesen sein**.	*He claims to have been ill.*

VERB USES IN CONTEXT

Die Hexe musste braten

Als Hänsel mager blieb, wollte die Hexe nicht länger warten. »Heda, Gretel«, rief sie dem Mädchen zu, »sei flink und trag Wasser: Hänsel mag fett oder mager sein, morgen wird er geschlachtet und gekocht.« Ach, wie jammerte das arme Schwesterchen, als es das Wasser tragen musste, und wie flossen ihm die Tränen über die Backen herunter! »Lieber Gott, hilf uns doch«, rief sie aus, »hätten uns nur die wilden Tiere im Wald gefressen, so wären wir doch zusammen gestorben.« »Spar nur dein Geplärre«, sagte die Alte, »es hilft dir alles nichts.«

Frühmorgens musste Gretel heraus, den Kessel mit Wasser aufhängen und Feuer anzünden. »Erst werden wir backen«, sagte die Alte, »ich habe den Backofen schon eingeheizt und den Teig geknetet.« Sie stieß das arme Gretel hinaus zu dem Backofen, aus dem die Feuerflammen schon herausschlugen. »Kriech hinein«, sagte die Hexe, »und sieh zu, ob recht eingeheizt ist, damit wir das Brot hineinschieben können.« Und wenn Gretel darin war, wollte sie den Ofen zumachen, und Gretel sollte darin braten, dann wollte sie Gretel auch aufessen. Aber Gretel merkte, was sie im Sinn hatte, und sprach: »Ich weiß nicht, wie ich's machen soll; wie komm ich da hinein?« »Dumme Gans«, sagte die Alte, »die Öffnung ist groß genug, siehst du wohl, ich könnte selbst hinein«, kam heran und steckte den Kopf in den Backofen. Da gab ihr Gretel einen Stoß, dass sie weit hineinfuhr, machte die eiserne Tür zu und schob den Riegel vor. Hu! da fing sie an zu heulen, ganz grauselich; aber Gretel lief fort, und die gottlose Hexe musste elendiglich verbrennen.

(Aus: Brüder Grimm, „Hänsel und Gretel", *Kinder- und Hausmärchen*, 1819/1857)

THE TENSES AND THEIR USE

present	Die Öffnung **ist** groß.
	Es **hilft** alles nichts.
	Ich **weiß** es nicht.
past	Gretel **jammerte**. Sie **merkte** es.
	Hänsel **blieb** mager.
	Da **gab** ihr Gretel einen Stoß.
perfect	Ich **habe** den Backofen **eingeheizt**.
(present of *haben* or	Ich **habe** den Teig **geknetet**.
sein + past participle)	[Wir **sind** zusammen **gestorben**.]
pluperfect	[Nachdem die Hexe den Kopf in den Backofen
(past of *haben* or	**gesteckt hatte**,] gab ihr Gretel einen Stoß.
sein + past participle)	[Als Gretel die Tür **zugemacht hatte**,] schob sie den Riegel vor.
future	Wir **werden backen**.
(*werden* + infinitive)	

PASSIVE VOICE

werden-passive	Hänsel **wird geschlachtet**. Hänsel **wird** morgen **gekocht**.
(*werden* + past participle)	
sein-passive	Es **ist eingeheizt**.
(*sein* + past participle)	

IMPERATIVE

Sei flink!	**Trag** Wasser!	**Hilf** uns doch!	**Kriech** hinein!

SUBJUNCTIVE

pluperfect subjunctive	Ich **könnte** selbst hinein, …
	[Wenn uns die Tiere **gefressen hätten**,]
	wären wir zusammen **gestorben**.
reported speech	[Die Hexe sagte, sie **hätte** den Ofen eingeheizt.]

THE MODAL AUXILIARIES

können	Wir **können** das Brot **hineinschieben**.
mögen	Hänsel **mag** fett **sein**.
müssen	Gretel **musste** das Wasser **tragen**.
sollen	Gretel **sollte** darin **braten**.
wollen	Die Hexe **wollte** nicht länger **warten**.

Valency and cases 8

The VALENCY of a verb refers to the type and number of COMPLEMENTS needed by the verb to make a meaningful and grammatically complete clause or sentence (see chapter **1**). Complements are distinct from ADVERBIALS, even though they may sometimes look the same. Compare:

Stefan *wohnt* in der Stadt.	***wohnen* + place complement** (**Stefan wohnt* would be ungrammatical)
Stefan *trifft* in der Stadt seinen Freund.	***treffen* + accusative object** (*in der Stadt* is added information)

▶ Complements **complete the meaning of the verb** and form an essential part of the clause or sentence.

▶ Adverbials are **optional extras**, providing added information (e.g. about time or place) without being necessary to make the sentence meaningful (see **4.8–4.14**).

The concept of valency allows you to identify the main elements of a clause or sentence (remember that each clause has its own main verb with its own valency). **Valency relates to the MAIN VERB of the clause, which conveys the action**, not to an auxiliary or modal auxiliary verb. For example, in the following sentences it relates to the main verbs *akzeptieren* and *kämpfen*, not to the FINITE VERBS *haben* and *müssen*:

subject + *akzeptieren* + accusative object
Im letzten Moment *hat* **der Regisseur** kurz vor Beginn der Dreharbeiten **das Angebot** der Produktionsfirma *akzeptiert*.
At the last moment **the director** (*has*) ***accepted*** **the offer** of the production company, shortly before the start of shooting.

subject + *kämpfen* + prepositional object
Der junge Fußballspieler *muss* jetzt nach seiner dritten Knieoperation **um seine Karriere** *kämpfen*.
The young football player *must* now ***fight*** **for his career** following his third knee operation.

This chapter explains the common **sentence patterns** and complements – in particular those German constructions which differ from English – and also other uses of the cases:

◆ sentence patterns (**8.1**)

◆ reflexive verbs (**8.2**)

◆ the dative case (**8.3–8.4**)

◆ the genitive case (**8.5–8.6**)

◆ prepositional objects (**8.7**)

◆ other complements (**8.8–8.10**).

8.1 Sentence patterns

The VALENCY of the MAIN VERB of a sentence **determines the pattern** of that sentence. There are a limited number of possible combinations of verbs and complements, and therefore a limited number of possible sentence patterns. Some verbs can be used with more than one sentence pattern (see **1.1**).

It is useful to know the most common sentence patterns and to **learn the valency** of each verb, since this is what shapes the sentence – not knowing the possible uses of a verb is like working with a blunt tool. The meaning and the standard translation of a verb into English will sometimes give you an indication. For example, neither *schwimmen* nor 'swim' need an object, while both *kaufen* and 'buy' require 'something' to be bought (a direct object – in the accusative case in German). You should concentrate in particular on learning the valency of verbs that are used with complements other than an accusative object.

▶ Especially with the more complicated sentence patterns, it is best to **learn the verb together with a sentence** that shows how it is used.

The subject

The basis of all the sentence patterns is a verb and its subject. The SUBJECT always **agrees** with the FINITE VERB (see **1.2**), but this may be an auxiliary or modal auxiliary verb rather than the main verb that conveys the action and determines the sentence pattern.

Transitive and intransitive verbs

All verbs which are **used with an accusative object** (often called the DIRECT OBJECT – sentence patterns **B**, **D**, **F**, **H** and **L**) are known as TRANSITIVE VERBS. Those which are **not used with an accusative object** (sentence patterns **A**, **C**, **E**, **G**, **I**, **J**, **K** and **M**) are INTRANSITIVE VERBS. Only the accusative object of transitive verbs can be turned into the subject of a verb in the passive (see section **7.4**).

▶ The role of a subject or an object can be taken by a SUBORDINATE CLAUSE as well as by a noun phrase (see section **10.3**).

A	subject + Der Mann	verb schwimmt		
B	subject + Der Mann	verb + kauft	**accusative object** den Fernseher	
C	subject + Der Mann	verb + hilft	**dative object** seinem Bruder	
D	subject + Der Mann	verb + gibt	**dative object +** seinem Bruder	**accusative object** den Fernseher
E	subject + Der Mann	verb + bedarf	**genitive object** der Ruhe	
F	subject + Der Mann	verb + würdigt	**accusative object** seinen Kollegen	**genitive object** keines Blickes
G	subject + Der Mann	verb + wartet	**prepositional object** auf seinen Bruder	
H	subject + Der Mann	verb + hindert	**accusative object +** seinen Bruder	**prepositional object** an der Arbeit
I	subject + Der Mann	verb + dankte	**dative object +** seinem Bruder	**prepositional object** für seine Hilfe
J	subject + Der Mann	verb + wohnt	**place complement** in einem Hausboot	
K	subject + Der Mann	verb + fährt	**direction complement** in die Stadt	
L	subject + Der Mann	verb + bringt	**accusative object +** seinen Bruder	**direction complement** in die Stadt
M	subject + Der Mann	verb + ist	**predicate complement** nett/ein netter Mensch	

NB Note that if a sentence with a transitive verb is in the passive, the accusative object of the active sentence acts as the subject of the passive sentence (see **7.4**), e.g. **Der Fernseher** *wird (von dem Mann) gekauft.*

A: Subject + verb

As in English, some verbs can stand on their own, without any complements other than the subject, e.g. *schwimmen, sterben, lachen.*

B: Subject + verb + accusative object

This is the **most common type of verb** in German, with a DIRECT OBJECT, in the accusative case. Verbs with this sentence pattern are the commonest equivalent for English verbs that indicate an action being done to, or affecting, something or someone:

Sie *küsst* **ihn.**	**She** *is kissing* **him.**
Ich *baue* **ein Haus.**	**I** *am building* **a house.**

C, D: Subject + verb + dative object

There are two kinds of verbs with an object in the dative case (see **1.4** and **8.3**):

▶ Some verbs have only a dative object (sentence pattern **C**), e.g. *helfen* and *dienen*.

▶ Other verbs have both a dative object (a so-called **INDIRECT OBJECT**) and an accusative object (**DIRECT OBJECT**, sentence pattern **D**). These are often similar to English:

Er *gab* dem Hund einen Knochen.	He *gave* the dog a bone./He *gave* a bone to the dog.
Die Sekretärin *brachte* ihm den Brief.	The secretary *brought* him the letter.

E, F: Subject + verb + genitive object

Very few verbs are used with a genitive object, and they are confined to formal registers and set phrases, e.g. *Er bedarf **der Ruhe*** (He needs peace and quiet), *Er würdigte ihn* (acc.) ***keines Blickes*** (gen.) (He did not deign to look at him). Most of those in general use are **REFLEXIVE VERBS**, e.g. *Er rühmt sich* (acc.) *seiner Taten* (gen.) (He prides himself on his deeds) (see **8.5**).

G, H, I: Subject + verb + prepositional object

Like English (e.g. 'think of...', 'ask for...'), German has many verbs that are used with a specific **PREPOSITION**, as a **set phrase** (e.g. *denken an...*, *bitten um...*). **The case of the following noun depends on the preposition**. Verbs with a prepositional object may have an accusative or dative object with them as well (see sections **1.5** and **8.7**).

J, K, L: Subject + verb + place/direction complement

▶ A few verbs indicating **position** need a place complement.

▶ Most verbs of **motion** can have a direction complement.

These complements generally look like adverbials, but unlike adverbials they are closely **linked to the action of the verb**, and in some cases they are required to make the clause or sentence grammatically complete:

Anja *lebt* jetzt in der Stadt/auf dem Land/zu Hause.	Anja now *lives* in the city/in the country/at home.
Lutz *ging* gestern in die Stadt/zum Friseur/nach Hause.	Yesterday Lutz *went* into town/to the hairdresser's/home.

Some verbs with a direction complement have an accusative object as well (see section **8.8**).

M: Subject + verb + predicate complement

A very small number of important verbs – notably ***sein*** and ***werden*** – have a predicate complement consisting of a **NOUN PHRASE** or an **ADJECTIVE**. If the predicate complement is a noun phrase, this is in the **NOMINATIVE** case, i.e. in the **same case as the subject**. These are called **COPULAR** ('linking') verbs (see **1.6** and **8.10**).

8.2 Reflexive verbs

A large number of verbs are used with a REFLEXIVE PRONOUN (see section **3.8**) in the ACCUSATIVE case, e.g. **sich beeilen** 'hurry', or **sich waschen** 'wash oneself':

ich	beeile	mich	*I hurry*
	wasche		*I wash myself*
du	beeilst	dich	*you hurry*
	wäschst		*you wash yourself*
er/sie/es	beeilt	sich	*he/she/it hurries*
	wäscht		*he/she/it washes himself/herself/itself*
wir	beeilen	uns	*we hurry*
	waschen		*we wash ourselves*
ihr	beeilt	euch	*you hurry*
	wascht		*you wash yourselves*
sie/Sie	beeilen	sich	*they/you hurry*
	waschen		*they wash themselves/you wash yourself/yourselves*

NB See also **3.8**, and the accusative forms of the personal pronouns (**3.7**).

The sentence pattern is essentially that of SUBJECT + VERB + ACCUSATIVE OBJECT (**B**), with the object always being a **pronoun that refers back to the subject**.

With *sich waschen* and a few other reflexive verbs, the meaning is clearly that the action of the verb affects the subject of the sentence (i.e. = '**oneself**'):

| jemanden überzeugen | *convince somebody* | sich überzeugen | *convince oneself* |
| jemanden waschen | *wash somebody/something* | sich waschen | *wash oneself* |

With most reflexive verbs, the meaning of the reflexive pronoun is less distinct, although it is often possible to detect the sense in which the action is directed back at the subject of the verb.

▶ Some verbs can be used either **transitively**, with an accusative object, or **reflexively**.

When used transitively, they correspond to an English transitive verb. When used reflexively, they correspond to an **English intransitive** verb or an **English passive** construction:

jdn./etw. ändern	*change sb./sth.*	sich ändern	*change*
jdn. ärgern	*annoy sb.*	sich ärgern	*be annoyed*
jdn./etw. drehen	*turn sb./sth.*	sich drehen	*turn*
jdn. interessieren	*interest sb.*	sich interessieren	*be interested*
etw. öffnen	*open sth.*	sich öffnen	*open*

NB jdn. (*jemanden*) = somebody (accusative case)
jdm. (*jemandem*) = somebody (dative case)
etw. (*etwas*) = something

▶ Other verbs have a **different meaning** depending on whether they are used transitively, with an accusative object, or reflexively, with a reflexive pronoun:

jdn. **erinnern**	*remind sb.*	sich **erinnern**	*remember*
jdn. **fragen**	*ask sb.*	sich **fragen**	*wonder, ask oneself*
jdn./etw. **setzen**	*put sb./sth.*	sich **setzen**	*sit down*
jdn. **unterhalten**	*entertain sb.*	sich **unterhalten**	*have a chat*

▶ Certain verbs, such as *sich beeilen*, are only ever used with the accompanying reflexive pronoun.

These reflexive verbs have no direct equivalent in English, and the REFLEXIVE PRONOUN **is an integral part of the verb**. Other common reflexive verbs of this type are:

sich **bedanken** (für)	*say 'thank you' (for)*	sich **entschließen** (zu)	*decide (to)*
sich **befinden**	*be (situated)*	sich **erholen**	*recover*
sich **benehmen**	*behave*	sich **erkälten**	*catch a cold*
sich **beschweren** (über)	*complain (about)*	sich **irren**	*be mistaken*
sich **eignen** (für)	*be suited (to)*	sich **weigern**	*refuse*

NB Some of these typically also take a prepositional object (sentence pattern **H**, see **8.7**). *Sich befinden* usually takes a place complement (see **8.8**). *Sich entschließen* is often used with an infinitive clause: *Ich entschloss mich (dazu), sie zu treffen.*

„Nein, der Swimmingpool befindet sich weiter oben."

Dative reflexive pronouns

A dative reflexive pronoun can be used in the same way, with verbs that have a **DATIVE OBJECT** (see **8.3**), to refer back to the **SUBJECT** of the sentence (for a table of the pronouns see **3.8**). They can be used for certain verbs that take only a dative object, e.g. *sich widersprechen* (contradict oneself), and for certain verbs that also take an accusative object, e.g. *sich etwas nehmen* (to take something (for oneself)):

Du *widersprichst* dir immer wieder.	*You constantly contradict yourself.*
Darf **ich mir eine Praline *nehmen*?**	*May I take a chocolate (for myself)?*

A reflexive dative pronoun is often used in German to indicate that a part of the **body** or article of **clothing** belongs to the subject of the clause (see section **8.4**). In this kind of construction German **rarely** uses a POSSESSIVE DETERMINER, unlike English:

Ich *putze* mir die Zähne.	*I'm cleaning **my** teeth.*
Wann *hast* du dir das Bein *gebrochen*?	*When did you break **your** leg?*

▶ A very few verbs always have a dative reflexive pronoun, as well as an accusative object, e.g. *sich etwas einbilden, sich etwas vorstellen, sich etwas vornehmen*:

sich etwas einbilden *imagine sth. (unreal)*	**Das *hast* du dir nur *eingebildet*.** *You only imagined that.*
sich etwas vorstellen *imagine, visualize*	**Ich** kann **mir das** sehr gut ***vorstellen*.** *I can imagine that very well/visualize that very clearly.*
sich etwas vornehmen *resolve*	**Wir *nehmen* es uns** fest ***vor*.** *We are firmly resolved to do that.*

8.3 Dative objects

▶ Some German verbs only have a dative object, and no accusative object (sentence pattern **C**):

Sabine *hilft* mir.	*Sabine is helping **me**.*
Der Termin *passt* seinem Chef nicht.	*The date doesn't suit **his boss**.*

It is necessary to learn verbs which are used in this way. The following are the most common:

ähneln	*resemble*	**folgen**	*follow*
antworten	*answer*	**gehorchen**	*obey*
begegnen	*meet*	**gehören**	*belong*
danken	*thank*	**gleichen**	*resemble*
dienen	*serve*	**gratulieren**	*congratulate*
drohen	*threaten*	**helfen**	*help*
einfallen	*occur* (e.g. thought)	**imponieren**	*impress*
entkommen	*escape*	**kündigen**	*fire, sack*

nutzen	*be of use*	trauen	*trust*
passen	*fit, suit*	vertrauen	*trust*
passieren	*happen*	wehtun	*hurt*
schaden	*harm*	widersprechen	*contradict*
schmeicheln	*flatter*	widerstehen	*resist*

With several verbs, a German dative object corresponds to the subject of the verb in the nearest English equivalent:

etwas **fällt** mir **auf**	*I notice sth.*	etwas **gelingt** mir	*I succeed in sth.*
etwas **fällt** mir schwer	*I find sth. difficult*	etwas **genügt** mir	*I have had enough of sth.*
etwas **fehlt** mir	*I lack/miss sth.*	etwas **tut** mir **Leid**	*I regret sth.*
etwas **gefällt** mir	*I like sth.*	etwas **schmeckt** mir	*I like sth.* (food)

'Einem etwas' *verbs*

A large number of verbs have a DATIVE object ('indirect object') as well as an ACCUSATIVE object ('direct object') (sentence pattern **D**).

▶ The INDIRECT OBJECT is almost always a **person** (*einem/jemandem*).

▶ The DIRECT OBJECT is typically a **thing** (*etwas*).

This group of verbs typically includes

▶ verbs of **giving** and **taking** (in the widest sense):

anbieten	**Sie** *haben* **mir eine Stelle** *angeboten*.	*They offered **me** a job/a job **to me**.*
beweisen	**Er** *wollte* **es (seinem Freund)** *beweisen*.	*He wanted to prove it **to his friend**.*
bringen	**Ich** *bringe* **(ihm) die Bücher**.	*I'm taking the books **to him**.*
empfehlen	**Ich** *kann* **(Ihnen) das Buch** *empfehlen*.	*I can recommend the book **to you**.*
geben	**Er** *gibt* **mir seine Adresse**.	*He's giving **me** his address.*
leihen	**Wir** *leihen* **euch die CD**.	*We'll lend the CD **to you**.*
schicken	**Wer** *hat* **(ihr) das Paket** *geschickt?*	*Who sent **her** the parcel?*
schulden	**Ich** *schulde* **dir noch etwas Geld**.	*I still owe **you** some money.*
stehlen	**Der Dieb** *hat* **(mir) meine Uhr** *gestohlen*.	*The thief stole my watch **from me**.*
verkaufen	**Ich** *habe* **(ihm) mein Fahrrad** *verkauft*.	*I sold **him** my bicycle.*
(weg)nehmen	**Er** *hat* **(mir) den Teddy** *weggenommen!*	*He's taken the teddy away **from me**!*
zeigen	**Wir** *werden* **dem Arzt die Wunde** *zeigen*.	*We'll show the wound **to the doctor**.*

▶ many verbs of **speaking**, with the accusative object often consisting of a **dass**-CLAUSE or an INFINITIVE CLAUSE (see **10.3** and **10.6**):

antworten	Er *antwortete* (mir), dass er es weiß.	*He replied (**to me**) that he knows it.*
erzählen	Ich *erzählte* (den Kindern) ein Märchen.	*I told **the children** a fairy-tale.*
raten	Wir *raten* Ihnen, nicht zu warten.	*We advise **you** not to wait.*
sagen	Ralf *hat* (mir) *gesagt*, dass er kommt.	*Ralf told **me** that he's coming.*
versichern	Sie *versicherte* ihm, dass sie nicht friert.	*She assured **him** that she wasn't cold.*
verzeihen	Das *wird* er dir nie *verzeihen*.	*He'll never forgive **you** that.*

As you can see, the dative object can be left out with some of the above verbs.

With a few verbs, the German '*einem etwas*' construction is quite different to that of the nearest English equivalent:

Das *hat* **sie mir** gestern *mitgeteilt*.	*She informed **me** of that yesterday.*
Die Polizei *konnte* **ihr nichts** *nachweisen*.	*The police couldn't prove anything **against her**.*
Das *hat* **sie mir** aber *verschwiegen*.	*She didn't tell **me** about that, though.*

8.4 Other uses of the dative case

The dative has the **widest range of uses** of the German cases.

▶ The dative can indicate **a person on whose behalf** the action is done.

This often corresponds to an English phrase with *for*:

Sie schrieb **mir** seine Adresse auf.	*She wrote his address down **for me**.*
Fährt sie **dir** zu schnell?	*Is she driving too fast **for you**?*
Ich öffnete **ihr** die Tür.	*I opened the door **for her**.*

▶ The dative can indicate the **body** or articles of **clothing**.

In most contexts, it is much more usual in German to use this construction than a possessive. If the possessor is the subject of the sentence, the pronoun is reflexive (see section **8.2**):

Er sah **ihr** in die Augen.	*He looked into her eyes.*
Ich zog **dem Kind** den Mantel aus.	*I took the child's coat off.*
Er zog **sich** den Mantel an.	*He put on his coat.*
Wann hast **du dir** das Bein gebrochen?	*When did you break your leg?*

For the use of the dative case with ADJECTIVES, see section **3.11**.

8.5 Genitive objects

A few verbs have a **single** object in the genitive case (sentence pattern **E**). They are restricted to **formal written** language and not used in everyday speech:

bedürfen	**Er *bedurfte* meiner Hilfe.**	*He needed my help.*
entbehren	**Die Anklage *entbehrt* jeder Grundlage.**	*The accusation lacks any basis.*
gedenken	**Wir *gedachten* der Opfer des** Nationalsozialismus.	*We remembered the victims of* *National Socialism.*

In practice, most verbs which are still commonly used with a genitive object are REFLEXIVE, i.e. they in effect have an accusative object and a genitive object (sentence pattern **F**):

Er *nahm* sich des Kindes *an*.	*He took the child under his wing.*
Sie *erfreut* sich noch bester Gesundheit.	*She is still enjoying excellent health.*

It is best to learn such verbs as a **phrase**, e.g. *sich jemandes/einer Sache annehmen* 'to look after someone/something' – or simply *sich einer Sache annehmen*. The following verbs are used with a genitive object:

sich einer Sache **annehmen**	*look after sth.*
sich einer Sache **bedienen**	*use sth.*
sich einer Sache **bemächtigen**	*seize sth.*
sich einer Sache **entsinnen**	*remember sth.*
sich einer Sache **erfreuen**	*enjoy sth.*
sich einer Sache **rühmen**	*boast of sth.*
sich einer Sache **schämen**	*be ashamed of sth.*
sich einer Sache **vergewissern**	*make sure of sth.*

NB Some of these verbs can also be used transitively, with an accusative object: *etw. annehmen, jdn. bedienen, jdn. erfreuen, jdn./etw. rühmen.*

8.6 Other uses of the genitive case

In practice, the main use of the genitive case in modern German is not to mark a complement of the verb, but to **link nouns**. A phrase in the genitive most often corresponds to an **English possessive construction with apostrophe + 's'**, or a construction with the preposition '**of**':

das Haus meines Bruders	*my brother's house*
die Rede des Bundeskanzlers	*the Chancellor's speech*
die Abfahrt des Zuges	*the departure **of the** train*
die Beschreibung des Urlaubs	*the description **of the** holiday*
viele der Anwesenden	*many **of the** people present*

▶ In German, the noun phrase in the genitive normally **follows** the noun it qualifies. The only exception is with names: *Peters Hemd*, *Helgas Katze*, *Deutschlands Straßen*.

As the above examples show, the function of the genitive is often but not always to indicate possession. The genitive is also frequently used:

▶ to **link a verbal noun** to its SUBJECT or OBJECT, e.g. *die Erfindung des Ingenieurs* (the engineer's invention), *die Erfindung des Elektromotors* (the invention of the electric motor);

▶ after a word indicating **quantity** or **proportion**, e.g. *einige der Verletzten* (some of the injured), *die Hälfte des Apfels* (half the apple).

The use of the genitive to link nouns is more common in written German. In everyday speech, a phrase with *von* is often used rather than a genitive: *das Haus von meinem Bruder*, *viele von den Anwesenden*.

In writing, on the other hand, the genitive is usual and phrases with *von* are avoided if possible. However, in some contexts a **genitive cannot be used**:

If a noun stands by itself, without an article or any other word with an ending to show the case	der Bau von Kraftwerken der Preis von fünf Videos der Geruch von Seetang	*the construction of power stations* *the price of five videos* *the smell of seaweed*
With personal pronouns	jeder von uns eine Tante von mir	*every one of us* *an aunt of mine*
After indefinites	viel/nichts von dem Geld etwas von dem Wein	*much/nothing of the money* *some of the wine*

8.7 Prepositional objects

As in English, many verbs have a prepositional object consisting of a PREPOSITION and a following NOUN PHRASE (sentence pattern **G**). Prepositional objects are quite different from usual prepositional phrases, as the preposition in them is generally not used with its usual meaning, but is **idiomatic**.

▶ In practice this means learning individual verbs with their **special prepositions**.

In addition to the prepositional object, some verbs have an accusative object or a dative object (sentence patterns **H** and **I**). These are best learnt with example sentences.

You will often find that the prepositional object consists not of a preposition and noun but of a PREPOSITIONAL ADVERB (see **5.5**). This may be referring to a NOUN mentioned previously or to a SUBORDINATE CLAUSE (see section **10.3** for *dass*-clauses and **10.6** for infinitive clauses):

Heute *kam der Brief*. Ich *warte* schon seit über einer Woche *darauf*.
Today the letter came. I've been waiting for it for over a week.
Ich *warte darauf*, dass er mir die Adresse sagt.
I'm waiting for him to tell me the address.
Ich *freue* mich *darauf*, euch in Frankfurt zu sehen.
I'm looking forward to seeing you in Frankfurt.

In this section you will find examples of the **most common prepositions used in prepositional objects**, with a selection of the most frequent verbs they are used with. **The preposition always determines the case of the following noun** (see chapter **5**). Note also that some verbs can be used with more than one preposition (e.g. *sich freuen*) and some may also be used with sentence patterns other than those given here. Many of the verbs are reflexive:

sich *spezialisieren auf* (+ accusative) Die Firma spezialisiert sich auf innovative Software.	***specialize in*** *The firm specializes in innovative software.*
sich *interessieren für* (+ accusative) Wir interessieren uns für den neuen Toyota.	***be interested in*** *We are interested in the new Toyota.*
sich *fürchten vor* (+ dative) Er fürchtet sich vor großen Spinnen.	***be afraid of*** *He's afraid of large spiders.*

An

an (+ dative)			
arbeiten an	*work at/on*	sich rächen an	*take revenge on*
erkranken an	*fall ill with*	riechen an	*smell*
interessiert sein an	*be interested in*	sterben an	*die of*
leiden an	*suffer from*	teilnehmen an	*take part in*
mitwirken an	*play a part in*	zweifeln an	*doubt*

an (+ accusative)			
denken an	*think of*	glauben an	*believe in*
sich erinnern an	*remember*	sich gewöhnen an	*get used to*

NB Verbs with *an* + accusative mostly denote mental processes.

an (+ dative) + accusative object	
jemanden an etwas erkennen **Er erkannte den Verbrecher an seiner Nase.**	*He recognized the criminal by his nose.*
jemanden an etwas hindern **Das Radio hindert mich am Arbeiten.**	*The radio is preventing me from working.*

Auf

auf (+ accusative)			
achten auf	*pay attention to*	drängen auf	*press for*
aufpassen auf	*look after*	sich erstrecken auf	*extend to*
sich berufen auf	*refer to*	folgen auf	*succeed, follow after*
sich beziehen auf	*relate to*	sich freuen auf	*look forward to*

auf (+ accusative) — cont.

sich gründen auf	*be based on*	schwören auf	*swear by*
hinweisen auf	*point to*	sich spezialisieren auf	*specialize in*
hoffen auf	*hope for*	sich stützen auf	*lean on, count on*
sich konzentrieren auf	*concentrate on*	sich verlassen auf	*rely on*
reagieren auf	*react to*	verzichten auf	*do without*
rechnen auf	*count on*	warten auf	*wait for*
schimpfen auf	*grumble about*	zählen auf	*count on*

auf (+ dative)

basieren auf	*be based on, rest on*	bestehen auf	*insist on*
beruhen auf	*be based on, rest on*		

Für

für (+ accusative)

sich begeistern für	*be/get enthusiastic about*	sich interessieren für	*be interested in*
sich eignen für	*be suitable for*	sich schämen für	*be ashamed for*
sich entscheiden für	*decide on*	sorgen für	*take care of*

NB also: *sich wegen jemandem/etwas schämen* (be ashamed of sb./sth.)
sich vor jemandem schämen (be ashamed in front of sb.)

other constructions with für

jemandem für etwas danken **Sie hat mir für die Blumen gedankt.**	*She thanked me for the flowers.*
sich (bei jemandem) für etwas bedanken **Sie hat sich (bei mir) für die Blumen bedankt.**	*She thanked me for the flowers.*
jemanden/etwas für jemanden/etwas halten **Sie halten ihn für sehr intelligent.** **Ich halte ihn für einen Idioten.** **Wir hielten das für eine gute Idee.**	*They consider him to be very bright.* *I consider him to be an idiot.* *We thought that was a good idea.*

Mit

mit (+ dative)

sich abfinden mit	*come to terms with*	sich befassen mit	*deal with, treat*
anfangen mit	*start with*	beginnen mit	*start, commence with*
aufhören mit	*stop, cease*	sich beschäftigen mit	*occupy oneself with*

mit (+ dative) — cont.

rechnen mit	*count on*	sich unterhalten mit	*converse with*
sprechen mit	*speak to/with*	zusammenstoßen mit	*collide with*
telefonieren mit	*speak on the phone with*		

NB also the use of *mit* for 'to compare sb./sth. with/to sb./sth.':
jemanden/etwas mit jemandem/etwas vergleichen: Sie verglich dich mit ihm.

Nach

nach (+ dative)

sich erkundigen nach	*ask after*	streben nach	*strive for/after*
riechen nach	*smell of*	suchen nach	*search for*
rufen nach	*call after/for*	telefonieren nach	*telephone for*
schmecken nach	*taste of*	verlangen nach	*ask/long for, crave*
sich sehnen nach	*yearn for*		

NB With verbs of calling, enquiring, longing, *nach* generally has the sense of 'after/for', e.g. *Er erkundigte sich nach dem Weg* (He asked for directions). With verbs relating to the senses it typically corresponds to 'of', e.g. *Es roch nach Teer* (There was a smell of tar).

Über

über (+ accusative)

sich ärgern über	*be annoyed about*	spotten über	*mock, make fun of*
sich beklagen über	*complain about*	sprechen über	*talk about*
sich beschweren über	*complain about*	sich täuschen über	*be mistaken about*
sich freuen über	*be glad about*	urteilen über	*judge*
lachen über	*laugh about*	sich wundern über	*be surprised at*
nachdenken über	*think about*		

NB also: *sich täuschen in jemandem/etwas* 'be mistaken about sb./sth.'.
NB See **5**.3 for the variable case of the preposition *über* in other contexts.

Um

um (+ accusative)

sich ängstigen um	*be worried about*	sich kümmern um	*take care of*
sich bemühen um	*take trouble over*	sich sorgen um	*be worried about*
bitten um	*ask for*	sich streiten um	*argue about*
kämpfen um	*fight for*		

other constructions with um

jemanden um etwas beneiden	
Ich beneide euch um eure Sauna.	*I envy you your sauna.*

other constructions with um — cont.	
gehen um etwas (used only in impersonal constructions, sometimes with additional dative object) **Es geht um Geld.** **Es geht mir nicht ums Geld.**	*It's a question of/It concerns money.* *It's not the money that concerns me.*
sich handeln um etwas (used only in impersonal constructions) **Es handelt sich um den Banküberfall.**	*It concerns the bank robbery.*

NB Distinguish *sich handeln um etwas* from *handeln von: Der Film handelt von einer Liebesaffäre* (The film is about a love affair).

Von

von (+ dative)			
abhängen von **abraten von** **ausgehen von** **sich distanzieren von** **sich erholen von**	*depend on* *advise against* *start by assuming* *distance oneself from* *recover from*	**handeln von** **herrühren von** **träumen von** **zeugen von**	*be about* *stem from* *dream of* *show, demonstrate*

NB Some of these are only used in impersonal constructions: *es hängt von jemandem/etwas ab, es rührt von jemandem/etwas her, es zeugt von etwas.*

other constructions with von	
jemanden von etwas abhalten **Er hielt sie von der Arbeit ab.**	*He kept her from her work.*
jemanden von etwas befreien **Der Ritter befreite sie von ihren Fesseln.** **sich von etwas befreien** **Ich habe mich von dem Druck befreit.**	*The knight liberated her from her bonds.* *I freed myself from the pressure.*
jemanden von etwas überzeugen **Er überzeugte den Richter von seiner Unschuld.**	*He convinced the judge of his innocence.*
sich von etwas überzeugen **Ich überzeugte mich von seiner Unschuld.**	*I satisfied myself as to his innocence.*

Vor

vor (+ dative)			
sich drücken vor **sich ekeln vor**	*dodge, shirk* *have a horror of*	**fliehen vor** **sich fürchten vor**	*flee from* *fear*

vor (+ dative) — cont.			
sich hüten vor	*beware of*	schützen vor	*protect from*
retten vor	*save from*	verstecken vor	*hide from*
sich scheuen vor	*shy away from*	warnen vor	*warn against*

NB Related expressions use the same preposition, e.g. *Warnung vor dem Hunde* (Beware of the dog), *Er hat Angst vor dem Hund* (He's afraid of the dog).

NB See **5.3** for the variable case of the preposition *vor* in other contexts.

Zu

zu (+ dative)			
berechtigen zu	*entitle to*	herausfordern zu	*challenge to*
dienen zu	*serve as*	neigen zu	*tend to*
einladen zu	*invite to*	raten zu	*advise to*
ermutigen zu	*encourage to*	treiben zu	*drive to*
führen zu	*lead to*	überreden zu	*persuade to*
gehören zu	*be part/one of*	verführen zu	*tempt to*
gratulieren zu	*congratulate on*	zwingen zu	*compel to*

Many of these verbs are commonly used with an additional object:

zu (+ dative) + accusative object	
jemanden zu etwas ermutigen/herausfordern/ treiben/überreden/verführen/zwingen **Sie überredeten mich zu dem Ausflug.**	*They persuaded me to go on the trip.*
jemanden zu jemandem/etwas einladen **Ich lade dich zu meiner Party ein.**	*I'll invite you to my party.*

zu (+ dative) + dative object	
jemandem zu etwas raten **Sie riet mir zu dem billigeren Modell.**	*She recommended (that I buy) the cheaper model.*
jemandem zu etwas gratulieren **Wir gratulierten ihm zu dem Erfolg.**	*We congratulated him on his success.*

8.8 Place complements

A few verbs which indicate **position** have a complement indicating where something is situated – a PLACE COMPLEMENT (sentence pattern **J**).

Place complements look like adverbials, but whereas adverbials are optional, place complements are closely linked to the **meaning of the main verb**. This affects their **place in the sentence** (see section **9.8**).

Unlike prepositional objects, place complements can **vary** the PREPOSITION used, e.g. *Die Lampe steht **auf dem Tisch/im Regal/unter dem Fenster/zu Hause***. The prepositions that form part of place complements usually belong to the group of prepositions used with either the accusative or the dative case (e.g. *an, auf, unter*, see section **5**.3).

▶ Place complements need the DATIVE because they show **position**:

Er *wohnt* seit Januar in diesem Haus.	*He has been living in this house since January.*
Paris *liegt* im Norden Frankreichs.	*Paris is in the north of France.*
Sie *hielt* sich in einem Dorf *auf*.	*She was staying in a village.*

Common verbs used with a place complement are:

sich aufhalten	*stay*	**parken**	*park*
sich befinden	*be (situated)*	**sitzen**	*sit*
bleiben	*stay, remain*	**stattfinden**	*take place*
hängen	*hang*	**stehen**	*stand*
leben	*live*	**übernachten**	*spend the night*
liegen	*lie, be lying*	**wohnen**	*live, dwell*

NB Most of the above verbs (but not *sich aufhalten, sich befinden, wohnen*) can alternatively be used without any object or other complement (sentence pattern **A**), in some cases with a variation in meaning. Compare *Er lebt in Ulm* ('He lives in Ulm'), and *Er lebt* ('He's alive').

NB *bleiben* can instead be used with a PREDICATE COMPLEMENT, see **8**.10.

8.9 Direction complements

Verbs of motion typically have a phrase with them which indicates where something is going or being put or taken. This is a DIRECTION COMPLEMENT (sentence patterns **K** and **L**).

Direction complements look like adverbials, but whereas adverbials are optional, direction complements are closely linked to the **meaning of the main verb**. This affects their **place in the sentence** (see section **9**.8).

Unlike prepositional objects, direction complements can **vary** the PREPOSITION used, e.g. *Sie geht **auf den Turm/ins Konzert/nach Hause***. The prepositions that form part of direction complements usually belong to the group of prepositions used with either the accusative or the dative case (e.g. *an, auf, unter*, see section **5**.3).

▶ Direction complements need the ACCUSATIVE because they convey **directional movement**.

Most verbs expressing the idea of **going** somewhere have the direction complement as their only complement (sentence pattern **K**):

Das Mädchen *ist* in den Bach *gefallen*.	*The girl fell into the stream.*
Sie *kam* in das Zimmer.	*She came into the room.*
Er *fuhr* gestern Abend nach dem Kartenspiel nach Hause.	*He drove home last night after the card game.*

Common verbs used with a direction complement are:

fahren	*go (by transport)*	**kriechen**	*creep, crawl*
fallen	*fall*	**reisen**	*travel*
fliegen	*fly*	**rennen**	*run*
fließen	*flow*	**sinken**	*sink*
gehen	*go*	**springen**	*jump*
kommen	*come*	**steigen**	*climb*

NB The above verbs are all INTRANSITIVE verbs of **motion**, which can also be used with sentence pattern **A**. They form their perfect tenses with *sein* (see **6**.7), and all these common verbs are strong or irregular (see **6**.11).

Some other verbs have a direction complement and additionally an accusative object (sentence pattern **L**). These are typically verbs which express the idea of **putting** or **taking** something somewhere:

Er *legte* das Buch auf den Tisch.	*He put the book on the table.*
Sie *hat* den Stein in den Bach *geworfen*.	*She threw the stone into the stream.*
Sie *brachte* ihn nach Hause.	*She took him home.*

Common verbs used in this way are:

befördern	*convey*	**schieben**	*push*
bringen	*take, bring*	**setzen**	*set, place*
hängen	*hang*	**stellen**	*stand, place*
heben	*lift*	**tragen**	*carry*
legen	*lay*	**werfen**	*throw*
schicken	*send*	**ziehen**	*pull*

NB Some verbs correspond to others that are used with a place complement, e.g. compare *legen* with *liegen* and *stellen* with *stehen*. *Hängen* can be used with a place complement or a direction complement, e.g. *Ich hänge das Bild **an die Wand** (acc.), Das Bild hängt **an der Wand** (dat.).*

8.10 Predicate complements

A few verbs have a predicate complement which describes the subject (sentence pattern **M**). This may consist either of a NOUN PHRASE in the nominative case, or of an ADJECTIVE.

Such verbs are called COPULAR VERBS because they typically **link two nouns** which are **both** in the NOMINATIVE case (see section **1**.6). The most important ones are *sein* and *werden*. Other verbs used in this way are *bleiben*, *heißen* and *scheinen*:

sein	**Der Song *ist* der Hit** des Jahres.	*The song is the hit of the year.*
	Das Buch *ist* langweilig.	*The book is boring.*
werden	**Er *wird* Automechaniker.**	*He is going to be a car mechanic.*
bleiben	**Er *bleibt* mein Freund.**	*He remains my friend.*
heißen	**Der Roman *heißt* „Der Prozess".**	*The novel is called 'The Trial'.*
scheinen	**Der Bericht *schien* unglaubwürdig.**	*The report seemed implausible.*

NB *werden* is here used not as an auxiliary verb but as a **main verb** meaning 'become'. It can also be used with the prepositional object *zu* (see **8**.7).

NB *scheinen* tends to be used with an infinitive clause, e.g. *Es scheint heute kalt zu sein*. It can also be used intransitively or with a direction complement, with the meaning 'shine'.

VALENCY AND CASES IN CONTEXT

Das verlorene Gleichgewicht

Die Bevölkerungsexplosion verdanken wir der Intelligenz und der Potenz des Menschen. Von allen Primaten hat der „Nackte Affe" den größten Penis und das größte Hirn. Sie sorgten dafür, dass es immer weniger Tod und immer mehr Leben gab.

Wie nur wenige Säugetiere hat der Mensch permanent Paarungszeit. Und der Intelligenz des Homo sapiens gelang es, durch Forschung, Medizin und Hygiene den Tod immer weiter hinauszuschieben.

Chinesische Ein-Kind-Propaganda

Als Julius Cäsar geboren wurde, konnte er statistisch damit rechnen, 30 Jahre alt zu werden. Heute beträgt die durchschnittliche Lebenserwartung in Deutschland rund 76 Jahre. Das Resultat des menschlichen Doppelsieges von Trieb und Verstand, in Bett und Labor: Jede Sekunde, jede Stunde, jede Woche werden rund doppelt so viele Zweibeiner geboren wie sterben.

Das menschliche Dasein hat seine Balance verloren. Das Gleichgewicht von Geburt und Tod besteht nicht mehr. Jede zusätzliche Milliarde Menschen bedeutet neue gigantische Zerstörungen von Natur und Umwelt, von Atmosphäre und Elementen. Nichts wird das Antlitz der Erde in den nächsten 50 Jahren nachhaltiger verändern als der zunehmende Bevölkerungsdruck.

(Aus: Claus Jacobi, „Des Teufels Alternative", *Der Spiegel*)

6000

2500

1950

1625

1900

900

545

360

200

170

Quelle: Atlas of World Population History

Liebe zum Leben?
Bevölkerungszunahme in Millionen

400 v.Chr.   0   200   400   600   800   1000   1200   1400   1600   1800   2000 n.Chr.

VALENCY/VALENCE

A term adapted from chemistry: the property of an element that determines the number of other atoms with which an atom of the element can combine, e.g. under normal conditions, chlorine has a valency of one, magnesium has a valency of two, etc. Accordingly, a verb forms bonds with other elements to make a complete sentence:

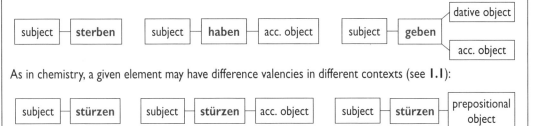

As in chemistry, a given element may have difference valencies in different contexts (see **1.1**):

Valency allows you to concentrate on the core components of a sentence – the complements needed by the main verb to make the sentence grammatical.

subject+	verb	
Zweibeiner	sterben	
Das Gleichgewicht	besteht	

subject+	verb+	accusative object
Der Nackte Affe	hat	den Penis/das Hirn
Es	gibt	Tod/Leben
Der Mensch	hat	Paarungszeit
[Die Intelligenz]	[hinausschieben]	den Tod
[subject]	gebiert	Julius Cäsar
Die Lebenserwartung	beträgt	76 Jahre
[subject]	gebiert	Zweibeiner
Das Dasein	verliert	die Balance
Jede Milliarde	bedeutet	Zerstörungen
Nichts	verändert	das Antlitz

subject+	verb+	dative object
Es	gelingt	der Intelligenz

subject+	verb+	dative object	accusative object
Wir	verdanken	der Intelligenz	die Explosion

subject+	verb+	prepositional object
Sie	sorgen	für + noun phrase (here: *dass*-clause)
Julius Cäsar	rechnet	mit + noun phrase (here: infinitive clause)

subject+	verb+	predicate complement
[Er]	wird	alt

The table has the verbs in the **present tense**. Identify their infinitive forms with the help of a dictionary.

NB Every verb needs a 'doer' of the action – the subject. If the sentence appears in the **passive form**, the 'doer' may remain implicit, and the ACCUSATIVE OBJECT shifts into the nominative case: *Julius Cäsar **wurde geboren**. Zweibeiner **werden geboren**.*

Word order 9

You saw the basic structure of clauses and sentences in chapter **1** (sections **1.7–1.10**). This chapter tells you more about the **order of words and phrases within the sentence**. At the end of the chapter you will find a comprehensive **word order table** for reference. It's helpful to use this together with the table of **sentence patterns** (**8.1**): the VALENCY of the main verb determines what objects and other complements form part of the clause or sentence.

German word order can be **more flexible** than English word order because the function of each noun phrase in the sentence is defined by its CASE (indicated by endings), not by its position. There are **four principles** to remember, and these are explained in this chapter:

▶ The MAIN VERB determines the main elements of the clause and its parts form a BRACKET round the other words, which make up the CENTRAL SECTION of the clause (**9.1–9.2**):

Ingenieure **haben** jetzt für das Handy der Zukunft ein neues Konzept **entwickelt**.   *Engineers **have** now **developed** a new concept for the mobile of the future.*
Dieses Jahr **werden** 135 000 Menschen in Deutschland an Alzheimer **erkranken**.   *This year 135 000 people **will become ill** with Alzheimer's disease in Germany.*

▶ In MAIN CLAUSES, the FINITE VERB comes in **second position**. There is only one element before the finite verb. This is the word or phrase you want to say something about (the 'topic'). This may be the subject (the 'doer' of the action) but it does not have to be (**9.3**):

Ingenieure haben jetzt für das Handy der Zukunft ein neues Konzept entwickelt.   Für das Handy der Zukunft **haben Ingenieure** jetzt ein neues Konzept entwickelt.
Dieses Jahr **werden** 135 000 **Menschen** in Deutschland an Alzheimer erkranken.   135 000 **Menschen werden** dieses Jahr in Deutschland an Alzheimer erkranken.

▶ In SUBORDINATE CLAUSES, **all parts of the verb** come at the **end** but the order of the other words is the same as for the central section of a main clause (**9.1–9.2**):

Experten schätzen,   dass 135 000 Menschen dieses Jahr in Deutschland an Alzheimer erkranken **werden**.

▶ Inside the central section, **the words that are most important for the action of the verb** and/or give the most important new information tend to **come last in the central section**, i.e. closest to the second part of the main verb (**9.4–9.9**):

> Ingenieure haben jetzt für das Handy der Zukunft **ein neues Konzept** entwickelt.
> Dieses Jahr werden 135 000 Menschen in Deutschland **an Alzheimer erkranken.**

What this means is that you always need to **consider the clause as a whole**. You should not assume that the subject will come first and you should not assume that the most important (stressed) information comes near the start of the clause or sentence. Generally, German speakers will exploit the flexibility of German word order to vary the emphasis. Observe how this works in practice, and avoid getting frustrated. This is not just a difficulty for the learner, but also an interesting linguistic difference between English and German. It requires a different way of thinking while you speak or write, listen or read.

9.1 The 'bracket' construction

You saw in sections **1.8–1.10** that there are three types of clause structure in German:

▶ MAIN CLAUSES: the FINITE VERB is the **second** element

▶ QUESTIONS and COMMANDS: the FINITE VERB is the **first** element

▶ SUBORDINATE CLAUSES: the FINITE VERB is the **last** element

In all these clause types, most of the words and phrases in the clause are enclosed in a CENTRAL SECTION. The enclosing words form a kind of BRACKET around the central section. **This bracket construction is typical of all German clauses.** However, if the verb consists of only one part, the 'closing bracket' may be a virtual one!

Main clauses

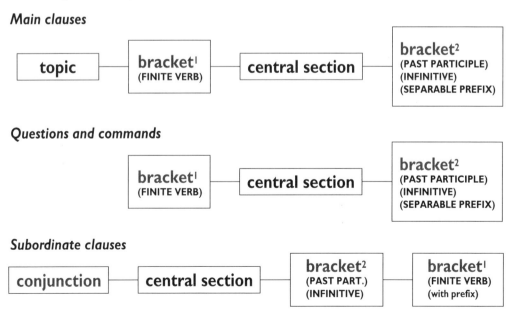

Questions and commands

Subordinate clauses

THE VERBAL BRACKET

	topic	bracket[1]	central section	bracket[2]
main clause	Gestern	hat	er in der Stadt	gearbeitet.
	Heute	arbeitet	er in der Stadt.	
	Anke	soll	ihn sofort zu Hause	anrufen.
	Um acht	rufe	ich meine Oma	an.
question/ command		Hat	er gestern in der Stadt	gearbeitet?
		Arbeitet	er heute in der Stadt?	
		Soll	Anke ihn zu Hause	anrufen?
		Ruf	ihn sofort zu Hause	an!
subordinate clause		..., weil	er gestern in der Stadt	gearbeitet hat.
		..., dass	Anke ihn sofort zu Hause	anrufen soll.
		..., wenn	ich meine Oma	anrufe.

NB In 'w-questions' the finite verb comes second, after the question word, e.g. *Warum ruft er sie nicht an?*

9.2 Verbs at the end of the clause

There may be more than one verb in final position at the end of the clause. The order of these verbs is fixed.

▶ In MAIN CLAUSES and QUESTIONS, the infinitive or past participle of the main verb is followed by the auxiliary verb:

topic	finite verb	central section	main verb	auxiliary verb
Ich	werde	es ihr doch	sagen	müssen.
Der Computer	soll	heute noch	repariert	werden.
	Ist	dir das schon	erklärt	worden?

▶ In SUBORDINATE CLAUSES, all infinitives and participles of the main verb and the auxiliary verb are followed by the finite verb:

conjunction	central section	main verb	auxiliary verb	finite verb
..., nachdem	ich sie zufällig	gesehen		habe.
..., weil	sie mit uns ins Kino	gehen		wollte.
..., dass	mir das schon	erklärt	worden	ist.

▶ However, if there are **two infinitives** at the end of the SUBORDINATE CLAUSE (generally the infinitive of the main verb, and the infinitive of a modal verb), then the finite verb comes before both infinitives:

conjunction	central section	finite verb	main verb	auxiliary verb
..., da	ich es bald	werde	machen	müssen.
..., ob	sie diese Probleme	hatte	lösen	können.
..., damit	ich bis Montag	habe	bleiben	dürfen.

*„Ich hätte schwören können,
dass es eine Fata Morgana ist!"*

9.3 First position in main clauses

As you saw in **1.8**, one, and only one, element can come before the finite verb in a main clause. **The finite verb is always in second position**.

The first element is the TOPIC of the clause – something we are emphasizing because we want to say something about it. Many kinds of words and phrases can come in this first position:

	topic	bracket[1]	central section	bracket[2]
accusative or dative object	Den Lastwagen	hatte	Ursula nicht	bemerkt.
	Meinem Vater	wollte	sie sicher nicht	schmeicheln.
another verb complement	Ins Theater	bin	ich nur noch selten	gekommen.
	Auf Angela	mussten	sie noch lange	warten.
adverbial (word/phrase)	Eigentlich	wären	wir lieber heute	gefahren.
	Heute Morgen	sollte	sie früher	aufstehen.
subordinate clause	Wohin sie fuhren,	hat	sie nicht	gewusst.
	Da ich ihn kenne,	habe	ich das auch	erwartet.

The structure of German main clauses is different from English. In English, a number of words or phrases can come before the verb, and the subject is almost always immediately before the finite verb. In fact, as English has no case endings for the subject, this is the only way we can tell it is the subject.

In German, **the subject often comes after the verb**, inside the central section. It is important to learn to recognize what the subject is

▶ from its **ending: the subject is in the nominative case**;

▶ from the **ending on the verb: this agrees with the subject**.

You can see this from the following sentences, which are easy to misunderstand because there is an object or complement in first position, and the subject comes later in the sentence:

Polizisten **attackierte** gestern Abend in Amstetten **ein alkoholisierter Arbeitsloser.** *Yesterday evening an unemployed drunk attacked policemen in Amstetten.*
Diesen Nachbarn **begegnete mein Bruder** nun öfters. *My brother met these neighbours frequently from then on.*
Dieser Frau **hat er** dann das Handy von seiner Schwester gegeben. *He then gave this woman his sister's mobile phone.*
Den Ministern **erschien diese Politik** unmöglich. *These policies seemed impossible to the ministers.*
Auch die dringend notwendige neue Heizung **können** sich **die Eheleute** nicht leisten. *The married couple cannot even afford the new heating which they so urgently need.*
Auch über diese Geschichte **kann** in Rudolstadt kaum **jemand** lachen. *Hardly anyone in Rudolstadt is able to laugh about this story either.*

There is nothing unusual or out of the ordinary about these sentences. They have this order because of where the writer (or speaker) wants to put the emphasis.

9.4 The order of words and phrases in the central section

Except for the verbs and the element in first position in main clauses, all the words and phrases in a German clause normally come in the CENTRAL SECTION, between the 'brackets'. The words in the central section tend to appear in the order summarized in the **word order table** at the end of the chapter. The sequence given there can be treated as a reliable guideline for your own use, but you will sometimes find Germans changing it slightly for reasons of emphasis.

More details about this sequence are given in the following sections (**9.5–9.8**). You should remember that **this order is the same for the central section of all clause types**, in questions and subordinate clauses as well as in main clauses.

9.5 The position of pronouns

PERSONAL PRONOUNS usually follow immediately after the finite verb or the conjunction. In other words, they are usually the **first words in the central section** of the clause.

▶ Personal pronouns have the order NOMINATIVE – ACCUSATIVE – DATIVE:

topic	bracket[1]	nom.	acc.	dat.	other elements	bracket[2]
Gestern	hat	er	sie	ihm	zum Geburtstag	gegeben.
	Hast	du	es	uns	nicht	gesagt?
	..., dass	er	sich	mir	auf diese Weise	vorgestellt hat.

▶ Personal pronouns come **before** DEMONSTRATIVE PRONOUNS

Thus personal pronouns like *ich*, *er*, *sie*, *es*, *Ihnen*, etc. – and the reflexive pronoun *sich* – come before demonstrative pronouns like *das*, *dieser*, etc., **irrespective of case**:

Wollen Sie ihm das gleich **sagen?**	*Do you want to tell him that straight away?*
Hat ihn dieser erkannt?	*Did he recognise him?*
Soeben **hat sich das ereignet.**	*That has just happened.*
Hast du den mitgebracht?	*Have you brought that?*

9.6 The position of the noun subject and objects

▶ If the subject (i.e. nominative case) and the dative and accusative objects of the verb are NOUN PHRASES, they usually **follow** the PRONOUNS in the central section (unless one of them is in initial 'topic' position):

Ich **wollte** es **meinem Vater erzählen.**	*I wanted to tell it to my father.*
Trotzdem **hat** er **den Fernseher gekauft.**	*Nevertheless, he bought the television.*
Das **hat** ihm **der Lehrer gezeigt.**	*The teacher showed him that.*
Gestern **hat** ihn **meine Mutter** hier **gesehen.**	*Yesterday my mother saw him here.*

An exception to this general rule is that the noun SUBJECT can precede or follow the personal pronouns:

Gestern **hat** ihn **mein Mann** hier **gesehen.**	Gestern **hat mein Mann** ihn hier **gesehen.**
Warum **will** ihm **dein Freund helfen?**	Warum **will dein Freund** ihm **helfen?**

▶ Subject and object noun phrases have the order NOMINATIVE – DATIVE – ACCUSATIVE:

topic	bracket[1]	nominative	dative	accusative	bracket[2]
Gestern	hat	der Nachbar	meinem Vater	diese Videos	geliehen.
	Hat	Monika	seiner Freundin	etwas	gesagt?
	..., dass	die Chefin	den Angestellten	mehr Geld	versprach.

9.7 The position of adverbials

▶ Adverbials in the central section are usually positioned **after** a DATIVE noun object and **before** an ACCUSATIVE noun object:

topic	bracket[1]	pron.	dative	adverbial	accusative	bracket[2]
Dann	hat	er	meinem Vater	trotzdem	diese Videos	geliehen.
	Hat	er	seiner Freundin	am Sonntag	kein Geschenk	gebracht?
	..., dass	sie	den Angestellten	vielleicht	mehr Geld	versprach.

▶ If there is more than one adverbial in the central section of the clause, they tend to be placed in the order **attitude – time – reason – place – manner**:

topic	bracket[1]	attitude	time	reason	place	manner	bracket[2]
Uwe	musste	leider	am Montag	wegen des Unfalls			operiert werden.
Ihr	werdet	wohl	nachher		zu Hause	fest	schlafen.
Sie	haben	offenbar	heute	trotz des Wetters	in Köln	gut	gespielt.

NB The traditional rule for the order of adverbials, **time – manner – place**, is misleading since it ignores the distinction between adverbials and complements. DIRECTION/PLACE COMPLEMENTS come **after** adverbials of manner, but ADVERBIALS **of place** normally come **before** adverbials of manner.

▶ Adverbials of **manner** tend to **follow all other adverbials** and also follow an accusative noun object since they directly define the action of the verb:

topic	bracket[1]	other elements	accusative	manner	bracket[2]
Dann	hat	er dem Spieler	den Ball	unvorsichtig	zugeworfen.
	Hat	die Feuerwehr	den Brand	schnell	gelöscht?
	..., dass	sie	das Stück	zu langsam	gespielt haben.

▶ The order of adverbials and noun objects can vary for **emphasis**. The neutral word order given above tends to place the emphasis on the action of the verb with its objects and complement.

If an adverbial is placed **later** in the clause than in its usual place, it becomes **more heavily stressed**:

Sie **hat** im Sommer **diesen neuen Wagen** gekauft.	*That's **what** she bought/did.*
Sie **hat** diesen neuen Wagen **im Sommer** gekauft.	*That's **when** she bought it.*
Er **hat** im Internet **die neue Adresse** gefunden.	*That's **what** he found/did.*
Er **hat** die neue Adresse **im Internet** gefunden.	*That's **where** he found it.*

9.8 The position of complements

The subject (nominative case) and any dative and accusative objects have special positions in the central section (see **9.6**). **All other** COMPLEMENTS **are placed at the end of the central section**, immediately before the closing 'bracket'. This applies to:

▶ genitive objects

▶ prepositional objects

▶ place and direction complements

▶ the predicate complement.

complement type	topic	bracket¹	other elements	complement	bracket²
genitive object		..., weil	der Verletzte dringend	eines Arztes	bedurfte.
prepositional obj.		Hat	sie lange im **Café**	auf ihren Mann	gewartet?
direction compl.	Sie	ist	mit dem **BMW** zu schnell	in die Kurve	gefahren.
place compl.	Sie	wollten	auf keinen Fall	in Wuppertal	wohnen.
predicate compl.	Hans	ist	erstaunlicherweise	Dolmetscher	geworden.

NB The noun portions of set verb phrases also come at the end of the central section. They can in fact be considered similar to separable prefixes, e.g. *Christian konnte sehr gut Klavier spielen.*

9.9 The position of *nicht*

If *nicht* refers to **the whole clause** – i.e. if it negates the action of the verb in general – it normally comes **before those elements** in the central section that **directly define the action of the verb**:

▶ **after** place or time adverbials, but **before** manner adverbials

▶ **after** an accusative noun object

▶ **before** all other complements.

topic	bracket¹	adverbials	accusative	*nicht*	manner	complement	bracket²
Alfred	will	trotzdem		nicht	lange		schlafen.
Sylvia	hat	allerdings	den Film	nicht			gesehen.
Lucia	hat	heute	die Rolle	nicht	gut		gesungen.
Ich	wollte	doch		nicht		auf diesen Mann	warten.
Wir	sind	gestern		nicht		nach Stuttgart	gefahren.

Other negating words, like **kaum** 'hardly', 'scarcely' and **nie** 'never', come in the **same position** in the clause as *nicht*:

Sylvia **kann** jedoch den Film **kaum gesehen haben**.	*But Sylvia can hardly have seen the film.*
Lucia **hat** jedoch die Rolle **nie** gut **gesungen**.	*But Lucia has never sung that part well.*

In some contexts, *nicht* refers not to the clause as a whole, but to a specific word or phrase. If *nicht* refers to a **specific element in the clause**, it comes **immediately before the word(s) in question**:

Sie **hat** mir dieses Buch **nicht geliehen**.	*[She didn't lend me the book.]*
Sie **hat** mir **nicht dieses Buch** geliehen, **sondern das andere**.	*[not **this** book]*
Sie **haben** am Freitag **nicht gespielt**.	*[They didn't play on Friday]*
Sie **haben nicht am Freitag gespielt, sondern am Samstag**.	*[not on **Friday**]*

9.10 Placing elements after the verbal bracket

As a general rule, the final part of the verb concludes a German clause, acting as the 'closing bracket'. However, in some contexts it is usual or possible to place an element after this closing bracket:

▶ SUBORDINATE CLAUSES are normally not enclosed within the verbal bracket.

▶ COMPARATIVE PHRASES introduced by **als** or **wie** are normally placed after the verbal bracket.

▶ PREPOSITIONAL PHRASES are sometimes placed after the verbal bracket, especially in colloquial speech.

Die Firma **will** Solaranlagen **entwickeln, die möglichst billig sind**.
The company wants to develop solar plants that are as cheap as possible.
Diese Technologie **wird** in zehn Jahren sicher **billiger sein als heute**.
In ten years' time this technology will undoubtedly be cheaper than today.
Letzte Woche **haben** wir einen ganz tollen Film **gesehen in dem neuen Kino**.
Last week we saw a brilliant film in the new cinema.

WORD ORDER

	topic	bracket[1]	pronouns N A D	noun subject	dative noun object	most adverbials	accusative noun object	nicht	manner adverbials	complements	bracket[2]
MAIN CLAUSE	Heute	hat	ihr	mein Freund		sicher	eine E-Mail				geschickt.
	Jan	soll			dem Chef	jetzt	den Bericht				bringen.
	Wir	sind				danach		nicht		klüger	geworden.
QUESTION/ COMMAND		Hat	sie es ihm			denn			richtig		erklärt?
		Hat	er Ihnen			trotzdem	den Weg	nicht			zeigen können?
		Geben	Sie mir			sofort	das Geld				zurück!
SUBORDINATE CLAUSE		…weil		der alte Herr	dem Mann					für seine Hilfe	gedankt hat.
		…da		meine Tante		meistens		nicht		vorsichtig	ist.
		…dass	sie			.	den Brief		schnell	in die Tasche	stecken wollte.

WORD ORDER IN CONTEXT

Beginn des Lebens auf der Erde

Es ist nicht sicher bekannt, wie die Erde entstanden ist. Die vorherrschende Vorstellung ist, dass sich kosmische Staubwolken in einem der unendlich vielen existierenden Milchstraßensysteme zusammenballten. Das Alter unserer Erde als fester Himmelskörper wird auf rund fünf Milliarden Jahre geschätzt. Es wird angenommen, dass der Erdball in den ersten fünfhundert Millionen Jahren aus glutflüssigem Gestein bestand. Dann begannen sich die Schmelzen allmählich abzukühlen, sodass sich an der Erdoberfläche eine feste Gesteinskruste bilden konnte. In den tieferen Zonen darunter blieb das Gestein flüssig.

In den nachfolgenden vier Milliarden Jahren kam es zu starken Veränderungen der Erdkruste. Ihre Oberfläche wurde an vielen Stellen gefaltet und ungleichmäßig zerbrochen. Zwischen riesigen Kontinentalplatten entstanden große Senken. Als die Kruste langsam abkühlte, sammelte sich hier Wasser. So bildeten sich die Ozeane, die sieben Zehntel der heutigen Erdoberfläche bedecken. Durch die Faltungsvorgänge entstanden Gebirge. Andere Gebirge wurden von Lava gebildet, und ausgeworfene Aschelagen türmten Vulkane auf.

Im Laufe der Erdgeschichte sind auch weite Teile Deutschlands immer wieder vom Meer bedeckt gewesen. Daher finden wir in vielen Gegenden unseres Landes fossile Meeresmuscheln.

(Aus: Christian Spaeth, *Säugetiere der Vorzeit*)

THE POSITION OF THE VERB

main clause **(finite verb appears as second element)**	*Es* ist nicht bekannt. *Die Vorstellung* ist X. *Das Alter* wird auf fünf Milliarden Jahre **geschätzt**. *Es* wird **angenommen**. Dann begannen sich *die Schmelzen* **abzukühlen**. In den Zonen darunter blieb *das Gestein* flüssig. In den nachfolgenden Jahren kam *es* zu Veränderungen. *Ihre Oberfläche* wurde **gefaltet**. Zwischen Kontinentalplatten entstanden *Senken*. [Als ….,] sammelte sich hier *Wasser*. So bildeten sich *Ozeane*. Durch die Faltungsvorgänge entstanden *Gebirge*. *Andere Gebirge* wurden von Lava **gebildet**. *Ausgeworfene Aschelagen* türmten Vulkane **auf**. Im Laufe der Geschichte sind *Teile* **bedeckt gewesen**. Daher finden *wir* fossile Meeresmuscheln.
subordinate clause **(finite verb appears as last element)**	…, wie *die Erde* **entstanden ist**. …, dass sich *Staubwolken* **zusammenballten**. …, dass *der Erdball* aus flüssigem Gestein **bestand**. …, sodass sich *eine Kruste* **bilden konnte**. Als *die Kruste* **abkühlte**, … …, [Ozeane], *die* sieben Zehntel … **bedecken**.

NB The FINITE VERB is in red. **Other parts of the verb** are in bold. The *subject* of the verb is in italics.

Complex sentences 10

As you saw in **1.7**, there are two basic types of clause:

▶ MAIN CLAUSES can stand on their own. The FINITE VERB is the **second element** in the main clause.

▶ SUBORDINATE CLAUSES depend on another clause. **All parts of the verb** come at the **end** of the subordinate clause.

Complex sentences are sentences which have **more than one clause**, at least one of which will be a main clause. This chapter explains how complex sentences are constructed in German:

◆ the construction of complex sentences **(10.1)**

◆ coordination **(10.2)**

◆ subordination **(10.3–10.5)**

◆ infinitive clauses **(10.6–10.8).**

10.1 Coordination and subordination

In complex sentences the clauses can be linked in two ways:

▶ Two (or more) main clauses may be joined by a **coordinating CONJUNCTION** ('linking' conjunction) like *und* or *aber*. In each of these clauses the verb is the second element. Each clause could be a simple sentence in its own right:

Magda war krank und deshalb konnte sie an dem Abend nicht kommen.   *Magda was ill and so she couldn't come that evening.*
Jochen starrte sie an, aber sie sagte immer noch nichts.   *Jochen stared at her but still she said nothing.*

▶ One (or more) subordinate clauses may be **embedded** in another clause, i.e.:

- clauses introduced by a **subordinating CONJUNCTION** like *dass, weil, wenn* or the RELATIVE PRONOUN *der/die/das*;

- INFINITIVE CLAUSES ending in an infinitive with *zu*.

A subordinate clause cannot form a sentence in its own right. It **substitutes** for a single word or phrase – a noun, adjective or adverbial – in the clause it depends on. In a subordinate clause all parts of the verb are at the end:

The subordinate clause plays the part of a noun phrase	**Ich habe gehofft, dass Sie kommen würden.** *I hoped that you would come.* **[Ich habe es gehofft.]**
The subordinate clause plays the part of an adjective	**Am liebsten mag ich Autos, die schnell fahren.** *Best of all I like cars that go fast.* **[Am liebsten mag ich schnelle Autos.]**
The subordinate clause plays the part of an adverbial	**Ich kann nicht kommen, weil ich krank bin.** *I can't come because I'm ill.* **[Ich kann deshalb nicht kommen.]**

10.2 Coordination

The following are the most important **coordinating** CONJUNCTIONS in German. Most of them can link single **words** or **phrases** as well as **clauses**:

aber	but	**Sie rief laut, aber der Junge kam nicht.** *She called loudly, but the boy didn't come.*
denn	for, since	**Wir blieben zu Hause, denn das Wetter war schlecht.** *We stayed at home since the weather was bad.*
oder	or	**Morgen können wir hier bleiben, oder wir können ins Kino gehen.** *Tomorrow we can stay here or we can go to the cinema.*
sondern	but	**Wir sind nicht ins Kino gegangen, sondern wir sind hier geblieben.** *We didn't go to the cinema but stayed here.*
und	and	**Elke liest die Zeitung und Johanna arbeitet im Garten.** *Elke is reading the newspaper and Johanna is working in the garden.*

NB The clauses are separated by a comma. This is optional before *und* (see **12.6**).

▶ *denn* gives a reason and is often translated as English 'because'. Unlike 'because', though, it is a coordinating conjunction introducing a main clause, and a clause with *denn* cannot begin a sentence.

▶ *sondern* and *aber* both translate English 'but' and need to be carefully distinguished. *Sondern* must be used if you are contradicting a preceding negative statement.

▶ The subject of the clause after **sondern** or **und** can be omitted ('understood') if it is the same as that of the first clause:

Angela kam um vier Uhr an und ging dann zu ihrer Tante.
Angela arrived at four and then went to her aunt's.

Wir gingen nicht ins Kino, sondern blieben zu Hause.
We didn't go to the cinema but stayed at home.

However, if there is a **word** or **phrase in front of the verb** in the second clause, the SUBJECT must be **repeated**:

Angela schrieb ein paar Briefe und dann ging sie zu ihrer Tante.
Angela wrote a few letters and then she went to her aunt's.

Coordinating conjunctions most often **link** MAIN CLAUSES, with the verb in second position in both, as the examples given so far show. But they can also **link** two parallel SUBORDINATE CLAUSES (introduced by a subordinating conjunction). In this case the verb is in final position in both clauses:

Ich weiß, dass sie gestern krank war und dass ihr Mann deswegen zu Hause geblieben ist.
I know that she was ill yesterday and that her husband stayed at home for that reason.

10.3 Subordination: noun clauses

Clauses introduced by the **subordinating** CONJUNCTION **dass** (that) substitute for a noun or noun phrase in the clause they depend on.

A **dass**-clause can **substitute** for a NOUN PHRASE in a number of ways:

verb subject	**Dass sie morgen kommt, erstaunt mich.** *I find it surprising that she's coming tomorrow.* **Dass er sie betrogen hat, steht jetzt fest.** *It is now certain that he betrayed her.*
accusative object	**Sie versicherte mir, dass alles in Ordnung war.** *She assured me that everything was all right.* **Ich weiß, dass sie das Examen bestanden hat.** *I know that she has passed the exam.*
prepositional object	**Sie ärgerte sich darüber, dass er so wenig getan hatte.** *She was annoyed that he had done so little.* **Er wartete darauf, dass Peter ihn grüßte.** *He waited for Peter to greet him.*
dependent on a noun or adjective	**Sie hatte das Gefühl, dass er bald kommen könnte.** *She had the feeling that he might come soon.* **Sie war böse, dass er es ihr nicht gesagt hatte.** *She was angry that he had not told her about it.*

„Wie oft habe ich dir schon gesagt, dass du mich während der Arbeit nicht anrufen sollst!"

▶ *dass* can be **omitted** in some contexts. The clause then has the word order of a main clause, with the **verb second**:

Sie sagte, sie würde es nicht tun. Sie sagte, dass sie es nicht tun würde.	*She said (that) she wouldn't do it.*
Sie hoffte trotzdem, er könnte noch kommen. Sie hoffte trotzdem, dass er noch kommen könnte.	*She hoped nevertheless that he might still come.*

In practice, *dass* is omitted much less often than English 'that'. It is frequently omitted after verbs of **saying** and, especially in spoken German, after verbs of **hoping** and **thinking**.

Anticipatory es

A *dass*-clause which is being used as the subject or object of a verb is sometimes **anticipated by *es*** in the **preceding clause**:

Es fiel mir auf, **dass sie plötzlich fehlte.**	*It struck me that she was suddenly missing.*
Dann fiel (**es**) mir auf, **dass sie plötzlich fehlte.**	*Then it struck me that she was suddenly missing.*
Ich bedaure (**es**), **dass sie nicht kommen konnte.**	*I regret that she couldn't come.*

This '**anticipatory**' *es* is common with a number of verbs, but it is only necessary if the subject is in initial position before the main verb, as in the first example above.

Dass preceded by a prepositional adverb

Some verbs, nouns or adjectives are followed by a PREPOSITIONAL OBJECT (see **8.7**), e.g. *Ich warte auf seinen Besuch; die Angst vor der Prüfung; Wir sind froh über die Nachricht.*

If a *dass*-clause is used instead of a noun phrase after the preposition, the **dass-clause** is often **anticipated in the preceding clause** by a PREPOSITIONAL ADVERB, i.e. the compound of **da(r)** + PREPOSITION (see **5.5**):

Ich warte **darauf, dass er mich besucht.**
I'm waiting for him to visit me.
Die Angst **davor, dass er bei der Prüfung durchfallen könnte,** machte ihn ganz krank.
The fear that he might fail the exam made him quite ill.
Wir sind sehr froh **darüber, dass ihr eure Katze gefunden habt.**
We're very glad that you've found your cat.

This prepositional adverb is most often included in written German, but it is often dropped in speech.

Conjunctions introducing indirect questions

The conjunction **ob** (whether, if) and the interrogative **w-words** like *was, wie, warum* or *wann* can be used in a similar way to *dass* to **introduce a noun clause** – usually an indirect question:

Maxi fragt, **ob wir mitkommen wollen.**	*Maxi is asking whether we want to come.*
Ich weiß nicht, **ob er eine Karte hat.**	*I don't know whether he's got a ticket.*
Es ist nicht sicher, **ob/wie sie kommt.**	*It isn't certain whether/how she's coming.*
Der Mann hat gefragt, **wo der Bahnhof ist.**	*The man asked where the station is.*
Ich weiß nicht, **warum ich so traurig bin.**	*I don't know why I'm so sad.*
Er hat keine Ahnung, **wann er fertig sein wird.**	*He has no idea when he'll be finished.*

10.4 Subordination: other conjunctions

Most subordinating conjunctions introduce a clause that has the same role as an adverbial, typically providing additional information about the **time**, **manner** or **reason**, etc. of the action expressed in the clause on which they depend.

Conjunctions of time

als when
Als ich ankam, habe ich sie auf dem Bahnsteig gesehen.
When I arrived I saw her on the platform.

NB *als* refers to a **single event in the past**. The following verb is never in the present tense.

NB *als* is also used as a conjunction of manner, to express a **comparison**, e.g. *Max läuft schneller **als** Moritz* (Max runs faster **than** Moritz).

bevor/ehe **before**

Großmutter fragte ihn immer, bevor sie etwas kaufte.
Grandmother always asked him before she bought something.

Ehe sie wegging, sah sie ihn noch einmal an.
Before she went off, she looked at him once more.

NB *bevor* is more frequent than *ehe*, especially in speech.
NB *bevor* only exists as a conjunction and always introduces a clause. The English preposition 'before', used simply with a noun, is equivalent to the preposition *vor*, e.g. *vor dem Essen* (before the meal).

bis **until, by the time**

Ich warte hier, bis du zurückkommst.
I'll wait here until you get back.

Bis du zurückkommst, habe ich das Fenster repariert.
By the time you get back, I'll have repaired the window.

nachdem **after**

Nachdem er gegessen hatte, legte er sich eine Weile hin.
After he'd eaten, he lay down for a while.

NB The following verb is always in the pluperfect tense.

seit/seitdem **since**

Seit er das Haus verkauft hat, wohnt er in einem Hotel.
Since he sold the house he's been living in a hotel.

NB *seitdem* is often used for *seit* in written German.

sobald **as soon as**

Sobald ich das merkte, ging ich zur Polizei.
As soon as I noticed it I went to the police.

solange **as long as**

Wir haben gewartet, solange wir konnten.
We waited as long as we could.

sooft **as often as, whenever**

Du kannst kommen, sooft du willst.
You can come as often as you like.

---

während while, whilst

Diese Probleme hat Erika gelöst, während wir in Urlaub waren.
Erika solved these problems while we were on holiday.

NB *während* can also be used as a conjunction of manner='whereas', 'while'.

---

wenn when, whenever

Ich bringe es, wenn ich morgen vorbeikomme.
I'll bring it when I come tomorrow.

Es wurde ihm jedes Mal schlecht, wenn er daran dachte.
Whenever he thought of it he felt quite ill.

NB *wenn* refers to the present, future, or repeated events in the past.
NB *wenn* can also be used as a conjunction of reason='if'.

Conjunctions of manner

als than = comparison

Wir fahren schneller, als du denkst.
We're going faster than you think.

NB *Als* expresses difference, with the comparative form of the adjective. *Wie* expresses similarity, usually as 'so… wie', e.g. *Wir fahren **so** schnell **wie** du* (We're going **as** fast **as** you).
NB *als* is also used as a conjunction of time, meaning 'when'.
NB see also *als ob* below.

---

als ob as if = hypothetical comparison

Das Kind weinte, als ob es Schmerzen hätte.
The child was crying as though it were in pain.

NB The following verb is normally in the subjunctive (though in less formal contexts it tends to be in the indicative). In written German, a common alternative is *als* (with *ob* omitted), in which case the verb is always in the subjunctive and follows *als*: *Das Kind weinte, **als hätte** es Schmerzen.*
NB *als wenn* and *wie wenn* are less common alternatives to *als ob*.

---

dadurch…, dass by…-ing = means

Sie hat die Probleme dadurch gelöst, dass sie ihn verließ.
She solved the problems by leaving him.

NB *dadurch…, dass* is similar to *indem*.

---

indem by…-ing = means

Sie hat die Probleme gelöst, indem sie ihm vergab.
She solved the problems by forgiving him.

NB *indem* is similar to *dadurch…, dass*.

soviel/soweit **as far as** = *limitation*
Soviel ich weiß, wohnt sie jetzt in Mannheim. *As far as I know she lives in Mannheim now.*
Ich werde dir helfen, soweit ich kann. *I'll help you as far as I am able.*

während **whereas, while** = *contrast*
Während wir uns gefreut haben, waren sie enttäuscht. *While we were pleased, they were disappointed.*

NB *während* can also be used as a conjunction of time, meaning 'while'.

wie/so... wie **as, like** = *similarity*
Der Film ist so gut wie das Buch. *The film is as good as the book.*
Der Film war nicht so spannend, wie ich erwartet hatte. *The film wasn't as riveting as I'd expected.*

NB *wie* expresses similarity in a comparison, usually as '*so... wie*'.
NB To express difference between two things with the comparative form of the adjective, *als* is used, e.g. *Der Film war **besser als** das Buch* (The film was **better than** the book).
NB *wie* can also be used to introduce an indirect question (see **10.3**), e.g. *Sie fragte, **wie** man dort hinkommt* (She asked how you get there).

Conjunctions of reason

da **as, since** = *cause*
Da er getrunken hatte, konnte er nicht fahren. *As/Since he'd been drinking, he couldn't drive.*

NB *da* can also be used as an adverb, meaning 'there', 'then'.

damit **so that** = *purpose*
Wir müssen uns beeilen, damit wir den Zug erreichen. *We'll have to hurry so that we catch the train.*

falls **in case, if** = *condition*
Ich besuche dich morgen, falls ich Zeit habe. *I'll visit you tomorrow if I have time.*

obwohl   although   = concession

Obwohl er mein Vetter ist, kann ich nichts für ihn tun.
Although he's my cousin, there's nothing I can do for him.

NB *obgleich, obschon, wenngleich* and *wiewohl* also mean 'although'. They are used mainly in written German and are less common than *obwohl*.

so dass   so that   = result, consequence

Er schob den Ärmel zurück, so dass wir die Narbe sehen konnten.
He pushed his sleeve back so that we could see the scar.

NB Don't confuse *so dass* with *damit*, which indicates a purpose. If you said *Er schob den Ärmel zurück, damit wir die Narbe sehen konnten* it would suggest that he rolled his sleeve back with the express purpose of showing us the scar.

weil   because   = reason, cause

Ich musste zu Fuß gehen, weil ich die letzte Straßenbahn verpasst hatte.
I had to walk because I'd missed the last tram.

NB In speech, *weil* is often used like *denn* with the word order of a main clause, i.e. the verb in second place rather than at the end of the clause, e.g. *..., weil ich **hatte** die letzte Straßenbahn verpasst*. Although common, this usage is usually thought of as incorrect and it is not used in written German.

wenn   if   = condition

Wenn ich nach Berlin komme, besuche ich meine alte Freundin.
If I get to Berlin, I'll visit my old friend/girlfriend.

Wenn ich Zeit hätte, käme ich gerne mit.
If I had the time, I'd love to come with you.

NB The verb in a *wenn*-clause is normally in the subjunctive if the condition is unreal or hypothetical (see **7.5**).
NB *wenn* can also be used as a conjunction of time, meaning 'when'.

10.5 Subordination: relative clauses

Subordinate clauses which **qualify a noun**, rather like adjectives, are called RELATIVE CLAUSES. They are introduced by a RELATIVE PRONOUN, corresponding to English 'who', 'which' or 'that':

Der Roman, den ich lese, ist interessant.	*The novel (which) I'm reading is interesting.*
Ich kannte **den Mann, der gestern gestorben ist**.	*I knew the man who died yesterday.*
Der Mann, dem ich helfe, ist sehr alt.	*The man (who[m]) I am helping is very old.*
Der Stuhl, auf dem ich sitze, ist wackelig.	*The chair on which I am sitting is wobbly.*

The most common **RELATIVE PRONOUN** in German is *der/die/das*. It indicates case, number and gender and has the same forms as the **DEMONSTRATIVE PRONOUN** *der/die/das* (see **3.9**):

RELATIVE PRONOUN

	masculine	feminine	neuter	plural	*closest equivalent*
nominative	der	die	das	die	*who*
accusative	den	die	das	die	*whom*
genitive	dessen	deren	dessen	deren	*whose*
dative	dem	der	dem	denen	*to whom*

The relative pronoun takes

▶ its **GENDER** and **NUMBER** from the noun it refers back to;

▶ its **CASE** from its **role in the relative clause** which it introduces.

This means that a relative pronoun referring back to a masculine singular noun (e.g. *der Mann*) will always be in the masculine singular form ('masculine' column in the table) but its case will depend on its role within the relative clause: if the man is the subject of the relative clause, the pronoun will be in the nominative case (*der*), if he is the direct object of the relative clause, the pronoun will be in the accusative case (*den*) etc:

THE CASE OF THE RELATIVE PRONOUN

nominative **subject of the verb in the clause**	der Mann, der kommt, … das Kind, das kommt, …	die Frau, die kommt, … die Leute, die kommen, …
accusative **object of the verb in the clause**	der Mann, den ich sehe, … das Kind, das ich sehe, …	die Frau, die ich sehe, … die Leute, die ich sehe, …
dative **object of the verb in the clause**	der Mann, dem ich es gebe, … das Kind, dem ich es gebe, …	die Frau, der ich es gebe, … die Leute, denen ich es gebe, …
genitive **dependent on a noun**	der Mann, dessen Frau ich liebe, … das Kind, dessen Oma ich kenne, …	die Frau, deren Mann ich liebe, … die Leute, deren Auto ich kaufe, …
accusative **or** dative **after a preposition**	der Mann, für den ich arbeite, … das Kind, mit dem ich spiele, …	die Frau, an die ich denke, … die Leute, über die ich spreche, …

▶ The relative pronoun is never omitted in German, unlike English.

▶ In a few contexts, **was is used as a relative pronoun** rather than *der*:

after the **demonstrative** *das*	**Ich hörte nichts von dem, was er sagte.** *I heard nothing of what he said.*
after *alles, etwas, nichts, viel(es)*	**Das ist alles, was ich sagen will.** *That's all that I want to say.*
after a **neuter adjective used as a noun**	**Das war das Erste, was sie sagte.** *That was the first thing that she said.*
to **refer back** to a whole clause	**Es ist ihm gelungen, was mich sehr erstaunt.** *He succeeded, which amazed me.*

▶ *was* is not normally used in combination with prepositions. Instead, the compound form **wo(r)** + PREPOSITION is used, e.g. *wovon, womit, worüber* (see **5.5**):

Genau *das* ist es, wofür ich mich interessiere.	*That's precisely what interests me.*
Das ist *alles*, woran ich mich erinnere.	*That's all I can remember.*
Sie liebt ihn, worüber Emil sich gar nicht freut.	*She loves him, which Emil is not pleased about.*

10.6 Infinitive clauses

Infinitive clauses are a type of subordinate clause that is constructed with the verb in the **INFINITIVE** form rather than with a **FINITE VERB**.

▶ In such constructions the infinitive is **preceded by *zu***, similar to English 'to' with an infinitive, and placed at the **end of the clause**:

| **Ich habe ihr geraten zum Arzt zu gehen.** | *I advised her to go to the doctor.* |
| **Es wird nicht leicht sein ihn davon zu überzeugen.** | *It won't be easy to convince him of it.* |

▶ With **SEPARABLE VERBS**, the *zu* is placed **between the prefix and the verb**, with the whole written as a single word:

| **Sie hatte vor ihren Freund anzurufen.** | *She intended to phone her friend.* |
| **Ich würde es vorziehen sofort wegzugehen.** | *I would prefer to leave straight away.* |

▶ If the infinitive is being used with an **AUXILIARY VERB** or a **MODAL AUXILIARY VERB**, the *zu* is placed **after the main verb** and **before the auxiliary verb**:

Er behauptet die Wahrheit gesagt zu haben.	*He claims to have told the truth.*
Ihr gefällt es nicht betrogen zu werden.	*She doesn't like being deceived.*
Es freut mich Sie hier begrüßen zu dürfen.	*It is a pleasure to be able to welcome you here.*

▶ Infinitive clauses most often **substitute** for a NOUN or NOUN PHRASE and can be used in the same way as clauses with *dass*:

verb subject	**Ihn *zu* überzeugen war völlig unmöglich.** **Eine Sprache *zu* erlernen ist nicht schwer.**	*It was impossible to convince him.* *It isn't difficult to learn a language.*
accusative object	**Ich riet ihr nach Hause *zu* gehen.** **Tom versprach ihr sie mitzunehmen.**	*I suggested she should go home.* *Tom promised to take her along.*
prepositional object	**Er träumte davon zum Mond *zu* fliegen.** **Sie bestanden darauf ihn *zu* interviewen.**	*He dreamed of going to the moon.* *They insisted on interviewing him.*
dependent on noun or adj.	**Er gab mir die Erlaubnis hierzubleiben.** **Ellen war bereit ihn nach Hause *zu* fahren.**	*He gave me permission to stay here.* *Ellen was willing to drive him home.*

▶ Infinitive clauses are usually quite **separate** from the clause they depend on.

They normally **follow all parts of the verb** in the clause they depend on and are not enclosed inside it:

Sie hatte beschlossen vor dem Rathaus *zu* warten. **NOT**: *Sie hatten vor dem Rathaus zu warten beschlossen.	*She had decided to wait in front of* *the town hall.*
Es fing um fünf Uhr früh an stark *zu* regnen. **NOT**: *Es fing um fünf Uhr früh stark zu regnen an.	*It began to rain hard at five o'clock in* *the morning.*
Ich weiß, dass sie versprochen hat ihm *zu* helfen. **NOT**: *Ich weiß, dass sie ihm zu helfen versprochen hat.	*I know that she promised to help him.*

However, separable prefixes can follow the infinitive clause if this only consists of *zu* plus the infinitive:

Es fing an *zu* regnen.	**OR**	**Es fing *zu* regnen an.**

Anticipatory es

An infinitive clause which is being used as the subject or object of a verb is often **anticipated by *es*** in the **preceding clause**:

Es fällt ihm nicht ein sich *zu* entschuldigen.	*It doesn't occur to him to apologize.*
Ihm fällt (es) nicht ein sich *zu* entschuldigen.	*It doesn't occur to him to apologize.*
Wichtig ist (es) den Begriff richtig *zu* verstehen.	*It's important to understand the term correctly.*

This 'anticipatory' *es* is common with a number of verbs, but it is only essential as a subject in initial position before the main verb, as in the first example above.

Infinitive clause preceded by prepositional adverb

An infinitive clause which depends on a verb, noun or adjective followed by a preposition is often **anticipated in the preceding clause** by a PREPOSITIONAL ADVERB, i.e. the compound of *da(r)* + PREPOSITION (see **5.5**):

Er hatte oft davon geträumt, allein auf dieser Insel zu sein.   *He'd often dreamed of being alone on this island.*
Wir haben uns darüber gefreut, euch wiederzusehen.   *We were pleased to see you again.*
Wir sind dazu bereit, Ihnen darüber Auskunft zu geben.   *We're prepared to give you information about this.*

This prepositional adverb is most often included in written German, but in speech it is often dropped especially with many common verbs.

10.7 Infinitive clauses after prepositions

An infinitive with *zu* is used after a few PREPOSITIONS: *(an)statt*, *außer*, *ohne* and *um*. The preposition is placed at the **beginning** of the clause (forming the first part of a 'bracket construction', see **9.1**) and the infinitive with *zu* at the **end**:

(an)statt ... zu   instead of
Er stand einfach da, (an)statt ihnen zu helfen.   *He just stood there instead of helping them.*

A clause with the conjunction *(an)statt dass* is an alternative. The subject must be the same for both clauses in either construction:

Er las Zeitung, (an)statt dass er das Auto reparierte.   *He read the newspaper instead of repairing the car.*

ausser ... zu   except, besides
Was konnten wir tun, außer heftig zu protestieren?   *What could we do except protest vehemently?*

If the subject of the clause is different from that of the main clause, the conjunction *außer dass* is used:

Ich habe nichts erfahren, außer dass sie abgereist ist.   *I couldn't find anything out, except that she has gone away.*

ohne ... zu   without

Er verließ das Haus, ohne von Emilie gesehen zu werden.
He left the house without being seen by Emilie.

If the subject of the clause is different from that of the main clause, the conjunction **ohne dass** is used:

Er verließ das Haus, ohne dass Emilie ihn sah.
He left the house without Emilie seeing him.

um ... zu in order to = *purpose*

Er zündete das Haus an, um die Versicherung zu kassieren.
He set fire to the house (in order) to collect on the insurance.

Da war kein Wasser, um das Feuer zu löschen.
There was no water to put the fire out.

NB In English it is not always necessary to say 'in order to' in such contexts – it is sufficient to say 'to'. In German it is normally necessary to use *um ... zu* if the idea of purpose is involved.

Um ... zu is also used after an adjective with *zu* or *genug*:

Er ist zu jung, um alles zu verstehen.
He is too young to understand everything.

Er ist alt genug, um alles zu verstehen.
He is old enough to understand everything.

NB If the subject of the two clauses is different, the conjunction *als dass* is used: **Er ist zu jung, als dass wir** *es ihm erklären könnten* (**He** is too young **for us** to be able to explain it to him).

10.8 The infinitive without *zu*

A few verbs can be followed by an **infinitive without *zu***. This infinitive is placed at the end of the main clause:

Ich darf heute nicht ausgehen.	*I'm not allowed to go out today.*
Ich sah ihn ins Zimmer kommen.	*I saw him come into the room.*
Er ließ mich das Buch behalten.	*He allowed me to keep the book.*
Ich musste heute früh aufstehen.	*I had to get up early today.*
Sie hörte das Kind weinen.	*She heard the child crying.*
Kommst du heute schwimmen?	*Are you coming swimming today?*

This 'bare infinitive' construction is used with the **following verbs**:

▶ The **modal auxiliaries** (see section **7.13**)

Wir können es nicht verhindern.	*We can't prevent it.*
Das sollte eine Überraschung sein.	*That was intended to be a surprise.*

▶ The verbs of **perception**, *sehen*, *fühlen*, *hören* and *spüren*

Ich sah sie aus dem Haus kommen.	*I saw her coming out of the house.*
Ich hörte sie durch das Haus gehen.	*I heard her going through the house.*

With these verbs, a clause with *wie* is a common alternative to the construction with the infinitive: *Ich sah, wie sie aus dem Haus kam.*

▶ *lassen*, which has two principal meanings when used with a bare infinitive

- 'let', 'allow'

Sie ließ mich ins Zimmer kommen.	*She let me come into the room.*
Lass mich bitte morgen ausschlafen.	*Please let me sleep in tomorrow.*

In this sense, *lassen* is often used with a reflexive *sich* with the force of a passive to express a possibility (see section **7.9**):

Das lässt sich leicht ändern.	*That can easily be changed.*
Das Problem lässt sich leicht lösen.	*The problem can be solved easily.*

- 'cause', 'make'

Sie ließ den Schlosser die Tür reparieren.	*She had the locksmith fix the door.*
Die Nachricht ließ ihn erblassen.	*The news made him turn pale.*

▶ Some verbs of **motion**, notably *gehen, kommen, fahren, schicken*

Ich ging mir die Hände waschen.	*I went to wash my hands.*
Sie fuhr vormittags einkaufen.	*She went shopping in the morning.*
Sie schickte den Großvater einkaufen.	*She sent grandfather shopping.*

▶ The verbs *helfen, lehren, lernen*

Sie half der alten Frau aufstehen.	*She helped the old woman to get up.*
Er lehrte mich schreiben.	*He taught me to write.*
Beim Militär lernte er Russisch sprechen.	*In the army he learnt to speak Russian.*

With these verbs **either** the bare infinitive **or** an infinitive with *zu* is possible, e.g. *Beim Militär lernte er Russisch zu sprechen*. The construction with *zu* tends to be preferred if the infinitive clause is relatively long:

Sie half der alten Frau ihren Koffer bis zum Auto zu tragen.
She helped the old woman carry her suitcase to the car.
Er lehrte mich diese komplizierte Maschine fachmännisch zu bedienen.
He taught me to use this complicated machine in an expert fashion.
Beim Militär lernte er diese schweren Lastwagen zu fahren.
He learned to drive these heavy lorries when he was in the army.

COMPLEX SENTENCES IN CONTEXT

Amerika

Als der sechzehnjährige Karl Rossmann, der von seinen armen Eltern nach Amerika geschickt worden war, weil ihn ein Dienstmädchen verführt und ein Kind von ihm bekommen hatte, in dem schon langsam gewordenen Schiff in den Hafen von New York

einfuhr, erblickte er die schon längst beobachtete Statue der Freiheitsgöttin wie in einem plötzlich stärker gewordenen Sonnenlicht. Ihr Arm mit dem Schwert ragte wie neuerdings empor, und um ihre Gestalt wehten die freien Lüfte.

»So hoch!« sagte er sich und wurde, wie er so gar nicht an das Weggehen dachte, von der immer mehr anschwellenden Menge der Gepäckträger, die an ihm vorüberzogen, allmählich bis an das Bordgeländer geschoben.

Ein junger Mann, mit dem er während der Fahrt flüchtig bekannt geworden war, sagte im Vorübergehen: »Ja, haben Sie denn noch keine Lust, auszusteigen?« »Ich bin doch fertig«, sagte Karl, ihn anlachend, und hob aus Übermut, und weil er ein starker Junge war, seinen Koffer auf die Achsel. Aber wie er über seinen Bekannten hinsah, der ein wenig seinen Stock schwenkend sich schon mit den andern entfernte, merkte er bestürzt, dass er seinen eigenen Regenschirm unten im Schiff vergessen hatte. Er bat schnell den Bekannten, der nicht sehr beglückt schien, um die Freundlichkeit, bei seinem Koffer einen Augenblick zu warten, überblickte noch die Situation, um sich bei der Rückkehr zurechtzufinden, und eilte davon.

(Aus: Franz Kafka, *Der Heizer*)

MAIN CLAUSE (finite verb appears as **second** element)

Can be linked by coordinating conjunction, e.g. *und*	[Als…,] **erblickte** er die Statue.
	Er **wurde** bis an das Bordgeländer **geschoben**.
	Ein junger Mann **sagte** [etwas].
	Ich **bin** fertig.
	Karl **hob** aus Übermut seinen Koffer auf die Achsel.
	[Wie…,] **merkte** er [es] bestürzt.
	Er **bat** den Bekannten um die Freundlichkeit.
	Er **überblickte** die Situation.
	Ihr Arm **ragte empor** *und* um ihre Gestalt **wehten** die Lüfte.

NB The **finite verb** is in red. **Other parts of the verb** are in bold.

SUBORDINATE CLAUSE (finite verb appears as **last** element)

***dass*-clauses**	…, *dass* er seinen Regenschirm **vergessen** hatte.
other subordinating conjunctions	*Als* Karl in den Hafen **einfuhr**, …
	…, *wie/als* er so gar nicht an das Weggehen **dachte**, …
	…, *weil* ihn ein Dienstmädchen **verführt** hatte, …
	…, *weil* er ein starker Junge **war**, …
	Wie/Als er über seinen Bekannten **hinsah**, …
relative clauses (introduced by relative pronoun)	…[Karl Rossmann], *der* nach Amerika **geschickt worden war**, …
	…[Gepäckträger], *die* an ihm **vorüberzogen**, …
	[Ein junger Mann], mit *dem* er **bekannt geworden war**, …
	[… seinen Bekannten …], *der* sich **entfernte**, …
	[… den Bekannten …], *der* nicht **beglückt schien**, …

INFINITIVE CLAUSE (infinitive with *zu* appears as **last** element)

[Sie haben keine Lust] **auszusteigen**.
[Er bat den Bekannten um die Freundlichkeit], bei seinem Koffer *zu* **warten**.
[Er überblickte die Situation], *um* sich **zurechtzufinden**.

Word formation 11

Knowing how complex words are made up in German is invaluable for extending your vocabulary. It allows you to **deduce the meaning** of a whole word from its parts, or to **recognize patterns** like *Dank – danken – dankbar – Dankbarkeit – Undankbarkeit*. Series of words like this are often more transparent in German, as we see when we compare the words above with their English equivalents: **thanks – to thank – grateful – gratitude – ingratitude**. Moreover, German is immensely rich in its patterns of word formation, so you can expand your vocabulary very efficiently by building up 'word maps' – e.g., by writing related words on cards using a system of arrows and colours.

It is a help, too, if you know the forms of the strong and irregular verbs (see **6.11**) since these often clarify such patterns: for example, the past tense of *sprechen* (*sprach*) gives you *die Sprache* and *das Gespräch*, and the past tense of *stehen* (*stand*) gives you *der Stand, standhaft, der Abstand, der Beistand, das Verständnis*, etc.

This chapter shows you the most common ways of **making up new words** in German:

◆ the basics of word formation (**11.1**)

◆ word formation: NOUNS (**11.2**)

◆ compounding (**11.3**)

◆ word formation: ADJECTIVES (**11.4**)

◆ word formation: VERBS (**11.5–11.8**).

11.1 The basics of word formation

New words are constructed in German in three main ways:

▶ by **adding** a PREFIX or a SUFFIX to a ROOT word

PREFIXES are most often used to create NOUNS from nouns, ADJECTIVES from adjectives, and VERBS from nouns, adjectives or other verbs:

prefixes			
der Instinkt	*instinct*	→ **der Urinstinkt**	*original instinct*
interessant	*interesting*	→ **uninteressant**	*uninteresting*
stören	*disturb*	→ **zerstören**	*destroy*
groß	*big, large*	→ **vergrößern**	*enlarge*

Suffixes are most often used to create **nouns** from adjectives or verbs, and **adjectives** from nouns or verbs. They are less common in forming verbs:

suffixes			
krank	*ill*	→ die **Krank**heit	*illness*
bedeuten	*mean*	→ die Bedeutung	*meaning*
der Freund	*friend*	→ freundlich	*friendly*
denken	*think*	→ denkbar	*thinkable*
das Ideal	*ideal*	→ idealisieren	*idealize*

▶ by **changing a vowel**

Umlaut occurs very often in word formation, sometimes in **combination with a suffix**:

Umlaut			
der Arzt	*doctor*	→ die Ärztin	*woman doctor*
der Bart	*beard*	→ bärtig	*bearded*
der Druck	*pressure*	→ drücken	*press*
scharf	*sharp*	→ schärfen	*sharpen*

Other vowel changes in word formation relate to the changes in the tenses of strong verbs. They are usually found with the **roots** of **strong verbs**, sometimes with a **suffix** as well:

strong verb vowel changes			
beißen	*bite*	→ der Biss	*bite*
		→ bissig	*biting, vicious*
binden	*bind, tie*	→ das Band	*ribbon, bond*
		→ das Bündnis	*alliance*
schwingen	*swing*	→ der Schwung	*swing, impetus*
		→ schwungvoll	*spirited*

▶ by **compounding**

Compounding involves putting two (or more) words together to form a new word. It is most commonly used to form **nouns**, but there are compound adjectives and verbs, too:

compounding			
der Staub + saugen	*dust + suck*	→ der Staubsauger	*vacuum cleaner*
der Rat + das Haus	*council + house*	→ das Rathaus	*town hall*
hell + blau	*light + blue*	→ hellblau	*light blue*
die Brust + schwimmen	*breast + swim*	→ brustschwimmen	*do breast-stroke*

11.2 The formation of nouns

▶ PREFIXES used to form nouns usually **narrow down the meaning** of the root noun in some way:

Erz-	*arch-, out and out*	der Feind → der Erzfeind *arch enemy*
Fehl-	*opposite or negative*	die Kalkulation → die Fehlkalkulation *miscalculation*
Ge- ... -(-e) (vowel change)	*from nouns: collectives*	der Berg → das Gebirge *mountain range* der Stern → das Gestirn *stars, constellation (of stars)*
Ge- ... -(-e)	*from verbs: repeated action*	schwätzen → das Geschwätz *chattering, drivel*
Grund-	*basic, essential*	die Tendenz → die Grundtendenz *basic tendency*
Haupt-	*main*	der Bahnhof → der Hauptbahnhof *main station*
Miss-	*opposite or negative*	der Brauch → der Missbrauch *misuse*
Mit-	*co-, fellow-*	der Reisende → der Mitreisende *fellow traveller*
Nicht-	*non-*	der Raucher → der Nichtraucher *non-smoker*
Riesen-	*augmentative (=huge)*	der Erfolg → der Riesenerfolg *huge success*
Schein-	*not real, imaginary*	der Erfolg → der Scheinerfolg *illusory success*
Un-	*opposite, abnormal*	der Mensch → der Unmensch *inhuman person*
Ur-	*original*	die Sprache → die Ursprache *original language*

▶ Many other '**augmentative**' prefixes are common in colloquial German, indicating that something is huge, enormous or important, often excessively so, e.g. *Affengeschwindigkeit, Bombengeschäft, Heidenlärm, Höllendurst, Mordsapparat, Spitzenbelastung, Superhit, Teufelskerl, Topmanager.*

▶ SUFFIXES commonly used to form nouns are almost always linked to a particular GENDER (see **2.2–2.4**):

-chen, -lein (+Umlaut) neuter	diminutives from nouns	die Stadt → das Städtchen *little town* das Buch → das Büchlein *little book*
-e (+Umlaut) feminine	abstract nouns from adjectives	groß → die Größe *size* lang → die Länge *length*
-e feminine	action or instrument from verbs	absagen → die Absage *refusal* bremsen → die Bremse *brake*
-ei feminine	place where something is done	der Bäcker → die Bäckerei *bakery* Bücher (pl.) → die Bücherei *library*
-erei feminine	annoying repeated action, from verbs	schreien → die Schreierei *constant screaming* angeben → die Angeberei *excessive boasting*

-er masculine	person performing an action, from verbs	fahren → der **Fahrer** *driver* lehren → der **Lehrer** *teacher*
-heit/-(ig)keit feminine	abstract nouns from adjectives	gesund → die **Gesundheit** *health* genau → die **Genauigkeit** *precision*
-in (+Umlaut) feminine	feminine person/ animal, from nouns	der Lehrer → die **Lehrerin** *female teacher* der Hund → die **Hündin** *bitch*
-schaft feminine	abstract or collective nouns, from nouns	der Freund → die **Freundschaft** *friendship* der Graf → die **Grafschaft** *county*
-tum neuter	collective nouns or categories	der Bürger → das **Bürgertum** *middle classes* der König → das **Königtum** *monarchy*
-ung feminine	nouns from verbs denoting the action	bedeuten → die **Bedeutung** *meaning* landen → die **Landung** *landing*

▶ Many nouns can be formed from VERBS (especially strong verbs) without a suffix, but often with a **vowel change** like that in the past tense of strong verbs. They usually express the **process** or **result** of the action. Almost all these nouns are MASCULINE:

ausgehen	→ der **Ausgang** *exit*	**schließen**	→ der **Schluss** *close*
brechen	→ der **Bruch** *break*	**schneiden**	→ der **Schnitt** *cut*
ersetzen	→ der **Ersatz** *replacement*	**stechen**	→ der **Stich** *stab, sting*

▶ The INFINITIVE of almost any verb can be used as a noun. These are always NEUTER and simply refer to the **action of the verb**, often corresponding to the English **-ing** form used as a noun:

das Bellen des Hundes	*the barking of the dog*
die Kunst des Schreibens	*the art of writing*
nach langem Warten	*after waiting a long time*

These infinitival nouns are often **compounded**: *das Zeitunglesen* 'reading the newspaper', *das Schlafengehen* 'going to bed'.

▶ Present and past PARTICIPLES, and many other ADJECTIVES, can be used as nouns. They have the **endings of adjectives** (see also **4.3**).

PRESENT PARTICIPLES used as nouns indicate a person actually carrying out the **action of the verb**:

der/die Reisende	*the person travelling*
der/die Lesende	*the person reading*
der/die Schlafende	*the person sleeping*

PAST PARTICIPLES used as nouns indicate **persons** who have done something or had something done to them, or **things** which have been done:

der/die Zugezogene	*new resident*
der/die Verlobte	*fiancé(e)*
das Vereinbarte	*something agreed*

11.3 Compound nouns

The ease with which compound nouns can be formed is a characteristic of German, and the use of compounds has increased over the last hundred years, so that even complex words like *Fahrpreisermäßigung* (fare reduction) or *Autobahnraststätte* (motorway service station/ restaurant) are in everyday use.

▶ Almost **any part of speech** can combine with a NOUN to form a compound. Compounds always have the GENDER of the **last element**:

noun + noun	**das Haar + die Bürste**	→ **die Haarbürste** *hairbrush*
adjective + noun	**edel + der Stein**	→ **der Edelstein** *jewel*
numeral + noun	**drei + der Fuß**	→ **der Dreifuß** *tripod*
verb + noun	**hören + der Saal**	→ **der Hörsaal** *lecture theatre*
preposition + noun	**unter + die Tasse**	→ **die Untertasse** *saucer*
adverb + noun	**jetzt + die Zeit**	→ **die Jetztzeit** *present day*

▶ Many noun + noun compounds need a **linking element**:

-e-	**das Pferd + der Stall**	→ **der Pferdestall** *stable*
-(e)s-	**das Kalb + das Leder**	→ **das Kalbsleder** *calf leather*
-(e)n-	**die Scheibe + der Wischer**	→ **der Scheibenwischer** *windscreen wiper*
-er-	**das Kind + der Garten**	→ **der Kindergarten** *kindergarten*

There are no fixed rules as to when you use one of these linking elements and you need to **learn the link** with each word.

▶ Although German forms compound nouns very readily, you need to be aware that you cannot simply put any two words together.

A compound always indicates a **type** of something, so *Krankenhaus* is a type of *Haus*, and *Schreibtisch* a type of *Tisch*. But a compound like **Blauhimmel* for 'blue sky' is not possible, because it is not a type of *Himmel* – it simply describes the sky, so you have to use the adjective with the noun as in English: *der blaue Himmel.*

In particular, ADJECTIVE + NOUN compounds are quite restricted and tend to have **special meanings** which are not just the sum of their parts. In this way, *eine Großstadt* is something more than simply *eine große Stadt* (officially, a city with more than 100 000 inhabitants) and *ein Junggeselle* 'bachelor' is not necessarily *jung*.

11.4 The formation of adjectives

▶ The following SUFFIXES are commonly used to form adjectives. Many of them have multiple meanings:

-bar	adjectives from verbs with the sense of English *-able, -ible*	brauchen → brauchbar *usable* essen → essbar *edible*
-en/-ern (-ern + Umlaut)	adjectives from nouns showing what something is made of	das Gold → golden *golden* das Holz → hölzern *wooden*
-haft	adjectives from nouns for persons indicating a quality (*like a …*)	der Held → heldenhaft *heroic* der Meister → meisterhaft *masterly*
-ig	adjectives from nouns indicating a quality (*like a …*)	das Eis → eisig *icy* das Haar → haarig *hairy*
-ig	adjectives from adverbs	dort → dortig *of/from there* heute → heutig *of today*
-ig (+Umlaut)	adjectives from time nouns indicating duration	drei Tage → dreitägig *lasting three days*
-isch (usu. + Umlaut)	adjectives from proper names and geographical names	Europa → europäisch *European* Sachsen → sächsisch *Saxon*
-isch	adjectives from nouns indicating a quality (often pejorative)	das Kind → kindisch *childish, puerile* der Wähler → wählerisch *choosy*
-isch	adjectives from foreign nouns	die Biologie → biologisch *biological* die Mode → modisch *fashionable*
-lich (often + Umlaut)	adjectives from nouns indicating a quality or a relationship	der Arzt → ärztlich *medical* der Tod → tödlich *fatal*
-lich (often + Umlaut)	adjectives from time nouns indicating frequency	der Tag → täglich *daily* die Stunde → stündlich *hourly*
-lich (often + Umlaut)	adjectives from verbs indicating ability, like *-able, -ible*, cf. -bar	bestechen → bestechlich *corruptible* verkaufen → verkäuflich *saleable*
-lich (often + Umlaut)	adjectives from adjectives indicating a lesser degree	klein → kleinlich *petty* rot → rötlich *reddish*
-los	adjectives from nouns indicating a lack of something	das Leben → leblos *lifeless* der Geschmack → geschmacklos *tasteless*
-mäßig	adjectives from nouns *in respect of / in accordance with*	der Plan → planmäßig *according to plan* der Verkehr → verkehrsmäßig *relating to traffic*

„Ich finde deine Geschenkverpackung geschmacklos!"

Many adjectives in modern German are built up with SUFFIXES which were originally **words in their own right**, but are now suffixed to a large number of nouns, and new ones are being created regularly:

having sth.	**rücksichtsvoll** *considerate*	**charakterstark** *of firm character*	**erlebnisreich** *eventful*
lacking sth.	**fettarm** *low-fat*	**alkoholfrei** *non-alcoholic*	**gedankenleer** *lacking in ideas*
protected from sth.	**hitzefest** *heatproof*	**kugelsicher** *bulletproof*	**waschecht** *washable, true-blue*
similar to sth.	**ringförmig** *circular, ringlike*	**lederartig** *leathery*	**maskenartig** *mask-like*
capable of sth.	**strapazierfähig** *hard-wearing*		
worth(y) of sth.	**nachahmenswürdig** *worthy of imitation*	**lesenswert** *worth reading*	
needing sth.	**korrekturbedürftig** *requiring correction*		

▶ Two common PREFIXES are used to form adjectives:

un-	**opposite (like English** *un-, im-, etc.)*	**reif** **möglich**	→ **unreif** *unripe* → **unmöglich** *impossible*
ur-	**intensifying meaning**	**alt**	→ **uralt** *very old*

▶ A number of PREFIXES used with adjectives, especially in colloquial German, have an **intensifying** meaning:

erzreaktionär **hochintelligent** **höchstbegabt**	*ultra-reactionary* *highly intelligent* *extremely talented*	**grundehrlich** **supercool** **affengeil**	*thoroughly honest* *really cool* *brilliant*

11.5 Inseparable verb prefixes

Verbs can be formed **from nouns or adjectives or other verbs** by the INSEPARABLE PREFIXES *be-, ent-/emp-, er-, ge-, miss-, ver-* and *zer-*.

▶ These prefixes are **unstressed** and always remain **attached** to the ROOT.

▶ The PAST PARTICIPLES of these verbs **do not add** *ge-*.

▶ In INFINITIVE CLAUSES (see **10.6**), *zu* **comes before the verb**:

Sie hat **versprochen ihn zu besuchen**.	*She promised to visit him.*

Most of these prefixes have a number of possible meanings. The verbs formed in this way can in turn form nouns, adjectives, adverbs and other verbs, e.g. *verstehen – Verstand – Verständnis – verständig – verständigen – verständnisvoll.*

Be-

▶ Makes intransitive verbs TRANSITIVE. The dative object or prepositional object of the root verb becomes the **accusative object of the verb with** *be-*:

jdn. **be**dienen	*serve sb.*	← *jemandem dienen*
eine Frage **be**antworten	*answer a question*	← *auf eine Frage antworten*
etw. **be**kämpfen	*combat sth.*	← *gegen etwas kämpfen*

▶ Makes verbs from nouns with the idea of **providing** with something. The vowel may have *Umlaut*, and the suffix *-ig-* is sometimes added:

bewässern	*irrigate*	← *das Wasser*
benachrichtigen	*notify*	← *die Nachricht*

▶ Makes verbs from adjectives with the idea of **endowing** something with that **quality**. The suffix *-ig-* is sometimes added:

befeuchten	*moisten*	← *feucht*
begradigen	*straighten*	← *gerade*

Ent-, emp-

The prefix *emp-* is a variety of *ent-*, but is only used with a few verbs: *empfangen, empfehlen, empfinden.*

▶ *Ent-* makes verbs from verbs of motion with the idea of **escaping** or **taking something away** with that motion (usually with a dative object):

jdm./etw. **ent**laufen	*run away from sb./sth.*	← *laufen*
jdm. etw. **ent**reißen	*snatch sth. from sb.*	← *reißen*

▶ Makes verbs from nouns or adjectives with the idea of **removing** something. Some of these verbs have *Umlaut*:

entgiften	*decontaminate* (take poison away)	← *das Gift*
enthärten	*soften*	← *hart*
entmilitarisieren	*demilitarize*	← *militarisieren*

Er-

▶ Makes verbs from nouns or other verbs with the idea of **gaining** something in that way:

etw. erbitten	*get sth. by asking for it*	← *bitten*
etw. erarbeiten	*get sth. by working for it*	← *die Arbeit*
etw. erforschen	*find out sth. by research*	← *forschen*

▶ Makes verbs from adjectives to express a **change of state** (i.e. 'becoming sth' or 'making sb. sth'):

erblinden	*go blind*	← *blind*
erröten	*blush (become red)*	← *rot*
erleichtern	*make easier*	← *leichter*

Ge-

▶ This prefix is no longer 'productive', i.e. no new verbs are formed with *ge-*. The following verbs are common:

gebrauchen	*use*	gehören	*belong*
gefallen	*please, like*	genießen	*enjoy*
gehorchen	*obey*	geschehen	*happen*

Miss-

▶ Makes verbs from verbs with the meaning '**opposite**', '**wrongly**':

missachten	*ignore, despise*	← *achten*
misshandeln	*ill-treat*	← *handeln*

Ver-

▶ Makes verbs from verbs with the idea of **finishing** or **going away**:

verblühen	*fade* (finish flowering)	← *blühen*
verhungern	*starve to death*	← *hungern*
verklingen	*fade away* (finish sounding)	← *klingen*

▶ Makes verbs from verbs with the idea of '**wrongly**' or '**to excess**':

verbiegen	*bend out of shape*	← *biegen*
verlernen	*forget how to do* (unlearn)	← *lernen*
versalzen	*over-salt* (put excessive salt on)	← *salzen*

▶ Makes verbs from nouns or adjectives to express a **change of state** (i.e. 'becoming sth.' or 'making sb. sth.'):

versklaven	*enslave*	← *der Sklave*
verlängern	*lengthen*	← *länger*
vereinfachen	*simplify*	← *einfach*

▶ Makes verbs from nouns with the idea of **providing somebody or something with something**:

| verglasen | *glaze* (provide with glass) | ← *das Glas* |
| verzaubern | *enchant* (make magical) | ← *der Zauber* |

Zer-

▶ Makes verbs from verbs with the idea of '**in pieces**':

| zerbeißen | *bite into pieces* | ← *beißen* |
| zerfallen | *fall to pieces, disintegrate* | ← *fallen* |

11.6 Separable verb prefixes

Verbs can be formed **from other verbs** by SEPARABLE PREFIXES (see also **6.4**). Most separable verb prefixes come from PREPOSITIONS or simple ADVERBS, and their meaning when linked with a root verb is often quite obvious, e.g. *abfahren* 'drive away', *hinauslaufen* 'run out', *mitkommen* 'come with sb.'.

▶ These prefixes are **stressed**.

▶ In the simple tenses (PRESENT, PAST), the prefix **separates from the verb** ROOT if it is in a main clause, and is placed at the end of the clause.

▶ In the PAST PARTICIPLE the syllable *ge-* is inserted **between the prefix and the verb**.

▶ In INFINITIVE CLAUSES (see **10.6**), *zu* is inserted **between the prefix and the verb**.

| Er **lief** im Schlafanzug **hinaus** | *He ran outside in his pyjamas.* |
| Sie hat **vorgeschlagen** ihn heute abend **ein**zuladen. | *She suggested inviting him this evening.* |

COMMON SEPARABLE PREFIXES

ab-	*away, down or off*	**absetzen** *put down* **abdrehen** *switch off*
an-	*at, on, starting, approaching or doing something partially*	**anreden** *address* (speak to/at) **andrehen** *switch on*
auf-	*up, on, open, or a sudden start*	**aufessen** *eat up* **auflachen** *burst out laughing*
aus-	*out, off, from, often the completion of an action*	**ausbrennen** *burn out* **ausdorren** *dry up*
ein-	*in(to), become accustomed to sth.*	**einfahren** *run in* (new car) **sich einleben** *settle down*
entgegen-	*towards*	**entgegenkommen** *come towards*
fort-	*away*	**fortbleiben** *stay away*
hinzu-	*in addition*	**hinzusagen** *add* (say in addition)
los-	*off, setting out*	**losgehen** *set off, start*
mit-	*with*	**mitarbeiten** *cooperate*
nach-	*after, often imitating or repeating*	**nachmachen** *copy, do the same*
vor-	*ahead, forward, demonstrating*	**vorgehen** *go on ahead* **vormachen** *show sb. how to do sth.*
weg-	*away*	**weglaufen** *run away*
zu-	*to, towards, closing*	**zusehen** *look at/towards, watch* **zumachen** *shut*
zurück-	*back*	**zurückfahren** *drive back*
zusammen-	*together, up, down*	**zusammensetzen** *put together* **zusammenfalten** *fold up* **zusammenbrechen** *collapse*

11.7 Variable verb prefixes

A few prefixes can be used to form **SEPARABLE** or **INSEPARABLE VERBS**. There is usually a difference in meaning, with the separable verb tending to have the more concrete, physical meaning. The separable prefix is stressed (e.g. '*über*setzen, 'ferry across, cross (water)') whereas the inseparable prefix is unstressed (e.g. *über'setzen*, 'translate').

Durch-

▶ **SEPARABLE** verbs with *durch-* usually have the idea of '**all the way through**':

'durchblicken	*look through*	'durchfahren	*drive (right) through*
'durchfallen	*fall through, fail*	'durchrosten	*rust through*

▶ INSEPARABLE verbs with *durch-* usually have the idea of **penetrating** into something without necessarily going all the way through:

durch'dringen	*penetrate*	durch'setzen	*infiltrate*
durch'reisen	*travel through*	durch'wachen	*remain awake*

Particularly with verbs of motion, the distinction between separable and inseparable verbs with *durch-* can be very slight.

Hinter-

▶ Verbs with *hinter-* '**behind**' are normally INSEPARABLE:

hinter'gehen	*deceive*	hinter'lassen	*bequeath, leave*

▶ SEPARABLE verbs with *hinter-* are regional and colloquial, e.g. (Austrian) 'hintergehen 'go to the back'.

Über-

▶ SEPARABLE verbs with *über-* are usually intransitive, with the literal meaning '**over**':

'überfahren	*cross over*	'überkochen	*boil over*
'überhängen	*overhang*	'überlaufen	*overflow, desert*

▶ INSEPARABLE verbs with *über-* are usually transitive, with a rather less literal meaning:

über'arbeiten	*rework*	über'setzen	*translate*
über'treiben	*exaggerate*	über'sehen	*overlook*

Um-

▶ SEPARABLE verbs with *um-* usually express the idea of **turning**, or a **change of state**:

'umblicken	*look round*	'umschreiben	*rewrite*
'umdrehen	*turn round*	'umsteigen	*change* (trains, etc.)

▶ INSEPARABLE verbs with *um-* express **encirclement** or **going round**:

um'armen	*embrace*	um'gehen	*avoid, go round*
um'geben	*surround*	um'schreiben	*paraphrase*

Unter-

▶ SEPARABLE verbs with *unter-* have the literal meaning '**under(neath)**':

'untergehen	*sink, decline*	'unterkommen	*find accommodation*
'unterlegen	*put underneath*	'untersetzen	*put underneath*

▶ INSEPARABLE verbs with *unter-* express the idea less than enough, or a variety of figurative meanings:

unter'schätzen	*underestimate*	**unter'brechen**	*interrupt*
unter'drücken	*suppress*	**unter'richten**	*teach*

Voll-

▶ SEPARABLE verbs with *voll-* normally have the literal meaning '**full**':

'vollstopfen	*cram full*	**'volltanken**	*fill up (petrol)*

▶ INSEPARABLE verbs with *voll-* mean '**complete**':

voll'bringen	*complete, achieve*	**voll'ziehen**	*execute, carry out*

Wider-

▶ Verbs with *wider-* '**against**' are mainly INSEPARABLE:

wider'legen	*refute*	**wider'stehen**	*resist*

▶ Only two verbs with *wider-* are SEPARABLE:

'widerhallen	*echo*	**'widerspiegeln**	*reflect*

Wieder-

▶ Verbs with *wieder-* '**again**' are mainly SEPARABLE:

'wiederkehren	*return*	**'wiedersehen**	*see again*

▶ Only one verb with *wieder-* is INSEPARABLE: *wieder'holen* 'repeat'.

11.8 Other ways of forming verbs

▶ Many verbs are formed from nouns or adjectives simply by **adding verb endings** to the ROOT (sometimes with *Umlaut*). The meaning is usually clearly related:

die Falte	→ **falten** *fold*	**grün**	→ **grünen** *become green*
der Film	→ **filmen** *film*	**hart**	→ **härten** *harden*
der Hammer	→ **hämmern** *hammer*	**reif**	→ **reifen** *ripen*
der Regen	→ **regnen** *rain*	**scharf**	→ **schärfen** *sharpen*
die Schraube	→ **schrauben** *screw*	**schwarz**	→ **schwärzen** *blacken*
die Tünche	→ **tünchen** *whitewash*	**trocken**	→ **trocknen** *dry*

▶ The SUFFIX -(*is*)*ieren* is mainly used to form verbs from originally **foreign** nouns and adjectives, but occurs with a few German roots:

das Ideal	→ **idealisieren** *idealize*	**brüsk**	→ **brüskieren** *snub*
das Interesse	→ **interessieren** *interest*	**halb**	→ **halbieren** *halve*
das Thema	→ **thematisieren** *take as a topic*	**ironisch**	→ **ironisieren** *ironize*

▶ Verbs ending in -*eln* (usually with ***Umlaut***) from other verbs, or from nouns or adjectives, express a **weaker** form of the action. They can be pejorative:

husten	→ **hüsteln** *cough slightly*	**der Sachse**	→ **sächseln** *talk like a Saxon*
lachen	→ **lächeln** *smile*	**fromm**	→ **frömmeln** *affect piety*
tanzen	→ **tänzeln** *prance*	**krank**	→ **kränkeln** *be sickly*

WORD FORMATION IN CONTEXT

DEUTSCHES

WÖRTERBUCH

VON

JACOB GRIMM UND WILHELM GRIMM

ABC, *n., die von den drei ersten buchstaben entnommne be-
nennung der ganzen reihe derselben, wie der name alphabet
nach den beiden ersten gebildet ist, mhd. âbc, â bê cê,* BEN.
1, 3. *doch wird in der grammatik und sonst im edlen sprach-
gebrauch stets* alphabet, abc *hingegen mehr von dem ersten
lernen der kinder gesagt.* er ist noch im abc; er kommt
nun aus dem abc. sie fiengen an das paternoster zu lernen,
wenn sie hetten das abc schon gelernt. PAULI *schimpf* 136*.
*es wird dann auch angewandt auf die anfangsgründe aller an-
dern erlernbaren dinge:*

bedenkt in wol und weh
dies goldne abc. GÖTHE 10, 218.

dasz Newton erst hier bemerkt, was zu dem abc der prisma-
tischen erfahrungen gehört. GÖTHE 59, 157; *er fängt mit einem
abc der empfindungen an.* J. PAUL *bücherschau* 1, 111.
ABCEBANK, *f.* auf der abcebank sitzen, *auf der untersten
schulbank.*
ABCEBUBE, *m. puer abecedarius, was* abcknabe, abceschütz.
ABCEBUCH, *n. das erste dem kind in die hände gegebne
buch, gewöhnlich mit lockenden und belehrenden bildern ge-
schmückt, früher mit heiligenbildern* (s. namenbüchlein). abce-
buchs angesicht, *unschuldiges, einfältiges aussehn, oder grell
und bunt gemahlt?* BÜRGER 40*.

Source: J. und W. Grimm, *Deutsches Wörterbuch*, 1854.

Die Dokumentation der Gegenwartssprache

Mit ihrem *Großen Wörterbuch der deutschen Sprache* legt die Dudenredaktion die sowohl aktuellste als auch umfassendste Dokumentation zum Wortschatz der deutschen Gegenwartssprache vor. Zur Bewältigung der komplexen lexikographischen Arbeit stand der Dudenredaktion neben einer umfassenden Fachbibliothek die Sprachkartei zur Verfügung.

Bei der Duden-Sprachkartei handelt es sich um eine in Jahrzehnten gewachsene Sammlung, die derzeit über drei Millionen Querbelege aus dem gegenwartssprachlichen deutschen Schrifttum enthält – auf ebenso vielen Karteikarten. Die Sprachbelege werden von einer wechselnden Zahl freiberuflich tätiger Exzerptorinnen und Exzerptoren nach Kriterien gesammelt, die von der Dudenredaktion vorgegeben werden. Diese »Sammler(innen)« sind unablässig auf der Suche nach neuen Wörtern, Wortbedeutungen und -verwendungsweisen. Parallel zum weiteren Ausbau dieser Zettelkartei entsteht eine entsprechende elektronische Datenbank.

Diese Datenbank eröffnet eine Vielzahl von Zugriffs- und Nutzungsmöglichkeiten und ist überdies mit dem elektronischen Redaktionssystem kompatibel. Darüber hinaus werden die vielfältigen Möglichkeiten genutzt, mithilfe des Internets in computerlesbar aufbereiteten Textkorpora und Datenbanken gezielt nach Wörtern und Wortformen zu suchen.

(Aus: *Duden. Das große Wörterbuch der deutschen Sprache*, 3. Auflage)

Abc [a(:)be(:)'tse:], das; -, - ⟨Pl. selten⟩ [mhd. ābēcē, abc, nach den ersten drei Buchstaben des Alphabets]: **1.** *festgelegte Reihenfolge aller Buchstaben der deutschen Sprache, Alphabet:* das Abc lernen, aufsagen. **2.** *Buch mit alphabetisch geordneten Stichwörtern:* Abc der Fotografie. **3.** *Anfangsgründe, Elemente:* dieses Wissen gehört zum Abc der Wirtschaft; das Abc der Unternehmensgründung beherrschten die beiden Entrepreneure aus dem Osten schneller als gedacht (SZ 19. 8. 98, 26).
ABC-Ab|wehr, die [ABC = Abk. für atomar, biologisch, chemisch]: *Abwehr gegen ABC-Kampfmittel.*
ABC-Ab|wehr|trup|pe, die: (bei der Bundeswehr) *Kampfunterstützungstruppe des Heeres, die bes. zum Entstrahlen, Entseuchen u. Entgiften eingesetzt wird.*
ABC-Alarm, der: *bei Einsatz von ABC-Kampfmitteln ausgelöster Alarm.*
Abc-Buch, das [zu ↑Abc] (veraltet): *Fibel.*

Source: *Duden*, 1999.

NOUN FORMATION

prefixes		
-e *(fem.)*	sprechen	→ die **Sprache**
	suchen	→ die **Suche**
-er *(masc.)*	sammeln	→ der **Sammler**
-in *(fem.)*	der Exzerptor	→ die **Exzerptorin**
	der Sammler	→ die **Sammlerin**
-keit *(fem.)*	möglich	→ die **Möglichkeit**
-tum *(neut.)*	die Schrift	→ das **Schrifttum**
-ung *(fem.)*	bewältigen	→ die **Bewältigung**
	sammeln	→ die **Sammlung**
	bedeuten	→ die **Bedeutung**

from verb stems	
arbeiten	→ die **Arbeit**
ausbauen	→ der **Ausbau**
belegen	→ der **Beleg**
formen	→ die **Form**
greifen	→ der **Griff**

compound nouns	
das Wort + der **Schatz**	→ der Wort**schatz**
das Wort + die **Form**	→ die Wort**form**
die Wörter *(pl.)* + das **Buch**	→ das Wörter**buch**
das Wort + die Verwendung + die **Weise**	→ die Wortverwendung**sweise**
die Gegenwart + die **Sprache**	→ die Gegenwarts**sprache**
die Sprache + der **Beleg**	→ der Sprach**beleg**
die Daten *(pl.)* + die **Bank**	→ die Daten**bank**

ADJECTIVE FORMATION

suffixes		
-bar	lesen	→ **lesbar**
-ig	die Tat	→ **tätig**
	die Vielfalt	→ **vielfältig**
-isch	die Elektronik	→ **elektronisch**
	der Lexikograph	→ **lexikographisch**
-lich	die Sprache	→ **sprachlich**
	der Beruf	→ **beruflich**

VERB FORMATION

inseparable prefixes		separable prefixes	
be-	bedeuten	auf-	aufbereiten
ent-	enthalten, entstehen, entsprechen	vor-	vorlegen, vorgeben
er-	eröffnen	zu-	zugreifen
ver-	verwenden		

Spoken and written German 12

This chapter tells you first about the most important features of **pronunciation**, **spelling** and **punctuation** in German. The last sections deal with the difference between spoken and written German and introduce the idea of REGISTER:

◆ the relationship between **pronunciation** and **spelling (12.1)**

◆ rules of **spelling (12.2–12.5)**

◆ rules of **punctuation (12.6–12.7)**

◆ REGISTER: spoken and written, formal and informal German **(12.8–12.11).**

12.1 The relationship between pronunciation and spelling

Try to develop a good German pronunciation from the start, with the help of a teacher – it's much easier to make yourself understood if you 'sound German'. Here it is only possible to outline the main features of the relationship between the pronunciation and spelling of the main **vowels** (**a**, **e**, **i** etc.) and **consonants** (**b**, **d**, **f** etc.). In general, German spelling reflects pronunciation more directly than is the case in English, and **most sounds are represented by a unique letter or group of letters**. However, in some cases this relationship is not precise.

Vowels

German vowels can be **short** or **long**. The difference between short and long vowels is much more distinct than in English – compare, for instance, *in* (short) and *ihn* (long) with English 'tin' and 'teen'. You need to make a conscious effort to **pronounce all German long vowels clearly**.

The indication of long and short vowels is the least consistent aspect of German spelling. The following general guidelines apply:

vowels are short	before more than one consonant	unten, Rippe, selten, Ebbe, Fluss
	before *sch* and *ch*	waschen, Fisch, Krach, Koch
vowels are long	before a single consonant	Tag, sagen, Igel, Mut, Fuß
	when followed by 'silent' *h*	wohnen, Bühne, Draht, Höhle
	when doubled	Saal, Boot, Beet, Haar, Tee

There are a few important variations on these guidelines:

▶ Some words in *sch* and *ch* have a **long** vowel: *Sprache, hoch, Buch, wusch*.

▶ The **long** 'i' vowel is most often spelled *ie*: *bieten, liegen*.

▶ **Inflected** words with a **long vowel in the** ROOT keep their long vowel before a consonantal ending: *sagte, hört*.

▶ Some common **short words** have a short vowel before a single consonant: *an, in, das, man*.

ä   is pronounced like *e* when **short**: *kräftig, mächtig*. When **long** it often has a distinctive pronunciation, like the vowel in English 'h**air**': *spät, während, zäh*. However, many German speakers simply pronounce it like long *e* and make no distinction between, for example, *zäh* and *Zeh*.

e, o   are **pure vowels** in German, e.g. *Beet, Boot*. The apparently similar English vowels in 'b**ai**t' and 'b**oa**t' are diphthongs and actually sound quite different. You should practise the German vowels carefully with a native speaker or your German teacher.

e   the typical unstressed vowel in German is usually spelled *-e*, e.g. *bedeuten, bitte*. It is pronounced like the unstressed English vowel (which is spelled in many different ways) in words like 'political' or 'pollen'.

er   **unstressed -er**, e.g. in *verbessert, bitter*, is pronounced as a vowel rather like southern British or American pronunciations of the vowel spelled 'u' in 'b**u**tter' and 'c**u**p'. It is not like English 'er' in words like 'farm**er**'. Listen carefully to the difference a German speaker makes between the unstressed vowels in *bitt**e*** and *bitt**er*** and practise these with your teacher.

u   is a **pure vowel**, e.g. *Fuß, Blut*. It is pronounced rather like English '**ooh**', but the lips are even more strongly pursed, and the tongue pulled further back in the mouth.

ö, ü   are pronounced differently from *o* and *u*, and you will need to practise that difference with a native speaker or your German teacher. The lips are strongly pursed for all four vowels. The difference in the sounds is produced by the tongue, which is at the back of the mouth for *o* and *u* and at the front for *ö* and *ü* (try producing *ü* by saying English '**ee**' but pursing your lips!).

y   is pronounced like *ü*: *typisch, Physik*.

Diphthongs

German has a number of diphthongs, where the sound changes from one vowel to another within a syllable. The shift is shown in the spelling by **combining two vowels**:

au   is pronounced similarly to the diphthong in English 'h**ou**se', though with a deeper 'a' sound, e.g. *Haus, laufen*.

ei, ai   are pronounced like the English pronoun 'I', e.g. *Feile, Mai*. The diphthong *ei* needs to be carefully distinguished from *ie*, which simply indicates a long 'i' sound., e.g. *viele*.

eu, äu   are pronounced like English 'o**i**', e.g. *Eule, käuflich*.

Consonants

German consonants tend to be **pronounced more strongly** than their English equivalents, and you should always aim to pronounce them clearly. The following list indicates the main points to watch out for in the relationship between spoken sounds and spelling:

b, d, g are pronounced like 'p', 't' and 'k' at the end of a syllable: *Sieb, Tod, Tag, abfahren, tödlich*. However, the SUFFIX *-ig* is generally pronounced *-ich*: *König, ruhig*.

ch represents **two distinct sounds**:

- The so-called **ach-Laut**, like Scots *ch*, is used after *a, o, u* and *au*: *Bach, Loch, Buch, Rauch*.

- The so-called **ich-Laut** is like the hard 'y' sound at the beginning of English 'huge'. It is used after the **other vowels**, and after *l, n* and *r*: *mich, Bücher, Löcher, Pech, Milch, manchmal, Kirche*.

The group *chs* is pronounced like English 'x': *wachsen, Fuchs*.

qu is pronounced like 'kv': *Quelle, bequem*.

r varies considerably depending on the position in the word (and from region to region). The pronunciation is **quite different from English 'r'** and needs to be practised.

- The most widespread pronunciation of *r* is **at the back of the throat**, similar to the **ach-Laut**, e.g. *Rose, Rache, groß, größere, streiten, Werk, Kirche, Herr*.

- After a **long vowel**, written *r* is usually pronounced more like a very short unstressed 'a' sound: *der, mir, Heer, werden, stört* (pronounced as though written *dea, mia, Heea, weaden, stöat*).

s is pronounced like English 's' except in the following environments, where it is pronounced like English 'z':

- at the beginning of a word before a vowel: *Sand, sagen*;

- in the middle of a word between vowels or at the start of a syllable: *lesen, blasen, Ferse, Felsen*.

ss is always pronounced like English 's'.

sch is pronounced like English 'sh': *Schuh, waschen*.

sp, st The consonant groups *st-* and *sp-* are pronounced *schp-* and *scht-* at the beginning of a word or root: *spielen, spät, versprechen, Straße, besteigen*.

ß is pronounced like English 's'. It is only used **after a long vowel** or **diphthong**: *Straße, Maß, Fuß, ließ, beißen*.
   This is the letter most affected by the spelling reform: the old spelling system always had *ß* rather than *ss* at the end of words or syllables, even if the preceding vowel was short, e.g. *daß, Fluß, faßte*.

w is pronounced like English 'v': *Wasser, warten*.

z is pronounced like strong 'ts': *Zeitung, faszinierend*.

12.2 German spelling

A reformed spelling of German was introduced in schools in 1998 (with a transitional period until 2005). Most printed materials now use the new spellings, and this is the spelling being taught in schools in the German-speaking countries. However, the spelling reform was extremely controversial, and many people are still opposed to it. Moreover, all books printed since 1902 are in the old spelling, so you are likely to see both spellings for some time.

In practice, the changes are slight. The main areas affected by the spelling reform are:

▶ **The use of *ß* and *ss*:** in the old spelling, *ß* is used at the end of all words and syllables (e.g. *daß, mußte*). In the new spelling, *ß* is always used after long vowels and all dipthongs while *ss* is always used after short vowels, e.g. *heißen, Fuß, dass, Fluss, musste*.

▶ **Capitalization:** the general rule that all nouns are capitalized has been retained, but in areas where difficulties arise over whether a word is really a noun, some rules have been modified.

▶ **The use of the comma:** the rules have been simplified.

In this book we have followed the **new spelling** consistently, and this chapter introduces the main features of German spelling according to the revised rules.

12.3 The use of capital letters

The basic rules are:

▶ The **first word** in a sentence has an initial capital letter.

▶ All **nouns** are written with an initial capital letter.

▶ The 'formal' **second person pronoun** *Sie* and all its forms (*Ihnen*, *Ihr*, etc.) are written with an initial capital letter.

▶ All parts of **proper names** and **titles** have an initial capital letter: *das Schwarze Meer, das Rote Kreuz, der Schiefe Turm von Pisa, Iwan der Schreckliche, Elisabeth die Zweite*.

▶ All other words start with a small letter.

The rule that nouns are spelled with an initial capital letter is a characteristic feature of German. Difficulties arise when there are **doubts about whether a particular word is really a** NOUN. The following table gives the most important of these cases; a number have been altered in the reformed spelling:

capital letter	adjectives used as nouns	der Alte, der Vorsitzende, nichts Gutes, alles Gute, auf Deutsch, im Klaren sein, im Allgemeinen, das Weiß, ins Schwarze treffen, im Großen und Ganzen
	ordinals and indefinite adjectives used as nouns	der Letzte, der Erste, der Nächste, das Ganze, jeder Einzelne, das Übrige
	verbs used as nouns	das Essen, beim Lesen, das Inkrafttreten, das Fensterputzen, das Wegsehen, das Soll
	other parts of speech used as nouns	ein Etwas, das Nichts, das Du, eine Drei, ein großes Durcheinander, das Für und Wider
	nouns which are part of fixed phrases and idioms	Rad fahren, Eis laufen, Recht haben, Angst haben, heute Abend, außer Acht lassen, auf Grund, in Bezug

small letter	adjectives with a preceding or following noun understood	Das ist wohl das schnellste von diesen drei Autos. Mir gefällt das rote Kleid nicht, ich nehme das blaue.
	superlatives with *am*	am klarsten, am deutlichsten, am einfachsten
	ander and *beide*	der andere, anderes, die beiden, beides
	angst, bange, leid, pleite, schuld used with *sein, bleiben* and *werden*	Mir wird angst. Uns ist angst und bange. Er war das alles leid. Die Firma ist jetzt pleite. Sie bleibt schuld daran.
	idiomatic noun prefixes of separable verbs	heimkehren, teilnehmen, stattfinden, preisgeben. Ich kehre heim. Er nimmt teil. Es findet statt.
	nouns used as adverbs or prepositions	abends, anfangs, morgen, angesichts, dank, kraft, mittels, trotz
	ein bisschen and *ein paar*	ein bisschen Salz, ein paar Leute

There are also points of doubt with ADJECTIVES in titles and proper names. The following rules apply:

capital letter	adjectives in proper names, titles, designations, biological names	Kap der Guten Hoffnung, Wilhelm der Zweite, der Bayerische Wald, Deutscher Bundestag, die Vereinten Nationen, der Heilige Abend, die Schwarze Witwe
	adjectives in -er from names of towns and cities	der Kölner Dom, die Frankfurter Messe, das Wiener Rathaus, das Londoner Parlament
small letter	adjectives of nationality or from personal names	deutsches Bier, der italienische Meister, das ohmsche Gesetz, das brechtsche Drama
	adjectives in fixed phrases which are not proper names or unique things	erste Hilfe, der schwarze Markt, die silberne Hochzeit, der blaue Brief, das gelbe Trikot, die künstliche Intelligenz, das schwarze Brett

12.4 One word or two?

The general rule is that COMPOUND WORDS are written as a **single word** in German. In practice, though, there have always been some areas of doubt, some of which have been clarified in the revised spelling:

one word	noun + verb compounds used only as infinitives	bergsteigen, brustschwimmen, kopfrechnen, seiltanzen
	idiomatic adjective+verb compounds	bereithalten, fernsehen, hochrechnen, schwarzarbeiten, totschlagen, weismachen

	idiomatic noun+verb compounds	heimkehren, irreführen, preisgeben, standhalten, stattfinden, teilnehmen, wettmachen
	compounds with *irgend*	irgendein, irgendetwas, irgendjemand, irgendwer
two words	noun + verb combinations	Angst haben, Auto fahren, Eis laufen, Fuß fassen, Leid tun, Rad fahren, Rat suchen, Schuld tragen
	adverb + verb (especially adverbs in *-einander*)	abhanden kommen, beiseite legen, zunichte machen, zuteil werden, durcheinander kommen
	adjective or participle + verb (esp. adjs in *-ig, -isch, -lich*)	bekannt machen, fern liegen, gefangen nehmen, laut reden, leicht fallen, übrig bleiben
	verb infinitive + verb	bestehen bleiben, kennen lernen, liegen lassen, sitzen bleiben, spazieren gehen
	combinations with *sein*	beisammen sein, da sein, fertig sein, pleite sein, zufrieden sein
	combinations with *viel* and *wenig*	so viel, so wenig, wie viel, wie viele, zu viel, zu wenig

12.5 *-ss-* and *-ß-*

The spelling of *-ss-* and *-ß-* was simplified by the spelling reform, and the rule is now quite straightforward.

▶ Use *-ss-* **after** a **short vowel**.

▶ Use *-ß-* **after** a **long vowel** or **diphthong**.

Fluss	Flüsse	Fuß	Füße
gewiss	lassen	groß	Größe
dass	Messe	weiß	heißen

NB *ß* has no capitalized form, and *ss* is used instead.

This ruling reflects the general rule that **vowels are long before a single consonant** in the spelling, since *ß* counts as a single consonant.

12.6 Punctuation: the comma

The use of the **comma** in German is a matter of **rule**, unlike English, and it is considered incorrect to use commas in the wrong place. In principle, the comma is used to mark **grammatical units**, rather than a pause in speech, and the basic rule is straight-forward.

▶ **Every clause within a sentence begins/ends with a comma**:

main clauses linked by a coordinating conjunction	**Er starrte sie an, aber sie sagte nichts.** *He stared at her but she said nothing.* **In diesem Buch finden Sie keine Legenden, sondern Sie finden die blanke Wahrheit.** *In this book you won't find legends, you'll find the naked truth.*
main clauses together without a conjunction	**Dort trafen sich die Jungen, sie machten zusammen Schulaufgaben, sie spielten Volleyball und Poker.** *There the boys met, they did their homework together, they played volleyball and poker.*
subordinate clauses introduced by a conjunction	**Sie fragte, ob wir nach Köln mitfahren wollten.** *She asked if we wanted to come to Cologne.*
subordinate clauses with no conjunction	**Sie sagte, sie habe diesen Mann noch nie gesehen.** *She said she'd never seen this man before.*
infinitive clauses	**Ich bin gekommen, um meinen Freund wiederzusehen.** *I came in order to see my friend again.*

There are some areas of uncertainty with this rule, which has been much simplified in the reformed spelling. The following specific rules now apply.

▶ No comma is required before **und** or **oder** (although one can be used if the sense might not be clear otherwise), but a comma is needed before the other coordinating conjunctions:

Dieses Gerät kann kopieren(,) und es kann auch scannen.	*This machine can copy and it can also scan.*
Er kann zwar nicht malen, aber alle wollen seine Bilder kaufen.	*He can't paint but everyone wants to buy his pictures.*

▶ **INFINITIVE CLAUSES** with *zu* do not require a comma, although a comma can be used if the sense might not be clear otherwise:

Ich bin bereit(,) Sie bei Ihrem Vorhaben zu unterstützen.	*I'm willing to support you in your venture.*
Der General ordnete an(,) die Gefangenen zu entlassen.	*The general ordered that the prisoners should be released.*

▶ **Interjections**, **exclamations**, **explanatory phrases** and the like are separated off by commas:

Kurz und gut, die Lage ist kritisch.	*In short, the situation is critical.*
Herr Meyer, Bürgermeister der Stadt	*Herr Meyer, Mayor of the city of Karlsruhe,*
Karlsruhe, spricht heute Abend im Rathaus.	*is speaking this evening in the Town Hall.*
Die Länge beträgt, grob gerechnet, 350 Meter.	*Roughly speaking, the length is 350 metres.*
Er kam zu uns herüber, außer sich vor Freude.	*He came across to us, beside himself with joy.*

▶ **Comparative phrases** with *als* or *wie* do not have commas:

Sie ist jetzt größer als ihre ältere Schwester.	*She's taller than her elder sister now.*
Dieser Mann sah aus wie ein Schornsteinfeger.	*That man looked like a chimney sweep.*

▶ ADVERBS and ADVERBIAL PHRASES are not marked off by commas, unlike English:

Jedoch ist er nicht dort geblieben.	*However, he did not remain there.*
Eigentlich kann er es sich leisten.	*Actually, he can afford it.*
Nach einiger Zeit begann die Vorstellung.	*After a while, the show began.*

12.7 Other punctuation marks

Semi-colon

Some writers use the semi-colon to mark a pause which is more than a comma and less than a full stop, but its use is fairly rare:

43 Prozent der befragten Wessis lesen	*43 per cent of west Germans surveyed read a*
weniger als einmal im Monat ein Buch; im	*book less than once a month; in the east it is*
Osten liegt der Anteil bei 51 Prozent.	*51 per cent.*

Colon

A colon is used rather than a comma when **direct speech** is introduced by a **verb of saying**:

Dann sagte sie: „Ich liebe dich.“	*Then she said, "I love you."*

Otherwise, the colon is used, as in English, to introduce a list, or to introduce an idea, sometimes for special emphasis:

Schon 1961 hatten die Deutschen	*Already in 1961, the Germans had their*
ihren Mann im All: Perry Rhodan, den	*man in space: Perry Rhodan, the astronaut*
Astronauten, der durch immer neue	*who zooms through one new galaxy*
Galaxien düst.	*after another.*

Quotation marks

The **opening** set of quotation marks is placed **on the line**, not above it as in English. This applies to single and to double quotation marks:

Dann fragte er: „Ist es wichtig, dass sie den	*The he asked, "Is it important that it was*
Brief geschrieben hat?"	*she who wrote the letter?"*
Er fragte mich: „Kennen Sie Goethes ‚Faust'?"	*He asked me, "Do you know Goethe's 'Faust'?"*

This usage is the norm in handwriting and most printing. English-style quotation marks are occasionally used, but then principally because of keyboard configuration.

Exclamation mark

Commands, interjections and exclamations are followed by an exclamation mark. Generally, the exclamation mark tends to be used rather more frequently in German than in English:

Guten Morgen!	*Good morning.*
Hören Sie sofort damit auf!	*Please stop that at once.*
Bitte einsteigen, Türen schließen selbsttätig!	*Please board the train, the doors close automatically.*

12.8 Register

There are many differences between **spoken** and **written** German, as there are in English and most other living languages. Written language tends to be more complex and formal, whereas everyday spoken language is generally more casual and less precise. As with any language, native speakers of German, whatever their degree of education, vary their language usage according to the **situation** (e.g. party or business meeting, poetry or e-mail) and adjust it to the **person** they are addressing (e.g. best friend, grandmother or bank manager). These differences, or levels of language, are referred to as variations in REGISTER.

It is an important part of learning a language to know what you can say (but not write) – and vice versa – or how to speak more formally if the situation demands. Mixing up register features can result in what Germans call a *Stilbruch*. If you tell people that, for example, *Meine liebe Großmutter ist gestern nach langem Leiden krepiert*, they're going to think it (and you) a little odd.

Register differences shouldn't be confused with **regionalisms** or **dialect**. Most spoken German is regionally coloured in some way, especially in pronunciation, and in the South it can be very close to dialect (which doesn't have the social stigma in Germany that it has in England).

In this book we have focused on the common structural 'core' of the language. Without this, it is impossible to communicate effectively in any register. But you should listen out for all kinds of differences in usage – they make the language endlessly fascinating, and in this final part of the chapter we list some of the most common features of the spoken register which can be heard almost anywhere in the German-speaking countries.

12.9 Colloquial and formal pronunciation

Everyday spoken language is more casual and less precise than formal spoken language (as in public speaking), and formal letter-by-letter pronunciation can sound very stilted in the wrong situation. The following table shows how, in particular, unstressed common words are shortened and reduced in colloquial speech:

	colloquial	formal
unstressed -en	gebm, fragng gutn, eign'n, kommndn	geben, fragen guten, eigenen, kommenden
personal pronouns ·	hammer, simmer wissnse, isse haste, biste isses, gibt's	haben wir, sind wir wissen Sie, ist sie hast du, bist du ist es, gibt es
definite and indefinite articles	n Mann, ne Frau s Haus, nem Haus	ein Mann, eine Frau das Haus, einem Haus
articles fused with prepositions	bein, ausn, ausm innem, minnem nachm, durchn	bei den, aus den, aus dem in einem, mit einem nach dem, durch den
-e in verb endings dropped	ich hab, ich mach sie könnt, er müsst	ich habe, ich mache sie könnte, er müsste

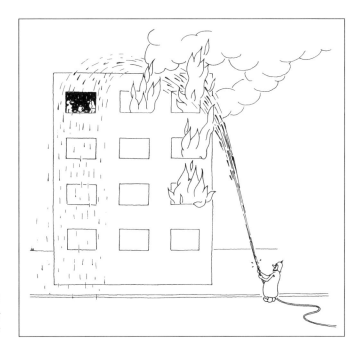

„Hab ich's nicht gesagt – nach dieser Affenhitze gibt's bestimmt noch einen Regenguss!"

12.10 Register differences in grammar

Some grammatical forms and constructions are restricted either to the spoken or to the written register. Some of the colloquial constructions are actually considered incorrect in writing:

	spoken	written
genitive case less usual in speech	der Beruf **von seinem Bruder**	der Beruf **seines Bruders**
	wegen **dem Wetter**	wegen **des Wetters**
simple past tense used more in writing, perfect tense in speech	Es **hat** ein bisschen **gedauert**, bis sie wieder eine Arbeit **gekriegt hat**.	Es **dauerte** ein bisschen, bis sie wieder eine Arbeit **bekam**.
subjunctive I used in written, indicative in spoken German	Man hat ihm gesagt, er **muss** sofort zur Polizei gehen.	Man sagte ihm, er **müsse** sofort zur Polizei gehen.
demonstrative used for personal pronoun in speech	Ich hab **die** nicht gesehen.	Ich habe **sie** nicht gesehen.
	Der kommt heute nicht.	**Er** kommt heute nicht.
definite article used with names in speech	**Der Christian** ist mit **der Petra Rittig** gekommen.	**Christian** kam mit **Petra Rittig**.
wie and *als* confused in spoken German	besser **wie** ich so bald **als** möglich	besser **als** ich so bald **wie** möglich
weil used with main clause word order in speech	..., **weil** sie **konnte** diesen Mann kaum verstehen	..., **weil** sie diesen Mann kaum verstehen **konnte**
elements placed after the 'verbal bracket'	Er **hat** Jakob *getroffen* **gestern in der Stadt**.	Er **hat** Jakob **gestern in der Stadt** *getroffen*.

12.11 Register differences in vocabulary

Many words are restricted to colloquial speech or formal writing, and often avoided in the other register. Some words are considered 'vulgar', and would tend to be perceived as rude in general discourse (marked with an asterisk below). The following table gives some common examples, together with neutral words which can be used both in speech and writing:

spoken/informal	neutral	written/formal
Schiss haben	**Angst haben** *be afraid*	sich fürchten
der Sprit	**das Benzin** *petrol*	der Treibstoff
der Knast	**das Gefängnis** *prison*	das Zuchthaus
die Visage*, die Fresse*	**das Gesicht** *face*	das Antlitz (*poetic*)
der Arsch*, der Po	**der Hintern** *behind*	das Gesäß
die Klamotten (*pl.*)	**die Kleider** (*pl.*) *clothes*	die Kleidung (*sg.*)
das Maul*, die Fresse*	**der Mund** *mouth*	
das Klo	**die Toilette** *toilet*	das WC

spoken/informal	neutral	written/formal
was, irgendwas	etwas, **irgendetwas** *something*	
blöd, doof	**dumm** *stupid*	einfältig, töricht
klasse, prima, toll, super	**gut, schön, großartig** *good, lovely, splendid*	hervorragend
bloß	**nur** *only*	lediglich
raus, rein, rauf	**heraus, herein, herauf** *out, in, up*	
total, echt	**sehr, wirklich** *very, really*	überaus
losgehen	**anfangen** *begin*	beginnen
(sich was) angucken	**(sich etwas) anschauen** *watch/look at sth.*	(sich etwas) ansehen
kriegen	**bekommen** *get*	erhalten
(sich was) reinziehen	**essen** *eat*	speisen
klappen	**gelingen** *succeed*	
klauen	**stehlen** *steal*	entwenden
krepieren*, abkratzen*	**sterben** *die*	entschlafen
pissen*, pinkeln	**[auf die Toilette gehen]** *urinate/*	urinieren
scheißen*, kacken	*defecate*	den Darm entleeren
kotzen, reihern	**sich übergeben** *vomit*	sich erbrechen
kapieren	**verstehen** *understand*	
abhauen	**weggehen** *go away*	sich entfernen
schmeißen	**werfen** *throw*	

Both in spoken and in written German, the vocabulary is changing fast owing to the readiness with which English words are being assimilated. Especially in colloquial speech and informal written contexts (e.g. e-mail), people are constantly experimenting. While some words may be one-offs (e.g. *trendig, gefeedbackt, translaten, upgraden*), the following words have now made it into *Duden*, the standard German dictionary: *das Fitnesscenter, das Outsourcing, die Wellness, trendy, antörnen, designen, downloaden, faken, recyceln, timen.*

REGISTER IN CONTEXT

BodyShaping, MuskelStyling- **TEST**

Bist du ein Fitness-Typ?

1. Was fällt dir spontan zu diesem Bild ein?

a. Klasse Body, echt gut gestylt …

b. Sieht ganz lecker aus …

c. Na ja, Opas alter Turnanzug scheint wieder in Mode zu sein, oder wie?

2. Was macht der Typ jetzt gleich, was glaubst du?

a. Seine Freundin wartet schon ganz ungeduldig im Bett, was wird er da wohl machen …

b. Keine Ahnung, vielleicht duschen gehen oder sowas?

c. Er hüpft raus aus dem Muskelanzug und rein in die Joggingklamotten, denn jetzt geht's ab zum Laufen.

3. Der Wecker klingelt – dein Kopf hämmert furchtbar von der feucht-fröhlichen Party gestern. Was tust du?

a. Ich dreh' mich noch mal um. Heute können mich alle mal …

b. Ich quäl' mich aus den Federn und werf' 'ne Aspirin ein. Irgendwie wird's schon gehen!

c. Kann mir nix anhaben. Ich spring' mit beiden Beinen ins Leben – schließlich will ich noch was haben von dem neuen Tag!

4. Der Stress fängt ja oft schon morgens beim Frühstück an. Was drückst du dir da rein?

a. Gar nix. So kurz nach Mitternacht bring' ich einfach nichts runter. Ich kauf' mir in der Pause dann 'nen Schokoriegel.

b. Na, was eben so rumliegt, ein Brot mit irgendwas – Hauptsache schnell!

c. Frühstück ist das Schönste überhaupt: heißer Kaffee, frischer O-Saft, Müsli …

5. Und wie kommst du danach in die Schule/Arbeit?

a. Mit dem Fahrrad – ich brauch' morgens einfach frische Luft.

b. Ich lass' mich von meinen Eltern hinkarren – ist immer noch das Angenehmste.

c. Meistens mit den Öffentlichen – Bus, Zug, U-Bahn …

6. Ein muskelbepackter(s) Boy/Girl macht dich im Schwimmbad ganz direkt an. Wie reagierst du?

a. Nix wie hin! Auf ihn/sie mit Geheul!

b. Na ja, erst mal gucken, was er/sie in der Birne hat.

c. Neeee. Auf Muskeln liegt man total unbequem. Und außerdem fällt neben so jemandem meine Schwabbelfigur noch mehr auf …

7. Wofür gibst du am meisten Geld aus?

a. Klamotten und CD's.

b. Pizzerias, Eisdielen – und außerdem für Zutaten: ich koch' total gern.

c. Auf der Piste – fast jeden Abend geb' ich da zu viel aus. Aber da ist wenigstens immer was los.

(Aus: *Popcorn*)

PRONUNCIATION/SHORTENED FORMS

colloquial	formal
'ne, 'nen, 's	eine, einen, es
ich dreh'/werf'/spring'	ich drehe/werfe/springe
nix, nee	nichts, nein

ELLIPTIC SYNTAX IN SPOKEN GERMAN

[Das] Kann mir nix anhaben.
[Er] Sieht ganz lecker aus.
[Er ist] echt gut gestylt.
[Ich habe] Keine Ahnung.
[Ich stürze mich] Auf ihn/sie mit Geheul!
[Er hat einen] Klasse Body.
[Die] Hauptsache [ist, es geht] schnell.
[Ich will] Nix wie hin [zu ihm/ihr]!
Heute können mich alle mal [am Arsch lecken!]

COLLOQUIAL AND FORMAL VOCABULARY

spoken/informal	written/formal
die Birne	der Kopf
die Federn (*pl.*)	das Bett
der Opa	der Großvater
der Typ	der Typ (*type*)/(junge) Mann
der Boy	der Junge/junge Mann
das Girl	das Mädchen/die junge Frau
die Klamotten (*pl.*)	die Kleider (*pl.*)
die Schwabbelfigur	die rundliche/vollschlanke Figur
die Piste	das Nachtleben
die Fitness	die gute körperliche Verfassung
der Body	der enganliegende Sportanzug/der Körper
klasse	gut, schön
echt, total	sehr, wirklich
gucken	sehen
hinkarren	hinfahren
stylen	gestalten, entwerfen
relaxen	sich entspannen
(Tablette) einwerfen	(Tablette) nehmen
sich was reindrücken	etwas essen
da ist was los	dort kann man sich gut amüsieren

Ein berühmter Stilbruch

Götz: Sag deinem Hauptmann, vor Ihro Kaiserlichen Majestät hab ich, wie immer, schuldigen Respekt. Er aber, sag's ihm, er kann mich – – – [=am Arsch lecken]   (J.W. Goethe, *Götz von Berlichingen*, 3. Akt)

TEST AUSWERTUNG

	a	b	c
1	7	5	2
2	4	5	9
3	0	5	10
4	0	3	8
5	10	0	4
6	1	5	0
7	5	5	10

2–22 Punkte:
Sport? Nicht dein Ding! Obwohl dich deine Rundungen wirklich ganz schön stören. Zum Glück bist du aber noch kein totaler Couch-Potatoe. Such dir also eine(n) Gleichgesinnte(n) und geht doch mal zusammen raus: ein bißchen Laufen, Radfahren, Rollerbladen kann total Spaß machen.

23–45 Punkte:
Gar nicht übel: Du hast für dich den idealen Mittelweg zwischen Fitness und Relaxen gefunden. Bleib so wie du bist – denn ganz zurecht stehen bei dir immer Freude und Fun ganz oben auf der Liste!

46–67 Punkte:
Erst ins Fitness-Studio, dann ab zum Joggen und hinterher noch ein kleines Squashmatch? Genau dein Tag! Auf deine perfekte Linie bist du stolz. Solange du dich wohlfühlst, ist deine Einstellung völlig o.k. – kritisch wird's erst, wenn das ganze zur Körperkultsucht wird. Deshalb: relax mal wieder!

Exercises

References are to the sections of the reference grammar (e.g. 'see 1.1' refers to section 1.1). Answers to exercises are given after the exercise section.

▮ Words and sentences

Have a stab at the exercises in this chapter, and see how your results match up with the answers. You should concentrate on the patterns rather than the meaning in detail. But don't worry if you get the answers wrong – try the exercises again once you've worked your way through the book!

1 Sentence patterns (see 1.1–1.6)
Match up the following sentences with the sentence patterns below.

1. Ich gebe dir eine Chance.
2. Fred ist ein unverbesserlicher Optimist.
3. Er erinnerte seinen Chef an den morgigen Termin.
4. Der Hund hat den Knochen gefressen.
5. Der Torwart hielt den Elfmeter.
6. Das Kind schläft.
7. Michael ist mein bester Freund.
8. Mein Sohn heißt Anton.
9. Dieses Auto gehört meinem Kollegen.
10. Wir kauften dem Jungen einen Gameboy.
11. Anne zeigte mir den Computer.
12. Ich laufe.
13. Sie kaufte den Tisch.
14. Mein Vater warnte meinen Bruder vor dem Pudel.
15. Meine Mutter arbeitet.
16. Sie liebt dich.
17. Der Schüler antwortete dem Lehrer.
18. Die Oma passt auf den Hund auf.
19. Das Kind ist müde.
20. Wir helfen unseren Eltern.

a. NP nom + verb
b. NP nom + verb + NP acc
c. NP nom + verb + NP dat
d. NP nom + verb + NP dat + NP acc
e. NP nom + verb + NP prep
f. NP nom + verb +NP acc + NP prep
g. NP nom + copula + NP nom/adj

2 The subject and the finite verb (see 1.2 and 1.8)
Look at the following text about a woman who has left Germany and now lives in Australia. Underline the finite verb and circle the subject. Adverbials have been put in brackets, and you can ignore them.

1. Kathrin Borchert hat Deutschland verlassen.   2. Australien war (schon immer) ihr großer Traum.
3. (Hier) lebt sie (jetzt).   4. Unser Reporter stellt ihr einige Fragen.   5. Was fasziniert sie an diesem Land?
6. Kathrin lächelt.   7. Sie liebt (einfach) diese grandiose Landschaft.   8. Sie liebt die tropischen Wälder

und die exotischen Klänge. 9. Ihre Heimat ist (jetzt) der kleine Ort Gold Coast. 10. Sie erzählt von unendlichen Nationalparks, von 300 Tagen Sonnenschein im Jahr. 11. Vermisst sie (hier) etwas? 12. Sie vermisst (nur) ihre Familie. 13. (In Deutschland) wünscht ihr niemand einen guten Tag. 14. (Hier) sind die Menschen anders. 15. Sie haben (immer) ein offenes Ohr, 16. und sie helfen ihr (immer). 17. Kathrin hat (zwar jetzt) weniger Geld, 18. (aber hier) ist sie glücklich. 19. An Deutschland hat sie kein Interesse (mehr). 20. Kathrin Borchert hat ihr Paradies gefunden.

(Fernsehwoche)

3 Sentence patterns (see **1.1–1.6**)

See if you can match up the individual sentences in exercise **2** with the sentence patterns below. Ignore any adverbials (in brackets) and concentrate only on the basic patterns, regardless of word order.

a. NP nom + verb
b. NP nom + verb + NP acc
c. NP nom + verb + NP dat
d. NP nom + verb + NP dat + NP acc

e. NP nom + verb + NP prep
f. NP nom + verb + NP acc + NP prep
g. NP nom + copula + NP nom/adj

4 Main clauses and subordinate clauses (see **1.7** and **1.10**)

No punctuation has been used in the following sentences. Identify main clauses (mc), subordinate clauses with a subordinating conjunction (sc) and infinitive clauses (ic) by putting (mc), (sc) or (ic) against the individual segments of the sentences.

1. Peters Frau schlief schon lange/als er nach Hause kam
2. Du brauchst mir nicht im Garten zu helfen/aber du könntest Tante Erna besuchen
3. Andrea weiß es schon/weil du es ihr gesagt hast
4. Ich muß meiner Mutter sagen/dass ich heute Abend etwas später komme
5. Anstatt immer nur vor dem Computer zu sitzen/könntest du mal ein bisschen Fußball spielen
6. Wenn du heute Nachmittag zu mir kommst/helfe ich dir mit den Hausaufgaben
7. Wir können anschließend noch Skateboard fahren/wenn du Lust hast
8. Es macht sicher viel Spaß/die neue Rollschuhanlage auszuprobieren.
9. Es wird nicht einfach sein/ihn von seinem Vorhaben abzubringen
10. Es ist sehr wichtig/ihm klar zu machen/dass er dadurch seinen Job verlieren kann
11. Ich will heute Abend mit meinem Sohn ins Konzert gehen/weil er dann vielleicht dazu animiert wird/auch ein Instrument zu spielen
12. Er ging zu der Besprechung/obwohl er nicht viel zu sagen hatte
13. Als Jonas von der Schule nach Hause kam/klingelte er mehrmals/aber niemand öffnete die Tür
14. Er bekam ziemliche Angst/weil seine Mutter nicht zu Hause war
15. Ich habe große Lust/mir den neuen James Bond Film anzusehen

5 Infinitive clauses (see **1.10**)

Form infinitive clauses from the following main clauses. These are the infinitive forms you will need, given here in alphabetical order: *besuchen, bringen, haben, haben, lassen, sein, sein, tun, verkaufen, werden.*

e.g. Ich gehe spazieren.
  Ich habe keine Lust, spazieren zu gehen.

1. Er wird mit seiner neuen Freundin gesehen.
   Er will vermeiden, ...
2. Er hat sie gestern in der Kirche getroffen.
   Er behauptete, ...
3. Ich besuche morgen meine Tante in Bochum.
   Ich habe vor, ...
4. Der Mann hat den Einbrecher nicht gesehen.
   Der Mann behauptete, ...
5. Mein Vater verkauft unser Auto.
   Es gelang meinem Vater nicht, ...

6. Ich bin mit meinen Freunden zusammen.
   Es macht immer viel Spaß, ...
7. Sie tut so etwas nie wieder.
   Sie versprach ihrer Mutter, ...
8. Der Kellner bringt dem Gast das Frühstück aufs Zimmer.
   Der Gast bat den Kellner, ...
9. Ich lasse mir die Haare schneiden.
   Ich habe beschlossen, ...
10. Er ist nicht in der Stadt gewesen.
    Er gab vor, ...

6 Subordinate clauses (see **1.7** and **1.10**)

Form one sentence from each of the following pairs of sentences with the conjunction given in brackets.

e.g. Ich weiß nicht genau (ob)/Er geht aufs Gymnasium.
  Ich weiß nicht genau, ob er aufs Gymnasium geht.

1. Wir müssen noch einige Dinge erledigen (bevor)/Wir können in Urlaub fahren.
2. Die Maschine aus Stuttgart hatte mehrere Stunden Verspätung (weil)/Dort war ein schlimmes Unwetter und niemand bekam Starterlaubnis.
3. Dein Vater macht einen sehr unglücklichen Eindruck (seitdem)/Er hat seine Arbeit verloren.
4. Du musst dich beeilen (wenn)/Du willst mitkommen.
5. Der Schüler öffnete das Fenster (damit)/Frische Luft kam ins Zimmer.
6. Sie fühlte sich ausgeruht (nachdem)/Sie hatte eine Stunde geschlafen.
7. Unser Nachbar spielt ziemlich schlecht Trompete (obwohl)/Er spielt schon seit 20 Jahren.
8. Ich hatte keine Ahnung (dass)/Dein Bruder lebt jetzt im Ausland.
9. Sie wollten dem Rektor nicht sagen (wie)/Der Unfall ist auf dem Schulhof passiert.
10. Die Kinder in der Schule bekamen hitzefrei (weil)/Die Temperaturen waren auf 32 Grad im Schatten gestiegen.
11. Du musst dich zuerst umziehen (bevor)/Wir gehen los.
12. Ich bin jeden Morgen gehetzt (obwohl)/Ich stehe immer rechtzeitig auf.

7 Main clauses (see **1.8**)

Rewrite the following sentences putting the italicized phrase in initial position. Remember that this has implications for the word order.

e.g. Wir gehen *morgen* ins Kino.
  Morgen gehen wir ins Kino.

1. Wir kommen *meistens* erst um Mitternacht nach Hause.
2. Man bekommt *in Secondhand-Shops* oft gute Kleidung für wenig Geld.
3. Ich sehe *meine Familie* leider nur sehr selten.
4. Ich glaube *Politikern* kein Wort.
5. Es hat *im letzten Winter* fast keinen Schnee gegeben.
6. Ich weiß leider nicht, *um wieviel Uhr der Zug ankommt.*
7. Sie wollte mir nicht sagen, *worum es in dem Brief ging.*
8. Er musste *leider* unerwartet nach Berlin fliegen.
9. Das Fest findet *bei schlechtem Wetter* drinnen statt.
10. Der öffentliche Verkehr muss *meiner Meinung nach* viel besser subventioniert werden.

8 Main clauses (see **1.8**)

Form main clause declarative sentences from the following elements, keeping in mind the general structure

topic – verb^1 – central section – verb^2

Put the element that functions as the topic (indicated in brackets) in initial position. Put the verb in its correct form and into the position(s) that reflect(s) the general structure pointed out above.

e.g. ich/lese/diese Zeitung (*topic*)/schon seit zehn Jahren
  Diese Zeitung lese ich schon seit zehn Jahren.

1. mein Bruder/fahren/nach Tübingen (*topic*)/mit dem Zug
2. ich (*topic*)/aufgestanden sein/heute erst um 11 Uhr
3. das Tennisturnier/angefangen haben/heute Nachmittag um 2 (*topic*)
4. ich/beneiden/dich nicht/um diese Arbeit (*topic*)
5. ich/gegessen haben/nichts mehr/seit heute Morgen um 8 (*topic*)
6. man/rechnen können/immer/mit seiner Hilfe (*topic*)
7. du/fahren müssen/allein in Urlaub/in Zukunft (*topic*)
8. man/nicht arbeiten dürfen/in diesem Land/ohne Arbeitsgenehmigung (*topic*)
9. ein schwerer Unfall/passiert sein/heute in den frühen Morgenstunden (*topic*)
10. die Züge/ankommen/in England (*topic*)/nicht immer pünktlich
11. mein Sohn/angenommen werden/hoffentlich (*topic*)/bei dieser Universität
12. ich/spazieren gehen/am liebsten (*topic*)/im Wald

9 Questions (see **1.9**)

Transform the following sentences into questions.

1. Du kommst morgen auch mit zu dem Fußballspiel.
2. Du machst das mit Absicht
3. Ihr schreibt morgen eine Klassenarbeit.
4. Ihr geht erst nächste Woche auf den Ausflug.
5. Sie putzen nie Ihre Fenster.
6. Du besuchst deine alte Tante.
7. Er will heute nach Lübeck fahren.
8. Er hat in der Stadt keine Erdbeeren bekommen.

10 Commands (see **1.9**)

Transform the following statements into commands.

1. Sie entschuldigen sich bei Ihrem Chef.
2. Sie spielen mir etwas auf der Gitarre vor.
3. Sie gehen zum Arzt .
4. Sie haben Geduld.
5. Sie machen das Fenster auf.
6. Sie sehen sich auch diesen neuen Film an.
7. Sie vergessen nichts.
8. Sie lassen mich in Ruhe.

2 Nouns

1 Gender by meaning (see **2.2–2.4**)

Decide whether the following nouns are masculine, feminine or neuter.

1. Arzt 2. Ferrari 3. Gold 4. Million 5. Ypsilon 6. Nebel 7. Frühling 8. Essen 9. Deutschland
10. Sekretärin 11. August 12. Baby 13. Sturm 14. Fünf 15. Europa 16. Harley Davidson 17. Grün
18. Mittwoch 19. Großvater 20. Concorde 21. Kuh 22. „Tirpitz" (ship) 23. VW 24. London
25. Krankenschwester 26. Wind 27. Eisen

2 Gender by ending (see **2.2–2.4**)

Decide whether the following nouns are masculine, feminine or neuter.

1. Fabrikant 2. Museum 3. Büchlein 4. Rassismus 5. Neuling 6. Version 7. Fakultät 8. Heilung
9. Fanatismus 10. Regiment 11. Bilanz 12. Botschaft 13. Humor 14. Heiterkeit 15. Anästhesie
16. Portion 17. Abitur 18. Wüterich 19. Häuschen 20. Argument 21. Bäckerei 22. Dogma
23. Bürgertum 24. Campus 25. Kontrast 26. Liebling 27. Frisur 28. Einheit 29. Fantasie
30. Viertel 31. Differenz 32. Verteilung 33. Villa 34. Stadium

3 Other clues to gender (see **2.5**)

Which gender would you expect for nouns

a. with the prefix *Ge-*

b. with the ending -e

Work with a partner and, with the help of a dictionary and/or this reference grammar, find some nouns that have the prefix *Ge-* or end in -e and do **not** have the expected gender.

4 The plural of masculine nouns (see **2.7**)

Use the two tables in section **2.6** about plural formation and put the following masculine nouns in the plural.

1. Berg 2. Wald 3. Tanz 4. Apfel 5. Garten 6. Schüler 7. Arm 8. Fisch 9. Finger 10. Kopf
11. Brite 12. Schmerz 13. Faden 14. Ring 15. Fernseher 16. Professor 17. Monat 18. Geist
19. Fall 20. Staat 21. Punkt 22. Artikel 23. Anzug 24. Rand 25. Bruder 26. König
27. Nachbar 28. Typ 29. Computer 30. Fuß

5 The plural of feminine nouns (see **2.8**)

Use the two tables in section **2.6** about plural formation and put the following feminine nouns in the plural.

1. Stadt   2. Gabel   3. Tochter   4. Arbeit   5. Freundin   6. Kenntnis   7. Wand   8. Nacht   9. Mauer   10. Mutter   11. Wohnung   12. Schulter   13. Bank   14. Hand   15. Blume   16. Universität   17. Einheit   18. Gewerkschaft   19. Regel   20. Wurst   21. Lösung   22. Explosion   23. Schwäche   24. Putzfrau   25. Faust   26. Tür   27. Kuh   28. Last   29. Frucht   30. Schwester

6 The plural of neuter nouns (see 2.9)

Use the two tables in section **2.6** about plural formation and put the following neuter nouns in the plural.

1. Kloster   2. Mädchen   3. Dach   4. Haus   5. Messer   6. Hemd   7. Rad   8. Floß   9. Land   10. Interesse   11. Argument   12. Jahr   13. Verbot   14. Büchlein   15. Auge   16. Bett   17. Schloss   18. Gespräch   19. Lamm   20. Blatt   21. Wort   22. Ohr   23. Licht   24. Klavier   25. Bein   26. Spiel   27. Buch   28. Bild   29. Schaf   30. Kissen

7 Plural (see 2.6–2.10)

Fill in gaps using the plural of the nouns in brackets.

1. [Radio, Kassettenrekorder] _____ und _____ sind im
   Allgemeinen billiger als [Videogerät, Computer] _____ und _____.
2. Ich tanze gern [Diskotanz] _____, aber auch lateinamerikanische [Rhythmus]
   _____ gefallen mir gut.
3. Auf den [Landstraße] _____ und in den [Stadtzentrum] _____ gibt es
   immer mehr [Auto] _____, und zwar sowohl [PKW] _____ als auch
   [LKW] _____.
4. An deutschen [Uni] _____ gibt es seit Jahren viel zu viele
   [Student] _____ und zu wenig [Professor] _____ und andere
   [Hochschullehrer] _____.
5. Die [Zimmer] _____ in den meisten [Hotel] _____ haben heutzutage
   [Balkon, Fernseher] _____ und _____.
6. Für ältere [Mensch] _____ scheinen die [Tag, Woche, Monat, Jahr]
   _____, _____, _____ und _____ immer
   kürzer zu werden.
7. Letzte Woche war ich mit meinem Sohn in zwei verschiedenen [Zoo] _____. Es
   gab dort viele wilde [Tier] _____ wie zum Beispiel [Löwe, Tiger, Bär,
   Leopard] _____, _____, _____
   und _____ zu sehen, aber mein Sohn hat sich am meisten für die [Vogel]
   _____ interessiert, besonders die [Taube, Spatz] _____
   und _____.
8. In mehreren [Museum] _____ finden [Ausstellung] _____ statt, in denen
   die [Besucher] _____ [Bild] _____ aus verschiedenen [Epoche]
   _____, aber auch andere [Ausstellungsstück] _____ bewundern können.
9. Heutzutage bekommen viele [Kind] _____, und zwar [Mädchen, Junge]
   _____ und _____ [Gameboy, Videospiel] _____
   und _____ geschenkt. Aber wenn sie draußen spielen, sind [Skateboard,

Fahrrad] _____, _____ und seit neuestem auch [Roller] sehr
beliebt.
10. Die meisten [Firma] _____ finden es wichtig, dass ihre [Mitarbeiter]
_____ gut in [Team] _____ arbeiten können und nicht so sehr als
[Individuum] _____.

8 Case (see **2.11** and **2.12**)

Look at the following sentences and for each italicized noun/noun phrase identify its case and its
function in the sentence.

e.g. Für *einen Euro* kann man heutzutage nicht sehr viel kaufen.
acc. (used after the preposition *für*)

1. Mit *diesem Kleid* kann ich unmöglich zu *der Party* gehen.
2. Ich war *den ganzen August* über im Urlaub.
3. Das Haus *meines Großvaters* musste abgerissen werden.
4. Ich gebe *dem Kassierer* später *das Geld*.
5. Er hat *den neuen Bürgermeister* in der Stadt getroffen.
6. *Den Ausflug* mit *deinem Freund* kannst *du* dir aus dem Kopf schlagen.
7. *Er* war schon immer *ein guter Zuhörer*.
8. Julia ist *ihrer Schwester* sehr ähnlich.
9. Niemand antwortete *den Kindern*.
10. *Dem Jungen* fiel *die Mütze* vom Kopf.
11. *Guten Appetit!*
12. Während *der Unterrichtsstunden* sind die Fenster geschlossen zu halten.
13. *Viele Leute* mögen *keinen Käse*.
14. *Dein Bruder*, den habe ich gestern zum ersten Mal gesehen.
15. Für *unsere Gäste* ist nur *das Beste* gut genug.

9 Weak masculine nouns and regular nouns (see **2.12**)

From the following list of nouns indentify the weak ones by putting a tick next to them.

1. Präsident   2. Regiment   3. Archäologe   4. Monolog   5. Soldat   6. Polizist   7. Gebäude   8. Gedanke
9. Fehler   10. Talent   11. Türke   12. Vase   13. Bär   14. Nase   15. Mensch   16. König   17. Stunde
18. Computer   19. Herr   20. Kabarettist

3 The noun phrase: determiners and pronouns

1 The definite and indefinite article (see **3.1–3.3**)

Fill in the correct form of the definite or indefinite article where necessary. If you decide
to use a definite article with a preposition it may sound better to use the contracted form
(*zu dem = zum*).

1. Wir wohnen schon seit 10 Jahren in _____ Bergstraße.
2. Ich hätte gern _____ Kaffee und _____ Stück Kuchen.
3. _____ Zeit vergeht schneller, je älter man wird.
4. Mein Sohn ist _____ Lehrer, aber er möchte sich umschulen lassen und _____ Pfarrer werden.
5. _____ Leute gehen heute nicht mehr so oft in _____ Kirche wie früher.
6. Übersetzen Sie bitte aus _____ Englischen in _____ Deutsche.
7. Volker war früher _____ Protestant, aber er ist letztes Jahr konvertiert, und jetzt ist er _____ Katholik.
8. Ich fahre meistens mit _____ Auto zu _____ Arbeit, aber manchmal fahre ich auch mit _____ U-Bahn.
9. _____ wieder vereinigte Berlin hat viele Veränderungen erfahren.
10. Für _____ erfahrenen Arzt ist diese Operation ein Kinderspiel.
11. Kannst du dich noch an _____ schönen Alfred erinnern? Der hat doch immer in _____ Schweiz gewohnt. Und letzte Woche ist er plötzlich in _____ Türkei gezogen.
12. _____ Leben ist manchmal ganz schön hart, aber _____ Mensch gewöhnt sich an alles.
13. Früher nahmen _____ Männer immer _____ Hut ab, wenn sie _____ Frau trafen.
14. Er ging in _____ Bett, machte _____ Augen zu und schlief ein.
15. Ich bin _____ Deutscher, meine Frau ist _____ Engländerin, und unsere Tochter hat die doppelte Staatsbürgerschaft.

2 The definite and indefinite article (see **3.1–3.3**)

Look at the following original titles of American films. Translate them into German, and then compare your answers with the answer section to find out under which title they were released in German-speaking countries. Remember that there are some discrepancies in the use of the article in English and German.

1. Little Caesar (1931, Edward G. Robinson, James Cagney)
2. All That Heaven Allows (1955, Rock Hudson, Jane Wyman)
3. The Man Who Fell To Earth (1976, David Bowie)
4. Heaven Can Wait (1978, Warren Beatty, Julie Christie)
5. Victim of Love (1991, Pierce Brosnan)
6. Death Becomes Her (1992, Meryl Streep, Goldie Horn, Bruce Willis)

3 Demonstratives and other determiners (see **3.4–3.6** and **3.9**)

Supply the correct endings on the determiners in the following sentences.

1. Jed____ vernünftige Mensch bleibt bei so ein_____ Wetter zu Hause.
2. Wir bitten d____jenig____ Passagiere, die weiterfliegen, ein____ paar Minuten in der Maschine sitzen zu bleiben und all____ anderen Passagiere zuerst aussteigen zu lassen. Sie haben dann einig____ Minuten Aufenthalt, bevor wir mit d____selb____ Maschine weiterfliegen.
3. Nur wenig____ von Ihnen scheinen von dies____ Musik viel____· Ahnung zu haben.
4. Ich glaube, ich habe gestern zu viel____ von dies____ Cognac getrunken.

5. Ich bekam ein____ solch____ Schreck, als ich sah, dass bei uns eingebrochen worden war. Obwohl wenig____ Bargeld fehlte, hatten die Einbrecher einig____ Schmuckstücke im Wert von mehrere____ Tausend Mark gestohlen. Sie hatten natürlich auch unser____ beide____ Computer, den Fernseher, den Videorekorder und mehrere____ Videokassetten mitgenommen. Außerdem fehlten viel____ Antiquitäten und sämtlich____ Briefmarken aus unser____ Sammlung. Was für ein____ Schock! Aber das Schlimmste war all____ der Ärger, der noch auf uns zukommen sollte.

6. Es gibt nur wenig____, die sich in irgendein____ Weise mit dies____ Thema beschäftigt haben.

7. Max hat all____ mein____ Bonbons aufgegessen.

8. Mit welch____ Zug fährst du morgen nach München?

9. Wir waren im Urlaub in all____ möglichen Museen und mussten uns sämtlich____ Bilder von irgendwelch____ langweiligen Malern anschauen.

10. Viel____ Jugendliche haben heutzutage zu viel____ Geld und zu wenig____ Verstand. Aber das gilt natürlich nicht für all____.

4 (k)ein and possessives used as pronouns (see 3.5 and 3.9)

Complete the following sentences by supplying the correct endings.

1. Nur ein____ der Angeklagten gab die Tat zu.

2. Ist das hier mein____ Pullover oder dein____? – Ich glaube, es ist dein____. Mein____ wäre dir nämlich viel zu eng.

3. Könnten wir vielleicht ein____ von euer____ Fernsehern ausleihen? Unser____ ist leider kaputt gegangen.

4. Ich beneide mein____ Schwester wirklich um ihr____ Haus. Ihr____ ist viel größer als unser____.

5. Wir haben mit kein____ von unser____ Nachbarn sehr viel Kontakt.

6. Unser____ Haus war ein____ der ersten, die in dieser Gegend gebaut worden sind.

7. Fahren wir doch lieber mit unser____ Auto als mit ihr____. Ihr____ ist immer so unbequem.

8. Ich brauche ein____ Kugelschreiber. Weißt du, wo ein____ ist? – Auf mein____ Schreibtisch müsste ein____ liegen.

9. Kein____ von den Sportwagen gefällt mir besser als der kleine rote da in der Ecke.

10. Mein____ Bruder kann froh sein, dass er sein____ Lehrer hat und nicht mein____. Sein____ ist nämlich viel netter als mein____.

5 Other common pronouns (see 3.6 and 3.9)

Translate the following sentences into German.

1. No one knows that.
2. Which of the two boys is yours?
3. My mother said something to my father.
4. I forgot to buy coffee. Could you lend me some?
5. Who were you talking to on the phone?
6. I will not say anything to anyone.
7. It is always better to talk to someone when you have (one has) problems.
8. Who knows whose fault it was?
9. You can really get on people's (one's) nerves.
10. Did you see anyone?

6 Personal pronouns (see 3.7)

Rewrite the following sentences replacing all italicized noun phrases by third person pronouns in the correct case.

e.g. *Die Mutter* liebte *ihre Kinder* sehr.
    Sie liebte *sie* sehr.

1. *Der Direktor* dankte *seinem Mitarbeiter*.
2. *Mein Sohn* spielt am liebsten mit *den Nachbarskindern*.
3. *Die Oma* legte *das kleine Kind* in die Wiege.
4. *Petra* wollte *ihrem Freund* das Geheimnis nicht verraten.
5. *Die Kinder* hätten *Ihre Eltern* um Rat fragen können.
6. *Die Flutkatastrophe* hat *viele Menschen* obdachlos gemacht.
7. *Der Regisseur* sagte, dass *der Bösewicht* hinter *der Fee* stehen solle.
8. *Der Verlag* hat vorgeschlagen, dass ich *ein neues Buch* schreibe.
9. Bei *meiner Nachbarin* hängt *die Wäsche* immer im Garten.
10. *Meine Schwester* möchte nicht mit *diesem Mann* verheiratet sein.
11. *Die Nachricht* hat *allen Bewohnern* einen Schock versetzt.
12. Für *seine Kinder* würde *Christoph* alles tun.

7 Personal pronouns (see 3.7)

In the following sentences replace the first person pronoun in italics (singular or plural) with all three forms of the second person pronoun.

e.g. Johannes liebt *mich*.
    Johannes liebt *dich/euch/Sie*.

1. Er hat *mir* nicht die Wahrheit gesagt.
2. Die Gruppenleiterin erzählt *uns* eine Geschichte.
3. Ein Mensch wie *ich* könnte so etwas nie tun.
4. Ich bin sicher, dass der Kollege *mich* belogen hat.
5. Bei *mir* zu Hause sieht es noch ziemlich chaotisch aus.
6. Für *mich* würde er seine Hand ins Feuer legen.
7. Das Finanzamt hat *uns* die Unterlagen zugeschickt.
8. Einen Zaun streichen kann jeder genauso gut wie *wir*.
9. Die Gastgeberin hatte nicht mehr mit *mir* gerechnet.
10. Wohl niemand kann sich so sehr in einem Menschen getäuscht haben wie *ich*.
11. Der neue Filialleiter mag *mich* nicht besonders.
12. Die neuen Nachbarn werden sich sicher bald bei *uns* vorstellen.

8 Prepositional adverbs (see 3.7)

Decide whether to use a prepositional adverb (*da(r)* + preposition) or a preposition + personal pronoun to refer to the noun phrase in italics.

e.g. Der Junge freut sich so sehr über *sein fern gesteuertes Auto*, dass er den ganzen
    Tag _____mit_____ spielen will.
    Der Junge freut sich so sehr über sein fern gesteuertes Auto, dass er den ganzen Tag *damit* spielen will.

1. Jörg hat sich *ein neues Auto* gekauft und heute Morgen ist er das erste Mal _____mit_____ zur Arbeit gefahren.
2. Obwohl *das Wetter* kein besonders interessantes Thema ist, spricht man in England viel _____über_____.
3. *Mein Bruder* geht mir total auf die Nerven und ich muss mich ständig _____über_____ ärgern.
4. Hannelore ist ganz verliebt in *ihren kleinen Hund* und versucht so oft wie möglich _____mit_____ spazieren zu gehen.
5. Wir haben unserem Sohn einen *Computer* zu Weihnachten geschenkt, und jetzt sitzt er in jeder freien Minute _____vor_____.
6. Oma hat dir doch *50 Mark* zum Geburtstag geschenkt. Vergiss nicht, dich _____für_____ zu bedanken.
7. Ich glaube, Holger ist in *Christiane* verliebt. Ich habe ihn gestern _____mit_____ Händchen haltend im Park gesehen.
8. *Das Theaterstück* wird sicher ein Erfolg. Die Presse hat sehr positiv _____über_____ geschrieben.
9. *Der Ball* ist auf das Dach geflogen und jetzt können wir nicht mehr _____mit_____ spielen.
10. Obwohl *mein Mann* und ich uns nur am Wochenende sehen können, denke ich jeden Tag _____an_____.

9 Reflexive pronouns (see 3.8)

Replace the direct object in italics with a reflexive pronoun to refer back to the subject of the sentence.

e.g. Ich wasche mein Auto.

   Ich wasche *mich*.

1. Das Mädchen legt *die Puppe* ins Bett.
2. Manuela kämmt *ihre Katze* jeden Morgen vor dem Frühstück.
3. Du kannst *Daniel* schon mal ins Auto setzen.
4. Manchmal stelle ich *meine Freunde* vor und manchmal nicht.
5. Ich habe beschlossen, *meine Tochter* anders zu nennen.
6. Die Katze leckt *ihre Jungen*.
7. Ihr könntet *eure Haare* mal wieder waschen.
8. Die Mutter zieht *ihren kleinen Jungen* an.
9. Ich muß *die Kinder* rechtzeitig auf die Prüfung vorbereiten.
10. Mach *das Essen* für die Party heute abend fertig!

10 Reflexive pronouns (see 3.8)

Fill in the gaps using the correct reflexive pronoun. Remember that the reflexive pronoun can be in the accusative or dative.

e.g. Ich habe _____ die Sache nur eingebildet.

   Ich habe *mir* die Sache nur eingebildet.

1. Er hat _____ beim Skifahren den Fuß gebrochen.
2. Ich stelle _____ einen Urlaub in der Karibik herrlich vor.

3. Meine Eltern haben _____ beim Kauf des Hauses völlig verkalkuliert.

4. Wenn du _____ die Hände waschen gehst, kannst du _____ auch gleich die Zähne putzen.

5. Wir haben _____ eine kleine Überraschung für dich ausgedacht.

6. Ihr solltet _____ unbedingt diesen Film ansehen.

7. Könnte ich _____ bitte diese CD vorher anhören?

8. Du kannst _____ von dem restlichen Geld ein Eis kaufen.

9. Melanie hat _____ gestern den Finger in der Tür eingeklemmt.

10. Wir haben _____ solche Sorgen um dich gemacht.

4 Adjectives, adverbs and adverbials

I Adjective declension (see **4.1** and **4.2**)

Fill in the correct adjective endings.

1. a. Das war ein grob____ Fehler.
   b. Er ist wegen eines grob____ Fehlers bei der Operation gestorben.
   c. Sie ist durch einen grob____ Fehler bei der Fahrprüfung durchgefallen.
   d. Du hast da einen grob____ Fehler gemacht.

2. a. Das ist nicht das eigentlich____ Thema.
   b. Sie reden am eigentlich____ Thema vorbei.
   c. Wir sollten uns auf das eigentlich____ Thema beschränken.
   d. Statt des eigentlich____ Themas wird hier Ihre persönliche Meinung diskutiert.

3. a. Klein____ Kinder müssen früh ins Bett gehen.
   b. Sie kann überhaupt nicht mit klein____ Kindern umgehen.
   c. Ich mag klein____ Kinder.
   d. Meine Kollegin findet trotz vier klein____ Kinder noch Zeit für ihren Beruf.

4. a. Macht euch wegen unserer klein____ Probleme keine Sorgen.
   b. Wir werden unsere klein____ Probleme lösen.
   c. Unsere klein____ Probleme sollen euch nicht belasten.
   d. Wir werden mit unseren klein____ Problemen schon fertig.

5. a. Ist das ihr neu____ Auto?
   b. Trotz ihres neu____ Autos geht sie immer noch oft zu Fuß.
   c. Für ihr neu____ Auto bekommt sie bestimmt einen guten Preis.
   d. Fährt sie mit ihrem neu____ Auto in Urlaub?

6. a. Ich war mit vielen jung____ Leuten zusammen.
   b. Wir haben viele jung____ Leute kennen gelernt.
   c. In unserer Stadt leben viele jung____ Leute.
   d. Trotz vieler jung____ Leute rentiert sich hier ein Jugendzentrum kaum.

7. a. Er wurde wegen gut____ Führung vorzeitig aus dem Gefängnis entlassen.
   b. Ich verlange von Ihnen gut____ Führung.
   c. Was verstehen Sie eigentlich unter gut____ Führung?
   d. Gut____ Führung kann frühzeitige Entlassung bedeuten.

8. a. Viel fett____ Essen schadet der Gesundheit.
   b. Bei viel fett____ Essen nimmt man natürlich zu.

    c. Ich mag zu viel fett_____ Essen nicht.

    d. Trotz viel fett_____ Essens ist sie immer noch schlank.

9. a. Dieser blöd_____ Kerl hat mir die Vorfahrt genommen.

    b. Mit diesem blöd_____ Kerl will ich nichts mehr zu tun haben.

    c. Leider liebe ich diesen blöd_____ Kerl immer noch.

    d. Wegen dieses blöd_____ Kerls habe ich nächtelang nicht geschlafen.

10. a. Es gibt nichts Besseres als eine gut_____ Freundin.

    b. Mit einer gut_____ Freundin kann man über alles reden.

    c. Eine gut_____ Freundin ist mehr wert als alles Andere.

    d. Ich hätte auch gern so eine gut_____ Freundin wie du.

2 Adjective declension (see 4.1)

Fill in the adjective endings where necessary in the following text.

Hawaii – ich lebe im Paradies

Seit sechs Jahren lebt die Hamburgerin Arabelle Bottorff auf Maui und richtet Hochzeiten für deutsch_____ Paare aus. Ihr Leben – das ist ein tropisch_____ Traum mit 340 herrlich_____ Sonnentagen im Jahr und exotisch_____ Früchten, die an jedem Baum wachsen …

Hawaii – das klingt nach unendlich_____ Sonnenschein und tropisch_____ Nächten, nach endlos_____ Freiheit und ewig_____ Sehnsucht. Nach einem Klischee, das eigentlich zu schön_____ ist, um wahr_____ zu sein. Mit einem Unterschied: „Diese Inseln sind real_____ und das Leben hier ist wirklich paradiesisch_____", sagt Arabelle Bottorff.

Seit sechs Jahren lebt die 37-Jährig_____ auf Maui, dem zweitgrößt_____ Atoll der Inselkette. Der Zufall und eine zerbrochen_____ Liebe haben sie damals hierher verschlagen. Als ihr damalig_____ Freund sie verlässt, will sie alles vergessen und macht erst mal Urlaub auf der malerisch_____ Insel Hawaii. Am Strand verliebt sie sich in ihren jetzig_____ Ehemann Gary, sechs Monate später schwören sich die beid_____ ewig_____ Liebe – und weil dieser glücklich_____ Tag der schönst_____ in ihrem Leben ist, steigt die Hamburgerin in das Hochzeitsgeschäft ein. Mit ihrer gut gehend_____ Agentur „Hawaii Lei" richtet sie romantisch_____ Hochzeiten für eine deutsch_____ Klientel aus. Ein manchmal nicht ganz unkompliziert_____ Geschäft auf den Inseln: „Ein Paar wollte sich in einer versteckt_____ Bucht trauen lassen", erzählt die gebürtig_____ Hamburgerin. „Aber als wir dort ankamen, war die Bucht verschwunden – die stark_____ Wellen hatten den gesamt_____ Strand weggespült."

Arabelle Bottorff lächelt. Viele ungewöhnlich_____ Geschichten könnte sie erzählen, sagt sie. Aber am meisten faszinieren sie immer noch diese traumhaft_____ Inseln selbst. Als sei es das Selbstverständlichst_____ auf der ganz_____ Welt, berichtet sie dann von den abertausend bunt_____ Fischen in der klein_____ Bucht, die in Maui alle Einheimisch_____ nur „das Aquarium" nennen. Sie beschreibt die duftend_____ Mangos und Guaven. Und die unglaublich_____ Vielfalt einer Landschaft, die geprägt ist von Vulkanen und riesig_____ Lavafeldern, von weiß_____, golden_____, schwarz_____ und sogar grün_____ Stränden, von endlos_____ Urwäldern und mächtig_____ Bergen. Sie erzählt von den einsamst_____ Buchten, die am leichtest_____ zu finden sind, wenn man nicht der lang_____ Straße folgt, sondern sich direkt durch das dicht_____ Gebüsch schlägt und sie hört nicht mehr auf zu schwärmen: „Ich liebe diese weich_____ Luft", sagt sie, „den mild_____ Wind und das unvergleichlich_____ Licht." Hier auf dem paradiesisch_____ Hawaii hat sie ihr zweit_____ Zuhause gefunden.

(Fernsehwoche)

3 Adjective declension after some plural determiners (see 4.2)

Supply the correct endings on the plural determiners and the adjectives that follow.

1. Einige____ klein____ Jungen liefen an uns vorbei.
2. Es ist besser wenig____ gut____ Freunde zu haben als viel____ oberflächlich____.
3. Wir haben mit mehrere____ ander____ Ärzten gesprochen.
4. Das ist die Meinung viel____ deutsch____ Politiker.
5. In einige____ klein____ Städten ist das kulturelle Angebot besser als in manch____ groß____.
6. Ich habe schon bei viel____ ausländisch____ Firmen gearbeitet.
7. Trotz manche____ klein____ Meinungsverschiedenheiten verstehen wir uns mit wenig____ unwichtig____ Ausnahmen sehr gut.
8. In meiner Klasse gibt es wenig____ interessiert____ Schüler, aber dafür viel____ laut____.

4 Declension of adjectives ending in -el, -en, -er (see 4.2)

Fill in the gaps, supplying the correct form of the adjective.

1. Das ist eine sehr (heikel) _____ Angelegenheit, die für alle (übel) _____ Konsequenzen haben kann.
2. Die Qualität von (teuer) _____ Kleidung ist nicht immer besser als die von (billig) _____.
3. Wir gingen durch einen (dunkel) _____ Wald, wo wir viele (selten) _____ Vögel sahen.
4. Meiner Meinung nach gibt es keine (plausibel) _____ Erklärung für sein plötzlich so (unflexibel) _____ Verhalten.
5. Bei diesem (miserabel) _____ Wetter bleibe ich zu Hause.
6. Nur (rentabel) _____ Firmen können mit (hoch) _____ Gewinnen rechnen.
7. In diesem Film gab es einige (makaber) _____ Szenen.
8. Du wirst (ungeheuer) _____ Schwierigkeiten bekommen.
9. (sauer) _____ Äpfel schmecken mir überhaupt nicht.

5 Adjectives used as nouns (see 4.3)

Complete the following sentences with nouns formed from the adjectives in the box below.

1. Ich wünsche dir alles _____ und _____ zum Geburtstag.
2. Bei dem Erdbeben gab es leider sehr viele _____. Die _____ wurden alle in nahe gelegene Krankenhäuser gebracht.
3. Hast du etwas _____ von deinem Bruder gehört? Oder ist alles beim _____.
4. Mein Mann ist _____, aber ich selbst bin Schweizerin.
5. Du musst in der Nacht etwas _____ geträumt haben. Du hast nämlich im Schlaf ganz laut gelacht.
6. Die _____ des Patienten gaben ihre Zustimmung zu der Operation.
7. Hier werden nur die Pässe von _____ aus Ländern kontrolliert, die nicht zur EU gehören.
8. Die Predigt des _____ enthielt wenig _____.
9. Bei dem Zugunglück wurden fünf _____ leicht verletzt.
10. Das ist Timo. Noch ist er mein _____, aber wir wollen im Juli heiraten.

verwandt	neu	verlobt	lustig	geistlich	überlebend	deutsch	lieb
reisend	staatsangehörig	interessant	gut	alt	tot		

6 Adjectives with the dative (see 4.4)
Translate the following sentences into German.

1. This man was not known to her.
2. I am very grateful to you for your help. (*familiar form, singular*)
3. Do you think your husband is faithful to you? (*familiar form*)
4. It has always been clear to me that she is superior to her colleagues.
5. I find it embarrassing that I am so similar to my brother.
6. Unfortunately it is impossible for me to come.
7. I feel sick and dizzy.
8. Usually I am either too hot or too cold.
9. All of us find his behaviour incomprehensible.
10. I find it unpleasant to wear clothes made of polyester.

7 Adjectives with prepositions (see 4.5)
Fill in the gaps supplying the correct preposition.

1. Benjamin ist neidisch _____ alle, die _____ besseren Leistungen fähig sind als er.
2. Es ist typisch _____ Eltern, dass sie stolz _____ ihre Kinder sind.
3. Die Journalistin machte ihren Kollegen _____ seinen Fehler aufmerksam.
4. Die Ärzte waren sehr besorgt _____ den Zustand des Patienten.
5. Wir sind nur _____ ernst gemeinten Zuschriften interessiert.
6. Ich bin zwar _____ harte Arbeit gewöhnt, bin aber nicht besonders scharf da(r) _____.
7. Deutschland ist ein Land, das arm _____ Bodenschätzen ist.
8. In manchen Berufen ist die Bezahlung _____ der Leistung abhängig.
9. Meine Tante ist bettlägerig und ist _____ ständige Hilfe angewiesen.
10. In dieser Frage ist der Bundeskanzler _____ keinerlei Kompromissen bereit.

8 Comparison of adjectives (see 4.6 and 4.7)
Make up questions for a quiz by using the correct superlative form of the adjective in brackets.

1. Wie heißt der (groß) _____ See Deutschlands?
2. Wo befindet sich der (klein) _____ Knochen im menschlichen Körper?
3. Welches ist der (hoch) _____ Berg Deutschlands?
4. Welcher Planet ist am (weit) _____ von der Erde entfernt, und welcher ist ihr am (nah) _____ ?
5. Welche Universität gilt als die (alt) _____ Uni Europas?
6. Wer war beim letzten internationalen Wettkampf der (stark) _____ Mann der Welt?
7. Auf welches Datum fällt der (lang) _____ Tag und die (kurz) _____ Nacht?
8. Wo befindet sich das (heiß) _____ Klima der Erde?
9. In welchem europäischen Land ist Benzin im Moment am (teuer) _____ ?
10. Welches College in Oxford gilt im Moment als das (reich) _____ , welches als das (arm) _____ ?

9 Comparison of adjectives (see 4.6 and 4.7)

Complete the following sentences by supplying the correct comparative form of the adjective in brackets.

1. Diese Schuhe sind mir zu teuer. Haben Sie keine (billig) _____?
2. Für einen (gut) _____ Wein muss man natürlich bereit sein, ein paar Mark (viel) _____ zu bezahlen.
3. Viele Leute beklagen sich, dass die Lebenshaltungskosten immer (hoch) _____ werden und die Löhne im Verhältnis immer (niedrig) _____.
4. In Deutschland trinkt man sein Bier im Allgemeinen (kalt) _____ und seinen Kaffee (stark) _____ als in England.
5. Markenartikel sind zwar (teuer) _____ als andere Artikel, aber nicht unbedingt immer (gut) _____.
6. Wer (gesund) _____ lebt, lebt (lang) _____.
7. Der (klug) _____ gibt nach. (Sprichwort)
8. Die Stimmen nach (hart) _____ Strafen für Gewaltverbrechen werden immer (laut) _____.
9. Mit deiner neuen Frisur siehst du um 10 Jahre (jung) _____ aus.
10. Ich fühle mich in einem (warm) _____ Klima (wohl) _____ als in einem (kühl) _____.
11. Meine Schwester hat (dunkel) _____ Haare und eine (tief) _____ Stimme als ich.
12. Je (nah) _____ die Prüfung rückt, desto (groß) _____ wird meine Angst davor.

10 Time adverbials (see 4.9)

Decide which time adverb in brackets to use for the sentence to make sense.

1. Elmar und Veronika sind vor zwei Jahren ins Ausland gegangen, und _____ haben wir nichts mehr von ihnen gehört. (soeben, seitdem, gerade, augenblicklich)
2. Hör _____ auf mit dem Blödsinn! (lange, selten, sofort, bisher)
3. Im Moment haben wir zwei Kinder, aber _____ wird ein drittes zur Welt kommen. (gelegentlich, unaufhörlich, meistens, demnächst)
4. Sie bekommen _____ einen provisorischen Vertrag. Nach der Probezeit geben wir Ihnen dann einen festen Vertrag. (vorläufig, gestern, seitdem, neulich)
5. Wir haben _____ die Nachricht bekommen, dass ihr heiraten wollt. Herzlichen Glückwunsch! (demnächst, wieder, gerade, bald)
6. Wenn du das Bad putzt, mache ich _____ den Abwasch. (lange, inzwischen, gerade, neulich)
7. Mein Vater ist _____ im Krieg verletzt worden. (kurz, inzwischen, damals, bisher)
8. Ich gehe mal _____ rüber zu den Nachbarn. Es dauert nicht lange. (immer, oft, selten, kurz)
9. Ich habe _____ einen interessanten Artikel in der Zeitung gelesen. (morgen, bisher, neulich, augenblicklich)
10. Du darfst den Film im Fernsehen angucken, aber _____ müssen die Hausaufgaben fertig sein. (vorher, selten, seitdem, manchmal)
11. Ich trinke _____ eine Flasche Wein beim Fernsehen. (neulich, bisher, früher, gelegentlich)
12. In afrikanischen Ländern regnet es ziemlich _____. (wieder, selten, manchmal, nie)

13. _____ bin ich viel öfter ins Theater gegangen. (jetzt, gestern, früher, nochmals)
14. Mein Sohn hat versprochen anzurufen, aber _____ hat er sich noch nicht gemeldet.(meistens, gerade, irgendwann, bisher)
15. Mein Onkel erzählt _____ vom Krieg. Ich kann es wirklich nicht mehr hören. (unaufhörlich, nie, vorher, inzwischen)

11 Adverbs of place (see 4.10)

Fill in the gaps using the correct adverbs of place from the box below.

1. Wo sind nur meine Schlüssel? Ich habe _____ gesucht, aber ich kann sie einfach _____ finden. _____ müssen sie doch sein.
2. In den meisten englischen Häusern befinden sich Wohnzimmer, Esszimmer und Küche _____ und die Schlafzimmer _____.
3. Im Winter ist es _____ meist kälter als _____.
4. Sie können leider im Moment nicht mit Herrn Petersen sprechen. Er ist _____ in einer wichtigen Besprechung.
5. Ich habe das Haus nur von _____ gesehen.
6. In diesem Restaurant ist es mir zu verraucht. Ich würde lieber _____ essen.
7. Ist dieser Fleck _____ oder _____ an der Scheibe?
8. _____ in der Pampa blieb plötzlich unser Auto stehen.
9. In einem Brief steht _____ normalerweise das Datum und _____ die Unterschrift.
10. Frau Blessing ist heute leider nicht _____. Sie ist geschäftlich in Rom und kommt erst am Freitag wieder zurück.

außen außen draußen drinnen irgendwo nirgendwo/nirgends anderswo/woanders
da oben oben innen mitten mitten unten unten überall

12 Adverbs of direction (see 4.11)

Decide whether to use -hin- or -her- to form the correct directional adverb.

1. Das Auto fuhr in den Wald _____ein und kam eine halbe Stunde später wieder _____aus.
2. Ich möchte auf keinen Fall in diese Geschichte _____ein gezogen werden.
3. Ich war jetzt schon fünf Mal im Urlaub in Italien. Ich möchte endlich mal woanders_____ fahren.
4. Niemand weiß genau, wo_____ er kommt und wo_____ er geht.
5. Peter stand auf dem Balkon und rief zu uns _____unter, wir sollten doch zu ihm _____auf kommen.
6. Plötzlich krabbelte eine Spinne unter dem Sofa _____vor.
7. Am Wochenende fahren wir zwei irgendwo_____.
8. Der Fremde trat zu uns an den Tisch _____an und zog einen seltsamen Gegenstand aus seiner Tasche _____aus.
9. Sie gehen hier die Straße _____unter, durch die Brücke _____durch und dann auf der anderen Seite den kleinen Hügel _____auf.
10. Komm doch bitte _____aus und hilf mir, die Einkaufstaschen _____ein zu tragen.
11. Früher mussten die Schüler aufstehen, wenn der Lehrer _____einkam.
12. Mit dir würde ich überall_____ gehen, sogar bis ans Ende der Welt.

13 Adverbs of place and direction (see **4.10** and **4.11**)

Translate the following sentences into German.

1. He woke me up in the middle of the night.
2. I am not going anywhere. I am staying here.
3. She didn't know where to look.
4. Please come down now and eat your breakfast. (*singular*)
5. One moment, please. He's out in the garden but I'll call him in.
6. I know there's a party tonight but I'm not going (there).
7. The picture is slightly damaged at the top.
8. I would like to go somewhere else.
9. She must have moved somewhere else.
10. Please go in and wait there.
11. I will never go there again.
12. How did you get here? (*familiar singular*)
13. He came from far away.

14 Adverbials with the accusative case (see **4.9** and **4.11**)

Look at sections **4.9** and **4.11** of the reference part of this book very carefully and then, from the following sentences, identify those in which the italicized accusative is used to express **length of time**, a **point in time** or **distance** rather than, for example, a direct object.

1. Er ging *den steilen Berg* hinauf.
2. *Nächsten Mittwoch* ist keine Schule.
3. Wir sahen *den steilen Berg* schon von weitem.
4. Wir waren *den ganzen August* unterwegs.
5. Mein Sohn kommt *diesen Herbst* zur Schule.
6. Ich freue mich auf *einen Tag* zu Hause.
7. Bleiben Sie doch einfach *einen Tag* zu Hause.
8. Wir mussten *die letzten zwei Kilometer* zu Fuß gehen.
9. Ich denke oft an *die Woche* mit dir in der kleinen Pension.
10. Wir mussten anhalten. *Die letzten zwei Kilometer* haben wir einfach nicht mehr geschafft.
11. Ich werde *diesen Herbst* nie vergessen.

15 Adverbs of manner (see **4.8** and **4.13**)

Make the following noun phrases into proper sentences by using a verb in place of the italicized noun and making the adjective into an adverb.

e.g. Die schnelle *Fahrt* des Zuges.
   Der Zug fährt schnell.

1. Das ständige *Jammern* meiner Mutter.
2. Die schwere *Arbeit* meines Vaters.
3. Der unaufhaltsame *Aufstieg* des Arturo Ui.
4. Die rasende *Entwicklung* der Technik.
5. Der wunderschöne *Gesang* der Chorknaben.
6. Das unerträgliche *Dröhnen* der Maschinen.
7. Der laute *Schrei* der Eule.
8. Die freiwillige *Hilfe* der Feuerwehr.
9. Der unermüdliche *Einsatz* der Hilfskräfte bei der Flutkatastrophe.
10. Der regelmäßige *Spaziergang* der Familie.
11. Die freundlichen *Grüße* der Nachbarn.
12. Das absichtliche *Foul* des Fußballers.

16 Adverbs of attitude and manner (see **4.8**, **4.12** and **4.13**)
Rewrite the following sentences replacing the italicized phrase or clause by an adverb of manner.

e.g. *Ich hoffe, dass* er noch kommt.
   Hoffentlich kommt er noch.

1. *Es ist möglich, dass* er den Zug verpasst hat.
2. *Es besteht kein Zweifel, dass* er die Wahrheit sagt.
3. Da haben Sie sicher *zum Teil* Recht.
4. *Er bedauerte, dass* er ihr nicht helfen konnte.
5. Heute darfst du *als Ausnahme* etwas länger aufbleiben.
6. In Deutschland *ist es normal*, sich vor dem Essen „guten Appetit" zu wünschen.
7. *Es ist erstaunlich, dass* sie die Stelle bekommen hat.
8. *Es ist interessant, dass* er seine Einstellung plötzlich geändert hat.
9. Wir haben drei neue Mitarbeiter *auf Probe* eingestellt.
10. Wir könnten *zum Beispiel* mit den Kindern ein Picknick machen.
11. *Es ist komisch, dass* ihr nie zu Hause seid, wenn ich anrufe.
12. *Es ist natürlich, dass* sich Tiere in freier Wildbahn wohler fühlen als im Zoo.
13. *Wir hoffen, dass* es euch im Urlaub gefallen hat.
14. Er ist *als Zwangsmaßnahme* in eine andere Filiale versetzt worden.
15. *Ich bin glücklich, dass* die Operation gut verlaufen ist.
16. Bei dieser Beschäftigung wird man *pro Stunde* bezahlt.

17 Ordinal numbers (see **4.18**)
Write the following dates in words. Start by saying *Heute ist der ...*

1. 11.1.	3. 24.12.	5. 16.10.	7. 6.5.	9. 18.2.	11. 31.12.
2. 2.7.	4. 8.3.	6. 28.4.	8. 13.9.	10. 25.11.	12. 20.7.

18 Ordinal numbers (see **4.18**)
Write the following dates in words. Start by saying *Er ist am ... geboren.*

1. 28.1.1958	3. 3.11.1987	5. 22.8.1789	7. 23.9.1672	9. 16.3.1354	11. 7.2.1555
2. 12.7.1947	4. 30.4.1492	6. 5.12.1667	8. 18.11.1202	10. 1.1.2000	12. 20.6.2001

5 Prepositions

1 Prepositions and cases (see **5.1–5.4**)
Group the following prepositions according to the case they govern, i.e. accusative, dative, accusative or dative, genitive.

bis	für	gegenüber	vor	hinter	an	während	wegen
auf	aus	bei	durch	außerhalb	statt	mit	über
außer	von	ohne	ab	nach	um	unter	zu
gegen	in	zwischen	hinsichtlich	trotz	angesichts	seit	neben

2 Prepositions with the accusative (see **5.1**)

Decide whether to use the preposition *bis*, *durch*, *für*, *gegen*, *ohne* or *um* for each of the following sentences to make sense. You will have to use some prepositions several times.

1. Er hat _____ seine eigene Schuld seinen Führerschein verloren.
2. Ich werde immer _____ dich da sein.
3. _____ zu meiner Pensionierung dauert es noch eine Weile.
4. Er fuhr mit dem Auto _____ einen Baum.
5. Ich gehe _____ ein Jahr nach Amerika.
6. Ich kann _____ dich nicht leben.
7. _____ halb vier kommt meine Tochter aus der Schule.
8. In vielen Mittelmeerländern machen die Leute _____ Abend gern einen Spaziergang.
9. Das Geld, das ich ihr geliehen habe, hat sie mir _____ heute noch nicht zurückgezahlt.
10. Mein Freund wohnt gleich _____ die Ecke.
11. Hast du _____ oder _____ einen Streik gestimmt?
12. _____ Stuttgart dauert es mindestens noch zwei Stunden.
13. Gehen Sie _____ die Unterführung und dann immer geradeaus.
14. Wenn wir uns streiten, dann immer _____ Geld.

3 Prepositions with the dative (see **5.2**)

Decide whether to use the preposition *aus*, *außer*, *bei*, *gegenüber*, *mit*, *nach*, *seit*, *von* or *zu* for each of the following sentences to make sense. You will have to use some prepositions several times.

1. Viele Jugendliche wohnen lieber allein als _____ ihren Eltern.
2. Ich schenke meiner Schwester zum Geburtstag ein Armband _____ Gold.
3. _____ hier bis in mein Büro dauert es eine halbe Stunde _____ dem Auto.
4. Wo warst du denn? Ich warte _____ fast einer Stunde auf dich.
5. Ich habe _____ Florian gehört, dass du ein guter Tennisspieler bist.
6. Wir wollen morgen _____ Freunden _____ Trier fahren und sie dort in ihrem neuen Haus besuchen.
7. Ich muss unbedingt _____ Hause. Es ist ja schon _____ Mitternacht.
8. _____ ihrem Hund hat die alte Frau niemanden, _____ dem sie sprechen kann.
9. _____ so einem Wetter bleibe ich lieber _____ Hause.
10. Mein Mann kommt _____ Buxtehude. Das ist nicht weit _____ Hamburg.
11. Wir wohnen _____ letztem Jahr direkt _____ der Schule.
12. Er hat sich _____ der Gartenarbeit _____ dem Spaten auf den Fuß gehauen.
13. Man kann _____ mehreren Gründen den Beruf wechseln.
14. Was wünschst du dir _____ deinem achtzehnten Geburtstag?
15. Ich saß gestern im Zug einem Mann _____ , der aussah wie Humphrey Bogart.
16. _____ so vielen Musikern in der Familie ist es kein Wunder, dass auch der Sohn Musik studieren will.
17. Meiner Meinung _____ sollten wir unseren Mitmenschen _____ viel toleranter sein.
18. Der Junge kam _____ dem Haus gelaufen.
19. Meine Mutter arbeitet schon _____ mehreren Jahren _____ Aldi.
20. Wie komme ich am besten _____ den Kliniken?

4 Prepositions with the accusative or the dative (see **5.3**)

Supply the correct endings, deciding whether the accusative or the dative is needed after the preposition.

1. Der Unfall geschah an ein____ Freitag direkt neben d____ Gemüseladen.
2. Unter ein____ Million Franken bekommt man in d____ Schweiz kein Haus in dies____ Größe.
3. Vor ein____ Woche habe ich meine Freundin in d____ neu____ Kino an d____ Ecke eingeladen.
4. Häng das neue Bild lieber an d____ ander____ Wand. An dies____ Wand hängen schon viel zu viele Bilder.
5. Wir haben in unser____ Garten hinter d____ Haus eine kleine Terrasse.
6. Leg dich doch unter ein____ Baum. Da bist du nicht so in d____ Sonne.
7. Was ist der Unterschied zwischen ein____ Kamel und ein____ Dromedar?
8. Ich fahre lieber in d____ Berge als an d____ See.
9. Die Streikenden stellten sich vor d____ Fabriktor und blockierten es.
10. Ich würde gerne mal wieder auf ein____ Fest gehen.
11. Auf d____ Weg nach Italien fuhren wir über d____ Brennerpass.
12. Meine Mutter stellt sich immer zwischen mein____ Bruder und sein____ Frau.
13. Schicken Sie den Brief wieder an d____ Absender zurück.
14. Fahren Sie immer d____ Fluss entlang und dann links über d____ Brücke. An d____ Ampel fahren Sie rechts in d____ Goethestraße, bis Sie an ein____ Kreuzung kommen. Sie fahren über d____ Kreuzung immer geradeaus und an d____ Post vorbei. Das Hotel Sonnenhof ist nur ungefähr zweihundert Meter hinter d____ Post auf d____ recht____ Seite. Sie können es auf kein____ Fall verfehlen.
15. Es ist unter d____ heutig____ Bedingungen nicht immer angenehm, an ein____ deutsch____ Universität zu studieren.
16. Auf d____ Ärztekongress wurde über d____ neuest____ Forschungsergebnisse gesprochen.
17. Wenn Christian neben sein____ Mutter läuft, merke ich erst, wie groß er in letzt____ Zeit geworden ist.
18. In mein____ Zimmer sieht es meistens ordentlich aus, weil ich immer alles unter d____ Bett schiebe.
19. Stell die Einkaufstüten am besten neben d____ Kühlschrank.
20. Komm doch heute Nachmittag auf ein____ Sprung bei mir vorbei.
21. Du gehst mir auf d____ Nerven.

5 Prepositions (see **5**)

Supply the correct endings for the following idiomatic expressions, and match them up with their correct meaning.

1. jemanden auf d____ Palme bringen
2. etwas an d____ groß____ Glocke hängen
3. etwas auf d____ hoh____ Kante haben
4. hinter schwedisch____ Gardinen sitzen
5. jemandem auf d____ Schlips treten
6. ein Brett vor d____ Kopf haben
7. sich aus d____ Staub machen
8. unter d____ Räder kommen
9. bis in d____ Puppen etwas tun
10. in d____ Tinte sitzen
11. von d____ Hand in d____ Mund leben
12. sich auf d____ faul____ Haut legen
13. vor d____ eigen____ Türe kehren
14. sich nach d____ Decke strecken
15. nicht alle Tassen in d____ Schrank haben
16. kein Blatt vor d____ Mund nehmen
17. die Katze aus d____ Sack lassen

a. jemanden (unabsichtlich) beleidigen

b. verrückt sein

c. nichts verstehen

d. in Schwierigkeiten sein

e. jemanden wütend machen

f. faul sein/nichts tun

g. sehr arm leben

h. sich Mühe geben/ehrgeizig sein

i. sehr direkt alles sagen

j. seine eigenen Fehler erkennen

k. heimlich weggehen/verschwinden

l. etwas publik/öffentlich machen

m. Geld gespart haben

n. in ernste Schwierigkeiten kommen

o. im Gefängnis sein

p. bei einer Tätigkeit kein Ende finden

q. ein Geheimnis erzählen

6 Prepositions (see 5)

Use the correct preposition in brackets for the sentences to make sense. Remember that the case is also an indication of which preposition to use. Sometimes several prepositions are possible.

1. Als Katholik war er strikt _____ eine Scheidung. (auf, durch, gegen, nach)

2. Ich stehe hundertprozentig _____ meinem Mann. (auf, zwischen, seit, hinter)

3. _____ der anhaltenden Regenfälle konnte das Open-Air-Konzert nicht stattfinden. (statt, wegen, vor, bis)

4. Sie stellte sich schützend _____ die Kinder. (gegen, bei, auf, vor)

5. Die Sitzplätze _____ der U-Bahn waren alle besetzt. (in, auf, an, mit)

6. Bleiben Sie bitte _____ der Fahrt angeschnallt! (während, wegen, seit, bei)

7. Ich fahre morgen früh wieder _____ Hause. (zu, nach, von, in)

8. _____ sein Alter müsste er viel besser lesen können. (in, bei, für, um)

9. Er wurde _____ einen Schuss verletzt. (bei, von, durch, mit)

10. _____ dem Unfall gab es einen Verletzten. (bei, in, während, wegen)

11. Die Wohnungen sollen noch _____ diesem Jahr fertig werden. (seit, während, zu, in)

12. _____ seiner Rückkehr ist er ganz anders als früher. (seit, vor, bei, trotz)

13. Ich würde gern mal _____ die USA fliegen. (nach, zu, in, an)

14. _____ Sonntagen sitzen wir den ganzen Tag vor dem Fernseher. (auf, vor, seit, an)

15. Herr Seberich ist _____ dem fünften und dem achten April auf Geschäftsreise. (an, seit, während, zwischen)

16. Ich muss _____ zwei Uhr wieder im Büro sein. (gegen, um, bis, auf)

17. _____ guter Schulnoten bekam er keine Lehrstelle. (wegen, mit, trotz, ohne)

18. Ich übernachte heute _____ Freunden in Tübingen (bei, zu, mit, an)

19. Was macht ihr dieses Jahr _____ Weihnachten? (bei, auf, an, zu)

20. Ich kann Sie _____ Reutlingen im Auto mitnehmen. (zu, bis, nach, seit)

7 Prepositions (see 5)

Fill in the gaps using the prepositions in brackets at the end of each section of the following interview with the German pop star Udo Jürgens.

Udo Jürgens – jetzt gibt er Vollgas

1.   Dieser Mann ist wirklich ein Phänomen: _____ 30. September wird Udo Jürgens tatsächlich 66 Jahre alt – und bestätigt, was er _____ einem seiner größten Hits gesungen hat: „_____ 66 Jahren ist noch lange nicht Schluss!" Eine Woche _____ seinem Geburtstag geht der Mega-Entertainer wieder _____ große Deutschland-Tournee. _____ 50 Konzerte, schon jetzt sind alle Hallen ausverkauft. „Hätte mir _____ 20 Jahren jemand prognostiziert, dass ich noch _____ Jahre 2000 die Fans mobilisiere, ich hätte ihn für verrückt erklärt."

(*über, vor, nach, am, im, in, auf, mit*)

2.   *Interviewer:* **Karriere** _____ **Familie – bereuen Sie diese Entscheidung manchmal?**
Udo Jürgens: Nein. Ich lebe zwar allein, pflege aber einen gesunden Kontakt _____ meinen Kindern. Das ist die einzige Form _____ Familie, _____ der ein Egoist wie ich leben kann.
Fühlen Sie sich denn nie einsam?
Doch. _____ einer großen Tournee zum Beispiel: Plötzlich ist der ganze Trubel vorbei und du sitzt allein _____ Hause. Da fällst du _____ ein Loch. Aber ich habe gelernt, _____ solchen Situationen umzugehen.

(*zu, zu, nach, statt, in, von, mit, mit*)

3.   **Sie haben** _____ **Ihrer Karriere alles erreicht – Geld, Erfolg, Anerkennung. Was treibt Sie immer noch** _____ **die Bühne?**
Als älterer Mensch hat man nur zwei Möglichkeiten: entweder du setzt dich _____ den Ofen und stumpfst ab, oder du hältst Geist und Körper fit. Ich habe mich für die zweite Variante entschieden.
Aber muss es denn eine 35-Städte-Tour sein?
Es gibt Leute, die gehen _____ meinem Alter barfuß _____ die Sahara oder _____ Sauerstoff _____ den Mount Everest. Ich mache halt eine Tournee. _____ einem erfolgreichen Konzert stelle ich mich _____ den Spiegel und sage: Udo, du bist zwar nicht mehr der Jüngste, aber du zeigst es ihnen noch.

(*hinter, nach, durch, auf, auf, ohne, in, in, vor*)

4.   **Die Sucht nach Applaus?**
Nein. Es mag viele Kollegen geben, die danach süchtig sind. _____ mir ist es definitiv nicht die Eitelkeit, die mich _____ die Bühne treibt. Es ist der ungeheure Rückenwind, den ich _____ meine Fans habe. Das muss man sich mal vorstellen: Die zahlen viel Geld _____ eine Karte und fahren dann _____ dem Auto weiß Gott wohin, um schließlich _____ eine oft ungemütliche Halle reinzukommen. Und wenn das Licht dann ausgeht, will das Publikum _____ drei Stunden _____ einer anderen Welt sein.

(*durch, mit, für, für, in, in, bei, auf*)

5.   **Hat der Erfolg Sie verändert?**
Und wie! Ich war plötzlich ein Star. Das hieß: wilde Partys, hübsche Frauen, falsche Freunde. Wir haben gesoffen _____ spät _____ die Nacht – und _____ Anfang 30 hatte ich ein Alkoholproblem. Erst als ich kurz _____ dem Zusammenbruch war, änderte ich mein Leben.
Haben Sie Angst vor dem Tod?
Nein. Das Leben erlischt _____ Kopf, dann _____ Geist und irgendwann hört das Herz auf zu schlagen. Ich wünsche mir eine möglichst kurze Zeitspanne _____ der Verdunkelung des Geistes und dem Stillstand des Herzens.

Wann ist der Ruhestand ein Thema _____ Sie?

Das weiß ich nicht. Ich lasse die Dinge auf mich zukommen. Der Weg ist das Ziel – _____ diesem Motto habe ich immer gelebt.

(*in, im, im, für, mit, nach, bis, zwischen, vor*)

(*Fernsehwoche*)

8 Prepositional adverbs (see **5.5**)

Fill in the gaps where appropriate, deciding whether to use a third person pronoun with the preposition (e.g. *für ihn*) or whether to use a prepositional adverb (e.g. *dafür*).

1. Er bekam ein neues Fahrrad zum Geburtstag und bedankte sich _____ für _____.
2. Stefan wollte unbedingt einen Gameboy zu Weihnachten haben, und jetzt spielt er kaum _____ mit _____.
3. Frank ist sehr in Gabriele verliebt und würde alles _____ für _____ tun.
4. Ich bin meinen Nachbarn sehr dankbar, denn _____ durch _____ habe ich meinen neuen Freund kennen gelernt.
5. Meine Freundin hat als kleines Kind in Australien gelebt, aber sie erinnert sich kaum noch _____an _____.
6. Mein Onkel ist zwar schon lange tot, aber ich erinnere mich noch gut _____ an _____.
7. Ich kann mich nicht _____ an _____ erinnern, diesen Film schon einmal gesehen zu haben.
8. Als Rotkäppchen an das Bett der Großmutter trat, sah es, dass der Wolf _____ in _____ lag.
9. Sebastian war früher Alkoholiker, aber er spricht nicht gern _____ über _____.
10. Elke verbringt viel Zeit bei ihrer Freundin und geht auch heute Nachmittag wieder _____ zu _____.
11. Herr Kunert ist zwar sehr nett, aber man kann sich nicht _____ auf _____ verlassen.
12. Herr Kunert ist zwar sehr nett, aber man kann sich nicht _____ auf _____ verlassen, dass er die Arbeit richtig macht.
13. Wir freuen uns sehr _____ auf _____, bald in Urlaub fahren zu können.
14. Alle wussten, dass Paul schon einmal im Gefängnis war, nur ich habe nichts _____ von _____ gewusst.
15. Niemand mag den neuen Chef, aber ich habe nichts _____ gegen _____.

9 Prepositional adverbs (see **5.5**)

Construct sentences from the following elements using a prepositional adverb to anticipate the following *dass*-clause or infinitive clause.

e.g. ich/bestehen auf/dass du mitkommst

    Ich bestehe darauf, dass du mitkommst.

1. wir/rechnen mit/dass er noch kommt
2. meine Arbeit/bestehen in/Computer zu programmieren
3. du/sich gewöhnen an/in dem neuen Haus zu wohnen
4. ich/sich verlassen auf/dass du pünktlich wieder zu Hause bist
5. er/denken an/sich scheiden zu lassen

6. ich/überzeugt sein von/dass er das Auto nicht gestohlen hat

7. sie/sorgen für/dass ihre Kinder eine gute Ausbildung bekommen

8. wir/sich freuen auf/bald von Ihnen zu hören

9. ich/sein gegen/Frau Müller als neue Vorsitzende vorzuschlagen

10. er/wissen von/dass wir eine Party für ihn geben wollen

6 Verbs: forms

1 Present tense of weak, strong and irregular verbs (see 6.3, 6.5, 6.10 and 6.11)

Form sentences in the present tense according to the pattern given in the example, supplying the *du*-form of the verb used in the original sentence.

e.g. Ich bleibe lieber zu Hause.
Bleibst du auch lieber zu Hause?

1. Ich spiele gern Fußball. 2. Ich mache sofort meine Hausaufgaben. 3. Ich fahre mit dem Zug. 4. Ich wandere durch die Berge. 5. Ich warte auf einen Freund. 6. Ich rechne nicht mehr mit ihm. 7. Ich trage gern Anzüge. 8. Ich grüße den neuen Lehrer. 9. Ich muss jetzt nach Hause. 10. Ich studiere Geschichte. 11. Ich kann heute nicht kommen. 12. Ich habe keine Zeit. 13. Ich öffne das Fenster. 14. Ich bade jeden Tag. 15. Ich arbeite bei Karstadt. 16. Ich lese gern Kriminalromane. 17. Ich weiß viel über Amerika. 18. Ich werde schnell müde. 19. Ich gebe ihm einen Tip. 20. Ich laufe nach Hause. 21. Ich stoße mir oft den Kopf. 22. Ich darf nicht schwimmen. 23. Ich nehme mir noch ein Stück Kuchen. 24. Ich lebe allein. 25. Ich backe gern Kuchen. 26. Ich klingle an der Tür. 27. Ich ändere meine Meinung. 28. Ich lasse die Kinder in Ruhe. 29. Ich gieße die Blumen. 30. Ich reite seit einem Jahr.

2 Present tense of weak, strong and irregular verbs (see 6.3, 6.5, 6.10 and 6.11)

Form sentences in the present tense according to the pattern given in the example, replacing the third person plural verb form by the third person singular. The letter in brackets indicates gender.

e.g. Die Kinder (*n*) machen Hausaufgaben.
Das Kind macht Hausaufgaben.

1. Die Menschen (*m*) wissen zu viel. 2. Die Bäume (*m*) wachsen schnell. 3. Die Kinder (*n*) schlafen. 4. Die Lehrer (*m*) finden den Fehler nicht. 5. Die Engländer (*m*) sprechen Englisch. 6. Die Athleten (*m*) haben keine Chance. 7. Die Angler (*m*) fangen viele Fische. 8. Die Touristen (*m*) sehen viel im Urlaub. 9. Die Jungen (*m*) werfen Papier auf die Straße. 10. Die Äpfel (*m*) fallen auf den Boden. 11. Die Preise (*m*) dürfen nicht erhöht werden. 12. Die Gäste (*m*) werden ungeduldig. 13. Die Bäume (*m*) sterben. 14. Die Steuern (*f*) werden gesenkt. 15. Die Schüler (*m*) fahren ins Ausland. 16. Die Kinder (*n*) machen heute einen Ausflug. 17. Die Häuser (*n*) stehen schon lange hier. 18. Die Ärzte (*m*) wollen so schnell wie möglich operieren. 19. Im Regal fehlen zwei Bücher (*n*). 20. Die Skifahrer (*m*) brechen sich ein Bein. 21. Die Bienen (*f*) stechen das Mädchen. 22. Die Kunden (*m*) kaufen wenig. 23. Die Kinder (*n*) laufen nach Hause. 24. Die Politiker (*m*) lösen das Problem. 25. Die Nachbarn (*m*) treffen einen Bekannten. 26. Die Autos (*n*) halten. 27. Die Diebe (*m*) stehlen wertvolle Gemälde. 28. Die Sportler (*m*) gewinnen die Medaille. 29. Die Verletzten (*m*) brauchen Hilfe. 30. Die Italiener (*m*) essen viel Spaghetti.

3 Separable verbs (see **6.4**)

Form two sentences, one main clause and one subordinate clause, in the present tense using the verb in brackets in its correct form. Pay attention to the word order.

e.g. Der Zug (ankommen) um 2 Uhr 40. Ich weiß, dass ...
Der Zug kommt um 2 Uhr 40 an. Ich weiß, dass der Zug um 2 Uhr 40 ankommt.

1. Meine Schwester (aufmachen) mir die Tür.
   Ich will, dass ...
2. Die Premiere (stattfinden) schon morgen.
   Weißt du, dass ...
3. Fehler (vorkommen) auch bei Spitzenkräften.
   Es ist klar, dass ...
4. Du (anzünden) eine Kerze.
   Ich finde es schön, wenn ...
5. Ich (vorstellen) dir morgen meinen Freund.
   Ich verspreche dir, dass ...
6. Wir (aufgeben) die Hoffnung nicht.
   Es ist wichtig, dass ...
7. Mein Bruder (eintreten) in einen Karateklub.
   Mein Bruder hat uns erzählt, dass ...

8. Ich (ausmachen) einen Termin beim Arzt für dich.
   Es ist höchste Zeit, dass ...
9. Wir (einziehen) nächste Woche in unser neues Haus.
   Ich freue mich schon, wenn ...
10. Unsere Katze (weglaufen) uns immer.
    Ich verstehe nicht, warum ...
11. Mein Vater (zugeben) nie einen Fehler.
    Es ist ärgerlich, dass ...
12. Du (zurückgeben) das Geld sofort.
    Ich bestehe darauf, dass ...

4 Imperative (see **6.3** and **6.5**)

You come across the following rules of good behaviour in a school. The way they are phrased is by using the infinitive of the verb. Rephrase the rules using the imperative plural (familiar) form as if a teacher is talking to the children.

e.g. Die Hausaufgaben regelmäßig machen.
Macht die Hausaufgaben regelmäßig.

1. Höflich mit den Lehrern sprechen. 2. Kein Papier auf den Boden werfen. 3. Die Türen leise schließen. 4. Im Schulgebäude nicht rennen. 5. Vor Lehrern und Eltern Respekt haben. 6. Keine Schimpfwörter benutzen. 7. Dem Lehrer und anderen Mitschülern zuhören. 8. Während des Unterrichts nicht im Klassenzimmer herumrennen. 9. Andere Mitschüler nicht ärgern oder schlagen. 10. Keinen Kaugummi kauen. 11. Beim Sport keinen Schmuck tragen. 12. Verantwortungsbewusst und vernünftig handeln. 13. Keine frechen Antworten geben. 14. Die Pausenbrote nicht während des Unterrichts essen. 15. Allen Mitschülern gegenüber rücksichtsvoll sein. 16. Kein fremdes Eigentum beschädigen.

5 Imperative (see **6.3** and **6.5**)

You tell your friend about your unhealthy lifestyle, and (s)he suggests what you should do to make it healthier. Form sentences using the imperative singular form (familiar).

e.g. Ich schlafe zu wenig.
Schlaf mehr!

1. Ich gehe zu spät ins Bett.   2. Ich esse sehr unregelmäßig.   3. Ich trinke zu viel Alkohol.   4. Ich rauche zu viel.   5. Ich gehe nicht oft genug spazieren.   6. Ich nehme mir zu wenig Zeit für mich.   7. Ich mache mir zu viele Sorgen.   8. Ich treibe zu wenig Sport.   9. Ich entspanne mich zu wenig.   10. Ich bin sehr nervös.   11. Ich rege mich zu schnell auf.   12. Ich ernähre mich zu schlecht.   13. Ich schalte zu selten ab. 14. Ich arbeite zu viel.   15. Ich gebe zu wenig Geld für mich aus.   16. Ich fahre zu selten in Urlaub.   17. Ich gebe mir immer die Schuld, wenn etwas schief geht.   18. Ich zerbreche mir den Kopf über zu viele unnötige Dinge.

6 Imperative (see **6.3** and **6.5**)

Here is some police advice on how you can minimize the risk of being burgled while you are away on holiday. Rephrase the instructions using the polite imperative form in the plural.

e.g. Eine Alarmanlage einbauen lassen.
   Lassen Sie eine Alarmanlage einbauen!

1. Die Haustür abschließen.
2. Niemals die Fenster offen lassen.
3. Die Nachbarn bitten, ein Auge auf Ihr Haus zu halten.
4. Sich versichern, dass die Alarmanlage funktioniert.
5. Den Rasen mähen, bevor Sie wegfahren.
6. Einem Nachbarn/Bekannten einen Schlüssel geben.
7. Darauf achten, dass man nicht von außen durch die Fenster sehen kann.
8. Nicht alle Fensterläden schließen.
9. Nicht alle Vorhänge zuziehen.
10. Einen Timer einbauen, damit regelmäßig irgendwo ein Licht angeht.

7 Forms of strong and irregular verbs (see **6.10** and **6.11**)

Sort the verbs in each section into groups according to the pattern they follow.

1. **EI – IE – IE**   (*bleiben – blieb – geblieben*)
   or
   EI – I – I   (*beißen – biss – gebissen*)

verzeihen	schreien	schweigen	greifen	schleichen
streiten	schreiben	pfeifen	reißen	leihen
gleiten	treiben	steigen	vergleichen	streichen
meiden	reiben			

2. **I – A – U**   (*singen – sang – gesungen*)
   or
   I – A – O   (*schwimmen – schwamm – geschwommen*)

trinken	zwingen	beginnen	klingen
stinken	spinnen	dringen	gewinnen
binden	verschwinden	gelingen	rinnen
sinken	sinnen	springen	ringen

3. **A – U – A**   (*fahren – fuhr – gefahren*)
   or
   A – IE – A   (*braten – briet – gebraten*)

halten	lassen	blasen	schlafen	fallen
laden	tragen	raten	wachsen	graben
waschen				

4. **E – A – O**   (*helfen – half – geholfen*)
   or
   E – A – E   (*geben – gab – gegeben*)
   or
   E – A – A   (*kennen – kannte – gekannt*)

sprechen	rennen	vergessen	treten
befehlen	geschehen	brennen	treffen
lesen	stechen	brechen	fressen
nennen	werben	stehlen	empfehlen
werfen	sehen	messen	sterben
erschrecken	gelten	verderben	

8 Forms of strong and irregular verbs (see **6.10** and **6.11**)

Give the forms of the third person singular present tense and past tense, and the past participle of the following verbs.

e.g. gehen
   geht – ging – gegangen

1. verzeihen   2. nennen   3. bringen   4. tun   5. sitzen   6. tragen   7. vergleichen   8. stehen
9. denken   10. sprechen   11. schreiben   12. fangen   13. leiden   14. frieren   15. verlieren   16. fließen
17. lügen   18. laufen   19. schneiden   20. schließen   21. fliegen   22. kommen   23. heißen
24. verschwinden   25. liegen   26. ziehen   27. nehmen   28. rufen   29. schieben   30. schweigen
31. essen   32. heben

9 Forms of strong and irregular verbs (see **6.5**, **6.10** and **6.11**)

Rewrite the following sentences in the past tense.

1. Wir fliegen nach Rhodos, leihen uns dort ein Auto und fahren über die ganze Insel.
2. Immer wenn sie diesen Film sieht, fängt sie an zu weinen.
3. Wir wollen am Wochenende aufs Land fahren, aber unsere Kinder bleiben zu Hause.
4. Jedes Mal, wenn er vor dem Fernseher sitzt, schläft er ein.
5. Da der Hund keinen Namen hat, nenne ich ihn einfach Lumpi.
6. Sie wissen nicht, was sie tun.
7. Er hält meine Hand und sieht mich verliebt an.
8. Wir müssen ihn zum Arzt bringen, weil die Schmerzen immer schlimmer werden.

9. Wir kommen ins Zimmer und sehen viele Leute, die wir kennen.

10. Er schwimmt die 100 Meter in seiner persönlichen Rekordzeit und gewinnt damit die Goldmedaille.

11. Ich denke, du willst den Rasen mähen.

12. Er geht ins Badezimmer und nimmt ein Bad.

13. Sie trägt immer einen Hut, weil es ihr steht und auch gut gefällt.

14. Obwohl es im Klassenzimmer viel Lärm gibt und alle Kinder durcheinander schreien, lässt sich unser Lehrer nicht aus der Ruhe bringen.

15. Die Einbrecher brechen in das Haus ein und stehlen viele wertvolle Gegenstände.

16. Die Polizei betritt das Haus und erschrickt über den Zustand der Zimmer.

17. Er hilft mir oft bei der Gartenarbeit, auch wenn er es manchmal vergisst.

18. Er bittet seine Frau um Entschuldigung, aber sie verzeiht ihm seinen Seitensprung nicht.

19. Das Lied, das die Chorknaben singen, klingt sehr schön.

20. Samstag ist für Jürgen der schönste Tag der Woche. Er schläft immer bis um 10 Uhr. Dann steht er auf, wäscht sich und zieht sich an. Danach läuft er zum Bäcker, um sich frische Brötchen zu holen, die er dann gemütlich zum Frühstück isst. Dabei liest er natürlich auch die Zeitung, in der gerade am Samstag immer sehr viel Interessantes steht. Dann ruft er seine Freundin an und trifft sich mit ihr zum Mittagessen. Anschließend gehen sie im Park spazieren, und abends lädt Jürgen seine Freundin ins Theater oder Kino ein. Danach sitzen sie meistens noch in einem Lokal, trinken eine Flasche Wein und sprechen über alles Mögliche. Zum Schluss bringt Jürgen seine Freundin nach Hause, und beide finden, dass der Samstag der schönste Tag der Woche ist.

10 Past tense (see **6.3**, **6.5**, **6.10** and **6.11**)

The following article is written in the present tense to heighten the effect. Rewrite it using the past tense. The relevant verbs are in italics. Leave the sentences in quotation marks in the present tense.

Wir leben in ständiger Angst – unser Nachbar hat einen Kampfhund

Mittwoch, 14.00 Uhr. Monika Peschel *blickt* aus dem Küchenfenster. Wie jeden Tag, wenn sie Sebastian und Julia aus der Schule zurück *erwartet*. Doch an diesem Tag *erlebt* sie einen Schock: Die Kinder *rennen* in panischer Angst auf die Haustür zu. Keine 20 Meter hinter ihnen ein ausgewachsener Bullterrier.

In letzter Sekunde *können* sich die Kinder vor dem gefährlichen Kampfhund in Sicherheit bringen und die Haustür zuwerfen. Nur mit viel Geduld *gelingt* es Monika Peschel, ihre verstörten Kinder zu beruhigen.

Noch am selben Abend *erfahren* die Peschels von Nachbarn, dass der Kampfhund dem neuen Mieter von gegenüber *gehört*. Die Eltern *wollen* gleich am nächsten Tag mit dem neuen Bewohner über den Bullterrier reden. Doch sie *bekommen* eine dreiste Abfuhr: Der Hundebesitzer *denkt* nicht daran, das Tier anzuleinen. Der Hund *braucht* schließlich Auslauf – und mit seiner Angst *muss* nun einmal jeder selber fertig werden. Mit dieser Begründung *lässt* er seinen Hund fortan jeden Tag frei herumlaufen.

Und das *hat* Folgen: Die Kinder *trauen* sich nicht mehr zur Schule. Ans Spielen auf der Straße *ist* gar nicht erst zu denken. Sogar die Erwachsenen *haben* Angst. Sobald man die Tür *öffnet*, *steht* da der Kampfhund und *fletscht* die Zähne.

Schon nach kurzer Zeit *wirkt* die Straße wie ausgestorben. Es *scheint* nur eine Lösung zu geben: Der Kampfhund *muss* weg. Verzweifelt *wendet* sich Monika Peschel an einen Anwalt. Für den *ist* der Fall klar: „Kampfhunde in der Nachbarschaft sind nicht zumutbar."

Das Landgericht Krefeld *zeigt* Verständnis für die Familie: „In unserem Staat muss niemand in ständiger Angst leben." Und weil der Hundebesitzer die Gefahr beharrlich *abstreitet*, *schlagen* die Richter in Hundefachbüchern nach. Darin *steht* fast gleichlautend: „In unkundigen Händen und falsch erzogen, kann ein Bullterrier zu einer gefährlichen Waffe werden, von der man nie weiß, wann sie losgeht."

Das *reicht* für ein Urteil: Der Halter *muss* seinen Bullterrier sofort ins Tierheim abgeben.

(Fernsehwoche)

11 Past participles (see **6.1**, **6.10** and **6.11**)

Supply the past participle form of the verb in brackets.

1. Bevor mein Mann und ich (verheiraten) waren, haben wir uns viel weniger (streiten).
2. Meine Tochter hat gestern einen Geldbeutel auf der Straße (finden) und ihn (aufheben). Sie hat ihn aber nicht mit nach Hause (nehmen), sondern zum Fundbüro (bringen) und ihn dort (abgeben).
3. Nachdem das Geschirr für die Vorspeise (abräumen) war, wurde das Hauptgericht (servieren).
4. Obwohl die Feuerwehr sich sehr (beeilen) hatte, war das Haus schon (abbrennen).
5. Ich habe früher viel Sport (treiben). Ich habe Judo und Karate (machen), bin (schwimmen) und (rudern) und habe sogar einmal die bayerische Jugendmeisterschaft im Schwimmen (gewinnen).
6. Nachdem er sich um die Stelle (bewerben) hatte, wurde ihm (mitteilen), dass die Stelle schon (vergeben) war.
7. Ich habe meine neuen Rollschuhe (ausprobieren), bin aber leider (fallen). Dabei habe ich mir ziemlich Weh (tun), mir den Arm (brechen) und mich an der Hüfte (verletzen).
8. Mein Sohn hat die Prüfung (bestehen) und ist bei der Hochschule (annehmen) worden.
9. Der Zeuge hat (sehen), wie das Auto in die Schillerstraße (abbiegen) ist und dann vor dem Haus des Opfers (halten) hat.
10. Ich habe in der Nacht (träumen), dass es bei uns (klingeln) hat und der Postbote uns ein kleines Paket (bringen) hat, das in rotes Seidenpapier (einpacken) war. Wir haben es (öffnen) und haben uns wahnsinnig (freuen), als wir (feststellen) haben, dass uns jemand eine Million Mark (schicken) hat. Leider bin ich dann (aufwachen) und habe (merken), dass es nur ein Traum (sein) ist.

12 *haben* or *sein* in the perfect? (see **6.7**)

Decide whether to use a form of *haben* or *sein*.

1. Die Maschine aus London _____ mit 25-minütiger Verspätung angekommen.
2. Ich _____ heute Morgen erst um 10 Uhr aufgewacht, weil ich in der Nacht so schlecht geschlafen _____ .
3. Der Junge _____ vom Baum gefallen und _____ sich dabei den Arm gebrochen.
4. Ich _____ heute zu spät zur Arbeit gekommen, weil ich eine Freundin getroffen _____ und wir uns noch eine Weile unterhalten _____ .
5. Die Benzinpreise _____ gestiegen, weil der Finanzminister die Rohölsteuer erhöht _____ .
6. Ich _____ gestern einen Autounfall gehabt, aber Gott sei Dank _____ nicht viel passiert.
7. Das erste Mal _____ er leider bei der Fahrprüfung durchgefallen, aber beim zweiten Mal _____ er sie bestanden.
8. Frank _____ vom Direktor der Schule ausgezeichnet worden, weil er das beste Abitur seines Jahrgangs gemacht _____ .

9. Ich _____ Petra vor einer halben Stunde nach Hause gefahren.

10. Gestern _____ sich vor unserem Haus ein Unfall ereignet, bei dem ein Radfahrer leicht verletzt worden _____.

11. Seit ich deine Kinder das letzte Mal gesehen _____, _____ sie wahnsinnig gewachsen.

12. Die Katze _____ auf den Tisch gesprungen und _____ den ganzen Fisch aufgefressen.

13. Das Konzert _____ schon angefangen.

14. Es _____ ihm nicht gelungen sie zu überzeugen, obwohl er sich sehr viel Mühe gegeben _____.

15. Mein Mann _____ mit den Kindern ins Kino gegangen, aber ich _____ zu Hause geblieben.

16. Im Urlaub _____ wir viel geschwommen und _____ manchmal auch Rad gefahren. Wenn es geregnet_____, _____ wir uns Regenkleidung angezogen und _____ spazieren gegangen. Es_____ ein sehr ruhiger Urlaub gewesen, und wir _____ uns gut erholt.

17. Als ich den Fernseher eingeschaltet _____, _____ plötzlich das Licht im Aquarium ausgegangen.

18. _____ du das Buch schon gelesen, das du dir von mir ausgeliehen _____?

19. Die Nachbarn _____ ihr Haus verkauft und _____ umgezogen.

20. Meine Freundin _____ ziemlich sauer geworden, weil ich schon wieder mal ihren Geburtstag vergessen _____.

13 The forms of the subjunctive (see **6.9**)

Rewrite the following sentences in the subjunctive. Use the same tense as in the original sentence.

e.g. Ich kann dir nicht helfen.
　　Ich könne dir nicht helfen.

1. Er gibt mir keine Antwort. 2. Du hast keine Lust gehabt. 3. Er wird schlafen. 4. Sie war eingeschlafen 5. Wir sind in der Stadt gewesen. 6. Du musst zu Hause bleiben. 7. Ich war krank geworden. 8. Es wird regnen. 9. Ich bin ausgelacht worden. 10. Er saß im Cafe. 11. Wir hatten nichts gewusst. 12. Es gibt keine Ausnahme. 13. Wir wurden ins Haus gelassen. 14. Sie kennt viele Schauspieler. 15. Ich will einen Brief schreiben 16. Du sollst aufhören. 17. Der Zug war angekommen. 18. Er ist in Berlin geblieben. 19. Ihr habt euch umgezogen. 20. Er ist gesehen worden. 21. Wir haben uns verabredet. 22. Er heiratet bald. 23. Er hat sich verlaufen. 24. Du ziehst morgen um. 25. Ich wusste alles. 26. Sie kam um die Ecke. 27. Der Chef mußte auf Geschäftsreise sein. 28. Der Junge lässt seine Schwester nicht in Ruhe. 29. Er wird ungeduldig. 30. Er fährt mit dem Auto.

7 Verbs: uses

I The forms of the passive (see **6.8**)

Rewrite the following sentences using the passive. Use the same tense as in the active constructions and leave out the agent.

e.g. Ich habe diese Bilder gemalt.
　　Diese Bilder sind gemalt worden.

1. Man hat dich in der Stadt gesehen.
2. In der Kirche sang man viele Lieder.
3. Sylvia wird dich sicher morgen anrufen.
4. Die Nachbarn grüßen uns schon lange nicht mehr.
5. Wir hatten die Polizei alarmiert.
6. Die Eltern werden das Kind geschlagen haben.
7. Er wird das Fenster nicht zugemacht haben.
8. Du hast mich belogen.
9. Der Verkehr hat mich aufgehalten.
10. Ich hatte den Rasen gemäht.
11. Die Diebe brachen in die Schule ein.
12. Die Diebe stahlen mehrere Computer.
13. Der Arzt untersucht den Patienten.
14. Die Chirurgen werden nächste Woche die Operation durchführen.
15. Wie viele Karten habt ihr verkauft?
16. Der Chef hat ihn in eine andere Abteilung versetzt.
17. Man beschuldigte ihn des Diebstahls.
18. Wir besprechen gerade ihren Fall.

2 The *werden-* and the *sein-*passive (see **7.4** and **7.8**)

Decide whether to use a form of *werden* or *sein* in the following passive constructions. Choose a suitable tense.

1. Bei dem Zugunglück _____ einige der Passagiere leicht verletzt.
2. Er musste ins Krankenhaus gebracht _____, weil er verletzt _____.
3. Ich _____ von lauter netten Menschen umgeben.
4. Im zweiten Weltkrieg _____ 80% der deutschen U-Boote versenkt.
5. In England _____ es als unhöflich betrachtet, nicht in jedem Satz mindestens einmal „please" und „thank you" zu sagen.
6. Auf dem Fest _____ gefeiert bis in die späte Nacht.
7. In diesem Waschkorb ist die Wäsche, die schon gewaschen _____, aber noch gebügelt _____ muss.
8. Mir _____ gestern meine Brieftasche gestohlen.
9. Er _____ von allen für seinen Mut bewundert.
10. Da die Sitzplätze schon alle vergeben _____, mussten wir einen Stehplatz nehmen.
11. Seit mein Mann tot ist, _____ mein Leben zerstört.
12. In dem Orkan _____ ganze Städte weggefegt.
13. Da ihm die Tat nicht nachgewiesen _____ konnte, musste er frei gesprochen _____.
14. Dresden _____ während des Krieges fast völlig zerstört.
15. Als wir zur Grenze kamen, _____ uns gesagt, dass die weiter führende Straße gesperrt _____.

3 The subjectless passive (see **7.5**)

Rewrite the following sentences using a 'subjectless' passive construction, retaining the tense of the original. Leave out the agent.

e.g. Sie dürfen hier nicht rauchen.
   Hier darf nicht geraucht werden.

1. Wir werden für die Kinder sorgen.
2. Die Leute kaufen nicht mehr genügend bei C&A.
3. Das Schild warnt vor bissigen Hunden.

4. Wir haben auf dem Geburtstagsfest getrunken, getanzt und gelacht.
5. Seit der Entwicklung von E-Mails telefonieren die Leute weniger.
6. In Zeiten einer Wirtschaftskrise sparen die Leute mehr.
7. In Griechenland rauchen die Leute mehr als in Deutschland.
8. In der Diskussion sprachen die Teilnehmer über Finanzhilfe an Länder der dritten Welt.
9. Man muss auf gesunde Ernährung achten.
10. Die Polizei hatte drei Tage lang nach dem vermissten Kind gesucht.
11. Heutzutage fahren die Leute viel aggressiver Auto als früher.
12. Gestern hat man bei uns eingebrochen.
13. In diesem Waldgebiet joggen die Leute gern.
14. Morgen können wir mit den Umbauarbeiten beginnen.
15. In dieser Fabrik arbeiten die Leute rund um die Uhr.
16. Die Abgeordneten stimmten über den Gesetzentwurf ab.

4 The passive with dative objects (see 7.6)

Give passive equivalents for the following active sentences, retaining the tense of the original. Leave out the agent.

e.g. Wir können dir helfen.
   Dir kann geholfen werden.

1. Er gratulierte mir zur bestandenen Prüfung.
2. Sie strich dem kleinen Jungen über das Haar.
3. Er hatte dem Richter nur zögernd geantwortet.
4. Männer schmeicheln schönen Frauen oft.
5. Man dankte mir für meine Mühe.
6. Die Politesse hat dem Autofahrer mit einer Geldstrafe gedroht.
7. Niemand glaubt einem Lügner.
8. Mein Arzt hat mir empfohlen mich zu schonen.
9. Man hat mir von deinen Plänen erzählt.
10. Die Studiogäste widersprachen dem Politiker heftig.
11. Wir misstrauten ihm in jeder Hinsicht.
12. Alle Männer lächeln meiner Schwester zu.

5 von or durch with the passive (see 7.7)

Decide whether to use *von* or *durch* in the following passive constructions, and use the correct case after the preposition.

1. Der Einbrecher wurde _____ [die Polizei] auf frischer Tat ertappt.
2. Ich bin _____ [mein Bruder] gewarnt worden.
3. Ich fühle mich _____ [Ihr Rauchen] belästigt.
4. Das Haus wurde _____ [ein Blitz] getroffen.
5. Die Explosion wurde _____ [eine defekte Gasleitung] verursacht.
6. Der Fußgänger wurde _____ [ein Lastwagen] überrollt.
7. Sein Leben konnte _____ [eine Operation] gerettet werden.
8. Die Angehörigen des Patienten wurden _____ [die Ärzte] benachrichtigt.
9. Sie sind mir _____ [ein Freund] empfohlen worden.
10. Der erste Weltkrieg wurde _____ [die Ermordung] des Erzherzogs Franz Ferdinand ausgelöst.

11. Er wurde _____ [ein herabfallender Dachziegel] am Kopf getroffen.

12. Dieses Bild wurde dem Museum _____ [eine anonyme Spenderin] geschenkt.

13. Die Olympischen Spiele in München im Jahre 1972 wurden _____ [das Attentat] auf mehrere israelische Sportler überschattet.

14. Der Wahlsieger wird _____ [seine Anhänger] gefeiert.

15. Der Pokal für das Tennisturnier in Wimbledon wird immer _____ [die Herzogin von Kent] überreicht.

16. Ich bin _____ [eine Wespe] gestochen worden.

6 Subjunctive II: conditional sentences (see 7.11)

Make two conditional sentences from the following sentences using   a. the past subjunctive or the conditional and   b. the pluperfect subjunctive.

e.g. Wenn ich Geld habe, kaufe ich mir ein Auto.
   Wenn ich Geld *hätte, würde* ich mir ein Auto *kaufen.*
   Wenn ich Geld *gehabt hätte, hätte* ich mir ein Auto *gekauft.*

1. Wenn du die Tabletten nimmst, wirst du wieder gesund.
2. Wenn du gut aussiehst, hast du Erfolg bei Männern.
3. Wenn du dich informierst, weißt du es.
4. Wenn wir gleich losgehen, treffen wir ihn noch.
5. Wenn du vorsichtig bist, beißt der Hund nicht.
6. Wenn sie den Zug verpasst, ruft sie uns sicher an.
7. Wenn du schneller arbeitest, sind wir früher fertig.
8. Wenn du dich vorbereitest, bestehst du die Prüfung.
9. Wenn du dein Zimmer aufräumst, schenke ich dir eine Karte für das Rockkonzert.
10. Was machen wir, wenn wir den Schlüssel nicht finden?
11. Was gibst du mir, wenn ich deinen Aufsatz für dich schreibe?
12. Er kommt zu spät, wenn er zu Fuß geht.
13. Ich sage Ihnen Bescheid, wenn ich etwas von ihm höre.
14. Wenn du langsam fährst, passiert nichts.
15. Wenn er die Wahlen gewinnt, bleibt er für weitere 5 Jahre Präsident.
16. Wenn ich mehr als zwei Gläser Wein trinke, bekomme ich Kopfschmerzen.

7 Reported speech (see 7.12)

Rewrite the following sentences in reported speech. Do not use *dass*. Remember to change pronouns accordingly.

e.g. Er sagte zu mir: „Ich kann heute nicht kommen."
   Er sagte zu mir, er *könne* heute nicht kommen.

1. Der Journalist fragte seinen Kollegen: „Bis wann musst du den Artikel fertig haben?"
2. Der Patient sagte zum Arzt: „Ich habe ständig Kopfschmerzen, mir ist immer schwindelig, und ich fühle mich insgesamt schlapp und müde."

3. Die Kollegen beteuerten: „Die Arbeit macht uns Spaß, und wir wollen noch viele Jahre hier arbeiten."

4. In einer Studie stand: „80% aller 9-Jährigen haben einen eigenen Fernseher im Zimmer und verbringen bis zu 5 Stunden täglich davor. Nur vor dem Computer sitzen sie noch länger."

5. Ein Experte behauptete: „Das Internet wird mehr und mehr zum Familienkiller, da jeder fünfte Deutsche seine familiären Kontakte durch die Beschäftigung mit dem Internet deutlich einschränkt. Man kümmert sich deutlich weniger um andere Familienmitglieder, und im Extremfall kann eine Familie durch das Internet zerstört werden. Man darf das Internet aber nicht verteufeln, sondern man muss lernen, bewusst damit umzugehen."

6. Mein Freund sagte mir: „Meine Eltern kommen aus Italien, aber ich bin hier geboren. Ich spreche Deutsch besser als Italienisch, aber wenn ich eine Zeit lang in Italien bin, fällt mir auch Italienisch sehr leicht."

7. Der Minister kündigte an: „Wir werden auf eine Steuererhöhung verzichten."

8. Betroffene der Überschwemmung berichteten: „Der Fluss trat über die Ufer, und das Wasser wurde in wenigen Minuten so hoch, dass die Brücke unpassierbar war. Wir mussten mit Schlauchbooten zu unseren Häuser fahren, vor die wir Sandsäcke gelegt hatten. Aber das Wasser drang natürlich trotzdem in die Häuser, die wochenlang unbewohnbar waren. Wir wurden in Hotels einquartiert, bis die gröbsten Schäden beseitigt waren."

9. Der Richter fragte den Angeklagten: „Wo waren Sie in der fraglichen Nacht, und was haben Sie gemacht?"

10. Der Angeklagte behauptete: „Ich saß zu Hause vor dem Fernseher und war allein. Es tut mir Leid, dass ich kein besseres Alibi habe, aber so war es. Ich weiß überhaupt nicht, warum sie mich hierher bestellt haben. Ich habe mit der ganzen Sache nichts zu tun."

8 Reported speech (see 7.12)

Read what four women have to say about their obsession with their partners and rewrite their statements in reported speech. Remember that reported speech also affects the pronouns.

a. Charlotte Off, 32 Jahre alt:
   „Frauen lieben meinen Mann – er sieht fantastisch aus, ist erfolgreich und ein echter Charmeur. Das weiß er auch – und er benutzt diesen Charme wie eine Waffe. Wenn wir abends ausgehen, flirtet er hemmungslos mit anderen Frauen. Mich beachtet er kaum. Ich verachte mich dafür, dass ich trotzdem bei ihm bleibe, aber ich liebe ihn halt."

b. Hanne Kaars, 43 Jahre alt:
   „Ich habe morgens überlegt, was ich abends kochen kann, damit mein Mann zufrieden ist. Aber er war nie zufrieden. Irgendwann habe ich gar nichts mehr gekocht und bin ausgegangen, wenn er heimkam. Da tat es ihm Leid. Seitdem ist wieder Ruhe."

c. Joelie Holt, 24 Jahre alt:
   „Am Anfang hat mir die Eifersucht meines Freundes geschmeichelt. Ich nahm Rücksicht darauf: Ich traf mich nicht mehr mit alten Freunden. Es gab keinen Tag, an dem ich mich nicht bei ihm abmeldete. Irgendwann wachte ich auf und dachte, ich bin gefangen. Ich verließ ihn."

d. Hede Kühne, 53 Jahre alt:
   „Manchmal nach einem bösen Streit, redet mein Mann wochenlang nicht mit mir. Kein Wort, kein Blick. Er behandelt mich wie Luft. Wenn er dann wieder auftaucht, bin ich dankbar wie ein dressiertes Hündchen – und das Leben geht weiter wie vorher."

(Fernsehwoche)

9 Reported speech (see **7.12**)

Look at the following court rulings about the keeping of dangerous dogs and put them into indirect speech. You could start as follows: *Das Gesetz besagt, …*

a. Wenn ein Hundehalter einen vorher verhängten Leinen- und Maulkorbzwang missachtet, muss er mit einer Haftstrafe rechnen.

b. Städte dürfen die Haltung von Kampfhunden verbieten, wenn der Besitzer keine Sondergenehmigung dafür hat. Selbst dann, wenn der Hund noch nie negativ aufgefallen ist.

c. Die Haltung von Hunden gehört zumindest in Großstädten nicht zur vertragsmäßigen Nutzung von Mietwohnungen. Auch bei kleinen Hunden muss der Vermieter zustimmen.

d. Der Vermieter darf dem Mieter das unangeleinte Herumlaufen eines Hundes in den öffentlichen Grundstücksteilen verbieten.

e. Wenn ein Vermieter in einem Mietvertrag genau begründet, warum eine Hundehaltung nicht erlaubt ist, so gilt ein solches Verbot auch für kleine Rassen.

f. Wenn Tierhaltung laut Mietvertrag von der Zustimmung des Vermieters abhängt, kann er sie ohne Angabe von Gründen verweigern, es sei denn, die anderen Mieter haben Tiere.

g. Der Vermieter kann die Haltung von Kampfhunden verbieten, auch wenn ansonsten die Tierhaltung grundsätzlich erlaubt ist.

(*Fernsehwoche*)

10 The modal auxiliary verbs (see **7.14–7.19**)

Fill in the gaps using the correct modal verb.

1. Ich _____ keinen Alkohol mehr trinken. Der Arzt hat es mir verboten.
2. Du _____ nicht mitkommen, wenn du nicht _____. Ich zwinge dich nicht.
3. Mein Mann war um 20 Uhr mit mir zu Hause. Er _____ also nicht gleichzeitig am Tatort gewesen sein.
4. Die Reparatur _____ doch unmöglich so viel Geld kosten. Da _____ Sie sich geirrt haben.
5. _____ ich Ihnen unseren neuen Mitarbeiter vorstellen? Das ist Herr Schubert.
6. _____ Sie noch eine Tasse Tee, oder _____ ich Ihnen etwas Anderes anbieten?
7. Wenn du deinen Zug noch erreichen _____, _____ du jetzt gehen.
8. Das neue Theaterstück _____ ausgezeichnet sein. Ich habe schon viel Gutes darüber gehört.
9. Peter _____ gestern in 30 Minuten von Stuttgart nach Ulm gefahren sein. Na ja, er war schon immer ein Angeber.
10. Analphabeten _____ weder lesen noch schreiben.

11 The modal auxiliary verbs (see **7.14–7.19**)

Give English equivalents for the following pairs of sentences, making sure that the difference in meaning is quite clear.

1. Er will uns sehen. – Er will uns gesehen haben.
2. Er durfte nach Berlin fahren. – Er dürfte nach Berlin fahren.
3. Er hätte es tun können. – Er kann es getan haben.
4. Ich will ein Stück Schokolade. – Ich möchte ein Stück Schokolade.
5. Das hättest du ihm sagen dürfen. – Das hättest du ihm sagen müssen.

6. Wir konnten ihm helfen. – Wir könnten ihm helfen.
7. Er muss jetzt gehen. – Er soll jetzt gehen.
8. Ich muss arbeiten. – Ich müsste arbeiten.
9. Das muss meine Schwester sein. – Das dürfte meine Schwester sein.
10. Ich muss mir das nicht anhören. – Ich darf mir das nicht anhören.
11. Er soll ein guter Lehrer sein. – Er will ein guter Lehrer sein.
12. Sollen wir dir helfen? – Müssen wir dir helfen?
13. Ich möchte keine Pilze. – Ich mochte keine Pilze.

12 The modal auxiliary verbs (see 7.14–7.19)

Translate the following pairs of sentences into English and say what they express (e.g. ability, permission etc.). Use the relevant reference section in this book.

1. a. Ich dürfte eigentlich gar nicht hier sein.
   b. Das Haus dürfte nicht billig gewesen sein.
2. a. Wir müssen uns beeilen.
   b. Wir müssen uns verrechnet haben.
3. a. Da magst du Recht haben.
   b. Magst du noch ein Stück Kuchen?
4. a. Er könnte dein Auto reparieren.
   b. Er könnte krank sein.
5. a. Er soll eine Menge Geld haben.
   b. Ich soll ihm morgen das Geld bringen.
6. a. Was ich Sie schon immer mal fragen wollte, …
   b. Ich wollte Sie nicht beleidigen.
7. a. Er will zur Tatzeit bei seiner Freundin gewesen sein.
   b. Er will um 5 Uhr bei seiner Freundin sein.
8. a. Das sollten Sie eigentlich wissen.
   b. Das sollte eine Überraschung sein.
9. a. Hundert Mark müssten reichen.
   b. Wir müssten ihm einfach mal die Wahrheit sagen.

13 The syntax of modal verbs (see 7.13)

Form conditional sentences from the following pairs of sentences using the pluperfect subjunctive of the modal verb. Remember that the auxiliary *haben* precedes both infinitives.

e.g. Wir durften ihn nicht besuchen. Er war nicht froh.
   Wenn wir ihn hätten besuchen dürfen, wäre er froh gewesen.

1. Wir wollten nicht in Urlaub fahren. Wir haben es nicht getan.
2. Er wollte den Zug nicht erreichen. Er ist nicht früher gegangen.
3. Ich durfte kein Instrument lernen. Ich habe mich nicht gefreut.
4. Du musstest nicht so früh aufstehen wie ich. Du hast dich nicht geärgert.
5. Ich konnte nicht umsonst in das Konzert gehen. Ich habe den anderen Termin nicht abgesagt.

6. Ich musste meinen Eltern beim Umzug helfen. Ich konnte nicht mitkommen.

7. Das Fahrrad sollte keine Überraschung sein. Wir mussten es nicht verstecken.

8. Du wolltest den Film nicht sehen. Du musstest nicht früher nach Hause kommen.

9. Ich wollte mir kein neues Auto kaufen. Ich musste einen Kredit aufnehmen.

10. Du konntest es nicht sehen. Du musstest nicht lachen.

14 The modal auxiliary verbs (see **7.13–7.19**)

Translate the following sentences into German using a modal verb.

1. We mustn't forget to inform your parents.
2. You should have asked me beforehand.
3. The door wouldn't open.
4. He is said to be a weak candidate.
5. He will (most probably) be in bed by now.
6. Without your help I could not have done it.
7. You don't have to pay now.
8. She can't have read the book.
9. May I ask you a question?
10. I couldn't read the article yesterday.
11. We were going to go to Munich tomorrow.
12. He claims to speak 10 languages.
13. We don't want to live here any more.
14. You ought to go to the doctor's.
15. Are you allowed to play outside?
16. Shall we go for a walk?
17. I shouldn't have mentioned it.
18. I had to tell him the truth.
19. We should really tell him the truth.
20. What am I supposed to tell him.
21. We could hire a car.
22. As a child I didn't like spinach.

8 Valency and cases

1 Reflexive verbs (see **8.2**)

Rewrite the following sentences, replacing the italicized noun phrase with an appropriate reflexive verb from the box below.

e.g. Gestern *ist* hier ein schlimmer Unfall *passiert*.
Gestern *hat sich* hier ein schlimmer Unfall *ereignet*.

1. Ich habe mir gestern bei dem Regen *eine Erkältung geholt*.
2. Du hast vergessen „*danke*" *zu sagen*.
3. Er *ist eher für einen handwerklichen Beruf geeignet*.
4. Die Toiletten *sind* gleich rechts vom Eingang.
5. Da haben Sie bestimmt *einen Fehler gemacht*.
6. Ich habe *beschlossen* meine Arbeitsstelle zu kündigen.
7. Wir werden beim Chef *eine Beschwerde* gegen Sie *führen*.
8. Mein Sohn *war* gestern beim Einkaufen wieder *unmöglich*.
9. Er *ist nicht willig* zu kooperieren.
10. Sie *ist* von ihrer Krankheit *genesen*.

sich eignen	sich benehmen	sich entschließen
sich bedanken	sich weigern	sich beschweren
sich befinden	sich irren	sich erkälten
sich erholen	~~sich ereignen~~	

2 Reflexive verbs (see 8.2)

Match up the elements on the left with the elements on the right and insert a reflexive pronoun to form sentences that make sense. Remember that the reflexive pronoun can be dative or accusative.

e.g. Du drehst *dich* im Kreis. (1 d)

1. ~~Du drehst~~	a. selbst von der Sauberkeit der Zimmer!
2. Interessierst du	b. warum ich noch mit ihm verheiratet bin.
3. Du widersprichst	c. auf den Boden!
4. Ich erinnere	d. ~~im Kreis.~~
5. Wir unterhalten	e. die Haare.
6. Ich ärgere	f. einen Urlaub in der Karibik herrlich vor.
7. Setzt	g. über unser Geschenk?
8. Du bildest	h. für Politik?
9. Die Tür öffnet	i. mit Freunden über das Theaterstück.
10. Ich wasche	j. automatisch.
11. Freust du	k. in deinem Aufsatz an mehreren Stellen.
12. Ich stelle	l. gern an unsere Zeit in Italien.
13. Überzeug	m. jeden Tag über meinen Chef.
14. Ich frage	n. deine Schönheit nur ein.

3 Dative objects (see 8.1 and 8.3)

Translate the following sentences into German using verbs that govern the dative.

1. He will never forgive you for that.
2. He threatened the boy with a stick.
3. The dog doesn't obey its owner.
4. I couldn't resist the temptation.
5. He wanted to impress her with his new car.
6. We followed the instructions.
7. Smoking can seriously damage your health.
8. My daughter succeeded in getting a scholarship.
9. Have you noticed his strange accent?
10. That will not happen to me again.
11. Don't trust anyone over 40.
12. May I congratulate you on the birth of your son.
13. She informed me of that yesterday.

4 Genitive or *von*? (see 8.6)

Link the following nouns or noun phrases into a single phrase using the genitive case or a construction with *von* as appropriate. Sometimes both versions are possible.

e.g. der Bau/Häuser
    der Bau von Häusern

der Bau/unser Haus
    der Bau unseres Hauses

1. die Verspätung/der Zug
2. etwas/der Kuchen
3. die Beschreibung/das Kind
4. eine Reihe/Fragen
5. eine Reihe/interessante Fragen
6. der Geruch/frisch gekochtes Essen
7. ein Freund/ich
8. viele/meine Freunde
9. die Zahlung/das Gehalt
10. nichts/die Vorlesung

11. der Preis/ein Haus
12. der Preis/fünf Häuser
13. eine Kollegin/meine Mutter
14. eine Kollegin/uns
15. viel/der Nudelsalat
16. drei/seine Schulkameraden
17. die Reparatur/das Auto
18. der Vorschlag/du
19. die Entsorgung/der Müll
20. eine Folge/Ereignisse

5 Objects and cases (see **8.1** and **8.3–8.6**)

Use the correct case for the objects in brackets.

1. Wir haben zuerst [der Direktor] getroffen, und dann sind wir auch noch [der Abteilungsleiter] begegnet.
2. Wenn du [ich] jetzt hilfst, erlaube ich [du], [der Film] heute Abend im Fernsehen anzugucken.
3. Es fällt [ich] schwer, [er] [die Nachricht] mitzuteilen.
4. Es tut [wir] Leid, dass wir [Sie] [die Stelle] nicht anbieten können, aber wir danken [Sie] trotzdem für [Ihre Bewerbung].
5. Sein Verhalten bedurfte [eine Erklärung].
6. Ich glaube [du] [kein Wort].
7. Die Polizei konnte [er] [der Einbruch] nicht nachweisen.
8. Er gab [sein Sohn] [der Rat], [ein einfacher Handwerker] zu werden und [kein eigenes Geschäft] aufzumachen.
9. Du bist [ein netter Kerl], und ich möchte, dass du [mein Freund] bleibst, aber heiraten kann ich [du] leider nicht.
10. [Mein jetziges Gehalt] genügt [ich] nicht.
11. Sie wischte [das Kind] [der Mund] ab.
12. Die Leute behaupten, meine Freundin gleiche [die Gewinnerin] des Miss Germany Wettbewerbs, was [sie] natürlich sehr schmeichelt.
13. Natürlich gefällt [ich] [dieses Auto], aber im Moment kann ich [ich] leider so [ein teurer Wagen] nicht leisten.
14. Am Totensonntag gedenkt man [die Gefallenen] der letzten beiden Weltkriege.
15. Wir schicken [Sie] morgen [der Mietvertrag].

6 Prepositional objects (see **8.1** and **8.7**)

Fill in the appropriate preposition and use the correct case for the noun phrase in brackets.

1. Wir müssen uns leider _____ [die Situation] abfinden.
2. Ich zweifle _____ [seine Ehrlichkeit].
3. Er litt seit Jahren _____ [ein zu hoher Blutdruck]. Dann erkrankte er _____ [Krebs], aber letztendlich gestorben ist er _____ [eine Lungenentzündung].
4. Wir freuen uns _____ [Ihr Eintritt] in unsere Firma und hoffen _____ [eine gute Zusammenarbeit].
5. Das Kind rief _____ [seine Mutter].

6. Ich kann dir nur _____ [der Kauf] dieses Hauses abraten, weil du dich dann nicht mehr _____ [deine Schulden] erholen wirst.

7. Unsere neue Katze hält mich _____ [meine Arbeit] ab, weil ich mich ständig _____ [sie] beschäftigen muss.

8. Ich bin _____ [deine Fähigkeiten] überzeugt, will dich aber nicht _____ [ein Hochschulstudium] zwingen.

9. Ich habe gestern _____ [du] geträumt.

10. Ich halte einen Spontanurlaub _____ [eine ausgezeichnete Idee], und ich habe mich auch schon _____ [Flüge] erkundigt.

11. Ich möchte dich _____ [ein Gefallen] bitten. Könntest du vielleicht heute Abend _____ [unsere Kinder] aufpassen. Ich kümmere mich dann wieder _____ [eure Haustiere], wenn ihr in Urlaub seid.

12. In der Küche riecht es _____ [Essen].

13. Ich sorge mich _____ [meine Schwester]. Sie hat sich schon immer gern _____ [fremde Menschen] distanziert, aber jetzt scheint sie sich sogar _____ [sie] zu verstecken.

14. Christian gehört _____ [die Leute], die _____ [übertriebene Eifersucht] neigen. Das führt leider immer wieder _____ [Konflikte] mit seiner Frau.

15. Die Zahlung von Arbeitslosengeld hängt auch _____ [die Frage] ab, ob man sich _____ [eine neue Stelle] bemüht.

16. Ich würde mich natürlich _____ [eine Gehaltserhöhung] freuen, aber ich rechne eigentlich nicht da(r)_____.

17. In unserer Branche muss man schnell _____ [Veränderungen] reagieren.

18. Ich glaube _____ [ein wirtschaftlicher Aufschwung], der _____ [die Rezession] der letzten Jahre folgen wird.

19. Ich habe dich _____ [er] gewarnt. Ich habe dir gesagt, dass er sich _____ [jede Verantwortung] scheut.

20. Es genügt nicht, _____ [Politiker] zu schimpfen. Wenn man _____ [eine wirkliche Veränderung] der Zustände interessiert ist, muss man etwas tun, zum Beispiel _____ [Demonstrationen] teilnehmen.

7 Prepositional objects (see **8.1** and **8.7**)

Identify the main verb in the numbered section of each sentence, and then complete it with its prepositional object taken from (a)–(o).

1. In der Fernsehdiskussion gestern Abend ging es
2. In meiner Doktorarbeit befasse ich mich
3. Wenn ich koche, schmeckt das Essen immer
4. Achten Sie bitte
5. Im Abitur spezialisiert sich meine Tochter
6. Ich gewöhne mich langsam
7. Obwohl der Radfahrer durch die Schuld des Autofahrers verletzt wurde, verzichtete er
8. Hüten Sie sich
9. Wir gratulieren dir ganz herzlich
10. Er überredete sie
11. Fast alle Menschen suchen
12. Wir warten sehnsüchtig
13. Ich zweifle sehr
14. Bei dieser Pflanze handelt es sich
15. Der Arzt riet dem Patienten dringend

a. nach dem idealen Ehepartner.

b. zum bestandenen Examen.

c. nach nichts.

d. darauf, das Spray nicht in geschlossenen Räumen zu verwenden.

e. auf Post von unserem Sohn in Australien.

f. um Drogenmissbrauch bei Kindern.

g. um eine Helianthus intermedius.

h. daran, dass die neue Regierung viel besser sein wird als die alte.

i. an das Rentnerdasein.

j. zu einem gemeinsamen Abendessen.

k. auf Mathematik, Physik und Spanisch.

l. vor allzu schnellen Urteilen.

m. mit dem Einfluss des Internets auf das Familienleben.

n. darauf, Anzeige bei der Polizei zu erstatten.

o. zu dieser Operation.

8 Valency and cases (see 8)

Form sentences from the following elements, putting the noun phrases in the correct case and/or adding the right preposition to form a prepositional object. Use an appropriate tense and word order.

e.g. ANTWORTEN – er/der Junge/seine Frage

Er antwortete dem Jungen auf seine Frage.

1. EMPFEHLEN – ich/können/Sie/dieser Wein
2. ÜBERZEUGEN – er/können/der Kommissar/nicht/seine Unschuld
3. VERSCHWEIGEN – du/ich/die Wahrheit
4. SICH ERFREUEN – der Vater/mein Freund/beste Gesundheit
5. AUFSCHREIBEN – sie/ich/ihre neue Adresse
6. HINDERN – du/ich/die Erfüllung/meine Pflicht
7. FEHLEN – meine Arbeit/ich/sehr
8. BEGEGNEN – wir/gestern/dein Bruder
9. SICH KONZENTRIEREN – ich/können/nichts
10. VERKAUFEN – wir/müssen/das Haus/meine Tante
11. ANBIETEN – ich/dürfen/Sie/ein Glas Sekt (question)
12. SCHMECKEN – Kartoffeln/ich/am besten
13. ANFANGEN – wir/morgen/die Umbauarbeiten
14. SICH VERLASSEN – Sie/können/meine Diskretion
15. DENKEN – er/oft/seine Jugendzeit
16. SICH WUNDERN – ich/das musikalische Talent/dein Sohn
17. VERBIETEN – der Arzt/der Patient/zu viel Anstrengung
18. GEHÖREN – dieser Mantel/ich/nicht
19. ABRATEN – ich/du/ein Treffen mit ihm
20. EINLADEN – ich/dürfen/Sie/hoffentlich/Essen
21. HERRÜHREN – seine Angst/die Erfahrungen/seine Kindheit
22. RECHNEN – Sie/müssen/eine Erhöhung/Ihre Miete
23. HOFFEN – wir/baldige Besserung/sein Zustand
24. ERZÄHLEN – ich/du/morgen/die Geschichte
25. ERKENNEN – du/können/sie/ihre tiefe Stimme

9 Place complements and direction complements (see **8.1**, **8.8** and **8.9**)
Decide whether the italicized elements in the following sentences are direction/place complements (comp) or whether they are adverbials (adv).

1. Ich lebe schon seit 15 Jahren *in England.*
2. Ich habe ihn gestern *in der Stadt* getroffen.
3. Wir fahren dich *zum Flughafen.*
4. Die Katze sitzt *auf meinem Sessel.*
5. Ich lese gern Krimis *im Bett.*
6. Ich lese dir eine Geschichte vor, wenn du *im Bett* bist.
7. Wir haben vorige Woche einen tollen Film *im Kino* gesehen.
8. Er fliegt morgen *nach Amsterdam.*
9. Stellen Sie bitte das Buch wieder *ins Regal.*
10. Ich muss die Äpfel *im Garten* aufsammeln.
11. Wohnt er nicht *in der Bachstraße?*
12. *In der Bachstraße* sollen fünf neue Häuser gebaut werden.

9 Word order

1 Main clauses (see **9.1–9.3**)
Rewrite the following sentences putting the italicized element in initial position.

1. Sie hat *gestern* einen wunderschönen Blumenstrauß bekommen.
2. Ich habe schon lange nicht mehr *Fußball* gespielt.
3. Ich kann überhaupt nicht verstehen, *warum er das getan hat.*
4. Man verlässt sich am besten nicht *auf meinen Bruder.*
5. Ich kenne *Sabine* schon seit mehreren Jahren.
6. Wir haben ihn *das letzte Mal* vor einer Woche gesehen.
7. Es ist jetzt *bei Karstadt* viel teurer als früher.
8. Du hast *dieses Buch* doch schon vor zwei Monaten gelesen.
9. Ich würde *deiner Mutter* vorerst nichts sagen.
10. Ich bin schon lange nicht mehr *mit dem Zug* gefahren.

2 First position in main clauses (see **9.3**)
Look at the following sentences very carefully and translate them into English.

1. Den Rasenmäher hat mein Vater immer noch nicht repariert.
2. Mit dir gehe ich nie wieder ins Kino.
3. Einen Urlaub im Ausland kann er sich nicht leisten.
4. Angezogen bist du noch nicht, und die Zähne hast du dir auch noch nicht geputzt.
5. Diesen Namen wird man sich merken müssen.
6. Der Junge konnte der Frau gerade noch entkommen.

7. Auf dich muss man immer warten.
8. Angela hat Petra im Kino getroffen.
9. Die drei Brüder konnte die Polizei endlich finden.
10. Dieser Frau gab er den Brief seiner Mutter.
11. Seine Vorlesungen versuchen alle Studenten zu meiden.

3 Subordinate clauses (see **9.1** and **9.2**)

Make the following main clauses into subordinate clauses. Start all sentences with *Ich glaube, dass* ...

1. Seine Tochter hat vor ungefähr einem Jahr schwimmen gelernt.
2. Er will seinen Sohn nächstes Jahr auf eine Privatschule schicken.
3. Auch die Politiker werden diese Probleme nicht lösen können.
4. Die Baupläne sind in der Besprechung erklärt worden.
5. Er hatte von den Plänen seiner Frau nicht wissen können.
6. Mein Vater würde sich gerne einen neuen Anzug machen lassen.
7. Wir sollten mal wieder für ein Wochenende wegfahren.
8. Wolfgang und Margret haben sich scheiden lassen.
9. Er will nichts von der Affäre gewusst haben.
10. Die Häuser hätten schon letztes Jahr fertig sein sollen.
11. Es soll morgen regnen.
12. Der Unfall ist durch Trunkenheit am Steuer verursacht worden.
13. Er hat seinen Freund nie wieder gesehen.
14. Sie konnte nicht anders handeln.
15. Du hättest nicht so lange warten dürfen.

4 The position of pronouns, noun subjects and objects (see **9.5** and **9.6**)

Answer the following questions, replacing the subject and objects with personal pronouns.

e.g. Hast du Annemarie das Buch zurückgegeben?
  Ja, *ich* habe *es ihr* zurückgegeben.

1. Hat Herr Braun seinem Sohn das Motorrad gekauft?
2. Hast du der Firma das fehlerhafte Gerät schon zurückgeschickt?
3. Hat man den Angehörigen die traurige Nachricht schon mitgeteilt?
4. Sollte Frank seiner Mutter diesen Kummer nicht ersparen?
5. Kannst du deinem Vater mal bitte die Schere holen?
6. Zeigst du unserem Gast vielleicht unseren Garten?
7. Hat Thomas seinen Eltern schon seine neue Freundin vorgestellt?
8. Muss die Krankenschwester dem Patienten die Wunde verbinden?
9. Willst du Oma das neue Stück auf dem Klavier vorspielen?
10. Haben die Müllers nicht allen Nachbarn eine Einladung versprochen?

5 The position of pronouns (see **9.5**)

Make sentences according to the pattern in the example, using the modal auxiliary verb *sollen*. Replace the personal pronoun *es* with the demonstrative pronoun *das*. This has implications for the word order.

e.g. Sie hat *es mir* gesagt.
Sie hätte *mir das* nicht sagen sollen.

1. Er hat es ihm erlaubt.
2. Du hast es mir versprochen.
3. Sie haben es uns gezeigt.
4. Wir haben es euch verschwiegen.
5. Ich habe es mir gewünscht.
6. Wir haben es uns anders überlegt.
7. Ihr habt es euch leicht gemacht.
8. Er hat es mir erzählt.
9. Sie haben es uns vorgeworfen.
10. Er hat es ihr geschenkt.

6 The position of adverbials and noun objects (see **9.6** and **9.7**)

Replace the personal pronouns in the following sentences by the nouns given in brackets. This also has implications for the position of the adverbial.

e.g. Ich habe *sie ihm gestern* gesagt. (die Wahrheit, Oliver)
Ich habe *Oliver gestern die Wahrheit* gesagt.

1. Ich habe *es ihm schon heute* gegeben. (das neue Fahrrad, Andreas)
2. Der Kellner kann *ihn ihm manchmal* empfehlen (ein guter Wein, der Gast)
3. Wir würden *ihn ihr gern* verbieten. (der Umgang mit diesem Kerl, unsere Tochter)
4. Er wird *sie euch sicher* mitteilen. (die Ergebnisse, du und dein Mann)
5. Sie hat *ihn ihnen für morgen* versprochen. (ein Besuch im Zoo, die Kinder)
6. Ich habe *ihn ihm vor zwei Tagen* geschickt. (ein Beschwerdebrief, mein Chef)
7. Er hat *es ihr unerwartet* hinterlassen. (sehr viel Geld, seine Frau)
8. Er hat *sie ihnen vorsichtshalber* verheimlicht. (die Trennung von Gabriele, seine Eltern)
9. Sie hat *sie ihr aus unerfindlichen Gründen* verweigert. (die Bitte, ihre Freundin)
10. Die Firma muss *sie ihm auf jeden Fall* anbieten. (eine neue Stelle, Ihr Sohn)
11. Ich leihe *sie ihnen nie* aus. (Bücher, Freunde)
12. Er hat *sie ihnen am Lagerfeuer* erzählt. (eine spannende Geschichte, die Pfadfinder)

7 The position of adverbials and complements (see **9.7** and **9.8**)

Construct sentences from the elements below, putting them in an appropriate order. The nouns and pronouns should be put in the right case and the perfect tense should be used unless otherwise stated. The subject of the sentence should be in initial position.

e.g. SICH GEWÖHNEN AN – sie/das feuchte Klima/nie
Sie hat sich nie an das feuchte Klima gewöhnt.

1. FRAGEN NACH – Herr Meier/du/in der Schule/gestern
2. WERDEN – dein Zeugnis/viel schlechter/in letzter Zeit/leider

3. BEDÜRFEN – der Verletzte/medizinische Hilfe/dringend/bei dem Unfall/gestern (past tense)
4. SICH ERKUNDIGEN NACH – ich/wollen/Billigflüge in die Türkei/gleich morgen früh (present tense)
5. SICH INTERESSIEREN FÜR – er/Fußball/noch nie/bekanntlicherweise
6. ARBEITEN – ich/wollen/in einer Fabrik/auf keinen Fall/natürlich (past tense)
7. KOMMEN – wir/nach Hause/um halb zwei/heute Morgen
8. WARTEN AUF – ich/müssen/er/über eine Stunde/gestern/in der Kälte (past tense)
9. SEIN – er/Lehrer/sehr gern/schon früher/nicht
10. SICH FÜRCHTEN VOR – das Kind/der große Hund/sehr/bei dem Spaziergang/gestern
11. GEHEN – mein Onkel/in Pension/vorzeitig
12. SICH FREUEN AUF – er/das Rockkonzert/wahnsinnig
13. SICH ERHOLEN VON – ich/die Krankheit/gut/Gott sei Dank
14. TRÄUMEN VON – wir/ein Millionengewinn im Lotto/schon lange
15. UMZIEHEN – wir/wollen/in ein größeres Haus/bald/auf jeden Fall (present tense)

8 The position of adverbials (see **9.7**)

Insert the adverbials in brackets in an appropriate place in the central section of the sentence and in the right order.

e.g. Wir haben gespielt. (lustig, im Park, heute)
  Wir haben *heute im Park lustig* gespielt.

1. Die Studentin konnte zu der Vorlesung gehen. (nicht, heute Morgen, wegen ihrer Erkältung)
2. Du hast die Sonate gespielt. (bei dem Konzert, viel zu langsam, gestern)
3. Er wollte arbeiten. (in der Schule, fleißig, deshalb)
4. Die Konferenz musste abgesagt werden. (leider, wegen zu geringer Teilnehmerzahl, vorgestern)
5. Das Bierfest fand statt. (trotz des schlechten Wetters, gestern, draußen)
6. Ich werde nach Hause kommen. (heute Abend, etwas später, leider)
7. Der Mord wurde begangen. (in der Nähe des Parks, um 22 Uhr, wahrscheinlich)
8. Man hat ihn gefunden. (Gott sei Dank, bei seinem Vater, heute Morgen)
9. Die Straße muss gesperrt werden. (wegen dringender Reparaturarbeiten, für zwei Wochen, leider)
10. Mein Mann fliegt ins Ausland. (nur einmal im Jahr, geschäftlich, glücklicherweise)
11. Ich habe geschlafen. (vor lauter Aufregung, sehr schlecht, letzte Nacht)
12. Ich kann arbeiten. (unmöglich, leider, bei dieser Hitze)

9 The position of *nicht* (see **9.9**)

Negate the following sentences (i.e. the whole clause) by inserting *nicht* in the right place.
1. Ich kann mich leider an ihn erinnern.
2. Das hast du mir gesagt.
3. Er fährt morgen nach Südtirol.
4. Er fährt morgen allein nach Südtirol.
5. So eine Bemerkung hätte er machen dürfen.
6. Bring das Auto in die Werkstatt!

7. Bring das Auto heute in die Werkstatt!
8. Kauf das Auto!
9. Sie ist für diese Stelle geeignet.
10. Ich steige gern auf hohe Türme.
11. Du musst das Buch in die Bibliothek zurückbringen.
12. Mein Vater wollte Lokomotivführer werden.
13. Man darf sich dieser Frage entziehen.
14. Wir kommen mit.
15. Ich kann dir morgen das Geld bringen.
16. Sie lagen träumend im Gras.
17. Ich will mich scheiden lassen.
18. Kinder aus sozial niedriger gestellten Familien haben die gleichen Chancen.
19. Er hatte das Klingeln des Telefons gehört.
20. Du musst dich für alles entschuldigen.

10 The order of words and phrases in the central section (see 9.4–9.9)

Construct main clause sentences from the following elements with the subject in initial position. Put all nouns and pronouns in the right case and use the perfect tense unless otherwise stated. An appropriate word order should be used.

e.g. ANTWORTEN AUF – ich/mein Sohn/sein Brief/sofort
Ich habe meinem Sohn sofort auf seinen Brief geantwortet.

1. WARNEN VOR – die Bürgerrechtler/die Politiker/die Gefahr der Atomenergie/schon immer
2. RETTEN VOR – er/können/seine Familie/der Tornado/glücklicherweise (past tense)
3. ANBIETEN – der Lehrer/der Schüler/Nachhilfeunterricht/wegen seiner schlechten Note in Chemie
4. FALLEN – die Gartenschere/ich/auf den Fuß/bei der Gartenarbeit/gestern Nachmittag
5. UNTERSUCHEN – der Arzt/der Junge/gründlich
6. SITZEN – mein Vater/vor dem Fernseher/am liebsten/abends
7. BETRÜGEN UM – der Vertreter/die alte Dame/5000 Mark/skrupellos
8. SICH BEDANKEN FÜR – ich/bei den Großeltern/das Geschenk/schon vor einer Woche
9. ZWINGEN ZU – man/können/ein Mensch/sein Glück/nicht (present tense)
10. SICH ERINNERN AN – er/können/seine Tante/nicht mehr/leider
11. EINFALLEN – sein Name/ich/gerade noch rechtzeitig
12. STERBEN AN – er/Herzversagen/nach langer Krankheit/gestern/im Marienhospital
13. SICH BEFINDEN – Alice/in einem langen schmalen Tunnel/plötzlich (past tense)
14. FAHREN – meine Frau/auf der Autobahn/bei Glatteis/gern/nicht
15. HOLEN – ihr/die Bücher/ihr/aus der Bibliothek/unerlaubt/gestern
16. RATEN ZU – ich/Ihr Sohn/eine praktische Tätigkeit/schon immer
17. ACHTEN AUF – die Wissenschaftler/müssen/die Temperatur/bei dem Experiment (past tense)
18. BEGINNEN MIT – wir/können/die Straßenarbeiten/noch nicht/voraussichtlich (present tense)

10 Complex sentences

1 Coordination (see **10.2**)

Fill in the gaps using the coordinating conjunctions *aber, denn, oder, sondern* or *und* so that the sentences make sense. You need to use the conjunctions several times.

1. Wir fahren dieses Jahr nicht in Urlaub, _____ wir müssen für ein neues Auto sparen.
2. Ich wollte nicht *Nabucco* im Theater sehen, _____ *Aida*.
3. Wir gehen nicht immer in dasselbe Restaurant, _____ ziemlich oft.
4. Ich bin gerade dabei, meinen Aufsatz zu schreiben, _____ es dauert nicht mehr lange.
5. Nach dem Abitur möchte ich entweder Wirtschaft studieren, _____ ich mache eine Banklehre.
6. Mit diesem Gerät können Sie zwar Kassetten und CDs hören, _____ Sie können keine Schallplatten abspielen.
7. Ich habe eine gute Idee: Du mähst den Rasen, _____ ich sehe dir dabei zu.
8. Er entschied sich für eine Karriere in der Unternehmensberatung, _____ auch sein Vater arbeitete in dieser Branche.
9. Ulm ist nicht nur eine reizvolle Universitätsstadt, _____ es ist auch verkehrspolitisch sehr günstig gelegen.
10. Ich würde gern Geschichte, Französisch _____ Sport als Leistungskurs machen, _____ das geht leider nicht, _____ Sport wird an unserer Schule nicht als Leistungskurs angeboten.
11. Du hast nicht mich, _____ wahrscheinlich meine Schwester auf dem Oktoberfest gesehen.
12. Sollen wir zu Hause kochen, _____ möchtest du lieber in der Mensa essen?

2 Coordination (see **10.2**)

Combine the two sentences using *und*. Omit the subject of the second sentence where possible.

e.g. Ich komme nach Hause. Ich gehe sofort ins Bett.
Ich komme nach Hause und gehe sofort ins Bett.

Ich komme nach Hause. Meistens gehe ich sofort ins Bett.
Ich komme nach Hause und meistens gehe ich sofort ins Bett.

Ich komme nach Hause. Du gehst zur Arbeit.
Ich komme nach Hause und du gehst zur Arbeit.

1. Petra machte den Haushalt. Dann ging sie einkaufen.
2. Wir gehen gern wandern. Manchmal machen wir auch eine Radtour.
3. Er kam ins Büro. Er sah mit Entsetzen, dass alle Dokumente verstreut auf dem Boden lagen.
4. Ich hatte mir ein neues Videospiel ausgeliehen. Ich wollte es natürlich sofort ausprobieren.
5. Bei den Müllers kümmert sich der Mann um die Kinder. Die Frau geht arbeiten.
6. Tagsüber arbeite ich. Abends treffe ich mich mit Freunden.
7. Sie können schon mal ins Wohnzimmer gehen. Sie können mit dem Staubsaugen anfangen.
8. Draußen ist das Wetter so schön. Wir müssen in der Schule sitzen.
9. Mein Computer ist kaputt gegangen. Er muss dringend repariert werden.
10. Ingrid kannte niemanden auf der Party. Sie ging deshalb bald wieder nach Hause.
11. Michael arbeitet immer bis spät in die Nacht. Am nächsten Tag ist er natürlich müde.
12. Mein Bruder ist ein ausgezeichneter Geiger. Er spielt schon seit mehreren Jahren im Schulorchester.

3 Anticipatory *es* (see **10.3** and **10.6**)

Rewrite the following sentences, making the subordinate clause or infinitive clause the subject of the sentence. This has implications for the 'anticipatory' *es*.

e.g. Es steht dir nicht zu, darüber zu entscheiden.
Darüber zu entscheiden steht dir nicht zu.

1. Es hat mich sehr geärgert, dass er den Termin so kurzfristig abgesagt hat.
2. Es ist mir völlig unwichtig, ob du Geld hast oder nicht.
3. Es ist mehr als leichtsinnig, ein 5-jähriges Kind allein zur Schule gehen zu lassen.
4. Es freut uns sehr, dass Sie uns heute endlich besuchen kommen.
5. Es ist fraglich, ob er jemals wieder laufen kann.
6. Es ist mir ein Rätsel, wie man so lange die gleiche monotone Arbeit machen kann.
7. Es ist eine Zumutung, mit dir zusammenzuarbeiten.
8. Es ist allen positiv aufgefallen, dass er viel ausgeglichener geworden ist.
9. Es interessiert mich nicht, mit wem du deine Abende verbringst.
10. Es ist nicht zu empfehlen, die beiden Rottweiler zu streicheln.
11. Es ist durchaus möglich, dass er den Termin vergessen hat.
12. Es war unübersehbar, dass er familiäre Schwierigkeiten hatte.

4 Relative clauses (see **10.5**)

Supply the correct relative pronoun (i.e. *der* in its correct form). In some cases *was* has to be used as a relative pronoun.

1. Das ist Susanne, mit _____ ich nach der Schule immer Badminton spiele.
2. Hunde, _____ bellen, beißen nicht.
3. Gestern ist unsere Waschmaschine, für _____ es keine Ersatzteile mehr gibt, kaputt gegangen.
4. Die Hotelgäste, _____ sich über den Lärm beschwerten und _____ das Hotel auch sonst nicht gefiel, brachen ihren Urlaub vorzeitig ab.
5. Der Busfahrer, durch _____ Schuld fünf Menschen verletzt wurden, wurde vom Dienst suspendiert.
6. Ich bin mit allem, _____ du vorschlägst, einverstanden.
7. Die Studenten verstanden nicht viel von dem, _____ der Professor in der Vorlesung sagte.
8. Das Thema, mit _____ wir uns heute befassen, betrifft uns alle.
9. Was machst du mit dem ganzen Geld, _____ du in der Quizshow gewonnen hast?
10. Wir bereiten für meine Eltern, _____ am kommenden Samstag Silberhochzeit haben, ein großes Fest vor.
11. Es gibt Leute, _____ nie zuhören und mit _____ zu reden deshalb keinen Spaß macht.
12. Toni arbeitet in der Fabrik, in _____ schon sein Vater und Großvater gearbeitet haben.
13. Die Ziele, für _____ wir damals gekämpft haben, interessieren heute niemanden mehr.
14. Ein Kind, _____ Eltern viel Zeit mit ihm verbringen, wird später im Leben selbstsicherer sein als ein Kind, _____ sich meistens selbst überlassen bleibt.
15. Josef ist nicht der talentierte Schauspieler, für _____ er sich hält.
16. Er hat die Stelle bekommen, _____ mich sehr gewundert hat.
17. Man kann mit dem, _____ ich verdiene, beim besten Willen nicht auskommen.

18. Ab morgen läuft der Film im Kino, von _____ ich dir kürzlich erzählt habe.
19. Ich würde lieber ein Auto fahren, _____ mit Strom betrieben wird.
20. Ich denke gern an die Jahre zurück, in _____ wir zwar weniger Geld, aber mehr Freizeit hatten.

5 Relative clauses (see **10.5**)

Make a single sentence from the following pairs of sentences, using a relative pronoun and changing the word order as appropriate.

e.g. Das Fahrrad ist total verrostet. Das Fahrrad stand monatelang im Regen.
Das Fahrrad, das monatelang im Regen stand, ist total verrostet.

1. Unsere Tochter geht auf eine Schule. In der Schule werden Jungen und Mädchen in manchen Fächern getrennt unterrichtet.
2. Ich wundere mich über den Enthusiasmus. Er betreibt diesen Sport mit Enthusiasmus.
3. Er besuchte seine Heimatstadt. Er hatte viele widersprüchliche Erinnerungen an die Stadt.
4. Die Menschen wurden vorübergehend in einer Turnhalle untergebracht. Die Häuser der Menschen waren bei dem Unwetter völlig zerstört worden.
5. Der Roman ist ein reiner Unterhaltungsroman. Ich lese den Roman im Moment.
6. Umweltschutz ist eine Frage. Umweltschutz muss man ernst nehmen.
7. Die Freunde leben heute fast alle in anderen Städten. Ich war früher oft mit den Freunden zusammen.
8. Die Lehrstellen sind oft schon vergeben. Die Schulabgänger interessieren sich am meisten für die Lehrstellen.
9. Der Mann gab eine Anzeige in der Zeitung auf. Der Hund des Mannes war entlaufen.
10. Ohne sein Handy geht er nie aus dem Haus. Er trägt sein Handy immer am Gürtel bei sich.
11. Diese Kaffeemaschine ist heute schon kaputt. Ich habe die Kaffeemaschine erst gestern hier gekauft.
12. Für die Oper gab es keine Karten mehr. Die Oper hätten wir am liebsten gesehen.
13. In dieser Schule gibt es viele Kinder. Man muss den Kindern überdurchschnittlich viel helfen.
14. Die Firma hat meinen Vater gestern entlassen. Mein Vater war 27 Jahre bei der Firma angestellt.
15. Er machte mir ein Angebot. Mit dem Angebot hatte ich nicht gerechnet.

6 Conjunctions (see **10.4**)

Replace the prepositional phrase in italics with a subordinate clause introduced by an appropriate conjunction.

e.g. Wir müssen dieses Kapitel *vor Beginn der Ferien* abschließen.
Wir müssen dieses Kapitel abschließen, *bevor die Ferien beginnen.*

1. *Nach dem Mittagessen* mache ich gern einen Mittagsschlaf.
2. Ruf mich doch bitte *sofort nach deiner Ankunft* an.
3. Kurz *vor Sonnenuntergang* ist ein Spaziergang besonders schön.
4. Der Verkehr musste *wegen des Unfalls* umgeleitet werden.
5. Der Menschheit wäre *durch die Entwicklung eines Impfstoffes gegen Aids* sehr geholfen.
6. Er ging *trotz seiner Erkältung* zu dem Fußballspiel.
7. *Durch richtiges Einstellen des Motors* können die Abgase reduziert werden.

8. *Während der Operation des Jungen* mussten die Eltern draußen warten.

9. *Bei schönem Wetter* fahren wir morgen an den Chiemsee.

10. *Seit seinem Umzug in eine kleinere Stadt* fühlt er sich viel wohler.

11. *Bis zu unserem nächsten Besuch bei euch* ist es noch ein ganzes Jahr.

12. Sie stach sich *beim Nähen* in den Finger.

13. Ich habe das Buch *für dich zum Lesen* ausgeliehen.

14. *Im Falle einer Beitragserhöhung* werde ich aus dem Verein austreten.

15. *Nach meinem Wissen* wohnt er jetzt in Leonberg.

7 Conjunctions (see 10.4)

Choose the correct conjunction in brackets for the sentences to make sense.

e.g. Komm, _____ du Zeit hast. (weil, während, sooft, indem)
   Komm, *sooft* du Zeit hast.

1. Immer _____ ich diesen Film sehe, muss ich weinen. (während, wenn, als, damit)

2. Verlassen Sie bitte das Gebäude, _____ Sie das Alarmsignal hören. (während, obwohl, bevor, sobald)

3. Er sieht aus, _____ er Nächte lang nicht geschlafen hätte. (wie, wenn, als ob, als)

4. Er musste gestern ein Taxi bestellen, _____ er zu viel getrunken hatte. (da, wenn, solange, bis)

5. Wir sperren die Katze in die Küche ein, _____ sie uns in Ruhe lässt. (weil, damit, falls, so dass)

6. _____ wir vor 5 Jahren in Ägypten waren, haben wir natürlich auch die Pyramiden gesehen. (wenn, während, bis, als)

7. Sie spricht sehr schlecht Deutsch, _____ sie schon seit 10 Jahren in Deutschland lebt.(weil, obwohl, als ob, so dass)

8. Ich hatte den Schlüssel im Büro vergessen, _____ ich nicht in meine Wohnung kam (wie, so dass, damit, als)

9. Das Musical hat mir viel besser gefallen, _____ ich erwartet hatte. (wie, obwohl, wenn, als)

10. Sie können Geld sparen, _____ Sie nach 8 Uhr abends telefonieren. (als ob, damit, so dass, wenn)

11. _____ ich gewusst hätte, dass Astrid auch kommt, wäre ich nicht gekommen. (als, wenn, falls, als ob)

12. _____ ich informiert bin, ist er der neue Professor für Philosophie. (wie, da, sobald, soweit)

13. Sie ist viel kleiner, _____ man denkt. (wenn, als, als ob, wie)

14. Ich habe mich über die Wahlergebnisse sehr gefreut, _____ Manfred ziemlich enttäuscht war. (während, indem, solange, als)

15. _____ wir hier einen ganzen Monat lang Regen hatten, hast du dich am Mittelmeerstrand gesonnt. (als, wenn, solange, während)

16. Er ist genauso alt, _____ er aussieht. (wie, als, obwohl, so dass)

17. _____ du zu Hause wohnst, machst du, was ich dir sage. (während, solange, wenn, als)

18. Jeden Morgen, _____ der Briefträger kam, gingen wir ans Fenster und winkten ihm (wenn, als, während, solange)

19. Sein Abiturzeugnis fiel schlechter aus als erwartet, _____ er leider nicht sofort Medizin studieren konnte. (indem, damit, so dass, weil)

20. Du könntest mir helfen, _____ du den Tisch deckst. (wenn, da, während, indem)

21. Ich hoffe, sie bauen die neue Wohnsiedlung so weit weg von unserem Haus, _____ es nur geht (als, ob, dass, wie).

8 Conjunctions (see **10.4**)

Make a single sentence from the following pairs of sentences using an appropriate conjunction so that the meaning stays the same as expressed by the italicized adverbial.

e.g. Ich hatte ihn eingeladen. *Trotzdem* kam er nicht.

    Obwohl ich ihn eingeladen hatte, kam er nicht.

1. Wir fliegen nach Syrien. Wir müssen uns *vorher* gegen Typhus und Hepatitis impfen lassen.
2. Ich habe mir eine Eigentumswohnung gekauft. *Seither* kann ich mir nichts mehr leisten.
3. Du kommst aus dem Ausland zurück. *Bis dahin* kannst du deine Möbel bei mir unterstellen.
4. Die Zuschauer hatten sich gesetzt. *Sofort danach* ging der Theatervorhang auf.
5. Sein Pass war abgelaufen. *Deshalb* musste er seinen Urlaub um zwei Wochen verschieben.
6. In England war alles ruhig. *Währenddessen* tobte in Frankreich und Deutschland ein ungeheurer Sturm.
7. Er hat mich so oft enttäuscht. *Trotzdem* liebe ich ihn immer noch.
8. Christian war mit dem Zaun fertig. *Danach* baute er einen Kaninchenstall.

9 Infinitive clauses (see **10.6**)

Make the following sentences into infinitive clauses.

e.g. Sie ging zum Arzt. Ich riet ihr …

    Ich riet ihr zum Arzt zu gehen.

1. Ich fahre ihn in die Stadt. Ich habe ihm versprochen …
2. Er war um diese Zeit in einer Kneipe. Er behauptete …
3. Wir können euch bald besuchen. Wir freuen uns darauf …
4. Man wird für einen Oscar nominiert. Es ist für jeden Schauspieler eine Ehre …
5. Er hatte ihn schon einmal in Frankfurt gesehen. Er glaubte …
6. Sie trifft sich noch einmal mit Felix. Ihr Vater hatte ihr verboten …
7. Wir gehen für drei Jahre ins Ausland. Wir haben beschlossen …
8. Sie wird mit all diesen Schwierigkeiten fertig. Es ist nicht einfach …
9. Sie gehen mit mir essen. Darf ich Sie einladen …
10. Ich nehme bis Weihnachten mindestens 10 Kilo ab. Ich habe mir vorgenommen …
11. Ich gehe abends mit Freunden weg. Ich habe selten Zeit …
12. Man spekuliert an der Börse. Es ist eine unsichere Sache …
13. Er hatte die alte Dame mit Absicht um ihr Geld betrogen. Er gab zu …
14. Ich verhandle mit Ihnen über das Honorar. Ich bin bereit …
15. Sie arbeitete an dem Projekt mit. Sie lehnte es ab …
16. Ich darf Sie heute Abend hier begrüßen. Es freut mich außerordentlich …

17. Man wird abends nach 10 Uhr angerufen. Es ist sehr lästig ...
18. Wir sprechen immer über das gleiche Thema. Ich habe keine Lust mehr ...
19. Du kannst bald wieder Ski fahren gehen. Freust du dich darauf ...
20. Rauchen Sie während des ganzen Fluges nicht! Darf ich Sie bitten ...

10 Infinitive clauses (see **10.6**)

Construct sentences with infinitive clauses from the words given. Be careful about the word order.

e.g. Elke/vorhaben/ins Kino/gehen
Elke hat vor ins Kino zu gehen.

1. Jochen/anfangen/Mädchen/sich interessieren für
2. Gudrun/aufhören/der Computer/arbeiten an
3. ich/sich vornehmen/alles/nicht/immer/in letzter Minute/machen
4. wir/ablehnen/es/die Verantwortung/für den Schaden/übernehmen
5. ich/vorziehen/es/ein ruhiger Abend/verbringen
6. er/anbieten/sie/die Sache/sich kümmern um
7. ich/sich vorstellen/es/schön/mit/du/in Urlaub/fahren
8. sie/vorgeben/als Model/arbeiten
9. die Arbeit/anfangen/ich/Spaß machen
10. der Gastgeber/auffordern/die Gäste/das Essen/beginnen mit

11 Infinitive clauses (see **10.6**)

Now use the sentences that you have constructed in exercise 10 and make them into subordinate clauses. Start all sentences with *Sie wissen, dass* ...

e.g. Elke hat vor ins Kino zu gehen.
Sie wissen, dass *Elke vorhat ins Kino zu gehen.*

12 Infinitive clauses after prepositions (see **10.7**)

Rephrase the following sentences, making the subordinate clause into an infinitive clause where possible. Some sentences cannot be rephrased in this way because the main clause and subordinate clause have different subjects. Put an asterisk against such sentences.

e.g. Wir konnten nichts tun, außer dass wir zusahen.
Wir konnten nichts tun *außer zuzusehen.*

Ich habe nichts erfahren, außer dass *sie* abgereist ist.

1. Er musste nach Hause gehen, ohne dass er mit seinem Chef gesprochen hatte.
2. Er verließ das Haus, ohne dass jemand es bemerkte.
3. Anstatt dass sie sich um ihre eigenen Dinge kümmert, mischt sie sich immer in alles ein.
4. Er verließ das Zimmer, ohne dass er auch nur ein Wort sagte.
5. Außer dass das Wetter ein bisschen wechselhaft war, war der Urlaub eigentlich sehr schön.
6. Ich bin extra früh aufgestanden, damit ich den Eisvogel am Fluss beobachten kann.

7. Ich habe das Meiste von der Geschichtsstunde vergessen, außer dass Hannibal mit Elefanten über die Alpen gezogen ist.
8. Anstatt dass du dich ein bisschen amüsierst, sitzt du immer nur über deinen Büchern.
9. Sie macht nicht viel, außer dass sie den ganzen Tag vor dem Spiegel steht.
10. Außer dass man von morgens bis abends am Strand liegt, kann man in der Algarve nicht viel machen.
11. Man kann nicht sagen, dass man Italien kennt, ohne dass man in Florenz war.
12. Sie fuhren in ein warmes Klima, damit seine Frau sich besser von ihrer Bronchitis erholen konnte.
13. Er ist noch zu klein, als dass er das verstehen würde.
14. London ist viel zu weit weg, als dass ich dort oft ins Theater gehen würde.
15. Er ging an mir vorbei, ohne dass er mich grüßte.

13 The infinitive without *zu* (see **10.8**)

Translate the following sentences into German.

1. We saw him going into the house.
2. I have to work every other Saturday.
3. He wants to show you his new rabbit.
4. We always have our car repaired in a little garage in Milton Keynes.
5. She heard someone come up the stairs.
6. A nice man helped me carry my suitcase.
7. She sent her son to get some rolls.
8. I'll teach you to swim.
9. The children didn't let the new boy play with them.
10. That can easily be done.
11. When did you learn to drive?
12. I am not allowed to eat fatty food.

▮▮ Word formation

1 The formation of nouns (see **11.1** and **11.2**)

Fill in the gaps using a noun that is derived from the adjective/noun/verb in italics. Refer to the relevant reference section in this book.

e.g. Eine Person, die *Auto fährt*, ist ein _____.
      Eine Person, die Auto fährt, ist ein *Autofahrer*.

1. Ein Mensch, der sich *unmenschlich* benimmt, ist ein _____.
2. Das, was er sagt, *bedeutet* nicht viel. Das, was er sagt, hat nicht viel _____.
3. Die Leute, die *anwesend* sind, nennt man die _____.
4. Wenn man aus einem Gebäude *hinausgehen* will, geht man zum _____.
5. Diese Vase kann man nicht *ersetzen*. Für diese Vase gibt es keinen _____.
6. Der *größte und wichtigste Bahnhof* in einer Stadt ist der _____.
7. Wir sind alle sehr *gesund*. Wir erfreuen uns bester _____.
8. Jemand, der *nicht schwimmen kann*, ist ein _____.
9. Sagen Sie mir bitte, wie *lang* und wie *hoch* Ihr Wohnmobil ist. Sagen Sie mir bitte die _____ und die _____ Ihres Wohnmobils.
10. Um *bremsen* zu können, braucht ein Fahrzeug eine _____.
11. Ich brauche unbedingt ein Auto. Dieses *viele Laufen* macht mich ganz kaputt. Diese _____ macht mich ganz kaputt.

12. Ein *kleines Haus* ist ein _____.

13. Dieses Lied wurde ein *sehr großer Erfolg*. Dieses Lied wurde ein _____.

14. Er leugnet, dass er der *Vater* des Kindes ist. Er leugnet die _____.

15. Eine Person, die mir gut *bekannt* ist, ist ein _____ von mir.

16. Wenn man etwas *schneidet*, macht man einen _____.

17. Wenn man sehr *reich* ist, lebt man im _____.

18. Ein *weiblicher Rechtsanwalt* ist eine _____.

19. In Deutschland kann man sich nicht mehr darauf verlassen, dass die Züge *pünktlich* fahren. In Deutschland kann man sich nicht mehr auf die _____ der Züge verlassen.

20. Wenn Leute miteinander *sprechen*, führen sie ein _____.

21. Er hat die Regeln *nicht beachtet*. Das war eine _____ der Regeln.

2 Compound nouns (see 11.3)

Form compound nouns from the following descriptions.

e.g. Ein Tisch, an dem man schreibt, ist ein _____.
Ein Tisch, an dem man schreibt, ist ein *Schreibtisch*.

1. Der Finger, mit dem man auf etwas zeigt, ist der _____.

2. Eine Ermäßigung für Studenten ist eine _____.

3. Ein Saal, in dem man Vorlesungen hört, ist ein _____.

4. Ein Eimer, in den man Abfall wirft, ist ein _____.

5. Eine Leine für Hunde ist eine _____.

6. Eine Maschine, mit der man Löcher bohrt, ist eine _____.

7. Eine Bedeckung für den Kopf ist eine _____.

8. Ein Pulver, das man zum Waschen benutzt, ist ein _____.

9. Ein Spruch, mit dem man für ein Produkt Werbung macht, ist ein _____.

10. Ein Laden, in dem man Bücher kaufen kann, ist ein _____.

11. Eine Halle, in der man schwimmen kann, ist eine _____.

12. Eine Feile für die Nägel ist eine _____.

13. Marmelade aus Kirschen nennt man _____.

14. Ein Boot mit einem Motor ist ein _____.

15. Ein Experte für Versicherungen ist ein _____.

16. Ein Lehrer für Deutsch ist ein _____.

17. Ein Lokal in einem Garten ist ein _____.

18. Eine Feier, bei der das Abitur gefeiert wird, ist eine _____.

19. Ein Aufenthalt in einem Krankenhaus ist ein _____.

20. Ein Unfall im Verkehr ist ein _____.

3 The formation of adjectives (see 11.1 and 11.4)

Fill in the gaps using an adjective that expresses the same as the original sentence. Refer to the relevant reference section in this book.

e.g. Man kann die Pilze essen. Die Pilze sind _____.
Die Pilze sind *essbar*.

1. Dieses Bild ist nicht zu verkaufen. Dieses Bild ist _____.
2. Meine Uhr ist aus Gold. Ich habe eine _____ Uhr.
3. Der Zug fährt nach Plan. Der Zug fährt _____.
4. Ich kann deinen Vorschlag gut gebrauchen. Dein Vorschlag ist sehr _____.
5. Ihre Haare sind ein bisschen rot. Sie hat _____ Haare.
6. Er hat keine Arbeit. Er ist _____.
7. Der Bus fährt alle zwei Stunden. Der Bus fährt im _____ Abstand.
8. Er hat Geige gespielt wie ein Meister. Er hat _____ Geige gespielt.
9. Man kann sich auf ihn verlassen. Er ist sehr _____.
10. Man sollte sich jeden Tag zweimal die Zähne putzen. Man sollte sich _____ zweimal die Zähne putzen.
11. Ihre Kleidung entspricht immer der neuesten Mode. Ihre Kleidung ist immer sehr _____.
12. Der Wind war so kalt wie Eis. Der Wind war _____.
13. Das ist die Zeitung von gestern. Das ist die _____ Zeitung.
14. Mein Bruder denkt sehr viel nach. Mein Bruder ist ein sehr _____ Mensch.
15. Wir haben in unserem Urlaub viel erlebt. Unser Urlaub war sehr _____.
16. Ich trinke nur Bier ohne Alkohol. Ich trinke nur _____ Bier.
17. Kinder brauchen sehr viel Liebe. Kinder sind sehr _____.
18. Wir nehmen immer sehr viel Rücksicht. Wir sind immer sehr _____.
19. Die alte Frau benimmt sich wie ein kleines Kind. Die alte Frau benimmt sich sehr _____.
20. Diese Zigarette hat wenig Nikotin. Diese Zigarette ist _____.
21. Mein Vater ist äußerst konservativ. Mein Vater ist _____.
22. Seine Gegenwart ist mir nicht angenehm. Seine Gegenwart ist mir _____.

4 Inseparable verb prefixes (see **11.5**)

Form as many verbs as possible from the verbs, nouns, and adjectives below, using the inseparable prefixes *be-, ent-, er-, ver-, zer-*.

1. a. kommen b. arbeiten c. blühen d. reißen e. handeln f. schreiben g. schießen
   h. legen i. antworten j. fallen k. wirtschaften
2. a. Nachricht b. Gift c. Silber d. Sklave e. Wasser f. Hunger g. Glas h. Bau
3. a. besser b. blind c. lang d. feucht e. grau f. scharf g. kurz h. arm i. krank
   j. richtig k. hoch l. leicht m. einfach

5 Separable verb prefixes (see **11.6**)

Fill in the gaps using the correct separable prefix in brackets for the sentences to make sense.

e.g. Bevor wir heirateten, lebten wir fünf Jahre _____ (ab-, zusammen-, ein-, auf-).
   Bevor wir heirateten, lebten wir fünf Jahre *zusammen*.

1. Ich gehe heute Abend noch einmal _____ (nach-, weg-, ein-, auf-).
2. Heute Morgen kam mir ein Auto auf der falschen Fahrbahn _____ (zurück-, an-, mit-, entgegen-).
3. Der Arzt musste die Behandlung (zusammen-, an-, ab-, ein-) _____brechen.

4. Du kannst ja schon mal (nach-, vor-, weg-, ab-) _____ gehen, und wir kommen dann später _____ (zurück-, nach-, mit-, aus-).

5. Wir fliegen nach Lanzarote. Morgen früh um 8 Uhr geht es _____ (mit-, los-, ab-, aus-).

6. Wenn du später aus dem Haus gehst, schließ bitte die Tür hinter dir _____ (zu-, weg-, auf-, ein-).

7. Geben Sie beim Kochen einen Esslöffel Salz _____ (mit-, ein-, hinzu-, ab-).

8. Wenn sie ihre Nichte besucht, bringt sie ihr immer ein Geschenk _____ (entgegen-, mit-, weg-, an-).

9. Der Lehrer singt das Lied _____ (mit-, vor-, nach-, ein-), und die Kinder singen es _____ (vor-, nach-, mit-, ein-).

10. Alle Häuser in dieser Straße sollen (weg-, an-, auf-, ab-) _____ gerissen werden.

11. Bei der Flutkatastrophe wurden Wohnwagen und Autos vom Wasser (zurück-, mit-, ein-, los) _____ gerissen.

12. Er schickte der Firma den fehlerhaften Artikel _____ (aus-, ab-, zurück-, fort-).

13. Trink deinen Tee _____ (aus-, auf-, weg-, mit-) und iss deine Cornflakes _____ (weg-, aus-, auf-, ab-).

14. Bei dem Erdbeben stürzten unzählige Häuser _____ (zusammen-, ein-, ab-, los-).

15. Ihr Mann arbeitet viel zu viel. Irgendwann bricht er _____ (ein-, aus-, aus-, zusammen-).

16. Sie hatten eine Minute für die Beantwortung der Frage. Jetzt ist Ihre Zeit leider (weg-, ab-, an-, auf-) _____ gelaufen.

17. Hast du morgen Zeit? Ich würde dich gern zu meinem Geburtstag (aus-, ab-, vor-, ein-) _____ laden.

18. Die Tüte hatte ein Loch, und jetzt ist die ganze Milch (fort-, aus-, zu-, ein-) _____ gelaufen.

19. Der Pitbull Terrier hatte sich von der Leine (weg-, ab-, los-, ein-) _____ gerissen.

20. Hast du Lust, ein Stück mit uns (weg-, entgegen-, ab-, mit-) _____ zulaufen?

6 Variable verb prefixes (see 11.7)

Make sentences from the following elements, deciding whether the verb is separable or inseparable. Use either present tense or past tense.

e.g. Der Direktor/den Brief/unterschreiben
Der Direktor *unterschreibt* den Brief.

Das Schiff/in dem Sturm/untergehen
Das Schiff *ging* in dem Sturm *unter*.

1. er/seiner Frau/eine Menge Geld/hinterlassen
2. Männer/ihre Gefühle/unterdrücken
3. der Sportler/eine Höchstleistung/vollbringen
4. sie (sg.)/ der Versuchung/widerstehen
5. wir/in dem alten Haus/sich umsehen
6. die Autofahrer/die Großstadt/umfahren
7. er/mir/das Buch/wiedergeben
8. die Kinder/das Einmaleins/wiederholen
9. das/seine arrogante Haltung/widerspiegeln
10. ich/oft/Fehler/übersehen
11. Kinder/gern/den Mund/sich vollstopfen
12. der Soldat/zum Feind/überlaufen
13. der Politiker/seine Antwort/genau/überlegen
14. ich/dein Manuskript/morgen/durchsehen
15. der Geruch nach Kaffee/das ganze Haus/durchdringen
16. Änderungen/an dieser Universität/nur langsam/sich vollziehen

7 Verbs with separable, inseparable and variable prefixes (see **11.5–11.7**)

Fill in the gaps using the past participle form of the verbs in brackets.

1. In unserem letzten Urlaub sind wir in einer billigen Pension _____ (unterkommen), und von dort aus haben wir ziemlich viel _____ (unternehmen).

2. Da der Fahrschüler eine rote Ampel _____ (missachten) hatte, ist er bei der Fahrprüfung _____ (durchfallen).

3. Die Unterrichtstunden, die gestern _____ (ausfallen) sind, müssen nächste Woche _____ (nachholen) werden.

4. Ihr Auto ist _____ (zusammenbrechen), weil es total _____ (durchrosten) war.

5. Ich habe _____ (vergessen), wie diese grammatikalische Konstruktion _____ (übersetzen) wird.

6. Er war ziemlich _____ (erschöpfen) und _____ (übermüden), weil er die ganze Nacht _____ (durchfeiern) hatte.

7. Nachdem die Polizei das Haus _____ (umstellen) und der Terrorist _____ (aufgeben) hatte, konnten alle Zimmer _____ (durchsuchen) und mehrere Waffen _____ (beschlagnahmen) werden.

8. Zweimal im Jahr werden die Uhren _____ (umstellen). Im Frühjahr werden sie _____ (zurückstellen), und im Herbst _____ (vorstellen).

9. Falsche Antworten sollten nicht _____ (verbessern) werden, indem sie _____ (ausradieren), sondern indem sie _____ (durchstreichen) werden.

10. Das Essen war wieder total _____ (anbrennen), weil sich meine Mutter beim Kochen einen Film _____ (ansehen) und nicht _____ (aufpassen) hatte.

11. Ich hatte gerade mit der Arbeit _____ (aufhören) und mich _____ (umziehen), als ich _____ (anrufen) und _____ (benachrichtigen) wurde, dass mein Bruder in einen Unfall _____ (verwickeln) war.

12. Warten Sie bitte draußen, bis Sie _____ (aufrufen) werden!

13. Nachdem Sie die Bücher _____ (auslesen) haben, müssen sie ins Regal _____ (zurückstellen) werden.

14. Entschuldigen Sie, dass ich Ihre Nummer _____ (anrufen) habe. Da muss ich mich _____ (verwählen) haben.

15. ch bin leider in meiner Argumentation _____ (unterbrechen) worden, wahrscheinlich weil mein Argument auf faire Weise nicht _____ (widerlegen) werden kann.

16. Ich weiß nicht, ob ich die Benzinkrise _____ (unterschätzen) oder _____ (überschätzen) _____ habe; auf jeden Fall habe ich beide Autos erst mal _____ (volltanken).

17. Gestern hat ein Auto auf der Gegenfahrbahn ein anderes Auto _____ (überholen) und ist mir dann auf meiner Spur _____ (entgegenkommen).

18. Letzte Woche hat ein Freund von uns eine Katze _____ (überfahren), und das hat sie leider nicht _____ (überleben).

19. Bei der Gerichtsverhandlung sollte _____ (untersuchen) werden, ob er sie wirklich _____ (umbringen) hatte.

20. Wenn ein Pass _____ (abgelaufen) ist, kann er nicht mehr _____ (verlängern) werden, sondern muss neu _____ (ausstellen) werden.

8 The formation of verbs (see **11.1** and **11.8**)

Form verbs from the following nouns and adjectives.

1. Schnee 2. Kontrolle 3. Bruch 4. Gedanke 5. Säge 6. Fahrt 7. Wurf 8. Aufnahme
9. Thema 10. Schuss 11. Kellner 12. Fernseher 13. Interesse 14. Fotograf 15. Rede
16. spitz 17. bleich 18. besser 19. scharf 20. ironisch 21. kurz 22. trocken

12 Spoken and written German

1 Pronunciation and spelling (see **12.1**)

Decide whether the stressed vowel in the following words is long (l) or short (s).

1. a. Wagen b. rasch c. was d. machen e. Sprache f. fast g. kam h. Haare i. Schaf
   j. Masse k. Maß l. lang m. sagte n. Bahn
2. a. beten b. Bett c. retten d. echt e. Fest f. lesen g. Ekel h. Beet i. fehlen j. Wespe
   k. Kessel l. Weg m. weg n. Feder
3. a. Liebe b. finden c. Igel d. Kinder e. fliehen f. bitter g. in h. ihn i. dir j. Kirche k. wider l. wieder
   m. wischen n. Kitsch o. viel p. Insel
4. a. hoch b. Koch c. oben d. folgen e. Floß f. floss g. Boot h. Boden i. Flotte j. oft k. Kohle l. Frosch
   m. Ofen n. offen o. Chor p. Osten q. Ostern
5. a. Kuchen b. Busch c. unten d. Kummer e. Stube f. Bruch g. fluchen h. wusch i. kuscheln j. Ufer k.
   Futter l. Fuß m. Fluss n. Kunst
6. a. Bühne b. glühen c. dünn d. Künstler e. Büste f. Rücken g. fünf h. kühl i. Flügel j. schütteln k. Bücher
   l. Küche m. Büsche n. Flüsse o. Füße
7. a. Löwe b. Förster c. Flöte d. Röcke e. Töchter f. können g. König h. Fön i. köstlich j. hört k. trösten
   l. Österreich m. öffnen n. östlich o. österlich

2 Pronunciation and spelling (see **12.1**)

Decide whether the *-ch* in the following words has the quality of the *ach*-Laut (a) or the *ich*-Laut (i).

1. brauchen 2. Tochter 3. Töchter 4. Nacht 5. Nächte 6. doch 7. Dolch 8. Veilchen
9. Schicht 10. durch 11. echt 12. feucht 13. brauchen 14. gebräuchlich 15. Licht 16. Buch
17. Bücher 18. Wächter 19. Wache 20. brechen 21. lachen 22. Kachel 23. richtig
24. horchen 25. manchmal 26. Blech 27. Krach 28. Loch 29. auch 30. Fluch 31. sprechen
32. Sprache 33. leuchten 34. Leiche 35. Kuchen 36. Küche 37. Koch 38. Köche
39. suchen 40. Richter

3 The use of capital letters (see **12.3**)

Decide whether to use small letters or capitals according to the spelling reform.

1. Liebe Frau Brinkmann,
   Z/zu I/ihrem achtzigsten Geburtstag sende I/ich I/ihnen im N/namen der Stadt H/herzliche
   G/glückwünsche. Wir wünschen I/ihnen alles G/gute und hoffen, dass S/sie mindestens H/hundert
   Jahre alt werden.

2. Im D/deutschen Bundestag soll bald ein Gesetz in B/bezug auf die D/doppelte Staatsangehörigkeit verabschiedet werden. Wann man mit dem I/inkrafttreten rechnen kann ist noch ein B/bisschen unklar.

3. Rolls-Royce-Motoren gelten immer noch als die B/besten in der Welt.

4. Das E/erste, was ich in meiner Rede heute A/abend ansprechen möchte, ist die Arbeitslosigkeit, die auf G/grund der Schließung von zwei Fabriken in dieser Stadt am S/schlimmsten in dieser Gegend ist.

5. Wir fahren M/morgen zur F/frankfurter Buchmesse.

6. Mir wird A/angst und B/bange, wenn ich an den Prozess über den Unfall denke, an dem er S/schuld war.

7. Es tut mir sehr L/leid, dass ich gestern N/nachmittag T/trotz meiner Zusage nicht an I/ihrer Podiumsdiskussion T/teilnehmen konnte.

8. Du hast R/recht. Im G/großen und G/ganzen scheint es Petra nicht zu stören, dass I/ihr Mann selbst am H/heiligen Abend auf Geschäftsreise ist. Es scheint I/ihr sogar R/recht zu sein.

9. Ich bin die E/einzige, die sich beim E/essen eine Serviette auf den Schoß legt.

10. Obwohl ich immer eine E/eins in Physik hatte, habe ich vergessen, was das O/ohmsche Gesetz ist.

11. Ich weiß nicht mehr im E/einzelnen, was er gesagt hat, aber es hatte E/etwas mit den Preisen zu tun, die man auf dem S/schwarzen Markt für A/alles bezahlen muss.

12. Das A/allerschlimmste, was einer Frau passieren kann, ist, wenn I/hr Mann die gemeinsame S/silberne Hochzeit vergisst.

13. Mein Mann war früher beim R/roten Kreuz tätig und arbeitet seit A/anfang letzten Jahres bei den V/vereinten Nationen.

14. Elisabeth die Z/zweite ist nicht nur Königin G/großbritanniens, sondern des G/ganzen V/vereinigten Königreichs und einiger ehemaliger Kolonialgebiete.

15. Der S/schiefe Turm von Pisa ist nicht der E/einzige schiefe Turm in Norditalien.

16. Wir sind uns A/alle darüber im K/klaren, dass von dem neuen Regierungschef nichts G/gutes zu erwarten ist.

17. Im A/allgemeinen halte ich meine Vorträge auf D/deutsch, aber manchmal auch auf E/englisch.

18. Lass uns H/heute R/rad fahren und M/morgen E/eis laufen. Denn B/beides an einem Tag zu machen ist zu anstrengend.

19. Am S/schwarzen Brett stand eine Mitteilung über die Studienfahrt ans S/schwarze Meer.

20. Wir dürfen nicht ausser A/acht lassen, dass die A/abgeordneten des L/londoner Parlaments anders gewählt werden als die des D/deutschen Bundestages.

4 One word or two? (see **12.4**)

Decide whether in the following sentences the italicized words should be spelled as one word or two. Cross out the wrong version.

1. Schüler heutzutage können schlechter *kopfrechnen/Kopf rechnen* als früher, weil man *sowenig/so wenig* Wert darauf legt.

2. Mir ist gestern, als ich *spazierenging/spazieren ging*, mein neuer Schirm *abhandengekommen/abhanden gekommen*.

3. Friederike hat vor drei Wochen einen netten jungen Mann *kennengelernt/kennen gelernt*. Sie würde am liebsten jede Stunde mit ihm *beisammensein/beisammen sein* und hofft sehr, dass die Beziehung *bestehenbleibt/bestehen bleibt*.

4. Wenn ich mit der Schule *fertigbin/fertig bin*, werde ich mich nicht damit *zufriedengeben/zufrieden geben*, einfach *irgendwo/irgend wo* zu arbeiten, sondern ich werde versuchen, bei einer *gutgehenden/gut gehenden* Firma *fußzufassen/Fuß zu fassen*.

5. *Alleinerziehende/Allein erziehende* Mütter oder Väter müssen manchmal bei Erziehungsberatungsstellen *ratsuchen/Rat suchen*, auch wenn es ihnen nicht immer *leichtfällt/leicht fällt*.

6. Er beschloss, den Namen des Mannes *preiszugeben/Preis zu geben*, der vor zehn Jahren den Drogendealer *totgeschlagen/tot geschlagen* hatte.

7. Darf ich Sie mit unserer neuen Mitarbeiterin *bekanntmachen/bekannt machen*. Sie wird an allen wichtigen Sitzungen *teilnehmen/Teil nehmen*, und ich bin sicher, dass wir mit ihr *zufriedensein/zufrieden sein* werden.

8. Ich hätte schwören können, dass du die Dokumente hier *liegengelassen/liegen gelassen* hast. Aber da muss ich wohl *durcheinandergekommen/durcheinander gekommen* sein.

9. Es wird dir *irgendwann/irgend wann* *leidtun/Leid tun*, dass du mir mit Absicht meine Pläne *zunichtegemacht/zunichte gemacht* hast.

10. Experten weisen immer wieder darauf hin, dass Kinder heutzutage *zuviel/zu viel* *fernsehen/fern sehen* und sich *zuwenig/zu wenig* bewegen.

11. Es wird mir immer *fernliegen/fern liegen*, die Bevölkerung *irrezuführen/irre zu führen*, aber wenn man die Zahlen *hochrechnet/hoch rechnet*, gibt es dieses Jahr ein Drittel mehr Leute, die *schwarzarbeiten/schwarz arbeiten* als noch im vorigen Jahr.

12. Um die Umwelt zu schonen, sollte man mehr *radfahren/Rad fahren* und weniger *autofahren/Auto fahren*.

13. Das Wetter ist leider zu schlecht, um *bergsteigen/Berg steigen* zu gehen. Es wird uns nichts Anderes *übrigbleiben/übrig bleiben* als *eislaufen/Eis laufen* zu gehen.

14. Die Polizisten sollten sich *bereithalten/bereit halten*, um an diesem Nachmittag den Terroristen *gefangenzunehmen/gefangen zu nehmen*.

15. Er hat sich im Laufe der Jahre ein bisschen Geld *beiseitegelegt/beiseite gelegt*, weil er es *satthatte/satt hatte*, immer *pleitezusein/pleite zu sein*.

5 -ss- or -ß- (see **12.5**)

Decide whether, according to the spelling reform, the following words are spelled with *-ss-* or *-ß-*. Cross out the wrong version.

1. lassen/laßen   2. weiss/weiß   3. Grüsse/Grüße   4. blass/blaß   5. gewusst/gewußt   6. gross/groß   7. Kuss/Kuß   8. du musst/du mußt   9. er frass/er fraß   10. Massentourismus/Maßentourismus   11. Massnahme/Maßnahme   12. fliessen/ fließen   13. aussen/außen   14. Schluss/Schluß   15. Russland/ Rußland   16. Russ/Ruß (soot)   17. Bussgeld/Bußgeld (meaning *fine*)   18. Busse/Buße (meaning *buses*)   19. Fluss/Fluß   20. Fuss/Fuß   21. Rasse/Raße   22. reissen/reißen   23. heiss/heiß   24. Wasser/ Waßer   25. Hass/Haß   26. Fass/Faß   27. stossen/stoßen   28. Essen/Eßen   29. er ass/er aß   30. Esslöffel/Eßlöffel

6 The comma (see **12.6**)

Insert a comma in the following sentences where necessary. Where it is optional put it in brackets.

1. Nachdem sie ihn so beleidigt hatte wollte er jedoch unter keinen Umständen jemals wieder etwas mit ihr zu tun haben.

2. Er behauptete die Zeugin noch nie in seinem Leben gesehen zu haben. Außerdem gab er zu Protokoll er sei immer ein unbescholtener Bürger gewesen der sich noch nie etwas habe zu Schulden kommen lassen.

3. Empört über die Reaktion ihres Klassenlehrers ging Katharina zum Direktor der Schule und beschwerte sich über solch ein Verhalten.

4. Ein Gerichtsurteil besagt dass einem Schüler der auf dem Schulweg andere Kinder verprügelt angedroht werden darf ihn von der Schule zu verweisen um Mitschüler zu schützen.

5. Sie setzte sich ohne zu fragen zu diesem fremden Mann an den Tisch suchte in ihrer Handtasche nach ihrer Zigarettenschachtel nahm eine Zigarette heraus und bot auch dem Mann eine Zigarette an.

6. Ich würde dich gerne ins Kino einladen aber leider habe ich mein ganzes Taschengeld für diesen Monat schon ausgegeben.

7. Wenn ich heute Abend nach Hause komme und du hast dein Zimmer immer noch nicht aufgeräumt dann bekommst du entweder einen Monat lang kein Taschengeld mehr oder ich schließe dich so lange in dein Zimmer ein bis du es endlich aufräumst.

8. Manchmal wünschte ich ich hätte so wenig Geld wie vor zwanzig Jahren aber dafür auch so viel Zeit wie ich sie damals hatte.

9. Außer sich vor Freude über die Geburt seines Sohnes nahm er sein Handy und teilte allen Leuten die ihm einfielen die freudige Nachricht mit ob sie es hören wollten oder nicht.

10. Obwohl ich schon mehrere Jahre in England lebe und arbeite ärgert es mich immer noch sehr dass man hier im Durchschnitt viel weniger verdient als in Deutschland dafür aber für fast alles mehr bezahlt.

11. Ich kam sah und siegte. (Cäsar)

12. Als er von der Arbeit nach Hause kam sah er mit Entsetzen dass in seine Wohnung eingebrochen worden war und dass unter anderem auch das Medaillon fehlte das ihm seine Mutter bei ihrem Tod hinterlassen hatte.

13. Da er noch nie vorher im Ausland gewesen war fühlte er sich ziemlich fremd als er vorige Woche mutterseelenallein und ohne Freunde auf dem Berliner Flughafen Tegel ankam.

14. Ich finde wir dürfen uns nicht darauf beschränken Politiker nur verbal zu kritisieren sondern wir müssen uns aktiv für unsere Ziele engagieren wenn wir wollen dass sich die Dinge wirklich ändern.

Answers to exercises

1   Words and sentences

1   Sentence patterns   1. d   2. g   3. f   4. b   5. b   6. a   7. g   8. g   9. c   10. d   11. d   12. a
13. b   14. f   15. a   16. b   17. c   18. e   19. g   20. c

2   The subject and the finite verb   1. Kathrin Borchert hat   2. Australien war   3. sie lebt
4. Unser Reporter stellt   5. Was fasziniert   6. Kathrin lächelt   7. Sie liebt   8. Sie liebt   9. der
kleine Ort Gold Coast ist   10. Sie erzählt   11. sie vermisst   12. Sie vermisst   13. niemand
wünscht   14. die Menschen sind   15. Sie haben   16. sie helfen   17. Kathrin hat   18. sie ist
19. sie hat   20. Kathrin Borchert hat

3   Sentence patterns   1. b   2. g   3. a   4. d   5. f   6. a   7. b   8. b   9. g   10. e   11. b   12. b
13. d   14. g   15. b   16. c   17. b   18. g   19. f   20. b

4   Main clauses and subordinate clauses   1. mc/sc   2. mc/mc   3. mc/sc   4. mc/sc   5. ic/mc
6. sc/mc   7. mc/sc   8. mc/ic   9. mc/ic   10. mc/ic/sc   11. mc/sc/ic   12. mc/sc   13. sc/mc/mc
14. mc/sc   15. mc/ic

5   Infinitive clauses   1. mit seiner neuen Freundin gesehen zu werden   2. sie gestern in der
Kirche getroffen zu haben   3. morgen meine Tante in Bochum zu besuchen   4. den Einbrecher
nicht gesehen zu haben   5. unser Auto zu verkaufen   6. mit meinen Freunden zusammen zu sein
7. so etwas nie wieder zu tun   8. ihm das Frühstück aufs Zimmer zu bringen   9. mir die Haare
schneiden zu lassen   10. in der Stadt gewesen zu sein

6   Subordinate clauses   1. bevor wir in Urlaub fahren können   2. weil dort ein schlimmes
Unwetter war und niemand Starterlaubnis bekam   3. seitdem er seine Arbeit verloren hat   4. wenn
du mitkommen willst   5. damit frische Luft ins Zimmer kam   6. nachdem sie eine Stunde
geschlafen hatte   7. obwohl er schon seit 20 Jahren spielt   8. dass dein Bruder jetzt im Ausland
lebt   9. wie der Unfall auf dem Schulhof passiert ist   10. weil die Temperaturen auf 32 Grad im
Schatten gestiegen waren   11. bevor wir losgehen   12. obwohl ich immer rechtzeitig aufstehe

7   Main clauses   1. Meistens kommen wir erst um Mitternacht nach Hause.   2. In Secondhand-
Shops bekommt man oft gute Kleidung für wenig Geld.   3. Meine Familie sehe ich leider nur sehr
selten.   4. Politikern glaube ich kein Wort.   5. Im letzten Winter hat es fast keinen Schnee
gegeben.   6. Um wieviel Uhr der Zug ankommt, weiß ich leider nicht.   7. Worum es in dem Brief
ging, wollte sie mir nicht sagen.   8. Leider musste er unerwartet nach Berlin fliegen.   9. Bei
schlechtem Wetter findet das Fest drinnen statt.   10. Meiner Meinung nach muss der öffentliche
Verkehr viel besser subventioniert werden.

8   Main clauses   1. Nach Tübingen fährt mein Bruder mit dem Zug.   2. Ich bin heute erst um
11 Uhr aufgestanden.   3. Heute Nachmittag um 2 hat das Tennisturnier angefangen.   4. Um diese
Arbeit beneide ich dich nicht.   5. Seit heute Morgen um 8 habe ich nichts mehr gegessen.

6. Mit seiner Hilfe kann man immer rechnen.   7. In Zukunft musst du allein in Urlaub fahren.
8. Ohne Arbeitsgenehmigung darf man in diesem Land nicht arbeiten.   9. Heute in den frühen
Morgenstunden ist ein schwerer Unfall passiert.   10. In England kommen die Züge nicht immer
pünktlich an.   11. Hoffentlich wird mein Sohn bei dieser Universität angenommen.   12. Am liebsten gehe ich im Wald spazieren.

9 Questions   1. Kommst du morgen auch mit zu dem Fußballspiel?   2. Machst du das mit
Absicht?   3. Schreibt ihr morgen eine Klassenarbeit?   4. Geht ihr erst nächste Woche auf den
Ausflug?   5. Putzen Sie nie Ihre Fenster?   6. Besuchst du deine alte Tante?   7. Will er heute nach
Lübeck fahren?   8. Hat er in der Stadt keine Erdbeeren bekommen?

10 Commands   1. Entschuldigen Sie sich bei Ihrem Chef!   2. Spielen Sie mir etwas auf der
Gitarre vor!   3. Gehen Sie zum Arzt!   4. Haben Sie Geduld!   5. Machen Sie das Fenster auf!   6. Sehen
Sie sich auch diesen neuen Film an!   7. Vergessen Sie nichts!   8. Lassen Sie mich in Ruhe!

2 Nouns

1 Gender by meaning   1. der   2. der   3. das   4. die   5. das   6. der   7. der   8. das   9. das
10. die   11. der   12. das   13. der   14. die   15. das   16. die   17. das   18. der   19. der   20. die
21. die   22. die   23. der   24. das   25. die   26. der   27. das

2 Gender by ending   1. der   2. das   3. das   4. der   5. der   6. die   7. die   8. die   9. der
10. das   11. die   12. die   13. der   14. die   15. die   16. die   17. das   18. der   19. das   20. das
21. die   22. das   23. das   24. der   25. der   26. der   27. die   28. die   29. die   30. das   31. die
32. die   33. die   34. das

3 Other clues to gender   a. neuter   b. feminine

4 The plural of masculine nouns   1. Berge   2. Wälder   3. Tänze   4. Äpfel   5. Gärten
6. Schüler   7. Arme   8. Fische   9. Finger   10. Köpfe   11. Briten   12. Schmerzen   13. Fäden
14. Ringe   15. Fernseher   16. Professoren   17. Monate   18. Geister   19. Fälle   20. Staaten
21. Punkte   22. Artikel   23. Anzüge   24. Ränder   25. Brüder   26. Könige   27. Nachbarn
28. Typen   29. Computer   30. Füße

5 The plural of feminine nouns   1. Städte   2. Gabeln   3. Töchter   4. Arbeiten   5. Freundinnen
6. Kenntnisse   7. Wände   8. Nächte   9. Mauern   10. Mütter   11. Wohnungen   12. Schultern
13. Bänke/Banken (benches/banks)   14. Hände   15. Blumen   16. Universitäten   17. Einheiten
18. Gewerkschaften   19. Regeln   20. Würste   21. Lösungen   22. Explosionen   23. Schwächen
24. Putzfrauen   25. Fäuste   26. Türen   27. Kühe   28. Lasten   29. Früchte   30. Schwestern

6 The plural of neuter nouns   1. Klöster   2. Mädchen   3. Dächer   4. Häuser   5. Messer
6. Hemden   7. Räder   8. Flöße   9. Länder   10. Interessen   11. Argumente   12. Jahre   13. Verbote
14. Büchlein   15. Augen   16. Betten   17. Schlösser   18. Gespräche   19. Lämmer   20. Blätter
21. Wörter/Worte   22. Ohren   23. Lichter   24. Klaviere   25. Beine   26. Spiele   27. Bücher
28. Bilder   29. Schafe   30. Kissen

7 Plural   1. Radios, Kassettenrekorder, Videogeräte, Computer   2. Diskotänze, Rhythmen
3. Landstraßen, Stadtzentren, Autos, PKWs, LKWs   4. Unis, Studenten, Professoren, Hochschullehrer

5. Zimmer, Hotels, Balkons/Balkone, Fernseher 6. Menschen, Tage, Wochen, Monate, Jahre
7. Zoos, Tiere, Löwen, Tiger, Bären, Leoparden, Vögel, Tauben, Spatzen 8. Museen,
Ausstellungen, Besucher, Bilder, Epochen, Ausstellungsstücke 9. Kinder, Mädchen, Jungen,
Gameboys, Videospiele, Skateboards, Fahrräder, Roller 10. Firmen, Mitarbeiter, Teams, Individuen

8 Case 1. dat. (after preposition *mit*), dat. (after preposition *zu*) 2. acc. (length of time)
3. gen. (to show possession) 4. dat. (indirect object), acc. (direct object) 5. acc. (direct object)
6. acc. (direct object), dat. (after preposition *mit*), nom. (subject of sentence) 7. nom. (subject of
sentence), nom. (complement of copular verb *sein*) 8. dat. (with adjective *ähnlich*) 9. dat. (sole
dative object) 10. dat. (to show possession with clothing), nom. (subject of sentence) 11. acc.
(greetings, wishes) 12. gen. (after preposition *während*) 13. nom. (subject of sentence),
acc. (direct object) 14. nom. (noun in isolation) 15. acc. (after preposition *für*), nom. (subject of
sentence)

9 Weak nouns and 'normal' nouns The weak nouns are 1, 3, 5, 6, 8, 11, 13, 15, 19, 20

3 The noun phrase: determiners and pronouns

1 The definite and indefinite article 1. der 2. einen; ein 3. die 4. –; – 5. die; die
6. dem; das (= ins) 7. –; – 8. dem; der (= zur); der 9. das 10. einen 11. den; der; die
12. das; der 13. –/den; eine 14. das (= ins); die 15. –; –

2 The definite and indefinite article 1. Der kleine Cäsar 2. Was der Himmel erlaubt 3. Der
Mann, der auf die Erde fiel 4. Der Himmel kann warten 5. Opfer der Liebe 6. Der Tod steht
ihr gut

3 Demonstratives and other determiners 1. jeder; einem 2. diejenigen; ein; alle; einige;
derselben 3. wenige; dieser; viel 4. viel; diesem 5. einen solchen; wenig; einige; mehreren;
unsere beiden; mehrere; viele; sämtliche; unserer; ein; all 6. wenige; irgendeiner; diesem 7. alle
meine 8. welchem 9. allen; sämtliche; irgendwelchen 10. viele; viel; wenig; alle

4 *(k)ein* and possessives used as pronouns 1. einer 2. mein; deiner; deiner; meiner
3. einen; eu(e)ren; unserer 4. meine; ihr; ihres; unseres 5. keinem; unseren 6. unser; eines
7. unserem; ihrem; ihres 8. einen; einer; meinem; einer 9. keiner 10. mein; seinen; meinen;
seiner; meiner

5 Other common pronouns 1. Niemand weiß das. 2. Welcher von den zwei/beiden Jungen/
Welcher der zwei/beiden Jungen ist Ihrer/eurer/deiner? 3. Meine Mutter sagte etwas zu meinem
Vater. 4. Ich habe vergessen Kaffee zu kaufen. Könntest du mir welchen leihen? 5. Mit wem hast
du am Telefon gesprochen? 6. Ich werde (zu) niemandem etwas sagen. 7. Es ist immer besser
mit jemandem zu sprechen, wenn man Probleme hat. 8. Wer weiß, wessen Schuld es war? 9. Du
kannst einem wirklich auf die Nerven gehen. 10. Hast du (irgend)jemanden gesehen?

6 Personal pronouns 1. er; ihm 2. er; ihnen 3. sie; es 4. sie; ihm 5. sie; sie 6. sie; sie
7. er; er; ihr 8. er; es 9. ihr; sie 10. sie; ihm 11. sie; ihnen 12. sie; er

7 Personal pronouns 1. dir/euch/Ihnen 2. dir/euch/Ihnen 3. du/ihr/Sie 4. dich/euch/Sie
5. dir/euch/Ihnen 6. dich/euch/Sie 7. dir/euch/Ihnen 8. du/ihr/Sie 9. dir/euch/Ihnen
10. du/ihr/Sie 11. dich/euch/Sie 12. dir/euch/Ihnen

8 Prepositional adverbs 1. damit 2. darüber 3. über ihn 4. mit ihm 5. davor 6. dafür
7. mit ihr 8. darüber 9. damit 10. an ihn

9 Reflexive pronouns 1. sich 2. sich 3. dich 4. mich 5. mich 6. sich 7. euch 8. sich
9. mich 10. dich

10 Reflexive pronouns 1. sich 2. mir 3. sich 4. dir; dir 5. uns 6. euch 7. mir 8. dir
9. sich 10. uns

4 Adjectives, adverbs and adverbials

1 Adjective declension 1. a. grober b. groben c. groben d. groben 2. a. eigentliche
b. eigentlichen c. eigentliche d. eigentlichen 3. a. kleine b. kleinen c. kleine d. kleiner 4. a. kleinen
b. kleinen c. kleinen d. kleinen 5. a. neues b. neuen c. neues d. neuen 6. a. jungen b. junge c. junge
d. junger 7. a. guter b. gute c. guter d. gute 8. a. fettes b. fettem c. fettes d. fetten 9. a. blöde b.
blöden c. blöden d. blöden 10. a. gute b. guten c. gute d. gute

2 Adjective declension für deutsche Paare; ein tropischer Traum; mit 340 herrlichen
Sonnentagen; und exotischen Früchten; nach unendlichem Sonnenschein; und tropischen Nächten;
nach endloser Freiheit; und ewiger Sehnsucht; zu schön; wahr; real; paradiesisch; die 37-Jährige;
dem zweitgrößten Atoll; eine zerbrochene Liebe; ihr damaliger Freund; auf der malerischen Insel;
ihren jetzigen Ehemann; die beiden; ewige Liebe; dieser glückliche Tag; der schönste; gut gehenden Agentur; romantische Hochzeiten; eine deutsche Klientel; ein … unkompliziertes Geschäft;
in einer versteckten Bucht; die gebürtige Hamburgerin; die starken Wellen; den gesamten Strand;
ungewöhnliche Geschichten; diese traumhaften Inseln; das Selbstverständlichste; auf der ganzen
Welt; bunten Fischen; in der kleinen Bucht; alle Einheimischen; die duftenden Mangos; die
unglaubliche Vielfalt; riesigen Lavafeldern; von weißen, goldenen, schwarzen und sogar grünen
Stränden; von endlosen Urwäldern und mächtigen Bergen; von den einsamsten Buchten; am leicht-
esten; der langen Straße; das dichte Gebüsch; diese weiche Luft; den milden Wind; das unver-
gleichliche Licht; auf dem paradiesischen Hawaii; ihr zweites Zuhause

3 Adjective declension after some plural determiners 1. einige kleine 2. wenige gute;
viele oberflächliche 3. mehreren anderen 4. vieler deutscher 5. einigen kleinen; manchen
großen 6. vielen ausländischen 7. mancher kleinen/kleiner; wenigen unwichtigen 8. wenige
interessierte; viele laute

4 Declension of adjectives ending in -el, -en, -er 1. heikle; üble 2. teurer; billiger 3. dun-
klen; selt(e)ne 4. plausible; unflexibles 5. miserablen 6. rentable; hohen 7. makabre
8. ungeheure 9. saure

5 Adjectives used as nouns 1. Liebe; Gute 2. Tote; Überlebenden 3. Neues; Alten
4. Deutscher 5. Lustiges 6. Verwandten 7. Staatsangehörigen 8. Geistlichen; Interessantes
9. Reisende 10. Verlobter

6 Adjectives with the dative 1. Dieser Mann war ihr unbekannt. 2. Ich bin dir sehr dankbar für deine Hilfe. 3. Glaubst du, dass dir dein Mann treu ist?/dass dein Mann dir treu ist? 4. Es war mir (schon) immer klar, dass sie ihren Kollegen überlegen ist. 5. Es ist mir peinlich, dass ich meinem Bruder so ähnlich bin. 6. Leider ist es mir unmöglich zu kommen. 7. Mir ist schlecht/übel und schwind(e)lig. 8. Normalerweise ist mir entweder zu heiß oder zu kalt. 9. Uns allen ist sein Verhalten unverständlich/unbegreiflich. 10. Es ist mir unangenehm, Kleidung aus Polyester zu tragen.

7 Adjectives with prepositions 1. auf; zu 2. für; auf 3. auf 4. um 5. an 6. an; darauf 7. an 8. von 9. auf 10. zu

8 Comparison of adjectives 1. größte 2. kleinste 3. höchste 4. weitesten; nächsten 5. älteste 6. stärkste 7. längste; kürzeste 8. heißeste 9. teuersten 10. reichste; ärmste

9 Comparison of adjectives 1. billigeren 2. besseren; mehr 3. höher; niedriger 4. kälter; stärker 5. teurer; besser 6. gesünder; länger 7. Klügere 8. härteren; lauter 9. jünger 10. wärmeren; wohler; kühleren 11. dunklere; tiefere 12. näher; größer

10 Time adverbials 1. seitdem 2. sofort 3. demnächst 4. vorläufig 5. gerade 6. inzwischen 7. damals 8. kurz 9. neulich 10. vorher 11. gelegentlich 12. selten 13. früher 14. bisher 15. unaufhörlich

11 Adverbs of place 1. überall; nirgends/nirgendwo; irgendwo 2. unten; oben 3. draußen; drinnen 4. mitten 5. außen 6. woanders/anderswo 7. innen; außen 8. mitten 9. oben; unten 10. da

12 Adverbs of direction 1. hinein; heraus 2. hinein 3. woandershin 4. woher; wohin 5. herunter; hinauf 6. hervor 7. irgendwohin 8. heran; heraus 9. hinunter; hindurch; hinauf 10. heraus; hinein 11. herein 12. überallhin

13 Adverbs of place and direction 1. Er weckte mich mitten in der Nacht. 2. Ich gehe/fahre nirgendwohin. Ich bleibe hier. 3. Sie wusste nicht, wohin sie schauen sollte/wo sie hinschauen sollte. 4. Komm bitte jetzt herunter und frühstücke. 5. Einen Moment bitte. Er ist draußen im Garten, aber ich werde ihn hereinrufen. 6. Ich weiß, dass heute Abend eine Party ist, aber ich gehe nicht hin. 7. Das Bild ist oben leicht beschädigt. 8. Ich möchte gern woandershin/anderswohin gehen. 9. Sie muss woandershin/anderswohin gezogen sein. 10. Bitte gehen Sie hinein und warten Sie dort/da. 11. Ich werde nie wieder dorthin/dahin gehen. 12. Wie bist du dorthin/dahin gekommen? 13. Er kam von weit her.

14 Adverbials with the accusative case 1. distance 2. point in time 4. length of time 5. point in time 7. length of time 8. distance

15 Adverbs of manner 1. Meine Mutter jammert ständig. 2. Mein Vater arbeitet schwer. 3. Arturo Ui steigt unaufhaltsam auf. 4. Die Technik entwickelt sich rasend. 5. Die Chorknaben singen wuderschön. 6. Die Maschinen dröhnen unerträglich. 7. Die Eule schreit laut. 8. Die Feuerwehr hilft freiwillig. 9. Die Hilfskräfte setzen sich unermüdlich bei der Flutkatastrophe ein. 10. Die Familie geht regelmäßig spazieren. 11. Die Nachbarn grüßen freundlich. 12. Der Fußballer foult absichtlich.

16 Adverbs of attitude and manner 1. Möglicherweise hat er den Zug verpasst.   2. Ohne Zweifel/Zweifellos sagt er die Wahrheit 3. Da haben Sie sicher teilweise Recht. 4. Bedauerlicherweise konnte er ihr nicht helfen.   5. Heute darfst du ausnahmsweise etwas länger aufbleiben.   6. In Deutschland wünscht man sich normalerweise vor dem Essen „guten Appetit". 7. Erstaunlicherweise hat sie die Stelle bekommen.   8. Interessanterweise hat er seine Einstellung plötzlich geändert.   9. Wir haben drei neue Mitarbeiter probeweise eingestellt.   10. Wir könnten beispielsweise mit den Kindern ein Picknick machen.   11. Komischerweise seid ihr nie zu Hause, wenn ich anrufe.   12. Natürlich fühlen sich Tiere in freier Wildbahn wohler als im Zoo. 13. Hoffentlich hat es euch im Urlaub gefallen.   14. Er ist zwangsläufig in eine andere Filiale versetzt worden.   15. Glücklicherweise ist die Operation gut verlaufen.   16. Bei dieser Beschäftigung wird man stundenweise bezahlt.

17 Ordinal numbers 1. elfte erste   2. zweite siebte   3. vierundzwanzigste zwölfte   4. achte dritte 5. sechzehnte zehnte   6. achtundzwanzigste vierte 7. sechste fünfte 8. dreizehnte neunte 9. achtzehnte zweite 10. fünfundzwanzigste elfte 11. einunddreißigste zwölfte 12. zwanzigste siebte

18 Ordinal numbers 1. achtundzwanzigsten ersten neunzehnhundertachtundfünfzig 2. zwölften siebten neunzehnhundertsiebenundvierzig   3. dritten elften neunzehnhundertsiebenundachtzig 4. dreißigsten vierten vierzehnhundertzweiundneunzig 5. zweiundzwanzigsten achten siebzehnhundertneunundachtzig 6. fünften zwölften sechzehnhundertsiebenundsechzig 7. dreiundzwanzigsten neunten sechzehnhundertzweiundsiebzig   8. achtzehnten elften zwölfhundertzwei 9. sechzehnten dritten dreizehnhundertvierundfünfzig   10. ersten ersten zweitausend 11. siebten zweiten fünfzehnhundertfünfundfünfzig   12. zwanzigsten sechsten zweitausendeins

5 Prepositions

1 Prepositions and cases *accusative*: bis, gegen, für, ohne, durch, um; *dative*: außer, aus, von, gegenüber, bei, ab, nach, mit, seit, zu; *genitive*: hinsichtlich, außerhalb, trotz, statt, angesichts, während, wegen; *accusative or dative*: auf, in, zwischen, vor, hinter, an, unter, über, neben

2 Prepositions with the accusative 1. durch 2. für 3. bis 4. gegen 5. für 6. ohne 7. um 8. gegen 9. bis 10. um 11. für; gegen 12. bis 13. durch 14. um

3 Prepositions with the dative 1. bei 2. aus 3. von; mit 4. seit 5. von 6. zu; nach 7. nach; nach 8. außer; mit 9. bei; zu 10. aus; von 11. seit; an/bei 12. bei; mit 13. aus 14. zu 15. gegenüber 16. bei 17. nach; gegenüber 18. aus 19. seit; bei 20. zu

4 Prepositions with the accusative or dative 1. einem; dem 2. einer; der; dieser 3. einer; das neue; der 4. die andere; dieser 5. unserem; dem 6. einen; der 7. einem; einem 8. die; die 9. das 10. ein 11. dem; den 12. meinen; seine 13. den 14. den; die; der; die; eine; die; der; der; der rechten; keinen 15. den heutigen; einer deutschen 16. dem; die neuesten 17. seiner; letzter 18. meinem; das 19. den 20. einen 21. die

5 Prepositions 1. die; e · 2. die große; l 3. der hohen; m 4. schwedischen; o 5. den; a 6. dem; c 7. dem; k 8. die; n 9. die; p 10. der; d 11. der; den; g 12. die faule; f 13. der eigenen; j 14. der; h 15. dem (im); b 16. den; i 17. dem; q

6 **Prepositions** 1. gegen 2. hinter 3. wegen 4. vor 5. in 6. während/bei 7. nach 8. für
9. durch 10. bei 11. in 12. seit 13. in 14. an 15. zwischen 16. gegen/um/bis 17. trotz
18. bei/mit 19. an/zu 20. bis/nach

7 **Prepositions** 1. am; in; mit; nach; auf; über; vor; im 2. statt; zu; von; mit; nach; zu; in; mit
3. in; auf; hinter; in; durch; ohne; auf; nach; vor 4. bei; auf; durch; für; mit; in; für; in 5. bis; in;
mit; vor; im; im; zwischen; für; nach

8 **Prepositional adverbs** 1. dafür 2. damit 3. für sie 4. durch sie 5. daran 6. an ihn
7. daran 8. darin 9. darüber 10. zu ihr 11. auf ihn 12. darauf 13. darauf 14. davon
15. gegen ihn

9 **Prepositional adverbs** 1. Wir rechnen damit, ... 2. Meine Arbeit besteht darin, ... 3. Du
gewöhnst dich daran, ... 4. Ich verlasse mich darauf, ... 5. Er denkt daran, ... 6. Ich bin
überzeugt davon, ... 7. Sie sorgt/sorgen dafür, ... 8. Wir freuen uns darauf, ... 9. Ich bin dagegen, ... 10. Er weiß davon, ...

6 Verbs: forms

1 **Present tense of weak, strong and irregular verbs** 1. Spielst du 2. Machst du 3. Fährst
du 4. Wanderst du 5. Wartest du 6. Rechnest du 7. Trägst du 8. Grüßt du 9. Musst du
10. Studierst du 11. Kannst du 12. Hast du 13. Öffnest du 14. Badest du 15. Arbeitest
du 16. Liest du 17. Weißt du 18. Wirst du 19. Gibst du 20. Läufst du 21. Stößt du
22. Darfst du 23. Nimmst du 24. Lebst du 25. Backst/Bäckst du 26. Klingelst du 27. Änderst
du 28. Lässt du 29. Gießt du 30. Reitest du

2 **Present tense of weak, strong and irregular verbs** 1. Der Mensch weiß 2. Der Baum
wächst 3. Das Kind schläft 4. Der Lehrer findet 5. Der Engländer spricht 6. Der Athlet hat
7. Der Angler fängt 8. Der Tourist sieht 9. Der Junge wirft 10. Der Apfel fällt 11. Der Preis
darf 12. Der Gast wird 13. Der Baum stirbt 14. Die Steuer wird 15. Der Schüler fährt 16. Das
Kind macht 17. Das Haus steht 18. Der Arzt will 19. fehlt ein Buch 20. Der Skifahrer bricht
21. Die Biene sticht 22. Der Kunde kauft 23. Das Kind läuft 24. Der Politiker löst 25. Der
Nachbar trifft 26. Das Auto hält 27. Der Dieb stiehlt 28. Der Sportler gewinnt 29. Der
Verletzte braucht 30. Der Italiener isst

3 **Separable verbs** 1. Meine Schwester macht mir die Tür auf. ..., dass meine Schwester mir die
Tür aufmacht. 2. Die Premiere findet schon morgen statt. ..., dass die Premiere schon morgen
stattfindet? 3. Fehler kommen auch bei Spitzenkräften vor. ..., dass Fehler auch bei Spitzenkräften
vorkommen. 4. Du zündest eine Kerze an. ..., wenn du eine Kerze anzündest. 5. Ich stelle dir
morgen meinen Freund vor. ..., dass ich dir morgen meinen Freund vorstelle. 6. Wir geben die
Hoffnung nicht auf. ..., dass wir die Hoffnung nicht aufgeben. 7. Mein Bruder tritt in einen
Karateklub ein. ..., dass er in einen Karateklub eintritt. 8. Ich mache einen Termin beim Arzt für
dich aus. ..., dass ich einen Termin beim Arzt für dich ausmache. 9. Wir ziehen nächste Woche in
unser neues Haus ein. ..., wenn wir nächste Woche in unser neues Haus einziehen. 10. Unsere
Katze läuft uns immer weg. ..., warum unsere Katze uns immer wegläuft. 11. Mein Vater gibt nie

einen Fehler zu...., dass mein Vater nie einen Fehler zugibt. 12. Du gibst das Geld sofort zurück...., dass du das Geld sofort zurückgibst.

4 Imperative 1. Sprecht 2. Werft 3. Schließt 4. Rennt nicht 5. Habt 6. Benutzt 7. Hört... zu 8. Rennt nicht... herum 9. Ärgert und schlagt... nicht 10. Kaut 11. Tragt 12. Handelt 13. Gebt 14. Esst 15. Seid 16. Beschädigt

5 Imperative 1. Geh früher ins Bett! 2. Iss regelmäßiger! 3. Trink weniger Alkohol! 4. Rauch weniger! 5. Geh öfter spazieren! 6. Nimm dir mehr Zeit für dich! 7. Mach dir nicht so viele Sorgen! 8. Treib mehr Sport! 9. Entspann(e) dich mehr! 10. Sei nicht so nervös! 11. Reg(e) dich nicht so schnell auf! 12. Ernähr(e) dich besser! 13. Schalte öfter ab! 14. Arbeite nicht so viel! 15. Gib mehr Geld für dich aus! 16. Fahr öfter in Urlaub! 17. Gib dir nicht immer die Schuld...! 18. Zerbrich dir nicht den Kopf...!

6 Imperative 1. Schließen Sie die Haustür ab! 2. Lassen Sie niemals die Fenster offen! 3. Bitten Sie die Nachbarn, ...! 4. Versichern Sie sich, ...! 5. Mähen Sie den Rasen, ...! 6. Geben Sie einem Nachbarn/Bekannten einen Schlüssel! 7. Achten Sie darauf, ...! 8. Schließen Sie nicht alle Fensterläden! 9. Ziehen Sie nicht alle Vorhänge zu! 10. Bauen Sie einen Timer ein, ...!

7 Forms of strong and irregular verbs 1. **EI – IE – IE**: verzeihen, meiden, schreien, schreiben, treiben, reiben, schweigen, steigen, leihen **EI – I – I**: streiten, gleiten, pfeifen, greifen, reißen, vergleichen, schleichen, streichen 2. **I – A – U**: trinken, stinken, binden, sinken, zwingen, verschwinden, dringen, gelingen, springen, klingen, ringen **I – A – O**: spinnen, sinnen, beginnen, gewinnen, rinnen 3. **A – U – A**: laden, tragen, wachsen, graben, waschen **A – IE – A**: halten, lassen, blasen, raten, schlafen, fallen 4. **E – A – O**: sprechen, befehlen, werfen, erschrecken, stechen, werben, gelten, brechen, stehlen, verderben, treffen, empfehlen, sterben **E – A – E**: lesen, geschehen, sehen, vergessen, messen, treten, fressen **E – A – A**: nennen, rennen, brennen

8 Forms of strong and irregular verbs 1. verzeiht – verzieh – verziehen 2. nennt – nannte – genannt 3. bringt – brachte – gebracht 4. tut – tat – getan 5. sitzt – saß – gesessen 6. trägt – trug – getragen 7. vergleicht – verglich – verglichen 8. steht – stand – gestanden 9. denkt – dachte – gedacht 10. spricht – sprach – gesprochen 11. schreibt – schrieb – geschrieben 12. fängt – fing – gefangen 13. leidet – litt – gelitten 14. friert – fror – gefroren 15. verliert – verlor – verloren 16. fließt – floss – geflossen 17. lügt – log – gelogen 18. läuft – lief – gelaufen 19. schneidet – schnitt – geschnitten 20. schließt – schloss – geschlossen 21. fliegt – flog – geflogen 22. kommt – kam – gekommen 23. heißt – hieß – geheißen 24. verschwindet – verschwand – verschwunden 25. liegt – lag – gelegen 26. zieht – zog – gezogen 27. nimmt – nahm – genommen 28. ruft – rief – gerufen 29. schiebt – schob – geschoben 30. schweigt – schwieg – geschwiegen 31. isst – aß – gegessen 32. hebt – hob – gehoben

9 Forms of strong and irregular verbs 1. flogen; liehen; fuhren 2. sah; fing 3. wollten; blieben 4. saß; schlief 5. hatte; nannte 6. wussten; taten 7. hielt; sah 8. mussten; wurden 9. kamen; sahen; kannten 10. schwamm; gewann 11. dachte; wolltest 12. ging; nahm 13. trug; stand; gefiel 14. gab; schrien; ließ 15. brachen; stahlen 16. betrat; erschrak 17. half; vergaß 18. bat; verzieh 19. sangen; klang 20. war; schlief; stand... auf; wusch sich; zog sich an; lief; aß; las; stand; rief... an; traf sich; gingen... spazieren; lud... ein; saßen; tranken; sprachen; brachte; fanden; war

10 Past tense blickte; erwartete; erlebte; rannten; konnten; gelang; erfuhren; gehörte; wollten; bekamen; dachte; brauchte; musste; ließ; hatte; trauten; war; hatten; öffnete; stand; fletschte; wirkte; schien; musste; wandte; war; zeigte; abstritt; schlugen; stand; reichte; musste

11 Past participles 1. verheiratet; gestritten 2. gefunden; aufgehoben; genommen; gebracht; abgegeben 3. abgeräumt; serviert 4. beeilt; abgebrannt 5. getrieben; gemacht; geschwommen; gerudert; gewonnen 6. beworben; mitgeteilt; vergeben 7. ausprobiert; gefallen; getan; gebrochen; verletzt 8. bestanden; angenommen 9. gesehen; abgebogen; gehalten 10. geträumt; geklingelt; gebracht; eingepackt; geöffnet; gefreut; festgestellt; geschickt; aufgewacht; gemerkt; gewesen

12 *haben* or *sein* in the perfect? 1. ist 2. bin; habe 3. ist; hat 4. bin; habe; haben 5. sind; hat 6. habe; ist 7. ist; hat 8. ist; hat 9. habe 10. hat; ist 11. habe; sind 12. ist; hat 13. hat 14. ist; hat 15. ist; bin 16. sind; sind; hat; haben; sind; ist; haben 17. habe; ist 18. hast; hast 19. haben; sind 20. ist; habe

13 The forms of the subjunctive 1. gebe 2. habest … gehabt 3. werde schlafen 4. wäre eingeschlafen 5. seien … gewesen 6. müssest … bleiben 7. wäre … geworden 8. werde regnen 9. sei ausgelacht worden 10. säße 11. hätten … gewusst 12. gebe 13. würden … gelassen 14. kenne 15. wolle … schreiben 16. sollest aufhören 17. wäre angekommen 18. sei … geblieben 19. habet euch umgezogen 20. sei gesehen worden 21. haben uns verabredet 22. heirate 23. habe sich verlaufen 24. ziehest … um 25. wüsste 26. käme 27. müsste … sein 28. lasse 29. werde 30. fahre

7 Verbs: uses

1 The forms of the passive 1. Du bist in der Stadt gesehen worden. 2. In der Kirche wurden viele Lieder gesungen. 3. Du wirst sicher morgen angerufen werden. 4. Wir werden schon lange nicht mehr gegrüßt. 5. Die Polizei war alarmiert worden. 6. Das Kind wird geschlagen worden sein. 7. Das Fenster wird nicht zugemacht worden sein. 8. Ich bin belogen worden. 9. Ich bin aufgehalten worden. 10. Der Rasen war gemäht worden. 11. In die Schule wurde eingebrochen. 12. Mehrere Computer wurden gestohlen. 13. Der Patient wird untersucht. 14. Die Operation wird nächste Woche durchgeführt werden. 15. Wie viele Karten sind verkauft worden? 16. Er ist in eine andere Abteilung versetzt worden. 17. Er wurde des Diebstahls beschuldigt. 18. Ihr Fall wird gerade besprochen.

2 The *werden*- and the *sein*-passive 1. wurden 2. werden; war 3. bin 4. wurden 5. wird 6. wurde 7. ist; werden 8. wurde 9. wird 10. waren 11. ist 12. wurden 13. werden; werden 14. wurde 15. wurde; ist/sei/wäre

3 The subjectless passive 1. Für die Kinder wird gesorgt werden. 2. Bei C&A wird nicht mehr genügend gekauft. 3. Vor bissigen Hunden wird gewarnt. 4. Auf dem Geburtstagsfest ist getrunken, getanzt und gelacht worden. 5. Seit der Entwicklung von E-Mails wird weniger telefoniert. 6. In Zeiten einer Wirtschaftskrise wird mehr gespart. 7. In Griechenland wird mehr geraucht als in Deutschland. 8. In der Diskussion wurde über Finanzhilfe … gesprochen. 9. Auf gesunde Ernährung muss geachtet werden. 10. Nach dem vermissten Kind war drei Tage lang gesucht worden.   11. Heutzutage wird viel aggressiver Auto gefahren als früher.   12. Gestern ist bei uns eingebrochen worden.   13. In diesem Waldgebiet wird gern gejoggt.   14. Morgen kann mit den Umbauarbeiten begonnen werden.   15. In dieser Fabrik wird rund um die Uhr gearbeitet. 16. Über den Gesetzentwurf wurde abgestimmt.

4   The passive with dative objects   1. Mir wurde zur bestandenen Prüfung gratuliert.   2. Dem kleinen Jungen wurde über das Haar gestrichen.   3. Dem Richter war nur zögernd geantwortet worden.   4. Schönen Frauen wird oft geschmeichelt.   5. Mir wurde für meine Mühe gedankt. 6. Dem Autofahrer ist mit einer Geldstrafe gedroht worden.   7. Einem Lügner wird nicht geglaubt. 8. Mir ist empfohlen worden mich zu schonen.   9. Mir ist von deinen Plänen erzählt worden. 10. Dem Politiker wurde heftig widersprochen.   11. Ihm wurde in jeder Hinsicht misstraut. 12. Meiner Schwester wird zugelächelt.

5   *von* or *durch* with the passive   1. von der Polizei   2. von meinem Bruder   3. durch Ihr Rauchen   4. von einem Blitz   5. durch eine defekte Gasleitung   6. von einem Lastwagen 7. durch eine Operation   8. von den Ärzten   9. von einem Freund   10. durch die Ermordung 11. von einem herabfallenden Dachziegel   12. von einer anonymen Spenderin   13. durch das Attentat   14. von seinen Anhängern   15. von der Herzogin   16. von einer Wespe

6   Subjunctive II: conditional sentences   1. Wenn du die Tabletten nähmest/nehmen würdest,würdest du wieder gesund (werden). Wenn du die Tabletten genommen hättest, wär(e)st du wieder gesund geworden.   2. Wenn du gut aussähest/aussehen würdest, hättest du Erfolg bei Männern. Wenn du gut ausgesehen hättest, hättest du Erfolg bei Männern gehabt.   3. Wenn du dich informieren würdest, wüsstest du es. Wenn du dich informiert hättest, hättest du es gewusst. 4. Wenn wir gleich losgingen/losgehen würden, träfen wir ihn noch/würden wir ihn noch treffen. Wenn wir gleich losgegangen wären, hätten wir ihn noch getroffen.   5. Wenn du vorsichtig wär(e)st, würde der Hunde nicht beißen. Wenn du vorsichtig gewesen wär(e)st, hätte der Hund nicht gebissen.   6. Wenn sie den Zug verpassen würde, riefe sie uns sicher an/würde sie uns sicher anrufen. Wenn sie den Zug verpasst hätte, hätte sie uns sicher angerufen.   7. Wenn du schneller arbeiten würdest, wären wir früher fertig. Wenn du schneller gearbeitet hättest, wären wir früher fertig gewesen.   8. Wenn du dich vorbereiten würdest, bestündest du die Prüfung/würdest du die Prüfung bestehen. Wenn du dich vorbereitet hättest, hättest du die Prüfung bestanden.   9. Wenn du dein Zimmer aufräumen würdest, würde ich dir eine Karte für das Rockkonzert schenken. Wenn du dein Zimmer aufgeräumt hättest, hätte ich dir eine Karte für das Rockkonzert geschenkt.   10. Was würden wir machen, wenn wir den Schlüssel nicht fänden/finden würden? Was hätten wir gemacht, wenn wir den Schlüssel nicht gefunden hätten?   11. Was gäbest du mir/würdest du mir geben, wenn ich deinen Aufsatz für dich schriebe/schreiben würde? Was hättest du mir gegeben, wenn ich deinen Aufsatz für dich geschrieben hätte?   12. Er käme zu spät/würde zu spät kommen, wenn er zu Fuß ginge/gehen würde. Er wäre zu spät gekommen, wenn er zu Fuß gegangen wäre.   13. Ich würde Ihnen Bescheid sagen, wenn ich etwas von ihm hören würde. Ich hätte Ihnen Bescheid gesagt, wenn ich etwas von ihm gehört hätte.   14. Wenn du langsam führest/fahren würdest, würde nichts passieren. Wenn du langsam gefahren wärest, wäre nichts passiert.   15. Wenn er die Wahlen gewinnen würde, bliebe er für weitere 5 Jahre Präsident/würde er … bleiben. Wenn er die Wahlen gewonnen hätte, wäre er … geblieben.   16. Wenn ich … tränke/trinken würde, bekäme ich Kopfschmerzen/würde ich … bekommen. Wenn ich … getrunken hätte, hätte ich … bekommen.

7 Reported speech 1. …, bis wann er den Artikel fertig haben müsse. 2. …, er habe …, ihm sei …, und er fühle sich … 3. …, die Arbeit mache ihnen Spaß, und sie wollten noch viele Jahre dort arbeiten. 4. …, 80% Prozent aller 9-Jährigen hätten … und verbrächten … Nur vor dem Computer säßen sie noch länger. 5. …, das Internet werde … zum Familienkiller, da jeder fünfte Deutsche … einschränke. Man kümmere sich …, und im Extremfall könne eine Familie … zerstört werden. Man dürfe … verteufeln, sondern man müsse lernen, … 6. …, seine Eltern kämen …, aber er sei hier geboren. Er spreche …, aber wenn er … sei, falle ihm auch Italienisch sehr leicht. 7. …, sie würden … verzichten. 8. …, der Fluss sei über die Ufer getreten, und das Wasser sei … so hoch geworden, dass die Brücke unpassierbar gewesen sei. Sie hätten … zu ihren Häusern fahren müssen, vor die sie Sandsäcke gelegt hätten. Aber das Wasser sei … in die Häuser gedrungen, die wochenlang unbewohnbar gewesen seien. Sie seien in Hotels einquartiert worden, bis die gröbsten Schäden beseitigt gewesen seien. 9. …, wo er … gewesen sei und was er gemacht habe. 10. …, er habe … gesessen und sei allein gewesen. Es tue ihm Leid, dass er kein besseres Alibi habe, aber so sei es gewesen. Er wisse überhaupt nicht, warum sie ihn hierher bestellt hätten. Er habe mit der ganzen Sache nichts zu tun.

8 Reported speech a. Frauen liebten ihren Mann/würden … lieben – er sehe fantastisch aus, sei erfolgreich … Das wisse er auch, und er benutze diesen Charme … Wenn sie abends ausgingen/ausgehen würden, flirte er … Sie beachte er kaum. Sie verachte sich dafür, dass sie trotzdem bei ihm bleibe, aber sie liebe ihn halt. b. Sie habe morgens überlegt, was sie abends kochen könne, damit ihr Mann zufrieden sei. Aber er sei nie zufrieden gewesen. Irgendwann habe sie gar nichts mehr gekocht und sei ausgegangen, wenn er heimgekommen sei. Da habe es ihm Leid getan. Seitdem sei wieder Ruhe. c. … habe ihr die Eifersucht ihres Freundes geschmeichelt. Sie habe Rücksicht darauf genommen: Sie habe sich nicht mehr … getroffen. Es habe keinen Tag gegeben, an dem sie sich nicht bei ihm abgemeldet habe. Irgendwann sei sie aufgewacht und habe gedacht, sie sei gefangen. Sie habe ihn verlassen. d. Manchmal … rede ihr Mann wochenlang nicht mit ihr. … Er behandle sie wie Luft. Wenn er dann wieder auftauche, sei sie dankbar … – und das Leben gehe weiter …

9 Reported speech a. Wenn ein Hundehalter … missachte, müsse er … rechnen. b. Städte dürften … verbieten, wenn der Besitzer … habe. …, wenn der Hund … aufgefallen sei. c. Die Haltung von Hunden gehöre … . … müsse der Vermieter zustimmen. d. Der Vermieter dürfe … verbieten. e. Wenn ein Vermieter … begründe, warum eine Hundehaltung nicht erlaubt sei, so gelte ein solches Verbot … f. Wenn Tierhaltung … abhänge, könne er … verweigern, es sei denn, die anderen Mieter hätten Tiere. g. Der Vermieter könne … verbieten, auch wenn … die Tierhaltung … erlaubt sei.

10 The modal auxiliary verbs 1. darf 2. musst; willst 3. kann 4. kann; müssen 5. Darf 6. Möchten; darf/kann 7. willst; musst 8. soll 9. will 10. können

11 The modal auxiliary verbs 1. He wants to see us. – He claims to have seen us. 2. He was allowed to go to Berlin. – He would be allowed to go to Berlin (or: He will most probably go to Berlin). 3. He would have been able to do it. – He can have done it (i.e. it is possible that he did it). 4. I want a piece of chocolate. – I would like a piece of chocolate. 5. You would have been allowed to tell him. – You should have told him. 6. We were able to help him. – We would be able to help him. 7. He has to/needs to/must go now. – He is supposed to go home now (i.e. someone else wants him to go).   8. I must/have got to/need to do some work. – I should really do some work.   9. This must be my sister. – This will most probably be my sister.   10. I don't have to/need to listen to this. – I am not allowed to listen to this.   11. He is supposed to be a good teacher. – He claims to be a good teacher (or: He wants to be a good teacher).   12. Shall we help you (i.e. do you want us to help you)? – Do we have to help you?   13. I don't want any mushrooms. – I did not like mushrooms.

12   The modal auxiliary verbs   1. a. I should not really be here (permission) b. The house will not have been cheap (probability)   2. a. We have to / must hurry (necessity) b. We must have miscalculated it (logical deduction)   3. a. You may be right there (possibility with concessive force) b. Would you like another piece of cake (liking)   4. a. He could repair your car (ability) b. He could/might be ill (possibility)   5. a. He is said/supposed to have a lot of money (rumour/report) b. I am supposed to take the money to him tomorrow (obligation)   6. a. What I've always wanted to ask you (intention) b. I did not want/mean to offend you (desire)   7. a. He claims to have been with his girlfriend at the time of the crime (claim) b.He wants to be at his girlfriend's at 5 o'clock (intention)   8. a. You should really know that (possible obligation) b. This was supposed to be a surprise (intention)   9. a. One hundred marks should be enough (logical deduction) b. We should simply tell him the truth one of these days (possible necessity).

13   The syntax of modal verbs   1. Wenn wir in Urlaub hätten fahren wollen, hätten wir es getan.   2. Wenn er den Zug hätte erreichen wollen, wäre er früher gegangen.   3. Wenn ich ein Instrument hätte lernen dürfen, hätte ich mich gefreut.   4. Wenn du so früh hättest aufstehen müssen wie ich, hättest du dich geärgert.   5. Wenn ich umsonst in das Konzert hätte gehen können, hätte ich den anderen Termin abgesagt.   6. Wenn ich meinen Eltern nicht beim Umzug hätte helfen müssen, hätte ich mitkommen können.   7. Wenn das Fahrrad eine Überraschung hätte sein sollen, hätten wir es verstecken müssen.   8. Wenn du den Film hättest sehen wollen, hättest du früher nach Hause kommen müssen.   9. Wenn ich mir ein neues Auto hätte kaufen wollen, hätte ich einen Kredit aufnehmen müssen.   10. Wenn du es hättest sehen können, hättest du lachen müssen.

14   The modal auxiliary verbs   1. Wir dürfen nicht vergessen deine Eltern zu informieren.   2. Du hättest mich vorher fragen sollen/müssen.   3. Die Tür wollte nicht aufgehen.   4. Er soll ein schwacher Kandidat sein.   5. Er dürfte inzwischen/mittlerweile im Bett sein.   6. Ohne deine Hilfe hätte ich es nicht tun können.   7. Sie müssen nicht jetzt/sofort bezahlen.   8. Sie kann das Buch nicht gelesen haben.   9. Darf ich Sie etwas fragen?   10. Ich konnte den Artikel gestern nicht lesen.   11. Wir wollten morgen nach München fahren.   12. Er will 10 Sprachen sprechen.   13. Wir wollen hier nicht länger leben/wohnen.   14. Du solltest zum Arzt gehen.   15. Darfst du draußen spielen?   16. Sollen/Wollen wir einen Spaziergang machen?   17. Ich hätte es nicht erwähnen sollen.   18. Ich musste ihm die Wahrheit sagen.   19. Wir sollten/müssten ihm wirklich die Wahrheit sagen.   20. Was soll ich ihm sagen?   21. Wir könnten ein Auto mieten.   22. Als Kind mochte ich keinen Spinat.

8   Valency and cases

1   Reflexive verbs   1. Ich habe mich gestern bei dem Regen erkältet.   2. Du hast vergessen dich zu bedanken.   3. Er eignet sich eher für einen handwerklichen Beruf.   4. Die Toiletten befinden sich gleich rechts vom Eingang.   5. Da haben Sie sich bestimmt geirrt.   6. Ich habe mich entschlossen… 7. Wir werden uns beim Chef über Sie beschweren. 8. Mein Sohn hat sich gestern beim Einkaufen wieder unmöglich benommen. 9. Er weigert sich zu kooperieren. 10. Sie hat sich von ihrer Krankheit erholt.

2 Reflexive verbs 2. h,dich 3. k,dir 4. l,mich 5. i,uns 6. m,mich 7. c,euch 8. n,dir 9. j,sich 10. e,mir 11. g,dich 12. f,mir 13. a,dich 14. b,mich

3 Dative objects 1. Er wird dir das nie verzeihen. 2. Er drohte dem Jungen mit einem Stock. 3. Der Hund gehorcht seinem Besitzer nicht. 4. Ich konnte der Vesuchung nicht widerstehen. 5. Er wollte ihr mit seinem neuen Auto imponieren. 6. Wir folgten den Anweisungen. 7. Rauchen kann Ihrer Gesundheit ernsthaft schaden. 8. Meiner Tochter ist es gelungen ein Stipendium zu bekommen. 9. Ist dir sein seltsamer Akzent aufgefallen? 10. Das passiert mir nicht noch einmal./ Das wird mir nicht noch einmal passieren. 11. Traue keinem (niemandem) über 40. 12. Darf ich Ihnen zur Geburt Ihres Sohnes gratulieren. 13. Sie teilte mir das gestern mit.

4 Genitive or *von*? 1. die Verspätung des Zuges 2. etwas von dem Kuchen 3. die Beschreibung des Kindes 4. eine Reihe von Fragen 5. eine Reihe interessanter Fragen 6. der Geruch frisch gekochten Essens (*or* von frisch gekochtem Essen) 7. ein Freund von mir 8. viele meiner Freunde (*or* von meinen Freunden) 9. die Zahlung des Gehalts 10. nichts von der Vorlesung 11. der Preis eines Hauses 12. der Preis von fünf Häusern 13. eine Kollegin meiner Mutter (*or* von meiner Mutter) 14. eine Kollegin von uns 15. viel von dem Nudelsalat 16. drei seiner Schulkameraden (*or* von seinen Schulkameraden) 17. die Reparatur des Autos 18. der Vorschlag von dir 19. die Entsorgung des Mülls 20. eine Folge von Ereignissen

5 Objects and cases 1. den Direktor; dem Abteilungsleiter 2. mir; dir; den Film 3. mir; ihm; die Nachricht 4. uns; Ihnen; die Stelle; Ihnen; Ihre Bewerbung 5. einer Erklärung 6. dir; kein Wort 7. ihm; den Einbruch 8. seinem Sohn; den Rat; ein einfacher Handwerker; kein eigenes Geschäft 9. ein netter Kerl; mein Freund; dich 10. mein jetziges Gehalt; mir 11. dem Kind; den Mund 12. der Gewinnerin; ihr 13. mir; dieses Auto; mir; einen teuren Wagen 14. der Gefallenen 15. Ihnen; den Mietvertrag

6 Prepositional objects 1. mit der Situation 2. an seiner Ehrlichkeit 3. an einem zu hohen Blutdruck; an Krebs; an einer Lungenentzündung 4. über Ihren Eintritt; auf eine gute Zusammenarbeit 5. nach seiner Mutter 6. von dem Kauf; von deinen Schulden 7. von meiner Arbeit; mit ihr 8. von deinen Fähigkeiten; zu einem Hochschulstudium 9. von dir 10. für eine ausgezeichnete Idee; nach Flügen 11. um einen Gefallen; auf unsere Kinder; um eure Haustiere 12. nach Essen 13. um meine Schwester; von fremden Menschen; vor ihnen 14. zu den Leuten; zu übertriebener Eifersucht; zu Konflikten 15. von der Frage; um eine neue Stelle 16. über eine Gehaltserhöhung; damit 17. auf Veränderungen 18. an einen wirtschaftlichen Aufschwung; auf die Rezession 19. vor ihm; vor jeder Verantwortung 20. auf Politiker; an einer wirklichen Veränderung; an Demonstrationen

7 Prepositional objects 1. f 2. m 3. c 4. d 5. k 6. i 7. n 8. l 9. b 10. j 11. a 12. e 13. h 14. g 15. o

8 Valency and cases 1. Ich kann Ihnen diesen Wein empfehlen. 2. Er konnte den Kommissar nicht von seiner Unschuld überzeugen. 3. Du verschweigst mir die Wahrheit. 4. Der Vater meines Freundes erfreut sich bester Gesundheit.   5. Sie schrieb mir ihre neue Adresse auf.   6. Du hinderst mich an der Erfüllung meiner Pflicht.   7. Meine Arbeit fehlt mir sehr.   8. Wir begegneten gestern deinem Bruder.   9. Ich kann mich auf nichts konzentrieren.   10. Wir müssen das Haus meiner Tante verkaufen (*or* Wir müssen das Haus an meine Tante verkaufen).   11. Darf ich Ihnen ein Glas Sekt anbieten?   12. Kartoffeln schmecken mir am besten.   13. Wir fangen morgen mit den Umbauarbeiten an.   14. Sie können sich auf meine Diskretion verlassen.   15. Er denkt oft an seine Jugendzeit.   16. Ich wundere mich über das musikalische Talent deines Sohnes.   17. Der Arzt hat dem Patienten zu viel Anstrengung verboten.   18. Dieser Mantel gehört mir nicht.   19. Ich rate dir von einem Treffen mit ihm ab.   20. Ich darf Sie hoffentlich zum Essen einladen.   21. Seine Angst rührt von den Erfahrungen (in) seiner Kindheit her.   22. Sie müssen mit einer Erhöhung Ihrer Miete rechnen.   23. Wir hoffen auf baldige Besserung seines Zustandes.   24. Ich erzähle dir morgen die Geschichte.   25. Du kannst sie an ihrer tiefen Stimme erkennen.

9 Place complements and direction complements 1. comp 2. adv 3. comp 4. comp 5. adv 6. comp 7. adv 8. comp 9. comp 10. adv 11. comp 12. adv

9 Word order

You should note that there is some flexibility in the German word order system, and the order of elements may in some instances deviate from the answers given here, depending on emphasis.

1 Main clauses 1. Gestern hat sie…   2. Fußball habe ich…   3. Warum er das getan hat, kann ich…   4. Auf meinen Bruder verlässt man sich…   5. Sabine kenne ich…   6. Das letzte Mal haben wir…   7. Bei Karstadt ist es…   8. Dieses Buch hast du…   9. Deiner Mutter würde ich… 10. Mit dem Zug bin ich…

2 First position in main clauses 1. My father still hasn't repaired the lawnmower.   2. I will never go/I'm never going to the cinema with you again.   3. He can't afford a holiday abroad. 4. You aren't dressed yet, and you haven't brushed your teeth yet either.   5. People will have to remember that name./This is a name to remember.   6. The boy just managed to escape (from) the woman.   7. One always has to wait for you./You always keep people waiting.   8. Angela met Petra in the cinema.   9. The police found/managed to find the three brothers at last.   10. He gave that woman his mother's letter.   11. All the students try to avoid his lectures.

3 Subordinate clauses 1. …, dass seine Tochter… schwimmen gelernt hat.   2. …, dass er… schicken will.   3. …, dass auch die Politiker… nicht werden lösen können.   4. …, dass die Baupläne… erklärt worden sind.   5. …, dass er… nicht hatte wissen können.   6. …, dass mein Vater… würde machen lassen.   7. …, dass wir… wegfahren sollten.   8. …, dass Wolfgang und Margret sich haben scheiden lassen.   9. …, dass er… gewusst haben will.   10. …, dass die Häuser… hätten fertig sein sollen.   11. …, dass es morgen regnen soll.   12. …, dass der Unfall… verursacht worden ist.   13. …, dass er… gesehen hat.   14. …, dass sie… handeln konnte. 15. …, dass du… hättest warten dürfen.

4 The position of pronouns, noun subjects and objects 1. Ja, er hat es ihm gekauft.   2. Ja, ich habe es ihr schon zurückgeschickt.   3. Ja, man hat sie ihnen schon mitgeteilt.   4. Ja, er sollte ihn ihr ersparen.   5. Ja, ich kann sie ihm holen.   6. Ja, ich zeige ihn ihm.   7. Ja, er hat sie ihnen schon vorgestellt.   8. Ja, sie muss sie ihm verbinden.   9. Ja, ich will es ihr vorspielen.   10. Ja, sie haben sie ihnen versprochen.

5   The position of pronouns   1. Er hätte ihm das nicht erlauben sollen.   2. Du hättest mir das nicht versprechen sollen.   3. Sie hätten uns das nicht zeigen sollen.   4. Wir hätten euch das nicht verschweigen sollen.   5. Ich hätte mir das nicht wünschen sollen.   6. Wir hätten uns das nicht anders überlegen sollen.   7. Ihr hättet euch das nicht so leicht machen sollen.   8. Er hätte mir das nicht erzählen sollen.   9. Sie hätten uns das nicht vorwerfen sollen.   10. Er hätte ihr das nicht schenken sollen.

6   The position of adverbials and noun objects   1. Ich habe Andreas schon heute das neue Fahrrad gegeben.   2. Der Kellner kann dem Gast manchmal einen guten Wein empfehlen.   3. Wir würden unserer Tochter gern den Umgang mit diesem Kerl verbieten.   4. Er wird dir und deinem Mann sicher die Ergebnisse mitteilen.   5. Sie hat den Kindern für morgen einen Besuch im Zoo versprochen.   6. Ich habe meinem Chef vor zwei Tagen einen Beschwerdebrief geschickt.   7. Er hat seiner Frau unerwartet sehr viel Geld hinterlassen.   8. Er hat seinen Eltern vorsichtshalber die Trennung von Gabriele verheimlicht.   9. Sie hat ihrer Freundin aus unerfindlichen Gründen die Bitte verweigert.   10. Die Firma muss Ihrem Sohn auf jeden Fall eine neue Stelle anbieten.   11. Ich leihe Freunden nie Bücher aus.   12. Er hat den Pfadfindern am Lagerfeuer eine spannende Geschichte erzählt.

7   The position of adverbials and complements   1. Herr Meier hat gestern in der Schule nach dir gefragt.   2. Dein Zeugnis ist leider in letzter Zeit (*or* in letzter Zeit leider) viel schlechter geworden.   3. Der Verletzte bedurfte gestern bei dem Unfall (*or* bei dem Unfall gestern) dringend medizinischer Hilfe.   4. Ich will mich gleich morgen früh nach Billigflügen in die Türkei erkundigen.   5. Er hat sich bekanntlicherweise noch nie für Fußball interessiert.   6. Ich wollte natürlich auf keinen Fall in einer Fabrik arbeiten.   7. Wir sind heute Morgen um halb zwei nach Hause gekommen.   8. Ich musste gestern über eine Stunde in der Kälte (*or* in der Kälte über eine Stunde) auf ihn warten.   9. Er ist schon früher nicht sehr gern Lehrer gewesen.   10. Das Kind hat sich gestern bei dem Spaziergang sehr vor dem großen Hund gefürchtet.   11. Mein Onkel ist vorzeitig in Pension gegangen.   12. Er hat sich wahnsinnig auf das Rockkonzert gefreut.   13. Ich habe mich Gott sei Dank gut von der Krankheit erholt.   14. Wir haben schon lange von einem Millionengewinn im Lotto geträumt.   15. Wir wollen auf jeden Fall bald in ein größeres Haus umziehen.

8   The position of adverbials   1. Die Studentin konnte heute Morgen wegen ihrer Erkältung nicht zu der Vorlesung gehen.   2. Du hast die Sonate gestern bei dem Konzert (*or* gestern bei dem Konzert die Sonate) viel zu langsam gespielt.   3. Er wollte deshalb in der Schule fleißig arbeiten.   4. Die Konferenz musste leider vorgestern wegen zu geringer Teilnehmerzahl abgesagt werden.   5. Das Bierfest fand gestern trotz des schlechten Wetters draußen statt.   6. Ich werde leider heute Abend etwas später nach Hause kommen.   7. Der Mord wurde wahrscheinlich um 22 Uhr in der Nähe des Parks begangen.   8. Man hat ihn Gott sei Dank heute Morgen bei seinem Vater gefunden.   9. Die Straße muss leider wegen dringender Reparaturarbeiten für zwei Wochen gesperrt werden.   10. Mein Mann fliegt glücklicherweise nur einmal im Jahr geschäftlich ins Ausland.   11. Ich habe letzte Nacht vor lauter Aufregung sehr schlecht geschlafen.   12. Ich kann leider bei dieser Hitze (*or* bei dieser Hitze leider) unmöglich arbeiten.

9 The position of *nicht* 1.… leider nicht an ihn… 2.… nicht gesagt. 3.… nicht nach Südtirol. 4.… nicht allein nach Südtirol. 5.… nicht machen dürfen. 6.… nicht in die Werkstatt. 7.… heute nicht in die Werkstatt. 8. Kauf das Auto nicht! 9.… nicht geeignet. 10.… nicht gern… 11.… nicht in die Bibliothek… 12.… nicht Lokomotivführer… 13.… nicht entziehen. 14. Wir kommen nicht mit. 15.… nicht bringen. 16.… nicht träumend… 17.… nicht scheiden lassen. 18.… nicht die gleichen Chancen. 19.… nicht gehört. 20.… nicht für alles…

10 The order of words and phrases in the central section 1. Die Bürgerrechtler haben die Politiker schon immer vor der Gefahr der Atomenergie gewarnt. 2. Er konnte seine Familie glücklicherweise vor dem Tornado retten. 3. Der Lehrer hat dem Schüler wegen seiner schlechten Note in Chemie Nachhilfeunterricht angeboten. 4. Die Gartenschere ist mir gestern Nachmittag bei der Gartenarbeit auf den Fuß gefallen. 5. Der Arzt hat den Jungen gründlich untersucht. 6. Mein Vater hat abends am liebsten vor dem Fernseher gesessen. 7. Der Vertreter hat die alte Dame skrupellos um 5000 Mark betrogen. 8. Ich habe mich schon vor einer Woche bei den Großeltern für das Geschenk bedankt. 9. Man kann einen Menschen nicht zu seinem Glück zwingen. 10. Er hat sich leider nicht mehr an seine Tante erinnern können. 11. Sein Name ist mir gerade noch rechtzeitig eingefallen. 12. Er ist gestern nach langer Krankheit im Marienhospital an Herzversagen gestorben. 13. Alice befand sich plötzlich in einem langen schmalen Tunnel. 14. Meine Frau ist bei Glatteis nicht gern auf der Autobahn gefahren. 15. Ihr habt euch gestern unerlaubt die Bücher aus der Bibliothek geholt. 16. Ich habe Ihrem Sohn schon immer zu einer praktischen Tätigkeit geraten. 17. Die Wissenschaftler mussten bei dem Experiment auf die Temperatur achten. 18. Wir können voraussichtlich noch nicht mit den Straßenarbeiten beginnen.

10 Complex sentences

1 Coordination 1. denn 2. sondern 3. aber 4. aber 5. oder 6. aber 7. und 8. denn 9. sondern 10. und; aber; denn 11. sondern 12. oder

2 Coordination 1. … und dann ging sie… 2. … und manchmal machen wir… 3. … und sah… 4.… und wollte… 5.… und die Frau geht… 6.… und abends treffe ich… 7.… und (können) mit dem Staubsaugen anfangen. 8.… und wir müssen… 9.… und muss dringend… 10.… und ging deshalb… 11.… und am nächsten Tag ist er… 12.… und spielt schon…

3 Anticipatory *es* 1. Dass er… abgesagt hat, hat mich sehr geärgert. 2. Ob du Geld hast oder nicht, ist mir völlig unwichtig. 3. Ein… Kind… gehen zu lassen ist mehr als leichtsinnig. 4. Dass Sie uns… besuchen kommen, freut uns sehr. 5. Ob er jemals wieder laufen kann, ist fraglich. 6. Wie man… machen kann, ist mir ein Rätsel. 7. Mit dir zusammenzuarbeiten ist eine Zumutung. 8. Dass er viel ausgeglichener geworden ist, ist allen… aufgefallen. 9. Mit wem du deine Abende verbringst, interessiert mich nicht. 10. Die beiden Rottweiler zu streicheln ist nicht zu empfehlen. 11. Dass er… vergessen hat, ist durchaus möglich. 12. Dass er… hatte, war unübersehbar.

4 Relative clauses 1. der 2. die 3. die 4. die; denen 5. dessen 6. was 7. was 8. dem 9. das 10. die 11. die; denen 12. der 13. die 14. dessen; das 15. den 16. was 17. was 18. dem 19. das 20. denen

5 Relative clauses 1. Unsere Tochter geht auf eine Schule, in der Jungen und Mädchen in manchen Fächern getrennt unterrichtet werden. 2. Ich wundere mich über den Enthusiasmus, mit dem er diesen Sport betreibt. 3. Er besuchte seine Heimatstadt, an die er viele widersprüchliche Erinnerungen hatte. 4. Die Menschen, deren Häuser … völlig zerstört worden waren, wurden … in einer Turnhalle untergebracht. 5. Der Roman, den ich … lese, ist ein reiner Unterhaltungsroman. 6. Umweltschutz ist eine Frage, die man ernst nehmen muss. 7. Die Freunde, mit denen ich früher oft zusammen war, leben heute fast alle in anderen Städten. 8. Die Lehrstellen, für die sich die Schulabgänger am meisten interessieren, sind oft schon vergeben. 9. Der Mann, dessen Hund entlaufen war, gab eine Anzeige … auf. 10. Ohne sein Handy, das er immer … bei sich trägt, geht er nie aus dem Haus. 11. Diese Kaffeemaschine, die ich erst gestern hier gekauft habe, ist heute schon kaputt. 12. Für die Oper, die wir am liebsten gesehen hätten, gab es keine Karten mehr. 13. In dieser Schule gibt es viele Kinder, denen man … viel helfen muss. 14. Die Firma, bei der mein Vater … angestellt war, hat ihn gestern entlassen. 15. Er machte mir ein Angebot, mit dem ich nicht gerechnet hatte.

6 Conjunctions 1. Nachdem ich (zu) Mittag gegessen habe, mache ich gern einen Mittagsschlaf. 2. Ruf mich doch bitte an, sobald du angekommen bist. 3. Kurz bevor die Sonne untergeht, ist ein Spaziergang besonders schön. 4. Der Verkehr musste umgeleitet werden, da/weil sich ein Unfall ereignet hatte. 5. Der Menschheit wäre sehr geholfen, wenn man einen Impfstoff gegen Aids entwickeln könnte/würde. 6. Er ging zu dem Fußballspiel, obwohl er erkältet war (*or* obwohl er eine Erkältung hatte). 7. Die Abgase können reduziert werden, indem der Motor richtig eingestellt wird (*or* Die Abgase können dadurch reduziert werden, dass der Motor richtig eingestellt wird). 8. Während der Junge operiert wurde, mussten die Eltern draußen warten. 9. Wenn das Wetter schön ist, fahren wir morgen an den Chiemsee. 10. Seit/seitdem er in eine kleinere Stadt umgezogen ist, fühlt er sich viel wohler. 11. Bis wir euch das nächste Mal besuchen, ist es noch ein ganzes Jahr. 12. Sie stach sich, als/während sie nähte, in den Finger (*or* Sie stach sich in den Finger, als/während sie nähte). 13. Ich habe das Buch ausgeliehen, damit du es lesen kannst. 14. Wenn/Falls der Beitrag erhöht wird, (*or* Falls es eine Beitragserhöhung gibt,) werde ich aus dem Verein austreten. 15. Soviel/Soweit ich weiß, wohnt er jetzt in Leonberg.

7 Conjunctions 1. wenn 2. sobald 3. als ob 4. da 5. damit 6. als 7. obwohl 8. so dass 9. als 10. wenn 11. wenn 12. soweit 13. als 14. während 15. während 16. wie 17. solange 18. wenn 19. so dass 20. indem 21. wie

8 Conjunctions 1. Bevor wir nach Syrien fliegen, müssen wir uns … impfen lassen. 2. Seit/Seitdem ich mir … gekauft habe, kann ich mir nichts mehr leisten. 3. Bis du … zurückkommst, kannst du … unterstellen. 4. Sobald sich die Zuschauer gesetzt hatten, ging der Theatervorhang auf. 5. Da sein Pass abgelaufen war, musste er … verschieben. 6. Während in England alles ruhig war, tobte … ein ungeheurer Sturm. 7. Obwohl er mich so oft enttäuscht hat, liebe ich ihn immer noch. 8. Nachdem Christian mit dem Zaun fertig war, baute er einen Kaninchenstall.

9 Infinitive clauses 1. … ihn in die Stadt zu fahren. 2. … um diese Zeit in einer Kneipe gewesen zu sein. 3. … euch bald besuchen zu können. 4. … für einen Oscar nominiert zu werden. 5. … ihn schon einmal in Frankfurt gesehen zu haben. 6. … sich noch einmal mit Felix zu treffen. 7. … für drei Jahre ins Ausland zu gehen. 8. … mit all diesen Schwierigkeiten fertig zu werden. 9. … mit mir essen zu gehen? 10. … bis Weihnachten mindestens 10 Kilo abzunehmen. 11.… abends mit Freunden wegzugehen. 12.… an der Börse zu spekulieren. 13.… die alte Dame mit Absicht um ihr Geld betrogen zu haben. 14.… mit Ihnen über das Honorar zu verhandeln. 15.… an dem Projekt mitzuarbeiten. 16.… Sie heute Abend hier begrüßen zu dürfen. 17.… abends nach 10 Uhr angerufen zu werden. 18.… immer über das gleiche Thema zu sprechen. 19.… bald wieder Ski fahren gehen zu können? 20.… während des ganzen Fluges nicht zu rauchen.

10 Infinitive clauses 1. Jochen fängt an sich für Mädchen zu interessieren. 2. Gudrun hört auf am Computer zu arbeiten. 3. Ich nehme mir vor nicht immer alles in letzter Minute zu machen. 4. Wir lehnen es ab die Verantwortung für den Schaden zu übernehmen. 5. Ich ziehe es vor einen ruhigen Abend zu verbringen. 6. Er bietet ihr an sich um die Sache zu kümmern 7. Ich stelle es mir schön vor mit dir in Urlaub zu fahren. 8. Sie gibt vor als Model zu arbeiten 9. Die Arbeit fängt an mir Spaß zu machen. 10. Der Gastgeber fordert die Gäste auf mit dem Essen zu beginnen.

11 Infinitive clauses 1. Sie wissen, dass Jochen anfängt sich für Mädchen zu interessieren. 2.…, dass Gudrun aufhört am Computer zu arbeiten. 3.…, dass ich mir vornehme nicht immer alles in letzter Minute zu machen. 4.…, dass wir es ablehnen die Verantwortung für den Schaden zu übernehmen. 5.…, dass ich es vorziehe einen ruhigen Abend zu verbringen. 6.…, dass er ihr anbietet sich um die Sache zu kümmern. 7.…, dass ich es mir schön vorstelle mit dir in Urlaub zu fahren. 8.…, dass sie vorgibt als Model zu arbeiten. 9.…, dass die Arbeit anfängt mir Spaß zu machen. 10.…, dass der Gastgeber die Gäste auffordert mit dem Essen zu beginnen.

12 Infinitive clauses after prepositions 1.…, ohne mit seinem Chef gesprochen zu haben. 2. * 3. Anstatt sich um ihre eigenen Dinge zu kümmern,… 4.…, ohne auch nur ein Wort zu sagen. 5. * 6.…, um den Eisvogel am Fluss beobachten zu können. 7. * 8. Anstatt dich ein bisschen zu amüsieren,… 9.…, außer den ganzen Tag vor dem Spiegel zu stehen. 10. Außer von morgens bis abends am Strand zu liegen,… 11.…, ohne in Florenz gewesen zu sein. 12. * 13.…, um das zu verstehen. 14. * 15.…, ohne mich zu grüßen.

13 The infinitive without *zu* 1. Wir sahen ihn ins Haus gehen (*or* Wir sahen, wie er ins Haus ging). 2. Ich muss jeden zweiten Samstag arbeiten. 3. Er will dir sein neues Kaninchen zeigen. 4. Wir lassen unser Auto immer in einer kleinen Werkstatt in MK reparieren. 5. Sie hörte jemanden die Treppe heraufkommen (*or* Sie hörte, wie jemand die Treppe heraufkam.) 6. Ein netter Mann half mir meinen Koffer tragen. 7. Sie schickte ihren Sohn Brötchen holen. 8. Ich lehre dich schwimmen (*or* Ich bringe dir schwimmen bei.) 9. Die Kinder ließen den neuen Jungen nicht mitspielen. 10. Das lässt sich leicht machen. 11. Wann hast du Auto fahren gelernt? 12. Ich darf nichts Fettes essen.

⟦11⟧ Word formation

1 The formation of nouns 1. Unmensch 2. Bedeutung 3. Anwesenden 4. Ausgang 5. Ersatz 6. Hauptbahnhof 7. Gesundheit 8. Nichtschwimmer 9. Länge; Höhe 10. Bremse 11. Lauferei 12. Häuschen 13. Riesenerfolg/Supererfolg/Bombenerfolg 14. Vaterschaft 15. Bekannter 16. Schnitt 17. Reichtum 18. Rechtsanwältin 19. Pünktlichkeit 20. Gespräch 21. Missachtung

2 Compound nouns 1. Zeigefinger 2. Studentenermäßigung 3. Hörsaal 4. Abfalleimer 5. Hundeleine 6. Bohrmaschine 7. Kopfbedeckung 8. Waschpulver 9. Werbespruch 10. Buchladen 11. Schwimmhalle 12. Nagelfeile 13. Kirschmarmelade 14. Motorboot 15. Versicherungsexperte 16. Deutschlehrer 17. Gartenlokal 18. Abiturfeier 19. Krankenhausaufenthalt 20. Verkehrsunfall

3 The formation of adjectives 1. unverkäuflich 2. goldene 3. planmäßig 4. brauchbar 5. rötliche 6. arbeitslos 7. zweistündigen 8. meisterhaft 9. verlässlich/zuverlässig 10. täglich 11. modisch 12. eisig 13. gestrige 14. nachdenklicher 15. erlebnisreich 16. alkoholfreies 17. liebebedürftig 18. rücksichtsvoll 19. kindisch 20. nikotinarm 21. erzkonservativ 22. unangenehm

4 Inseparable verb prefixes 1. a. bekommen; entkommen; verkommen b. bearbeiten; erarbeiten; verarbeiten c. erblühen; verblühen d. entreißen; verreißen; zerreißen e. behandeln; verhandeln f. beschreiben; verschreiben g. beschießen; erschießen; verschießen; zerschießen h. belegen; erlegen; verlegen; zerlegen i. beantworten; verantworten j. befallen; entfallen; verfallen; zerfallen k. bewirtschaften; erwirtschaften 2. a. benachrichtigen b. entgiften; vergiften c. versilbern d. versklaven e. bewässern; entwässern; verwässern f. erhungern; verhungern g. verglasen h. bebauen; erbauen; verbauen 3. a. verbessern b. erblinden c. verlängern d. befeuchten e. ergrauen f. entschärfen; verschärfen g. verkürzen h. verarmen i. erkranken j. berichtigen k. erhöhen l. erleichtern m. vereinfachen

5 Separable verb prefixes 1. weg 2. entgegen 3. ab- 4. vor-; nach 5. los 6. zu 7. hinzu 8. mit 9. vor; nach 10. ab- 11. mit- 12. zurück 13. aus; auf 14. ein 15. zusammen 16. ab- 17. ein- 18. aus- 19. los- 20. mit-

6 Variable verb prefixes 1. Er hinterlässt/hinterließ seiner Frau eine Menge Geld. 2. Männer unterdrücken/unterdrückten ihre Gefühle. 3. Der Sportler vollbringt/vollbrachte eine Höchstleistung. 4. Sie widersteht/widerstand der Versuchung. 5. Wir sehen/sahen uns in dem alten Haus um. 6. Die Autofahrer umfahren/umfuhren die Großstadt. 7. Er gibt/gab mir das Buch wieder. 8. Die Kinder wiederholen/wiederholten das Einmaleins. 9. Das spiegelt/spiegelte seine arrogante Haltung wider. 10. Ich übersehe/übersah oft Fehler. 11. Kinder stopfen/stopften sich gern den Mund voll. 12. Der Soldat läuft/lief zum Feind über. 13. Der Politiker überlegt/überlegte seine Antwort genau. 14. Ich sehe dein Manuskript morgen durch. 15. Der Geruch nach Kaffee durchdringt/durchdrang das ganze Haus. 16. Änderungen an dieser Universität vollziehen/vollzogen sich nur langsam.

7 Verbs with separable, inseparable and variable prefixes 1. untergekommen; unternommen 2. missachtet; durchgefallen 3. ausgefallen; nachgeholt 4. zusammengebrochen; durchgerostet 5. vergessen; übersetzt 6. erschöpft; übermüdet; durchgefeiert 7. umstellt; aufgegeben; durchsucht; beschlagnahmt 8. umgestellt; zurückgestellt; vorgestellt 9. verbessert; ausradiert; durchgestrichen 10. angebrannt; angesehen; aufgepasst 11. aufgehört; umgezogen; angerufen; benachrichtigt; verwickelt 12. aufgerufen 13. ausgelesen; zurückgestellt 14. angerufen; verwählt 15. unterbrochen; widerlegt 16. unterschätzt; überschätzt; vollgetankt 17. überholt; entgegengekommen 18. überfahren; überlebt 19. untersucht; umgebracht 20. abgelaufen; verlängert; ausgestellt

8 The formation of verbs 1. schneien 2. kontrollieren 3. brechen 4. denken 5. sägen 6. fahren 7. werfen 8. aufnehmen 9. thematisieren 10. schießen 11. kellnern 12. fernsehen 13. interessieren 14. fotografieren 15. reden 16. spitzen 17. bleichen 18. verbessern 19. schärfen 20. ironisieren 21. kürzen 22. trocknen

12 Spoken and written German

1 Pronunciation and spelling
1. a. l b. s c. s d. s e. l f. s g. l h. l i. l j. s k. l l. s m. l n. l
2. a. l b. s c. s d. s e. s f. l g. l h. l i. l j. s k. s l. l m. s n. l
3. a. l b. s c. l d. s e. l f. s g. s h. l i. l j. s k. l l. l m. s n. s o. l p. s
4. a. l b. s c. l d. s e. l f. s g. l h. l i. s j. s k. l l. s m. l n. s o. l p. s q. l
5. a. l b. s c. s d. s e. l f. s g. l h. l i. s j. l k. s l. l m. s n. s
6. a. l b. l c. s d. s e. l f. s g. s h. l i. l j. s k. l l. s m. s n. s o. l
7. a. l b. s c. l d. s e. s f. s g. l h. l i. s j. l k. l l. l m. s n. s o. l

2 Pronunciation and spelling
1. a 2. a 3. i 4. a 5. i 6. a 7. i 8. i 9. i 10. i 11. i 12. i 13. a 14. i 15. i 16. a 17. i 18. i 19. a 20. i 21. a 22. a 23. i 24. i 25. i 26. i 27. a 28. a 29. a 30. a 31. i 32. a 33. i 34. i 35. a 36. i 37. a 38. i 39. a 40. i

3 The use of capital letters
1. zu; Ihrem; ich; Ihnen; Namen; herzliche; Glückwünsche; Ihnen; Gute; Sie; hundert 2. Deutschen; Bezug; doppelte; Inkrafttreten; bisschen 3. besten 4. Erste; Abend; Grund; schlimmsten 5. morgen; Frankfurter 6. angst und bange; schuld 7. Leid; Nachmittag; trotz; Ihrer; teilnehmen 8. Recht; Großen und Ganzen; ihr; Heiligen; ihr; recht 9. Einzige; Essen 10. Eins; ohmsche 11. Einzelnen; etwas; schwarzen; alles 12. Allerschlimmste; ihr; silberne 13. Roten; Anfang; Vereinten 14. Zweite; Großbritanniens; ganzen; Vereinigten 15. Schiefe; einzige 16. alle; Klaren; Gutes 17. Allgemeinen; Deutsch; Englisch 18. heute; Rad; morgen; Eis; beides 19. schwarzen; Schwarze 20. Acht; Abgeordneten; Londoner; Deutschen

4 One word or two?
1. kopfrechnen; so wenig 2. spazieren ging; abhanden gekommen 3. kennen gelernt; beisammen sein; bestehen bleibt 4. fertig bin; zufrieden geben; irgendwo; gut gehenden; Fuß zu fassen 5. Allein erziehende; Rat suchen; leicht fällt 6. preiszugeben; totgeschlagen 7. bekannt machen; teilnehmen; zufrieden sein 8. liegen gelassen; durcheinander gekommen 9. irgendwann; Leid tun; zunichte gemacht 10. zu viel; fernsehen; zu wenig 11. fern liegen; irrezuführen; hochrechnet; schwarzarbeiten 12. Rad fahren; Auto fahren 13. bergsteigen; übrig bleiben; Eis laufen 14. bereithalten; gefangen zu nehmen 15. beiseite gelegt; satt hatte; pleite zu sein

5 -ss- or -ß-
1. lassen 2. weiß 3. Grüße 4. blass 5. gewusst 6. groß 7. Kuss 8. du musst 9. er fraß 10. Massentourismus 11. Maßnahme 12. fließen 13. außen 14. Schluss 15. Russland 16. Ruß 17. Bußgeld 18. Busse 19. Fluss 20. Fuß 21. Rasse 22. reißen 23. heiß 24. Wasser 25. Hass 26. Fass 27. stoßen 28. Essen 29. er aß 30. Esslöffel

6 The comma
1. Nachdem … hatte, wollte er … haben. 2. Er behauptete(,) die Zeugin … gesehen zu haben. Außerdem … Protokoll, er sei … gewesen, der … kommen lassen.

3. ... Klassenlehrers, ging ...   4. Ein Gerichtsurteil besagt, dass einem Schüler, der ... verprügelt, angedroht werden darf(,) ihn von der Schule zu verweisen, um Mitschüler zu schützen.   5. Sie setzte sich(,) ohne zu fragen(,) zu diesem ... Tisch, suchte ... Zigarettenschachtel, nahm ...   6. Ich ... einladen, aber leider ...   7. Wenn ... nach Hause komme(,) und du hast ... aufgeräumt, dann bekommst du ... mehr(,) oder ich schließe ... Zimmer ein, bis du ... aufräumst.   8. Manchmal wünschte ich, ich hätte ... zwanzig Jahren, aber dafür auch so viel Zeit, wie ich sie damals hatte.   9. Außer sich ... seines Sohnes, nahm er ... teilte allen Leuten, die ihm einfielen, die freudige Nachricht mit, ob sie ... oder nicht.   10. Obwohl ... lebe und arbeite, ärgert es mich immer noch sehr, dass man hier ... Deutschland, dafür aber ... mehr bezahlt.   11. Ich kam, sah und siegte.   12. ... kam, sah er mit Entsetzen, dass in seine Wohnung ... fehlte, das ihm seine Mutter ... hinterlassen hatte.   13. ... gewesen war, fühlte er sich ziemlich fremd, als er ... ankam.   14. Ich finde, wir dürfen ... beschränken(,) Politiker nur verbal zu kritisieren, sondern wir müssen ... engagieren, wenn wir wollen, dass sich ... ändern.

Grammar in context: translations

◼ Words and sentences in context

The Creation of the World

In the beginning God created the heaven and the earth.
And the earth was without form, and void;
and darkness was upon the face of the deep.
And the Spirit of God moved upon the face of the waters.
And God said, Let there be light: and there was light.
And God saw the light, that it was good.
(From: Genesis 1, 1–3, Authorized Version)

The Metamorphosis

When Gregor Samsa woke up one morning from uneasy dreams, he found himself transformed in his bed into a gigantic insect.
(From: Franz Kafka, *The Metamorphosis*)

Other Worlds

The ultra-modern luxury liner is stranded, the crew is running around in confusion, deep in the bowels of the vessel a time bomb is ticking. The interstellar computer game 'Spaceship Titanic', invented by British cult book author Douglas Adams, is now being launched onto the market in a German edition. German speakers gave the robots voices.
(From: *Der Spiegel*)

◼ Nouns in context

A modern Noah's Ark

Circus – also known as the people's theatre – is one of the oldest forms of entertainment and a medium for international culture. Circus – that means acrobats, clowns and, above all, animals, for the origin of the circus lies in the presentation of animals.

Our circus is rather like a modern Noah's Ark. The animals are our partners, our friends, and belong to our big family.

All our animals have the best care, good food, spacious stabling and outside enclosures, optimum care from qualified veterinary surgeons and farriers, and, above all, constant contact with animal trainers and keepers. All our acts are based on the natural behaviour of the animals. Partnership between man and beast is the foundation for the circus training.

In an age when more and more exotic species are being driven from their natural environment, it is extremely important that we are providing them with a habitat. In this way we are making a

contribution towards preserving the only form of entertainment for the whole family for future generations – the circus.
(From: Circus Krone Munich, *Programme*)

3 The noun phrase in context

Better than the 'Dream Team'?

The signs are good: Munich's team is top of the German League with a big lead. The probability that the Bavarian footballers will gain their 15th German championship is 99.9 per cent! And if everything runs according to plan, the Bayern team could achieve something that has never been done in Germany before: the Triple – German Champion, winners of the German Football Association Cup and Champions League winner – all in one year! Everyone in Munich is really hot on the idea of sunning themselves once again at the peak of European football – from the groundsman to the president!

There's no question about it, this extraordinary success would put the team into the footballing annals. Record-breaking national player Lothar Matthäus, who has long been assured of his place in the history books: 'We have the opportunity to introduce a big era for FC Bayern – that has to be motivation enough for any player.' Remember – Munich's footballers gained the world reputation they are enjoying today between 1974 and 1976, when the team around top stars Franz Beckenbauer, Gerd Müller and Sepp Maier took the European Cup of National Champions three times in a row…

The current team is supposed to be even better than the 'dream team' – at least that is what Franz Beckenbauer thinks, now advanced to president of Bayern München: 'At that time we had seven or eight good people. Today, we've got 15 to 17 top-class players!' Bayern München – stronger than ever?
(From: *Bravo Sport*)

4 Adjectives, adverbs and adverbials in context

Addiction trap Internet – the number of Internet surfers is growing

When do you become an Internet addict and how do you get to that state? Night after night you sit up until two in the morning in front of your screen. You want to get out of the Net, but you simply can't do it. If you're offline for any length of time, you become restless, depressed, and log on again. People are particularly at risk if they have a tendency towards depression or they are lonely. Some have marital problems, others are replacing an earlier addiction, e.g. abstinent alcoholics.

Are there any differences between men and women? While men tend to migrate to sex pages and spend hours downloading pictures, women prefer chat rooms. Many embark on virtual affairs in this way, because you can get closer much more quickly than in real life. That's why an Internet addiction can destroy a marriage within a few months.

What can you do if your partner can't get away from the computer? Then you have to confront the addicted surfer with their addiction. Unfortunately, addicts generally deny the problem.

Sport, trips to the cinema or a holiday for two can provide support. But if nothing helps, there's only one thing: professional help from a psychologist.
(From: *Cosmopolitan*)

5 Prepositions in context

Trainee journalist – a job with a future

The desire to earn your money as a journalist, to experience daily events at first hand, and always to be on the spot when it comes to current information from across the world, is the number one professional goal for many people! Without university entrance qualifications, the chances are slim. One is more likely to reach one's goal with a university degree (e.g. media studies), a training at a school of journalism, or a position as a trainee journalist on a newspaper that may take you on as an editor at the end. The future prospects are good, because there will always be newspapers, in spite of the Internet. Mirjam (22) was lucky. She reports on her experiences.

What stages do you go through as a trainee journalist? I started in the local editorial office. Initially on a student placement for a number of weeks, then as a freelancer, and later for five months when I was a trainee journalist. Now I've recently joined the business editor's staff. What I'm looking forward to most is the cultural section, because I'm interested above all in art and theatre.

What stories are you working on at the moment? I've recently been writing short reports on current share prices.

What do you recommend to people who are interested in becoming trainee journalists? If possible, you should have done some groundwork on a student placement. Don't be disheartened if your application to become a trainee journalist isn't immediately successful. You've got to be a bit persistent!
(From: *Popcorn*)

6 Verb forms in context

My parents love me to death

'So, you're the young man my daughter has been telling me about?' Sandra's mother asks with a shark's smile. 'Er, I don't know, yes', answers Tino. Silence. 'And what do you do? Are you still at school?' Sandra's mother uses the polite form of address and calls him 'young man', although at 17 he is hardly older than her daughter. Sandra now simply finds this embarrassing. 'No, I'm doing an apprenticeship as a carpenter at the moment,' drawls Tino. And then to Sandra: 'Can we go?' – 'Please be back at 11 o'clock. You know I'll worry!' her mother calls after them in a tone of voice that once again makes everything crystal clear: failed.

It's almost always like that. If Sandra is trying on clothes, her mother comes along and tells her what suits her and what doesn't – until she gets on Sandra's nerves so much that Sandra gives up and buys precisely the item of clothing that her mother likes. Or the time when she had to take those stupid ballet lessons. Because of her poor posture, said her mother. How she hated the lessons. She would have liked to chuck the ballet shoes in the corner and never go again. But she didn't do it – because she was afraid of disappointing her parents. 'I only want the best for you', said her mother. And: 'I would like to have a pretty daughter.'

All discussions go like this. Sandra knows that her parents would do anything for her. But they are always putting on pressure. By being disappointed, sad or over-protective. But with Tino she feels she is unconditionally accepted.

(From: *Brigitte Young Miss*)

7 Verb uses in context

The witch had to roast

When Hansel stayed thin, the witch didn't want to wait any longer. 'Hey, Gretel,' she called to the girl, 'look sharp and carry some water: It doesn't matter whether Hansel's fat or thin, tomorrow he's going to be slaughtered and cooked.' Oh dear, how the poor little sister wailed as she had to carry the water, and how the tears flowed down her cheeks. 'Dear God, please help us,' she called out, 'if only the wild animals had eaten us in the forest, at least we would have died together.' 'Save your whining,' said the old woman, 'it won't help you.'

Early in the morning Gretel had to get up, hang up the kettle full of water, and light the fire. 'First we'll do the baking,' said the old woman, 'I've already heated the oven and kneaded the dough.' She shoved poor Gretel out to the oven, from which the flames were already licking out. 'Crawl in,' said the witch, 'and see whether it's well and truly heated up, so that we can put the bread in.' And once Gretel had climbed in she wanted to close the oven, and Gretel was supposed to roast in the oven, and then she wanted to eat Gretel up, too. But Gretel realized what was in her mind and said: 'I don't know how to do it. How do I get in there?' 'Stupid girl,' said the old woman, 'the opening is big enough, look, I could even get in there myself.' She came and put her head in the oven. Then Gretel gave her a push so that she went right in, shut the iron door and drew the bolt. Oh! Then the witch started to howl, quite terribly; but Gretel ran away and the godless witch had to burn to death most wretchedly.

(From: Brothers Grimm, 'Hansel and Gretel', *Tales for Children and Home*)

8 Valency and cases in context

The lost equilibrium

The population explosion is all due to the intelligence and virility of mankind. Of all the primates, the 'naked ape' has the biggest penis and the biggest brain. They ensured that there was less and less death and more and more life.

Humans are among the few mammal with a permanent mating season. And the intelligence of Homo sapiens succeeded in postponing death further and further through research, medicine and hygiene.

When Julius Caesar was born, he could reckon statistically on living for 30 years. Today, the average life expectancy in Germany is around 76 years. The result of the human double victory of instinct and reason, in bed and in the laboratory: every second, every hour, every week around twice as many bipeds are born as die.

Human existence has lost its equilibrium. The balance between birth and death no longer exists. Each additional billion people entails new, gigantic destruction in nature and the environment, the atmosphere and the elements. Nothing will change the face of the earth more enduringly during the next 50 years than the increasing population pressure.
(From: Claus Jacobi, 'The Devil's Alternative', *Der Spiegel*)

9 Word order in context

The beginning of life on earth

It is not known for certain how the earth came into existence. The predominant idea is that cosmic dust clouds gathered together in one of the infinite number of existing galaxies. The age of our earth is estimated to be around 500 billion years. It is thought that the earth consisted of molten stone during the first 500 million years. Then the magma slowly began to cool, so that a firm stone crust was able to develop on earth's surface. In the deeper zones below, the molten rock remained liquid.

In the following four billion years considerable changes occurred in the earth's crust. Its surface was folded and irregularly broken up in many places. Between giant continental plates large dips developed. As the crust gradually cooled down, water collected in them. Thus oceans developed which now cover seven-tenths of the earth's surface. Through the folding processes, mountain ranges came into existence. Other mountains were formed from lava and the ejected ash layers piled up to form volcanos.

In the course of geological history large parts of Germany have repeatedly been covered by the sea. Fossilized sea shells are therefore found in many areas of our country.
(From: Christian Spaeth, *Mammals of Prehistoric Times*)

10 Complex sentences in context

America

Sixteen-year-old Karl Rossmann had been sent to America by his poor parents because a servant girl had seduced him and had had a child by him. As he came into New York harbour on the ship that had already slowed down, he suddenly saw the Statue of Liberty, which he had been watching for some time, as if the sunlight had got stronger. Her arm holding the sword stretched aloft as if for the first time, and the free air swept around her form.

'So high!' he said to himself. He had no thought of leaving, and was gradually pushed against the railings of the ship by the growing number of porters that were moving past him.

A young man he had made a fleeting acquaintance with during the crossing, said to him in passing: 'Well, don't you want to go on shore yet?' 'I'm ready,' said Karl, laughing at him. And because he was in high spirits, and a strong young man, he lifted his suitcase onto his shoulder. But as he looked over the head of his acquaintance, who was swinging his stick a little and moving away with the others, he remembered with consternation that he had forgotten his own umbrella below deck. He quickly asked his acquaintance – who didn't appear to be very happy about it – to be good enough to look after his case for a minute, quickly took in the situation, in order to be able to find his way back, and hurried off.
(From: Franz Kafka, *The Stoker*)

11 Word formation in context

The documentation of the contemporary language

With its *Big Dictionary of the German Language*, the Duden editorial board presents the most up-to-date and most comprehensive documentation of the vocabulary of the contemporary German language. Aside from a comprehensive specialist library, the Duden editorial board had the language card index as its disposal in order to master the complex lexicographical task.

The Duden language card index is a collection that has developed over a period of decades. It currently comprises more than three million cross references from contemporary written documentation in the Germany language – on the same number of cards. The language references are collected by a changing number of freelance language selectors on the basis of criteria that are specified by the Duden editorial board. These 'collectors' are constantly on the lookout for new words, word meanings and usages. An equivalent electronic database is being created in parallel with the ongoing expansion of this card index.

This database opens up a large number of options for access and use and is also compatible with the electronic editorial system. In addition, use is made of the wide range of opportunities for searching selectively for words and word forms with the help of the Internet, in machine-readable text corpuses and databases.

(From: *Duden. The Big Dictionary of the German Language, 3rd edition*)

12 Register in context

Are you a fitness freak?

1. **What occurs to you spontaneously as you look at this picture?**
   a. Great body, really well styled…
   b. Looks rather tasty…
   c. Well, looks like grandad's old gym suit is back in fashion, doesn't it?

2. **What is the guy about to do now, what do you think?**
   a. His girlfriend is already waiting for him impatiently in bed, it's not hard to imagine what he'll be doing…
   b. No idea, perhaps have a shower or something like that?
   c. He's hopping out of his muscle suit and into his jogging gear, because he's going running now.

3. **The alarm rings – your head is throbbing furiously from the wild party yesterday. What do you do?**
   a. I turn over again. Today, everyone can take a running jump [kiss my arse]…
   b. I drag myself out of bed and pop an Aspirin. Somehow it'll be all right!
   c. Doesn't affect me. I jump up and then have my feet firmly on the ground – after all, I want to make the most of the new day!

4. **Stress often starts in the morning at breakfast. What do you cram in?**
   a. Nothing. I can't eat anything so soon after midnight. I buy myself a chocolate bar during the break.
   b. Oh, anything that's lying around, a piece of bread with something – the main thing is it has to be quick!
   c. Breakfast is the best meal of the day: hot coffee, fresh orange juice, muesli …

5. **And how do you get to school/work after that?**
   a. By bike – I really need fresh air in the morning.
   b. I get my parents to take me – still the most comfortable way of doing things.
   c. Usually by public transport – bus, train, subway …

6. **A muscular boy/girl chats you up quite openly at the swimming pool. How do you react?**
   a. I can't wait! I'd throw myself at him/her!
   b. Well, take a look first, what he/she's got up top.
   c. Not likely. It's so uncomfortable lying on muscles. And what's more, my flabby figure is even more noticeable next to someone like that …

7. **What do you spend most money on?**
   a. Clothes and CDs.
   b. Pizzerias, ice cream parlours – and ingredients: I really like cooking.
   c. On the nightlife – I spend too much there virtually every evening. But at least there's always something going on there.

(From: *Popcorn*)

A famous lapse

Götz: Tell your leader, I have due respect for Your Majesty the Emperor, as always. But he, tell him, he can … [lick my arse].
(J.W. Goethe, *Götz von Berlichingen*, Act III)

Test Result

2–22 points:

Sport? Not your scene! Although your curves really do bother you quite a lot. However, luckily you are not yet a total couch potato. Look for someone with the same attitude and go outside with them: a bit of running, cycling, roller blading can be really good fun.

23–45 points:

Not bad: You have found the ideal compromise for yourself between fitness and relaxing. Stay as you are – it's quite right that you've always got happiness and fun at the top of the list!

46–67 points:

First into the fitness studio, then off jogging and afterwards a short squash match? Just your day! You're proud of your perfect figure. As long as you're comfortable with that, your attitude is perfectly OK – it only starts getting tricky if it all becomes an addictive body cult. So relax for a change!

Index